IN SEARCH OF A NEW HUMANISM

SYNTHESE LIBRARY

STUDIES IN EPISTEMOLOGY,

LOGIC, METHODOLOGY, AND PHILOSOPHY OF SCIENCE

VOLUME 282

IN SEARCH OF A NEW HUMANISM

The Philosophy of Georg Henrik von Wright

Edited by

ROSARIA EGIDI
Università Roma Tre, Rome, Italy

KLUWER ACADEMIC PUBLISHERS
DORDRECHT / BOSTON / LONDON

Library of Congress Cataloging-in-Publication Data is available.

ISBN 0-7923-5810-4

Published by Kluwer Academic Publishers,
P.O. Box 17, 3300 AA Dordrecht, The Netherlands.

Sold and distributed in North, Central and South America
by Kluwer Academic Publishers,
PO Box 358, Accord Station, Hingham, MA 02018–0358, U.S.A.

In all other countries, sold and distributed
by KIuwer Academic Publishers, Distribution Centre,
P.O. Box 322, 3300 AH Dordrecht, The Netherlands

Printed on acid-free paper

Printed and bound in Great Britain by MPG Books, Bodmin, Cornwall.

TABLE OF CONTENTS

ROSARIA EGIDI

VON WRIGHT AND "DANTE'S DREAM"
STAGES IN A PHILOSOPHICAL PILGRIM'S PROGRESS

I. ALBO LAPILLO NUMERATUS ANNUS: 1974 AS A STARTING POINT FOR "TWO NEW LINES" OF THOUGHT

The brief "Postscript 1980", which we find appended to the "Intellectual Autobiography" that von Wright wrote seven years before for the volume dedicated to him in *The Library of Living Philosophers*,[1] contains some valuable indications about the development of his research beginning from the mid-Seventies. Not published until 1989, and with a bibliographical update that goes up to 1988, Schilpp and Hahn's volume presents, in effect, a critical history of von Wright's vast and multiform philosophical activity up to 1974, putting the seal on his achievements in the fields of induction, probability, and philosophical logic (particularly deontics), as well as in the theories of norms, values and intentional action. The theses formulated in *Causality and Determinism*,[2] which were, to a large extent, innovative with respect to those in the preceding volume, *Explanation and Understanding*,[3] and to the results attained in the wide-ranging and passionate debate to which that work gave rise, may be considered the *terminus ad quem* of a systematic reconstruction of von Wright's thought, documented, in the Schilpp and Hahn volume, by a huge collection of essays dedicated to the various aspects of his reflections and accompanied by the Philosopher's "Replies", which were also composed, like the larger part of the critical studies, between 1974 and 1975.[4]

In the "Postscript" von Wright makes a direct reference to "two new lines" along which his thought had begun to move in those same years. The *first* line develops an analysis of the modal and temporal concepts first discussed in earlier writings, while the *second* is centered on the subject of determinism and constitutes an essential contribution to the reassessment to which von Wright gradually subjected the teleological scheme for action-explanation and the nature of the relation between the human sciences and the natural sciences.[5] At the end of the "Postscript", von Wright provides an indication, nonetheless significant, that there exists in his work an as yet unresolved tension between the strictly specialized intent behind his writings, on the one hand, and his "craving for a more 'visionary' grasp of the totality of human existence", on the other. It is to "the search for a *Weltanschauung*" able to fill the gap within the "double soul" of his philosophy and bring together the various elements that dwelt therein, that von Wright seems to tie the emergence of topics such as the man-nature relationship, the future of Western civilization, and the problems of scientific and technological progress, which have appeared more and more frequently in his work over the past two decades. It is, in effect, not difficult to recognize in the

1

R. Egidi (ed.), In Search of a New Humanism, 1–34.
©1999 *Kluwer Academic Publishers. Printed in Great Britain.*

two lines mentioned in the "Postscript" the first step toward significant system-
atizations which would later take form, above all in *Freedom and Determination*,[6] in
the essays included in *Truth, Knowledge, and Modality*[7] and, finally, in the various
papers collected in *The Tree of Knowledge and Other Essays*.[8] It is also true that these
works, in turn, manifest further lines of research that, while in large part linked to
earlier conceptions, reveal a strong tendency to integrate themselves in a unitary
perspective.

Over the twenty years that have passed from the contributions discussed in the
"Postscript" until his recent volume, *In the Shadow of Descartes: Essays in the
Philosophy of Mind*,[9] von Wright's philosophical activity has, in fact, interwoven
multiple directions of research, which have helped to create new links and to clarify the
articulation of essential points of reference. But of more interest, perhaps, than an
identification of the individual aspects of von Wright's research would be a search for the
unitary ground, if it exists, that runs through them. This could, in fact, be the same
ground that lies at the basis of his conception of natural determinism and human acting,
which had, even earlier, informed his attempts to identify the connections and
differences between acting and causation, between time and truth. It could concern the
"humanization of nature" which inspires, in his more recent work, his critique of the
misconceptions within the traditional dualisms of man-nature, freedom-necessity, good
and evil, values-facts, and mind-body, as well as his reformulation of the problem
regarding man's place in nature and the relationship between the human and the natural
sciences. To identify a guiding thread does not, however, signify a desire to enclose the
multiple and multi-branched aspects of von Wright's work within a closed philosophical
system, but, rather, to trace in them a dynamic and multidimensional perspective, whose
dominant trait could be summarized as the "search for a new humanist orientation"
which he himself, in his "Intellectual Autobiography", had indicated as characteristic of
the mature phase of his thought.[10]

My goal here is to offer a systematic overview of the main topics into which von
Wright's most recent research can be organized, trying in this way, against the
background of the great collection contained in Schilpp and Hahn's volume, to
present a framework of the later developments in his thought up to the end of the
Nineties. I will, in fact, try to group the substance of von Wright's reflections over
the past twenty years under three large headings: the *compatibility thesis*,
philosophical humanism, and the *mind-matter relationship* – with the intent of
showing how one might find one's way through them by using the guiding motif of
unmasking and dissolving what he calls the "deterministic illusion." Present in
different forms, and often hidden in the depths of the myths created by European
man, the illusion that one can bring together into a unified whole the intrinsic
doubleness of human rationality marks, according to von Wright, the entire history
of our civilization, and it is also responsible for the fatal consequences cognitive
hybris encounters when it absolutizes the power of reason and the results attained by
scientific and technological progress.

Up until the works prior to his mature period, it had been clear to von Wright – and
it is advantageous to underscore this immediately at this point – that understanding

this double, and hence tragic, nature of the human reason requires one both "to reject a *rationalism* which looks for the value of reason and truth in various possibilities to improve man's external conditions of life, and which holds that reason alone can make man and society perfect", and "to reject an *anti-rationalism* which blames reason for man's misfortunes, and which believes that of mankind only the child and the savage can be blessed."[11]

In one of his essays, which will be treated later,[12] von Wright links what he calls "Dante's dream," *i.e.*, the ideal of a complete restoration of lost innocence, to the deterministic illusion to which human reason is prey. It is an ideal which guides the other-worldly voyage of the poet and turns it into a metaphor of the very path that modern culture is following and of its quest for a knowledge that is not a road to self-annihilation, but a tool for emancipation and freedom.

II. SAVE CONTINGENCY, SAVE FREEDOM!

The two Tanner Lectures published in 1985 under the title, "Of Human Freedom," play a particularly important role in the context of von Wright's mature thought. Not only do they constitute, in fact, the point of arrival for the ideas that subtend the two lines of thought mentioned in "Postscript 1980," but also the starting point for a solution to the problem of congruence, or parallelism, between mind and matter. This is a problem which will occupy the field of his later reflections in "An Essay on Door-Knocking",[13] in "On Mind and Matter,"[14] and, finally, in various texts included in the volume *In the Shadow of Descartes*.

At first glance, it might seem risky to affirm that there is a link between such apparently heterogeneous areas of research as the theories of modality and of time, which are placed among the topics characteristic of philosophic logic, and the problems of determinism, which belong to the sphere traditionally ascribed to practical philosophy and philosophical anthropology. If, however, one considers the fact that the peculiar compatibilism of von Wright's approach is a corollary of his well known "dynamic" concept of human action, understood as the possibility for human interference in the external world and as the result of a change or a not-change of nature, then the apparent heterogeneity of his research areas ceases to pose a problem. Therefore, in order to understand fully the meaning of the version of the compatibility thesis that von Wright reached in "Of Human Freedom," it is worthwhile to elucidate the interweaving of themes that prepared the way for its formulation and that provide its conceptual background. Without such an explanation, it would be impossible not only to define the non-contradictory nature of the notions of "free action" and of "determinism," but also to shed light on related themes, such as the role of human phenomena in the natural order, or the approach to the mind-body problem, which von Wright calls "externalization," since it does not proceed from an internal, or subjective, point of view, but from the "output" aspect of an agent.

The centrality of the theory of action in von Wright's thought is indisputable, at least until the end of the Eighties, when, once again, "a new opening" develops in his philosophical itinerary, a shift of the center of gravity in his thought from practical philosophy to the philosophy of mind.[15] Beginning with the creative phase of his research into deontic logic,[16] it is the foundational role of the theory of action (both individual and collective) with respect to the logic of norms that increasingly attracts von Wright's theoretical interests. Nevertheless, the logic of action does not play a "fundamental" role in the hierarchy of the "logics" that he recognizes: the fact that the logic of action is, in turn, based on the logic of change is a nodal point in his systematic research between 1963 and 1974,[17] and he often repeats the point in later expositions, such as the 1983 essay "A Philosophical Pilgrim's Itinerary"[18] or the "Introduction" to the third volume of the *Philosophical Papers*, where a sort of family tree of the notion of "action" is outlined with a few strokes, highlighting its dependence on concepts of a modal and temporal nature:

> The discovery of deontic logic in the early 1950s had made me interested in *norms*. Norms are, primarily, rules of (human) *action*. And actions consist, normally, in the bringing about or prevention of *changes* in the world. I therefore came to the opinion that a (more) fully developed Logic of Norms (deontic logic) will have to be based on a Logic of Action and this, in turn, on a Logic of Change. In *Norm and Action* [...] a first attempt was made to work out this hierarchy of "logics" in some detail. A change is, in its simplest form, a transition in time from one stage in the history of a state of affairs to the next.[19]

The "genetic" profile of the theory of action shown in this passage, even if only sketchily, is sufficient, however, to evoke the logical-conceptual problems linked to its formulation. Von Wright argues that the theory of action is based on the logic of change from different visual angles. In *Norm and Action*, and in his other writings during the Sixties, the concept of "human act" is described as "the bringing about or *effecting* ('at will') of a change," and it is linked to the concept of an "event", which is defined, in turn, as the transition from one state of affairs to another:

> the notion of human act is related to the notion of an event, *i.e.*, a change in the world. What is the nature of this relationship? It would not be right, I think, to call acts a kind or species of events. An act *is* not a change in the world. But many acts may quite appropriately be described as the bringing about or *effecting* ('at will') of a change. To act is, in a sense, to *interfere* with the 'course of nature'. An event [...] is a transition from one state of affairs to another, or from a state to a process, or from a process to a state; or it is a transformation of processes. The Logic of Change [...] is primarily a logic of events of the first type [...] The acts of opening a window or of killing a person effect changes in states of affairs. Starting to run or stopping to talk may be acts which effect a change from a state to a process and from a process to a state respectively. But when a walking man starts to run, his action effects a transformation of processes.[20]

In *Explanation and Understanding*, von Wright's early interests in the logic of action expand into the themes of explanation and the relation between action and cause. The structure of practical inference and its use in intentional explanations is identified by its difference from causal explicative patterns and by the specific role it plays in the study of man, especially in history and in the social sciences. The description of human action, however, introduced in the passage quoted above, as provoking or preventing a change in the natural world, reaches its most significant development in *Causality and Determinism*.[21] In this work, the relation between action and causation is profoundly reworked, giving way to the famous "actionistic" thesis of causality, which marks the primacy of agency over causation, reaffirming that action is conceptually fundamental to causation. This represents a significant theoretical achievement, which not only recuperates for analytical philosophy the huge field of practical rationality, but which also, by linking action to the concept of change, reestablishes a contact, which had seemed broken, both with the great themes of the Hegelian and Marxian dialectic tradition and with the more recent Habermasian version of critical social theory.[22] Furthermore, by reaffirming the strict nexus between human act and the course of nature, and by emphasizing, therefore, the fact that our actions and, more generally, practical action, play a role in the constitution of the natural world, von Wright aligns himself, in keeping with the positions presented in large measure by Husserl and by Wittgenstein, with the project – broadly definable as "anti-naturalistic" – of bringing about a humanization of nature, and which carries to completion his critique of the deterministic illusion.

The richness of the philosophical implications of von Wright's "actionistic" conception would undoubtedly merit ample and detailed analysis; to do so is not, however, the direction my examination will take.[23] As I have already said, my attention in this paper is, rather, aimed at themes which, beginning with the mid-Seventies, specify the two new lines of research indicated in the "Postscript," in an attempt to show the fabric of arguments that function as a backdrop to von Wright's compatibilist conception and to identify, therefore, the point where the theory of action is welded to the problems of determinism and of freedom.

One group of essays belonging to the decade between 1974–1984[24] and that scans the turn von Wright's research takes from a logic of change to a logic of time, while also specifically treating the problem of the temporalization of the concept of truth, seems to offer a *trait d'union* between the themes of modality and temporality, on one hand, and the problems of the determination of the future and of free will, on the other. Let it be said at the outset that the treatment of modal and temporal concepts in these writings by von Wright is a continuation, from an epistemological and historical-critical perspective, of topics previously presented in specifically logical terms. In his important essay, "Time, Change, and Contradiction",[25] are condensed the results achieved up to that point in the field of temporal logic,[26] and an apparent paradox is identified by which a logic of change would violate the law of contradiction. While, according to that principle, the truth-value of a proposition must be true or false, there are phrases like "it is raining," "Socrates is taking a walk," *etc.*, that can be both true and false depending on their placement in space and time. Only by admitting that the truth-value might vary with the time can we avoid the contradiction. Kant had already affirmed that "only by virtue of the representation of time is it possible to find a way out of the contradiction, since contradictorily opposed or incompatible properties of one and the same object are exhibited at different times, namely, *one after the other*".[27] From the Kantian position, it follows, according to von Wright, that

if we start from the fact that changes occur and are familiar to us from experience, we must describe them by arranging contradictorily related states in an order of succession – or else we have contradictions. Time, one could say metaphorically, is man's *escape from contradiction*.[28]

But is it really imperative – von Wright would wonder – to eliminate contradiction from logic? The negative answer he gives to this question in his 1969 essay constitutes a solution model which he will apply in later works, in particular when it involves denying the violation of the principle of logic in the case of propositions expressed in the future tense.[29]

This is certainly not the place to give an account of von Wright's achievements in the fields of deontic logic and temporal logic. Let it suffice to recall that his contribution to establishing the analogy between modal and temporal concepts and the place that deontics, as well as the logic of time, occupy in the family of modal logics stands alongside – even if in a completely independent formulation – that of Arthur N. Prior, the first systematizer of tense-logic in our century.[30] The significance, however, as well as the novelty, of von Wright's contribution lies in having linked these themes to the theory of action and to the problems of determinism: the essays from 1974-1984 constitute precisely the link connecting them, offering simultaneously a logical and an epistemological basis for the thesis which is central to "Of Human Freedom."

The kind of "determinism" that has to do with the human act is, in fact, based, according to von Wright, on time-laden categories, or, as he says, on dynamic categories (and not on the static categories typically expressed in the laws that govern facts in the natural world). Intentionality as direction toward the future is the hallmark of human acting and the characteristic of the propositions that concern "the study of man." The fact that acting has its foundation in temporality also clarifies in what way a theory of action might involve the theory of determination or of freedom to act and might carry with it a kind of foreknowledge, a "knowledge of the future". In short, whether we are either determined or destined to live in a certain way depends on how the present is correlated with the future. But in what way is "determinism through foreknowledge" distinct from "determinism under laws"?[31] It seems necessary, therefore, to identify a meaning for "determinism" that is valid in the humanities and not in opposition to the meaning of free action.

The problem has already been clearly defined in *Causality and Determinism*:

The problem of reconciling determinism with free action can be put in the following form: It is conceivable, *i.e.*, logically possible, that every change or not-change which results from action has, whenever it occurs, a causally sufficient condition? The problem, at bottom, is whether the existence of such a condition is *compatible* with the possibility that the conditioned change or not-change is the result of an action. It is one of the complications of this problem that one cannot discuss it thoroughly without bringing in the notion of time.[32]

But even if the formulation of the *problem* here is perfectly clear, its *solution* was to take another decade of reflection. It is precisely the need to get to the root of the "complications" arising from the introduction of the concept of "time" that led von Wright to develop the *first* line of thought indicated in the "Postscript." Its more mature fruit is harvested in 1984 in "Determinism and Future Truth" and in the other essays linked to it.[33] Taken as a whole, they sketch out the interlacing of the concepts of modality (necessity, possibility, and contingency) and those of time with the problems of determinism and free action.

In the essay "Determinismus, Wahrheit und Zeitlichkeit. Ein Beitrag zum Problem der zukünftigen kontingenten Wahrheiten",[34] cited in "Postscript 1980" as the point of departure for the *first* line of thought he had announced, von Wright critically discusses the argument by which the truth of a proposition in the future tense would involve determinism. This essay opens a substantial series of texts dedicated to the relationships between modality and time, or, more precisely, to the "modal" solution von Wright gives to the problem of future contingents.[35] For my purposes, it is sufficient to consider "Determinismus, Wahrheit und Zeitlichkeit" as introducing what I would call a triptych, composed of "Time, Truth and Necessity", "Determinism and Future Truth" and "Possibility, Plenitude and Determinism",[36] all essays that start from the Aristotelian version of the problem of future contingencies and develop the idea that the alleged deterministic conclusions of that problem are an "illusion." In these works, von Wright puts into motion a problem-resolving strategy that consists of avoiding determinism without, however, denying the validity of the laws of logic. For the sake of convenience, from here on we will call this strategy "anti-deterministic." Its adoption in the field of logic will be incorporated into the later elaboration of the compatibility thesis.

The difficulties one encounters when the application of the Law of Excluded Middle is extended from propositions concerning present and past events to propositions about future events are precisely defined by Aristotle in Chapter IX of his *De Interpretatione* by means of various examples, the best known of which is the naval battle.[37] If, based on logical principles, we allow that it is true that tomorrow there will be a naval battle or that tomorrow there will not be a naval battle, then either it is true that tomorrow there will be a naval battle, or it is true that tomorrow there will not be a naval battle. From this antiphasis it is inferred that at least one (even if we do not know which) of the two disjunctive propositions is already true today. We are, therefore, faced with a serious aporia, and the choice of one or the other option carries with it a very high price. If we wish to keep faith with logical principles, we are bound to acknowledge that what is going to be in the future has already been determined before it occurs; if, instead, we want to escape from determinism, we must stop holding that logical principles are universally valid. What is absurd is that, in any case, *contingently* true or false propositions, such as "tomorrow there will be a naval battle" and "tomorrow there will not be a naval battle," should be, instead, if true, *necessarily* true, and, if false, *impossible*.

Hence, the problem is a complex one: it is not solely a matter of affirming or denying the validity of logic, but of saving or losing contingency, that is, of leaving the door open to the possibility of being and of not being, or else of denying or embracing determinism. The counterpart of contingencies, that is, of those things that can be different from what they are, is constituted, in the context of human conduct, by the concept of what could have been done otherwise or freely performed or deliberated. Aristotle used in a similar way the concept of *proairesis*[38] to mean the characteristics of human actions which can be omitted or performed differently. In a fatalistic or deterministic vision, the suppression of contingency would, therefore, have the paradoxical consequence of making man's practical activity itself meaningless, of frustrating the possibility of free choice in human acting.

According to "traditional"[39] interpretations, the problem of future contingents posed by Aristotle is resolved by showing that the passage from the first part of the antiphasis (that is, from the hypothesis "if it is true that tomorrow there will be a naval battle or that tomorrow there will not be a naval battle") to the second part (that is, to the apodosis "then it is true that tomorrow there will be a naval battle or it is true that tomorrow there will not be a naval battle") is undue. While the first part of the antiphasis is universally valid, based on the Principle of Excluded Middle, the second part is not valid for future contingents, with the consequence that the Principle of Bivalence, which it obeys, does not have universal validity. There is, for this reason, a conflict between the two logical principles, which is resolved by denying that the Principle of Bivalence is universally valid.

According to von Wright, the traditional argument does not resolve the Aristotelian puzzle, while it is possible to glimpse in the same Aristotelian text the "intuition" of a way to escape the difficulty. In von Wright's reading, the conclusive passage 19a36-38 of *De Interpretatione* IX would affirm that, "although the disjunction ('it is true that tomorrow there will be a naval battle and it is true that tomorrow there will not be a naval battle') is necessarily true, the disjuncts taken by themselves ('it is true that tomorrow there will be a naval battle and it is true that tomorrow there will not be a naval battle) are 'not yet' true or false. [...] this temporalization of the truth-values makes good sense and removes the impression of conflict with the Principle of Bivalence."[40]

Von Wright's solution to the Aristotelian puzzle makes appeal to modal elements which intervene in the propositions concerning future contingents and, therefore, do not in any way involve a negation of bivalence. The problem is, rather, placed within a context that differentiates the double use of the concept of "it is true that" in relation to the concepts of time and of necessity that are present in the antiphasis. While for statements about present and past events it is valid to assert the truth or falsity of the statements themselves, both in the disjunction and if taken in the alternative, the need for statements about future contingents to be true or false concerns *solely* the alternative of true or false, that is, a temporalized concept of truth. But, in this case, logical arguments are not the means by which we can be assured that the event in question occured or did not occur (whether or not the naval battle took place). Rather, we recognize the "truth" – or better, we are "certain" – of our statements on the basis of experience and tradition, of good reasons and consolidated and shared beliefs. It is, thus, with reference to the fixed, settled truth of statements of which we are "sure" that we can speak of foreknowledge, of a knowledge of the future. These expressions can, without a doubt, generate misunderstandings and confusion if the distinction between temporality as *omni-temporality* and temporality as *atemporality* is not clear.[41] Continuing with the example of the naval battle, the disjunction of the two propositions is necessarily true – let us say *atemporally* true – independent of the fact that it concerns propositions about present, past, or future propositions, while this is not the conclusion that is drawn from it, according to which either one proposition is true or its negation is true. In this second case, it does not concern an atemporal truth, a "plain truth," but rather a contingent truth, for which we have a reasonable, justifiable "certainty" based on consolidated pratices and institutionalized forms of behaviour, which we accept as fixed, settled truths.[42]

According to von Wright, once these two concepts of truth have been distinguished, any reason for repudiating the Principle of Bivalence in order to justify our foreknowledge disappears. Since the two concepts of truth belong to different logical uses, they do not interfere with, and do not contradict, each other. Consequently, the atemporal truth of the disjunction of the two propositions (tomorrow there will or there will not be a naval battle) is independent of the contingent and temporally determined truth that tomorrow there will be or that tomorrow there will not be a naval battle. Since one is independent of the other, the *necessary* truth is not incompatible with the *contingent* truth/falsehood.

The application of the principles of an atemporal logic to propositions that are contingently true or false is, therefore, the fruit of an undue transfer. Within the domain of contingency, the application of principles that are valid *semper et ubique*, such as the laws of logic and of universal determinism, is simply meaningless. The notion that all truths, including those of which we are certain are already written in the stars, or in the divine mind, or are pre-determined by iron laws, is the result of the deterministic illusion, which obscures the distinction between the different uses of "it is true that." Nevertheless, once the distinction is clarified, the deterministic illusion, too, is dispelled, and contingency resumes its proper role in the order of truths. It can be said, at this point, that the conclusion drawn by the essays that expound von Wright's first line of thought exhibits the application of a strategic model that will promptly be followed in the second line, with regard to the problems of determinism. His faithfulness to Aristotle's call to save contingency will mean, in fact, on the level of practical rationality, that he succeeds in saving freedom.

III. VON WRIGHT'S VERSION OF THE COMPATIBILITY THESIS

Von Wright's *second* line of thought – which begins in 1976 with "Determinism and the Study of Man" and, going through *Freedom and Determination*, culminates in "Of Human Freedom"[43] – constitutes, in substance, a continuation of his original intentionalistic theory of action, but it is also an attempt to integrate it in the light of a more articulate idea of the relation between determinants of action and action itself. As we have already said, the second line develops, on the level of practical philosophy, the "anti-deterministic" strategy he had formulated on the epistemological and logical level along the first line and applies it to action and to free will. If, in "Determinismus, Wahrheit und Zeitlichkeit" and in the triptych of essays that follow it, the "deterministic illusion" derived, according to von Wright, from a misconception of the notion of truth,[44] in his 1976 essay and in its amplified version, *Freedom and Determination*, the determinism to which human conduct seems doomed in so far as it is subjected to "laws" that govern the "factual regularities of individual and collective behaviour and of institutional change"[45] is the result of a misunderstanding of the conceptions and methods proper to the human sciences, as opposed to those that are valid for the natural sciences. And, just as the atemporal concept of truth belongs to contexts that are distinct from those where the temporalized concept is in force, and just as knowledge of future contingents does not presuppose the predetermination of their truth, so, too, the intentional-motivational context of man as agent is something other than the causal determinism to which man is subject as an entity of nature. The fact that the determinants of human acts and of natural events belong to a different kind of phenomena, which fall under the domains of social rules and laws of nature, respectively, makes it such that determinism in the study of man is profoundly different from determinism in the study of nature, and that a kind of "methodological parallelism" is in force between norms and the laws of nature, as von Wright points out at the beginning of "Determinism and the Study of Man":

> I shall argue that deterministic ideas in the human sciences have a relation to societal rules which is *analogous* to the relation in the natural sciences between deterministic ideas and natural laws. I am not, of course, saying that laws of the state and other social rules are, in themselves, like laws of nature. They are, on the contrary, very different. The former are normative, the latter descriptive, as we say. And from this profound difference between the two types of law it follows that, if the "methodological parallelism" I am making is at all correct, determinism in the study of man means something utterly different from determinism in the study of nature. (p. 35)

The objections that can be made against this methodological parallelism are based, according to von Wright, on presuppositions implicit in the old causal theory of action, which conceives the explanation of human phenomena as based on the inductive and deductive models used to explain natural phenomena. The critical task that opens von Wright's 1976 essay centers precisely on the legitimacy of these presuppositions. One of them is found in the misleading analogy traditionally instituted between causal laws and determinants or reasons for acting, with the result that only to those determinants or reasons that are also "causes" is any explicative power attributed. Another presupposition is what von Wright calls the methodological misunderstanding of "internalization". The problem of the relation between actions and their determinants, such as the will, desires, feelings, and intentions, is modeled on the relation that exists between neuro-physiological processes and macroscopic reactions in an individual's body, with the consequence that it involves an illegitimate transfer from a sphere proper to a natural science, in this case physiology, to that of a human science, such as sociology or psychology.

Rejecting these presuppositions and substituting them with others deemed more correct is not enough to provide a solution to the problems concerning free action. The "anti-deterministic" strategy that von Wright adopts is the same one he had followed in developing his first line of thought: it consists of clarifying the special meaning that the concept of "determinism" assumes in the "study of man". On a par with the fatalistic difficulties that load the problem of future contingencies, the obstacles that postulating behavioral laws seems to pose for the unfolding of free will can be dissolved if we unmask the misleading analogies that exist between the causal context of the laws of nature and the intentional context of those factors that determine actions. If we avoid confusing the two contexts by proving that the determinants of acting, unlike natural laws which are valid *semper et ubique*, are governed by dynamic categories dependent on a logic of change, the contradiction between natural necessity and freedom disappears. The acknowledgment of the one cannot therefore constitute a threat to the performance of the other. In a later text[46] von Wright will illustrate this conclusion by recalling the Kantian conception of man as a "citizen of two worlds," of the intelligible or noumenal world, in which he is a free agent, and the phenomenal world, in which he is a body subject to rigid causality.[47] In the same text by Kant, the incompatibility between the natural laws of phenomena and freedom in the practical use of reason had been declared "*an illusion*" (*eine Täuschung*).[48]

In effect, the problem of free action will take front stage only in "Of Human Freedom," after the formulation of the thesis of compatibility between freedom and determination, *i.e.* free action and determined action. Both in "Determinism and the Study of Man" and in *Freedom and Determination*, the problem of free will remains largely in the background. As we have already noted, in these first two texts von Wright's attention is turned mainly to the study of the determinants of action and to the specific "conceptual" relation they have with the actions themselves. The technical term "determinants" is used by von Wright "as a common name for all the factors which explain action [...] In colloquial language these factors are sometimes referred to as *causes*, sometimes as *grounds* or *reasons*, sometimes as *motives*".[49] He keeps the meanings of "cause" and of "reason" distinct, however, reserving the first term for *nomic* or *Humean* causes, so called because they are "related to their effects by a law which is an inductive generalization,"[50] while he associates the term "reasons" with what are called the *internal* and *external determinants* of action.

What are the causes or reasons that determine human acting, and what is their specificity? And what is the nature of the relation between the complex interweaving of the factors of determination and the action itself? In *Causality and Determinism* von Wright had explored the first of the two themes considered in *Explanation and Understanding*, that of causation. In the works that follow it, his interest centers, instead, on the second, on the theme of intentionality. It is, in fact, with the determinant that is closest to the action, that is, the "intention to do something," that von Wright begins a treatment he reserves, in the essays composed between 1976 and 1981,[51] to "internal determinants" of action as well as to the "intentionalist explanation," that is, the explanation of an action as determined by the intentions of its agent (the *volitional* attitudes), together with his thoughts, beliefs, and desires (the *epistemic* attitudes). According to the scheme of the "practical syllogism" introduced in *Explanation and Understanding*,[52] the volitional and epistemic attitudes (*A* intended to ventilate the room; and *A* thought/believed/wished that, unless he opened the window, he could not ventilate the room) together constitute the premises of a conclusion in which the action is expressed (therefore: *A* opened the window). In this example, the cause or the reason why *A* performed that action is, therefore, a characteristic combination of an intention and an opinion of how to make real the object of the intention:

One could also say that the determinant of A's action was a combination of a volitive and of a cognitive (or epistemic) attitude of an agent. This is a general characteristic of intentionalist action-explanations.[53]

The intentionalist explanation scheme exemplified above is applied to the action that A believes is a necessary means to obtain the end he has set for himself.[54] Von Wright considers at least two other schemes in which the means attain certain ends that are not believed necessary, but sufficient, or simply useful, or favorable to one's goal. If the agent believes that performing a certain action (for example, opening the window) is a sufficient, but not necessary, means to a certain end (for example, to ventilate the room), he obviously has an alternative means available (for example, opening air-conditioning), and, therefore, a possibility of choice, to achieve the same end. In this case, what A performs is a "disjunctive action" (A opens the window or A opens air-conditioning), as von Wright specifies:

When the performance of an action is the outcome of a choice between several total actions within an agent's horizon of intentionality the agent performs what I propose to call a *disjunctive action*.[55]

The proposed scheme thus allows a complete explanation for why an agent performed that action, even if it does not completely explain the choice of the particular way in which he did it. Performing a disjunctive action means, in fact, making a choice, and if the choice is not explained, the intentionalist explanation remains incomplete.

Von Wright's writings from 1976 to the late Eighties integrate and, in part, correct what he had maintained in *Explanation and Understanding* concerning the intentionalist explanation and the internal determinants of an action. First of all, the intentionalist model loses the privileged position it had held in that work, and a plurality of variants of it are introduced. As von Wright himself will acknowledge later in a passage that is almost autobiographical, there are, in reality, many determinants and various explanation models of action. Moreover, the external determinants exercise a direct influence on the action itself, one that is not mediated by the internal determinants:

For a long time I was held by the belief that *all* action explanation was, in the last resort, reducible to the intentionalist model – moreover in the special form of it which contemplates necessary means to a presumed end. This simply will not do – not even for explanations which make reference to *internal* determinants. As for explanations through external determinants, I believe there is a deeprooted tendency to think that these determinants can effect conduct only provided they first call forth intentions and similar determinants of an internal nature in the agent. On this view the external determinants work only indirectly on actions, through the "intermediary" of internal determinants. This too is a mistake.[56]

In von Wright's conception of action beginning with the 1976 essay, one can note, in effect, at least *three* new elements, which I will present briefly: (i) the attribution of an important role to external determinants of action; (ii) a revision of the logical-connection-argument; (iii) the advance from a "retrospective" view of action-explanation to a "prospective" view of action-prediction.

(i) Von Wright's attention to the external determinants of action, which runs throughout his whole treatment in *Freedom and Determination*, arises from the discovery of internal limitations in the intentional explanation model and from the need to correct the dominant tendency to privilege the internal determination of actions. In reality, not all actions can be understood as answers to why an agent intends to do something, and not all actions are performed as means intended to achieve an end. Executing an order, answering a question, and reacting to a signal (for example, a traffic signal) are actions determined through verbal or symbolic challenges that involve the agents' participation in practices and institutionalized forms of behaviour.[57] The explanation that appeals to this kind of reason, or external determinant, specifies what von Wright calls an *imperative* explanation model. Other actions are, rather, performed in keeping with rules or in obedience to legal or moral norms. The rules and norms that, in this case, determine conduct serve to institutionalize the behaviour; the explanation that makes use of this kind of determinant puts into play a *normative* explanation model.[58]

It is obvious that, presenting themselves in the form of challenges or of rules, the external determinants do not influence the conduct of the individual as an individual, but as a member of a community. To say that the practices in which he participates by responding (*if* he responds) to symbolic challenges or by obeying (*if* he obeys) rules are "institutionalized" means, in fact, that "they are shared by a community into which we are reared by being taught to participate."[59] The fact, however, that the forms of external determination, as opposed to the intentions and epistemic attitudes that constitute the internal determinants of action, "have to be taught and learnt" reveals, as von Wright emphasizes, that the agent's understanding of these challenges and norms and his mastery of the rules of conduct are not enough to determine the action. In specifying the factors that, in the one case and in the other, determine the intentional-motivational mechanism, von Wright introduces one of the most important "dynamic" concepts that characterize the context in which the reasons that explain human actions are to be sought and that thus make it possible to "rationalize" it: the concept of "normative pressure":

Learning to participate in institutionalized forms of behaviour is connected with a characteristic motivation. I shall call this motivational mechanism normative pressure.[60]

The nature of this mechanism is repeated in *Freedom and Determination*:

This additional element is related to the way in which people are taught to participate in the various institutionalized patterns of behaviour or to follow rules–and also to the purpose of the institutions (rules). I shall refer to this element with the name of normative pressure.[61]

For this reason, connected with the concept of normative pressure is the idea of participation in institutionalized forms of behaviour that exercise coercion on the agent or, in the case of non-conformity with the accepted norms or rules, call for unpleasant consequences (disapproval, ostracism, etc.) for the agent. The idea of the reward that follows participation in or obedience to social practices does not seem to be connected with the "aura of normative pressure" that surrounds an action. The coercion of normative pressure gives way to acceptance of the rules for the advantage of the community. In this case it can be said that the social rules have been "internalized" and that, since they are internalized, they retain the "freedom" of the agents which had, in some way, been annulled or limited under the influence of the normative pressure.[62] In short, it can be said that, by making the individual a participant in social games, this mechanism becomes, in some way, an intermediary for the internal and external reasons that determine an individual action.

It certainly is not difficult to recognize the influence of Wittgenstein's conception of *Sprachspiele* and the consonance with Habermas' most recent theory of "communicative action"[63] in this idea of participation in institutionalized forms of conduct. In any case, the articulated phenomenology of externally determined behaviour which von Wright develops in the second chapter of *Freedom and Determination* has theoretical goals that are very different from those pursued, for example, by the author of the *Philosophische Untersuchungen*. As the two other arguments formulated by von Wright beginning in 1976 will bring to light, his analysis of the complex network of motivations for acting has the purpose of identifying the peculiar notion of "determinism" used in the study of man and to prove, in short, that externally determined actions are, by definition, free actions.

(ii) The unilateral character which derives, as we have seen, from a general tendency to privilege internal determinants also brings to light the inadequacy of the two solutions traditionally given for the problem of the nexus between determinants (intentions, desires, beliefs, challenges, and norms) and actions. According to von Wright, this nexus is neither causal nor logical: the determinants of an action, *i.e.* the reasons that explain it, are connected to that action by means of a link of a "third kind," which cannot be assimilated to a relation between cause and effect, nor to an implication between ground and consequence. The traditional dichotomy between the *causal* because-relation and the *logical* because-relation has prevented us, according to von Wright, from stating the central problem of the philosophy of action correctly as the determination of actions through reasons, and thus also from fully understanding the meaning of the practical inference. In *Freedom and Determination*, not only does he repeat the critique of the causal theory of action that was already present in *Explanation and Understanding*, but a self-critique of the logical alternative he had introduced in that same work also appears.

The argument for why the relation between reasons (determinants) and actions is neither a causal nexus nor a logical entailment occupies the third chapter of *Freedom and Determination*. Causal relations are characterized (a) by the requirement of *nomicity*: cause and effect are connected by a general law; therefore, when a cause occurs, an effect necessarily follows; and (b) by the requirement of *independence*: the occurrence of a cause can be identified without needing to identify the occurrence of an effect, and *vice versa*. Of a very different nature is the relation between determinants and actions: their relation cannot be nomic, because that would presuppose, for example, that an order must always (by virtue of the law) be followed by its execution. We know, instead, that orders are not unfailingly executed, and that there exists a great variety of modes that predispose one to obey or disobey orders. Furthermore, actions and determinants cannot be considered as mutually independent, cannot be analyzed outside their context. Rather, they must be seen in the broadest possible context, in a "narration" about the agent[64] that connects the action to its entire life history.[65] If, then, the thesis of a logical entailment between determinants and actions were true, then it would be unthinkable (self-contradictory) for an agent to have received and understood an order and not to have executed it.[66] The reality, instead, is that actions do not logically follow upon orders, and that disobedience is a rather widespread practice.[67]

The *sui generis* connection that links an action with its internal and external determinants is, according to von Wright, of a "conceptual" nature, in the sense that it depends on the meaning of the concepts of intention, desires, challenges and norms that we have been taught and that we have learned to use, together with the concept of action itself:

The conceptual features which make intentions etc. action-determinants do not exist independently of the actual functioning of the determinants. It is also a conceptual feature of intentions, *etc.* that people normally do act on their intentions, reach out for things they want, respond to orders and requests, follow the rules of the society in which they live.[68]

To say, then, that an action is neither logical nor causal means that there is "no absolute, incorrigible or unshakeable truth ground" for the statement that links the action to factors of an internal and external nature, that there is no possibility that an atemporal validity might be attributed to such a statement, or that a sovereign power might exist – be it fate, or an inscrutable divine plan, or the unquestionable agent's first authority – that is capable of irrevocably determining it.[69] In other words, the conceptual connection, as such, is removed from the domain of the plain truth, which von Wright had carefully distinguished, in his modal essays, from that of the settled, fixed truths which are temporally (historically) determined.

(iii) The third argument, which centers on the theme of predicting actions, is interwoven with the second in Chapter III of *Freedom and Determination*. It, too, constitutes an attempt to shed light on a new aspect of the relation between actions and internal and external determinants, *i.e.* the aspect that von Wright calls *ex ante actu*,[70] as opposed to the other aspect, which is, to a large extent, the more frequently studied of the two, the *ex post actu*.[71] The first aspect refers to the *prediction* of actions, the second to their *explanation*. One can imagine that von Wright's interest in the prospective view of action-prediction arises from the need to extend to the realm of action those results he had achieved, within the first line of thought, regarding the knowledge of the future and the crucial distinction between foreknowledge and knowledge obtained through natural laws.

First of all, von Wright defines the thesis of the structural identity of explanation and prediction in the empirical sciences, supported by the epistemologies of neoempiristic derivation,[72] as an "oversimplification," that, in any case, does not reflect the situation within the framework of the human sciences and, in particular, in the theory of action. In what sense can one speak of a "prediction" of action based on reasons, or internal and external determinants? It is true that predicting actions seems to have "a certain resemblance with the prediction of effects from knowledge of their causes."[73] This similarity consists, however, in predicting that the volitional and epistemic background of an agent, *i.e.* his internal determinants, will not change before he executes the action. What we predict, therefore, is not that the agent will act, but that he will not change his mind. The use of the term "predict," in this case, appeals to a conceptual nexus (not a nomic one) between the intentions of an agent and his actions, a nexus that can be instituted only by one who knows and is familiar with those concepts and who can, therefore, affirm that, given the series of internal motivations in the agent, he will perform a certain action or he will not. As von Wright points out:

To say that such and such intentions and beliefs, assuming they do not change, will normally result in such and such behaviour is not to state an empirical generalization based on observations and experiments. It is to state a necessary truth to which anybody familiar with the concepts involved will agree off-hand.[74]

When one considers the case of external determinants of action, it might seem that, here, too, there is at least one statistical law that connects symbolic challenges and social rules to actions. However, the strenght of this connection can be used to measure a variety of characteristics of an agent's reactions to external determinats, but it does not explain predictability.[75] Why, then, are we so reluctant to give the name of "laws" to the correlations between symbolic challenges and actions? This is the question von Wright poses, and which he answers in an incisive passage from his 1976 essay, which also appears in *Freedom and Determination* at the end of his analysis of the *ex ante actu* aspect of the relation between an action and its external determinants:

It is of some interest to ponder why we do not willingly speak of such correlations as "laws". Is it because of their unprecise and statistical nature? Or because of their dependence upon individual agents and individual societies? An even weightier reason for not calling them "laws" is, I think, their dependence upon factors, *viz.*, norms and institutionalized patterns of behaviour, which are themselves susceptible to change in the course of history as a result of human action. "Scientific laws", we tend to think, must not for their validity be dependent upon historical contingencies. They should hold true *semper et ubique*.[76]

The truth of the prediction of actions, its reliability, is not founded, therefore, on general laws that are universally valid; rather, it is of a contingent and historically determined nature: it can change with reference to this or that agent and according to its role within a life history. Precisely because human actions are internally and externally determined, that is, because they are actions for reasons, in terms of which the agent can account for what he has done or has failed to do, we have the possibility of predicting, of explaining, and, more generally, of understanding actions. But if acting is acting for reasons, then the concept of human action is intrinsically linked to the concept of freedom:

The "freedom" or "free will" of a man consists in the *fact* that he acts, one could say. And that he *acts* – not just behaves – consists in the fact that he (we) can account for what he does in terms of what I have called determinants of human action. Therefore the concepts used for describing and explaining a man's actions, such as motive, reason, intention, choice, deliberation *etc.*, are all of them tied to the idea of "freedom". To deny that an *agent* is *free* is to commit a contradiction in terms. The "mystery" of freedom, if there is one, is the "mystery" of the fact that there *are* agents and actions.[77]

In "Explanation and Understanding of Action," the essay which lucidly and exhaustively brings to a conclusion the path taken by the second line that was begun in "Determinism and the Study of Man," von Wright expresses his conception of action for reasons in an exemplary passage:

Free action and action for reasons are twin concepts. "Determination" of action through reasons is, one could say, a precondition of human freedom. Without this type of determination our very notions of agent and action would not exist, or be quite different from those we have.[78]

The problem of freedom and determinism, which is only introduced in *Freedom and Determination* and in the essays that surround it, becomes central in "Of Human Freedom," where it is, in some way, "resolved" by showing that the irreconcilability traditionally accorded to these concepts is, in effect, a "pseudo-conflict." The notion of determinism in the framework of actions for reasons cannot be confused with the notion of universal determinism used in the framework of the natural sciences. As Kant said, the liberty of the practical use of reason and submission to natural laws are not contradictory and therefore not incompatible. The clarification offered by this distinction, which von Wright proposes as a "solution," is, in reality, a very special version of the classical thesis, known as the *compatibility thesis*. Von Wright is not proposing a theory that defends, with new arguments, the reconciliability of determinism and free will; rather, he is showing how the "problem" of that reconciliation, once the differences are made clear, simply disappears, and the "solution" to the problem is precisely this.

Rather than define von Wright's compatibilism as a thesis, I would say it is a corollary to his conception of action for reasons, and, thus, as we have already seen, of free action. In the context provided by "Of Human Freedom," von Wright's view, as presented in the Second Lecture, occupies a "central" place in a more specific sense as well: it is, in fact, placed between his treatment, in the First Lecture, of actions for reasons that determine the range of a man's freedom, and the discussion, developed in the Second Lecture, of psycho-physical parallelism, or, as it is often called, the "problem of congruence" between the physical and the mental. In this way the special importance that "Of Human Freedom" assumes in von Wright's writings over the last decade is confirmed, since it constitutes, on one hand, the point of arrival of his reflections on the themes of human action and, on the other, a new opening to the problems of the philosophy of mind.

In the First Lecture, certainly the themes that characterize *Freedom and Determination* dominate, in particular the topic of the internal and external determinants in terms of an analysis of "actions for reasons" that are "up to the agent" and of "reasons for acting" that, instead, are not up to the agent. Nevertheless, these themes seem to have been reconstructed here in order to clear the terrain of the numerous misunderstandings linked to the traditional definitions of free will and to put to the test the fundamental idea of § 48 of *Freedom and Determination*, according to which the very concept of action for reasons is intrinsically linked to the concept of freedom.

Two arguments of the First Lecture act as a prologue to the compatibilist thesis and to the problem of congruence; with them, von Wright denounces the inadequacy and, in a certain sense, the obsolescence of the "classical" posing of the problems of the freedom-of-the-will. *First*, von Wright rejects the voluntaristic conceptions of the problem of freedom: linking the concept of freedom to that of the agent's will or desires simply means abandoning any explanation of our actions; it is like saying, "It is none of your business to inquire into the motives for my action."[79] In other words, it means "obscuring" the existence of the motivational background of factors that really determine the agent, in particular, the set of "conditions, institutions, and practices in the society of which he is a member,"[80] *i.e.* the "reasons" we have for acting. *Second*, von Wright separates the context to which the concept of freedom should be attributed from the scientific and theological contexts within which it had originally been discussed. To define it in connection with traditional ideas about natural determinism or the omnipotence of God is to create an undue tension between the physical aspect of the action, which determines it causally according to the "iron laws" operating in the natural world, and the elements of freedom and responsibility, which we attribute, instead, to human acting.

In § 5, in analyzing the meaning of the concept of "free action" as what I could have omitted doing or what I could have done otherwise, von Wright again takes up the theme of the *contingent* character of action in analogy to the treatment he had offered earlier for future contingents. The action is *logically contingent* in a sense of the expression "it could have been omitted" (or "it could have been done otherwise"), which is different from the sense of the statement: "it is *logically necessary* that one performs or omits to perform the action". Although the meaning of logical contingencies attributed to performance and omission of actions seems to dispel in some way the aura of fatalism which is typical of some traditional theories of free will, "we feel istinctively – as von Wright says – that the meaning of "could have acted differently" is more interesting than this."[81] In fact there is a "stronger" sense according to which that phrase is involved in the concept of action for reasons:

That an agent acted for a certain reason normally means that something was, for this agent, a reason for doing something *and* that he set himself (chose, proceeded, maybe upon deliberation) to do this thing *for that reason*. To say this is to intimate that he could, in fact, have acted otherwise [...] Normally, it is, as one says, "up to the agent" to act or not on given reasons. Action for reasons is *self-determined*.[82]

In von Wright's language, the concept of *self-determination* is a property of action for reasons and, hence, by definition, also of *free action*. The phrase "self-determination" may, however, risk being misunderstood. It is worthwhile, therefore, to consider at least two topics in this regard presented in the First Lecture: one concerns the kind of explanation offered in terms of reasons; the other is related to the "boundless subjectivism" with which the explanation of the action for reasons seems to be involved. The point of view von Wright expresses on both these points further develops his view in *Freedom and Determination*, where action for reasons and free action are twin concepts. To say that an action for reasons is self-determined means that it does not have its basis in absolute truth, that is does not depend on a sovereign authority, but that it is determined by its own reasons and, as such, is an exercise in freedom. The first theme, introduced in §§ 9–11, has also been developed by von Wright in his more recent writings under the heading of "understanding explanations."[83] Instead of pursuing an *explicative* purpose, as is the case for explanations that have their basis in scientific theories, reason-giving explanations have an *evaluative* purpose. But the precondition for evaluating an action (for judging it good or bad, right or blameworthy) is to understand it in the context of its reasons. In this way von Wright corroborates his well known argument, whereby the relation between actions and reasons is neither causal nor logical, but conceptual, based, that is, on the understanding of the meaning of the concepts they involve.

The second theme, discussed in §§ 12–16, centers on his disagreement with the idea that a candidate exists who can act as a "supreme judge" for the better understanding of actions. By saying that the "truth" of an action for reasons can be understood by starting with the self-determination of the agent, von Wright wishes to maintain that it does not have a subjective or an objective foundation, that it is not the exclusive property of the individual agent or of an outside observer, and that it does not, therefore, depend on the authority of the first or of the third person (pp. 26–7). The "truth" of actions for reasons derives from the context into which they are inserted, and to understand that context, no one can be designated in advance and for all time as the best interpreter:

[...] the agent is not necessarily better equipped than the outsider. The outsider may be superior. To neither of the two belongs exclusively the right to pass a final judgement. (p. 26)

In conclusion: the self-determination of actions may be the key concept of the First Lecture, and it certainly constitutes a prototype of the very special version of "compatibilism" that von Wright would propose in the Second Lecture as a solution to the problem of congruence, or parallelism, of mind and matter, which the classical compatibility thesis had left open-ended. I call von Wright's version of compatibility "very special" because it is in no way associated with the prevalent use of the term, *i.e.* with its meaning as peaceful coexistence, as stability in principle, almost as mutual indifference. On the contrary, the compatibility of which von Wright speaks is his name for a relation that is anything but stable, anything but painless, perhaps for a balance that has always been sought and never achieved. The fact that human action is both free and determined is itself already a sign of its radical doubleness, of the instability and dramatic nature intrinsic to the condition of man in the world. In the same way, the "parallelistic" thesis of the Second Lecture forms part of this pervasive *Stimmung*, and it, too, is a "very special" version, as we shall see, of what is traditionally meant by psycho-physical parallelism. Intrinsically connected to the concept of action for reasons is, in fact, the concept of "somatic change," which is another way of saying that "actions which are performed for reasons also have a bodily aspect."[84] The parallelism, or congruence, between the bodily and mental aspects of the actions takes the form of a dynamic vision of man as an agent who is both subject and object of natural forces which he controls and by which he is controlled, of a creature who, as had been said in the 1976 essay, "is both slave and master of his own destiny." (p. 52). In substance, von Wright's view of compatibility is rooted in his conception of man and of the dialectic relationship that links him to the natural world. This basic orientation is certainly present throughout von Wright's work, but it becomes the object of independent reflection in a series of essays that I will call "humanistic" to distinguish them from those with a more specifically analytical subject. Although thematically they are characterized by a more general interest, from a philosophical point of view the humanistic essays have full right to be considered an integral part of the two lines of thought mentioned in "Postscript 1980."

IV. PROBLEMS OF PHILOSOPHICAL HUMANISM

Around the middle of the Seventies, and in ways that are singularly interwoven with the problems of temporality and determinism, von Wright published some writings on the themes of "humanism," the importance of which he himself mentions in "Postscript 1980". In reality, this interest in what he called the "neo-humanistic attitude" is anything but new in von Wright's thought.[85] Running throughout von Wright's entire itinerary is the practice of a philosophizing that is shaped, not only by the problems and methods of logic and of philosophical analysis, but also by the "study of man," and that pays heed to the themes which, from the pre-Socratics to Nietzsche, have oriented philosophy toward the search for a "Weltanschauung" and a "Sinn des Lebens." He himself has also recently acknowledged the "double track" of his research and, in the brief but illuminating "Introduction" to *The Tree of Knowledge*, attributes its existence, in large part, to the influence exercised on him by the personalities of his two masters: Kaila and Wittgenstein.

On one page of the "Replies" included in Schilpp's volume, he lists four phases in his investigation into humanism: the youthful phase of aesthetic humanism, the ethical phase of the Forties and Fifties, the rationalist one of the Sixties, and the social-humanist phase, which extends up to the mid-Seventies.[86] One can, therefore, reasonably assume that the 1976 Lindley Lecture mentioned in the "Postscript," "What is Humanism?", opens a fifth phase in his studies on humanism. But in what way is this phase "new" in the context of von Wright's production over the last two decades? In his writings from 1976-1977 up to the essays collected in *The Tree of Knowledge* and beyond,[87] it is clear that the "two tracks" of his research, while taking shape in ways of philosophizing that are distinct for their style and content, nonetheless present an affinity of conceptions and intents. Von Wright establishes a link, which had not been made explicitly in his previous writings, between his theses about free action and the problems of humanism. It could, perhaps, be said that, in the more recent "humanistic" essays, the problematic nucleus that had remained in the background of the "analytical" essays is laid bare and comes into the limelight.

In his "Reply" to the article by Tranøy that appears in Schilpp's volume,[88] von Wright assigns to what he then considered the "fourth" phase of his "search for a humanist attitude," the revision of his previous rationalist conception, according to which the science of man must be modeled on the exact sciences of nature and integrated into a more comprehensive family of the sciences.[89] This revision will be carried to its conclusion in *Explanation and Understanding*, where his dualistic vision of the study of man and of nature will mature, a vision that von Wright considers very close to what he calls the "Aristotelian" tradition and in opposition to the monistic and scientistic positions which have, instead, kept alive up to our days the "Galilean" tradition.[90] Nevertheless, in his writings on humanism in the past two decades, a perspective emerges which further corrects the point of view of *Explanation and Understanding*. Instead of the heritage of the Aristotelian tradition, one can easily recognize there the reflection of a new source of inspiration, precisely that of the "Kantian" tradition which we have seen underpinning von Wright's most recent investigations into man's place in nature, between the intelligible world of causal laws and the noumenal world of the ideals of reason. Significant traces of this inspiration are present in many works of the period, particularly in "Of Human Freedom."[91]

It is, perhaps, precisely in this agreement with the special form of "compatibility" between natural necessity and free will, between causality and freedom, which Kant recognized when he considered the condition of man as a "citizen of two worlds," that one can catch sight of the link that sums up von Wright's way to escape from the "deterministic illusion," on one hand, and from "Dante's dream," on the other, from the ideal pursued in the *Divine Comedy* of "restoring" a world that seemed lost and a human condition that had been fatally compromised by cognitive *hybris*.[92] His interpretation of this "dream" is, at heart, not so much with the view of "solving" it, in keeping with the style of problem-solving typical of the theoretical procedures of science, as it is to "dissolve" the illusion that pervades European culture in its most meaningful expressions – Greek and Judeo-Christian in origin – that it is possible to treat the ideals of the reason with the categories of the intellect, and the problems of metaphysics with the tools of science.

Von Wright's philosophical neo-humanism consists precisely in showing the irrealizability – the "dream" indeed – of fusing the varied forms of human rationality, of crystallizing them within a single and conclusive theoretical schema, which assumes the model of scientific knowledge as its paradigm. According to von Wright, the monistic tendencies present in the great traditions of the past survive in the positivistic and neo-positivistic programs of a unitary science, of the unification of the theories and methods of the natural and human sciences, and, above all, in the intellectual orientation of today's scientific and technological revolution. This tendency aims to obscure the multiple forms in which the human condition is expressed, and it "provides a quasi theoretical justification for dehumanizing manipulations of society by individuals and groups who are in a position to 'engineer' or 'steer' the social process."[93] Once the impracticability of the monistic expectation has been made clear and the illusion that lies at its base has been unmasked, the problem of avoiding the contradictions between nature and reason, between causality and freedom, reappears under a new form, not that of their mutual reduction or identification, but of "a more articulate schema of understanding"[94] which "dissolves," that is, makes meaningless, any form of dualism, as well as any form of reductionism.[95] The concepts involved in the old dualism do not refer to substances which can be reduced or identified, their meaning is, as we know, determined by the contexts in which they are used, by their reference to the symbolic challenges (institutions, rules, and norms) to which they respond.

In his essay published in 1960, "The Tree of Knowledge," which anticipates by about twenty years his more mature formulations on philosophical humanism, von Wright had manifested his first doubts about the optimistic belief in a positive outcome for the transformations in the style of human life stemming from scientific-technological progress and from the age-old search for a hegemonic form of rationality. Precisely because of the emblematic significance enjoyed by the biblical myth referring to the tree of the knowledge of good and evil in representing the destiny of man dominated by cognitive *hybris*, von Wright included this essay in the volume published in 1993 under the same title. In the two parts that constitute the book, he collected his autobiographical and historical-critical contributions to the formulation of the great themes of philosophical logic and analytical philosophy, as well as his considerations about the condition and the destiny of man in the modern age. Far from taking the form of a kind of "theory of culture," these considerations express, instead, his attempt to offer a "diagnosis of our time," the result of which is to bring to light those tendencies that, asserted throughout the course of Western culture, have proposed an illusory rationalization of the relation between science and reason, between man and nature, and have given credit to the prevalence of forces whose aim is the dehumanization and self-annihilation of man and of his environment. This is exemplified, according to von Wright, by the classical myths that narrate the expulsion from Eden, the punishment of Prometheus, and the damnation of Faust, and it is re-proposed, in one of von Wright's most charming essays, in his reference to Dante's tale of the final voyage of Ulysses and his shipwreck at the forbidden boundaries of the world.

What is the significance of the mythological stories from a philosophical point of view? First of all, they show the doubleness of human rationality and, hence, its intrinsically tragic nature: that is, that knowledge can, at the same time, be an instrument of good and of evil, of emancipation and of damnation. In the conclusion to "The Tree of Knowledge" von Wright states that the three myths

are all tragic, either in the sense – as in the Paradise myth and in the Faust saga – that they show us man torn between the two poles of light and darkness, or in the sense – as in the Prometheus myth – that they depict a struggle of man for a fundamentally just cause, but blinded by self-overconsideration. (p. 153)

The *leitmotiv* common to the three myths consists precisely of the double potential for good and evil intrinsic in the desire for knowledge that pervades human reason. In the biblical story, as in the myth of Prometheus and in the saga of Faust, von Wright sees a prefiguration of the human condition which he had so significantly expressed in "Determinism and the Study of Man," defining man as both a slave and master of his own destiny, and his actions as intrinsically marked by the requirement of being both free and determined. This basic doubleness cannot be eliminated without paying the price of progressive dehumanization, leading to self-destructive results: if man were not determined, he could not exercise his freedom; if he were not free, he could not act rationally. The risk to which the human condition is exposed, clenched between a desire for knowledge and the very limits of its nature, is obviously represented in the language of these myths: man in Eden, Prometheus, and Faust all share the human desire for knowledge, but, as their exemplary stories show, it can become a "lethal game" and, if turned into an absolute, can lead to sin, to damnation, and to death. Sin, damnation, and death are metaphors, or figures, for the destructive processes that man primes for firing when he tries to go beyond his nature, wishing to become omniscient and omnipotent, to be the equal of the gods of the natural domain, to surpass the limits of his temporality by making the fleeting hour eternal. In this gallery of myths, von Wright gives a place no less important to Dante's Ulysses, who, "in pursuit of virtue and knowledge," finds death by overstepping the boundaries of the inhabited world.

By digging into the rich mythology of the biblical account and the tales of Prometheus, of Ulysses, and of Faust, and into the interpretations that philosophy, literature, and art have given them over the centuries, von Wright brings to light the profound similarities that the truths hidden in the language of myth have with "modern" expressions of the human desire for knowledge: science unbound from any form of authority (the fruit of the knowledge of good and evil), progress as the bearer of happiness (the gift of fire to man still in the wild state), the victory over time and death (the pact with the devil in exchange for one's soul) – these are all images, in turn poetic, philosophical, and religious, of the destiny that awaits a world and a society threatened by the absolutization of the proper values of technological civilization.[96]

Is the aspiration to knowledge, therefore, fatally destined to become tragedy? Do science and technology, born from the need to liberate and emancipate mankind, inevitably lead to a new form of slavery? In the face of the urgency of these questions, the classical myths lose their apparent, banal meaning of illustrating divine abuses with regard to man, the triumph of violence over justice, and assume the dimension of a severe warning: human reason, in the complex formed by its abilities and cognitive acquisitions, can contribute to making man freer, but also to making him more of a slave. Dante had pointed to salvation, in the form of the intervention of a higher grace, and the restoration of a lost equilibrium. For modern man, it is not possible to return to paradise lost; Dante's dream is over: "der Traum ist ausgeträumt," as Husserl would say. Nevertheless, it remains a regulating ideal: no power exists if not that of human reason itself to turn knowledge into an instrument of salvation rather than damnation:

There is no way back for us moderns either to Ancient belief in a self-preserving cosmic harmony or to Dante's dream of the restoration of a universal Christian commonwealth. We must try to attain our own self-reflective understanding of our situation. And I have wanted to say that it belongs to this achievement that we take warning of the fate which the poet foresaw for the non-Homeric Ulysses who steered his vessel beyond the pillars of Hercules and thereby entered the road to self-annihilation.[97]

The "lesson" that von Wright seeks to draw from the warning implicit in the tales of the great myths is to conceive man's place in nature from a perspective that we will call "humanistic," with reference to a conception of the problem that harks back to the "Humanists" of the Renaissance, such as Pico della Mirandola, and reaches, I would say, up to Kant's Copernican revolution. Contrary to Kepler's later deterministic conceptions, Pico's man, as he presented him in his 1486 work "Oratio de hominis dignitate",

has no fixed place in the great order of things. It is up to man himself to choose his place, what he will be: beast or angel or something in between.[98]

Von Wright's humanism can be seen in this conception of the dynamic relationship between man and the natural world, a relationship that, to a certain extent, incorporates his "very special" idea of compatibility formulated in "Of Human Freedom".

V. THE MEANING OF THE MIND-MATTER RELATIONSHIP

On various occasions throughout this work, I have called attention to the fact that "Of Human Freedom" is not only the apex of von Wright's theory of action, but also the starting point for the philosophy of mind that he develops in the essays that follow it.[99] In a very recent text, von Wright reveals that, while he was working on the Tanner Lectures, his thoughts underwent a turnabout and were moving at the time in a field very different from the theories of action, of norms and of values.[100] His new opening toward the themes of the philosophy of mind, documented in "Of Human Freedom," undoubtedly confer on this work, and above all on the Second Lecture, a particular importance in the context of von Wright's mature thought. However, rather than dwell on these developments, whose traces can be found in some of his most recent essays, I will limit myself here to showing the continuity of von Wright's conception of the mind-matter relationship with his theory of free action.

In § 1 of the First Lecture, von Wright points out that the problem of the relationship between mind and matter is another way of posing the problem of freedom, or, at the very least, a face of it:

[...] if the bodily life of man is governed by "iron laws" of causal necessitation, how can it happen that his limbs, on the whole, move in a way which corresponds to the agent's free actions? The question is obscure. The way to answer it is, I think, to try to formulate it clearly – and then see that there is no question at all to be answered. I shall call this the Problem of Congruence. (§1, p. 3)

In the Second Lecture, he offers an "answer" that springs, as we will see, from von Wright's definition of action for reasons and from his view that freedom and determination are "compatible".

In §§ 3–8 of the Second Lecture, von Wright presents his solution to the problem of the congruence between the mental and bodily aspects of an action, going on, then, in §§ 9–12, to point out that this solution does not entail determinism. In two works that come shortly afterwards, "An Essay on Door-Knocking" and "Reflections on Psycho-Physical Parallelism," von Wright again takes up and isolates the two topics of the Second Lecture, offering us a clear synthesis of his way of setting forth and resolving the problem of congruence as of a "harmony" between mind and body, in a sense which is not that of a Leibnitian pre-established harmony but that of something achieved (when and if it is achieved) "in the course of the individual's life and necessary for its preservation over the span of time allotted to each of us."[101]

The example of the "knock on the door" (I hear a knock on the door, I get up, I go to the door, and I open it) describes the presence of physical and mental facts that intervene in the action and constitute the reasons why the agent performed it. In other words, in the action it is possible to distinguish a bodily aspect, consisting of a muscular activity that provokes a change in the external world and can, thus, be called an outer aspect, and a mental aspect, consisting of the volitional and epistemic background of the agent, which provokes the change and can also be called an inner aspect of the action. Just as the inner aspect constitutes the input of the action and the outer aspect is its output, so the reverse is true, where an outer event, like a knock on the door, constitutes the input, while the inner aspect is its output. This example clearly seems to place before us the problem of the existence of two distinct causal chains: mental (psychical) cause – bodily (physical) effect, and bodily (physical) cause – mental (psychical) effect:

Granting that reasons are causes, we seem to have two parallel but independent causal chains here. On the one hand we have reasons causing actions, and on the other hand we have innervations and other neural processes causing muscular activity. The two chains converge in the physical aspect of the actions.[102]

However, it is following this description that the problem arises:

How shall we understand the "congruence" or seeming "coincidence" that when I do a certain thing for one reason or other, the required physical aspect of my action makes its appearance under the influence of causes, perhaps acting from without my body, and in any case "external to my will"?[103]

As von Wright justly recalls, the existence of these two causal chains and the "mysterious" nature of their convergence in the action have lain at the center of philosophical reflection since Descartes and his conception of two substances that, nevertheless, interact. Passing through Hobbes, Spinoza, Leibniz and Berkeley, the entire history of Western thought seems to have been dominated by attempts to shed light on the obscure points of our Cartesian heritage and to reject interactionism. The phenomenology of "door-knocking," which von Wright carefully presented in his works at the end of the Eighties, responds to the need to unveil the "mystery" of the interaction between mind and body by showing that the distinction between the two causal chains is an illusion and that the link between mind and body is of *conceptual* nature. It is characteristic that, in considering the work of the three greatest philosophers of this century, Husserl, Heidegger and Wittgenstein, as an effort to get rid of the Cartesianism, von Wright defines his own research as "an independent track in the same direction".[104]

Certainly the knock on the door is the input of the action. But, in order for a pure sound to become a reason for action or a reason against action, it is necessary that determinate physical conditions for the performance of the action occur (for example, that the agent is not deaf, is not far from the door, and has heard the sound). This already provides a characteristic way in which, as von Wright emphasizes, "my body is involved in the context of my action".[105] With respect to the other condition that makes the performance of the action possible, i.e. understanding, here, too, it is possible to see how "my body is also involved, intrinsically".[106] For the performance of the action, it is, in fact, necessary that I understand the meaning of door-knocking, i.e. that I know (I have learnt) that a knock on the door is a reason for opening the door.[107] The action can be the output of the knock on the door only to the extent that it is the result of the agent's education, learning, and training, of his understanding of the characteristic language, practices and institutions of the community into which his life history is inserted. The "mysterious" passage between the intentional background of the action and the neural processes that constitute its bodily or physical aspect rests, then, on the fact that the acquisition of those practices that make understanding possible involves an "impact on my nervous system" and that "my brain becomes programmed to certain reactions to stimuli":

> To the understanding of the reasons (as reasons for or against an action) there answers a programmation of the neural apparatus, and to the existence of the reasons in the context of a certain action there answers a stimulation of this apparatus, and to the agent's proceeding to action there answers innervations of some muscles in the agent's body".[108]

The temptation to believe that the causal relation between sensory input and motoric output also pertains to the sound "understood as a reason for an action and its initiation," and that, in both cases, they involve a stimulus-response relation, is a *leitmotiv* that runs throughout the whole of modern philosophy's study of the mind-body problem. Descartes' interactionist solution is a corollary of his conception of two substances; obviously, his solution will not be embraced by anyone who, coming after him, denies the dualism of mind and matter. Von Wright rejects, not only interactionism, but also the alternative doctrines presented later as reductionist theories. In "On Mind and Matter" von Wright gives detailed arguments for why his position is different from the variants of such theories (materialism, behaviorism, and phenomenalism) and is especially different from the identity theory, according to which mental phenomena can be reduced to physical phenomena.[109] The fact that reasons for acting and their neural correlatives do not interact does not mean that they can be reduced to or identified with each other. According to von Wright, reductionism and identitism fall victim to an illusion, which is the fruit of a misleading picture of the mind-matter relationship. Only by clarifying the nature of that relationship can one dispel the reductionist illusion.

The heart of von Wright's argument, formulated in various forms in his works between 1985 and 1994, is that the connection between the bodily and mental aspects of the action is *conceptual* in nature, using the sense of "conceptual" that he had given it in his writings during the Seventies, as in opposition to what is *causal* or *logical*. The nexus between the agent's intentional (motivational) background and the causes of his muscular activity is to be understood based, not on experience or logic, but on the *meaning* of those concepts that work together to determine the notion of "reasons for acting." The example of the knocking on the door shows how both the bodily and mental aspects determine that the agent will act, *i.e.* they give him reasons for the action: they constitute *two* aspects of the *same* event in the world. The formulation of this argument, already present in "Of Human Freedom", has been expressed with great clarity in a passage from "An Essay on Door-Knocking", which merits being reread in its entirety:

The agent's action for a reason and his body's reception of the reason-giving stimulus and subsequent reaction to it are two aspects of the same (complex) event of the world. One could call them, with caution, the bodily and the mental aspect of this event. Their "connection" is not contingent: the knock would not be a reason for action unless it also were perceived and the agent's proceeding to opening the door would not be an action unless his body went through the appropriate movements. The connection of the two aspects is, to this extent, conceptual and therefore logically necessary. (p. 94)

If one calls to mind the centuries-old history of the mind-body problem, it is easy to associate von Wright's conception of the congruence of these two aspects of the same event with a form of parallelism, or even with a form of monism, reminiscent of Spinoza's doctrine of mind and body as properties of a unique substance, as well as of Russell's idea of a neutral stuff monism. In "An Essay on Door-Knocking", von Wright accepts the idea that one can use the term "parallelism" as the name of the *conceptual* relation of the mental and bodily aspects of action, on condition, however, that it not be confused with the conception of psycho-physical parallelism professed in scientific psychology, whose investigations concern the *contingent* relation between an action for a reason and the chain of neural events in an agent.[110] The conceptualization of these two aspects, *i.e.* the idea that the bodily and the mental aspects are intrinsic to the meaning of an action, makes any appeal to parallelism vacuous. The "lesson" that the case of door-knocking offers is suc-cinctly phrased in an exemplary passage from "Reflections on Psycho-Physical Parallelism":

Just as it is intrinsic to the notion of an action that an action has a somatic aspect, it is intrinsic to the notions of hearing and seeing that a man has ears and eyes ("sense organs"), intrinsic to the notion of perceiving that his body is oriented towards other objects in space, intrinsic to the notion of learning to grasp meanings that he is exposed to influences from and interacts with his surroundings. The full story of the agent who opened a door in response to a knock is an intrinsic mixture of features, some of which belong to what we call his mental, others to what we call his bodily life. That the mixture is intrinsic means that the two aspects cannot be separated and the full story told exclusively in terms belonging to one or to the other of them. (pp. 31–32)

More recently, von Wright has returned to this subject, reasserting that his conception of congruence cannot be completely assimilated to a form of monism *à la* Spinoza or *à la* Russell. Above all, in "Notes on the Philosophy of Mind", a broad and enlightening work done in preparation for "On Mind and Matter", he adds some important clarifications of the views contained in his 1988 essay. The congruence of the two aspects in a human action is to be unders tood as a "double relationship", one of mind to matter, the other of matter to mind. It would be a serious mistake to confuse the reversed role of the mental and bodily aspect, which is conceptual in character, with two parallel chains of the properties of the reality:

The attribution of mental phenomena to a person depends on a conceptualization of some physical phenomena under the aspect of intentionality. Similarly, one could say that the attribution of qualities to physical phenomena requires a conceptualization of some mental phenomena under an aspect of materiality. (p. 107)

In his essays between 1976 and 1985, von Wright had maintained that the deterministic illusion is dispelled as soon as the compatibility of freedom and determination is made clear, that is, as soon as it is shown that the notions of action for reasons and of free action are intrinsically related, are "twin concepts". However, we know that the doubleness within the notion of compatibility confers on it a meaning that is anything but peaceful, anything but painless: to attain a clear vision of the fact that action is both free and determined, we must become acquainted with the tragedy of liberty. In line with his version of compatibility and with his intent to dispel the deterministic illusion, in his writings over the last decade, von Wright shows that an equally dangerous illusion is that of removing the mind-body dualism in the style the reductionist and identitist theories have. The dualism between mind and body is an apparent conflict. In human action these two aspects are conceptually congruent; that is, they do not contradict each other, they are logically compatible. Von Wright says that they, literally, attain harmony (*when* and *if* they attain it). But once again this harmony carries a high price – namely, accepting the paradox that it involves, *i.e.* the paradox of a reality that is neither mind nor matter and that is both mind and matter. The formulation of the paradox is contained in an incisive passage in "Notes on the Philosophy of Mind", which concludes von Wright's critique of the victims of the reductionist illusion:

> And perhaps this is how things stand: materialism and phenomenalism are both false, but one can reject them both with the right arguments only at the cost of acquiescing in a paradox. It would be like saying that reality (the real) is neither mind nor matter and that it is both mind and matter. (p. 110)

In a very recent text, while summarizing the arguments with which in "On Mind and Matter" he had explained the interplay between the mental, neural and behavioral factors that determine the agent's actions for reasons, von Wright states that he agrees with the thesis of the supervenience of the causal relations between mental and physical phenomena on the causal relations between physical phenomena only. In "On Mind and Matter" he had qualified his position, linking it to what is called, in the history of philosophy, "epiphenomenalism". In what sense, however, does the epiphenomenal character of mental phenomena, *i.e.* the conception that they are by-products of basic neural phenomena, do complete justice to the idea of a double relationship of the mental to the bodily and of the bodily to the mental? It seems to me that an answer to this question has not been fully articulated in von Wright's work of the last ten years. His attempt to give a clear indication of the characteristics that would make epiphenomenalism an instrument for coming out from under the shadow of Descartes is probably still *in fieri*.

Università Roma Tre (Italy)

NOTES

[1] Schilpp and Hahn 1989.
[2] Von Wright 1974.
[3] Von Wright 1971.
[4] Among the essays included in the Schilpp volume, only that of Føllesdal was written some years later and, therefore, contains references to von Wright's work after 1975.

[5] In reference to the "two new lines" von Wright mentions his 1978 lecture, "Time, Truth, and Necessity" (von Wright 1979), and his 1976 essay, "Determinism and the Study of Man".

[6] Von Wright 1980.

[7] This is the title of Volume III of the *Philosophical Papers* (von Wright 1984), in which are collected, with few exceptions, various works on these topics from the Eighties.

[8] Von Wright 1993.

[9] Von Wright 1998.

[10] Schilpp and Hahn 1989, p. 41.

[11] Von Wright 1960, in von Wright 1993, p. 153 [italics mine].

[12] Von Wright 1990.

[13] Von Wright 1988.

[14] Von Wright 1994.

[15] Von Wright 1998, p. x. In one of his most recent works, von Wright recalls that, beginning with "Of Human Freedom," his thoughts "had already started to move into a different field of inquiry which no longer falls under the rubric 'Action, Norms, and Values'" (von Wright 1999, p. 28).

[16] According to von Wright, the conclusive contribution in this phase is his 1982 essay, "Norms, Truth, and Logic." See also the essay "Logic and Philosophy in the Twentieth Century", in von Wright 1993.

[17] See especially von Wright 1963; 1967; 1971, and finally, von Wright 1974.

[18] Von Wright 1983 B.

[19] Von Wright 1984, p. x.

[20] Von Wright 1963, pp. 35–6.

[21] See also von Wright 1967, p. 121.

[22] See especially the "Intellectual Autobiography", in Schilpp and Hahn 1989 and von Wright 1999.

[23] The arguments and implications of the actionistic thesis have been the subject of ample and systematic discussions in the essays by Stoutland, Prawitz, Donagan and others, contained in Schilpp and Hahn 1989, and more recently in the first section of the volume by Meggle 1999.

[24] See especially von Wright 1974 a; 1979; 1984 a.

[25] Von Wright 1969.

[26] In this respect, see the essays dedicated to the logic of the temporal connectives 'and next', 'and then' and 'always' in von Wright 1983 a.

[27] In von Wright 1969 reference is made (p. 124, footnote) to the following Kantian passage, taken from the "Transcendental Aesthetics":"[...] der Begriff der Veränderung und, mit ihm, der Begriff der Bewegung (als Veränderung des Orts) nur durch und in der Zeitvorstellung möglich ist: daß, wenn diese Vorstellung nicht Anschauung (innere) a priori wäre, kein Begriff, welcher es auch sei, die Möglichkeit einer Veränderung, d. h. einer Verbindung kontradiktorisch entgegengesetzter Prädikate (z. B das Sein an einem Orte und das Nichtsein eben desselben Dinges an demselben Orte) in einem und demselben Objekte begreiflich machen könnte. *Nur in der Zeit können beide kontradiktorisch-entgegengesetzte Bestimmungen in einem Dinge, nämlich nacheinander, anzutreffen sein*" (*Kritik der reinen Vernunft*, B 49, § 5) [italics mine].

[28] Von Wright 1969, p. 125. The defense of two different approaches to the theory of time is offered in recent writings by Le Poidevin 1991, though conducted from an angle different from that of von Wright, by Smith 1993 and Smith and Oaklander 1995. For the relationship of these two theories of time with physics see Dorato 1995.

[29] See the conclusion of von Wright 1969: "We can now answer the question [...] whether the 'escape from contradiction' which time was supposed to afford is successful. The answer is as follows: It is successful, provided that any given occasion in time is divisible into parts such that the world in every part can be univocally characterized in terms of all states which are applicable to its characterization (on that occasion). This is so, independently of whether division comes to an end in a finite number of steps or may be continued *ad infinitum*. But if time, when regarded as a change-propagated flow, is not thus divisible, we relapse into contradiction. We, so to speak, lose at the micro-level what we gained at the macro-level – a world free from contradiction" (pp. 130–31).

[30] See Prior 1957.

[31] Von Wright 1974, Part IV, 6.

[32] *Ibidem*, Part IV, 8.

[33] See, in particular, the essays "Determinism and Knowledge of the Future", "Knowledge and Necessity", "On Causal Knowledge", and "Diachronic and Synchronic Modality", included in von Wright 1984. See also the essays on modality cited in note 35.

[34] Von Wright 1974 a.

[35] See, in particular, the essays "Logical Modality", "Natural Modality", and "Laws of Nature", included in von Wright 1984.

[36] Von Wright 1979, 1984 a, 1991.

[37] *De Interpretatione*, 19 a 23–b 4. On the Aristotelian puzzle see the "classical" essay by Anscombe 1956, and Hintikka 1973.

[38] *Nicomachean Ethics*, III, 5, 1112–1113 a 30 ff. The Aristotelian definition is taken up again, with some precise statements, by Moore 1912 and by von Wright 1963a; 1995.

[39] Von Wright uses this term to qualify the versions given by Łukasiewicz 1920 and by others of the puzzle in *De Interpretatione* IX, versions with which he disagrees, countering them with his "modal" solution. See also von Wright 1974 a, 1979.

[40] Von Wright 1979, p. 240.

[41] Von Wright 1979, pp. 241–42; 1984 a, pp. 5–8.

[42] In this regard see von Wright 1974 a, p. 174–77; 1979, pp. 242–47; 1984 a, pp. 8–12. See also the continuation of these themes in von Wright 1991, which constitutes his most recent defense of contingency based on modal logic.

[43] The main essays that document the second line are von Wright 1979 a, 1980, 1981, 1985, 1985 a, 1985 b.

[44] In "Determinism and Knowledge of the Future" von Wright develops a parallel thesis of particular interest, in which the deterministic illusion is rooted in a misconception *not only* of the notion of *truth*, but also of the notion of *knowledge*. (von Wright 1984, p. 53 ff.). In this regard see also Egidi 1999.

[45] Von Wright 1976, p. 35.

[46] See the Preface to the Italian translation of von Wright 1980 (*Libertà e determinazione*, Pratiche Editrice, Parma 1984), p. 24.

[47] That man belongs to the *Sinnenwelt* and to the *Verstandeswelt* is argued in the *Grundlegung zur Metaphysik der Sitten* (*Kants Werke*, Akademie-Textausgabe, IV, 3. Absch., p. 457): "Denn daß ein Ding in der Erscheinung (das zur Sinnenwelt gehörig) gewissen Gesetzen unterworfen ist, von welchen eben dasselbe als Ding oder Wesen an sich selbst unabhängig ist, enthält nicht den mindesten Widerspruch".

[48] *Ibidem*, p. 456: "Daher ist es eine unnachläßliche Aufgabe der spekulativen Philosophie: wenigstens zu zeigen, daß ihre Täuschung wegen des Widerspruchs darin beruhe, daß wir den Menschen in einem anderen Sinne und Verhältnisse denken, wenn wir ihn frei nennen, als wenn wir ihn als Stück der Natur dieser ihren Gesetzen für unterworfen halten, und daß beide nicht allein gar wohl beisammen stehen können, sondern auch als nothwendig vereinigt in demselben Subjekt gedacht werden müssen, weil sonst nicht Grund angegeben werden könnte, warum wir die Vernunft mit einer Idee belästigen sollten, die, ob sie sich gleich ohne Widerspruch mit einer anderen, genugsam bewährten vereinigen läßt, dennoch uns in ein Geschäft verwickelt, wodurch die Vernunft in ihrem theoretischen Gebrauche sehr in die Enge gebracht wird."

[49] Von Wright 1980, II, § 13. For the distinction between reasons (grounds) and motives, see also von Wright 1985, First Lecture, §§ 7–8.

[50] *Ibidem.*

[51] See in particular von Wright 1976, 1979 a, 1980, 1981.

[52] See von Wright 1971.

[53] Von Wright 1979 a, p. 108.

[54] Von Wright 1980, II, § 21.

[55] *Ibidem*, § 16.

[56] Von Wright 1979 a, pp. 112–3.

[57] *Ibidem*, p. 110. See also Von Wright 1976, p. 38; 1980, II, § 24.

[58] See von Wright 1979 a, p. 109; 1980, II, § 14 and §§ 25–26.

[59] Von Wright 1980, II, § 25.

[60] Von Wright 1976, pp. 38–39

[61] Von Wright 1980, II, § 27.

[62] Von Wright 1976, pp. 39–40; 1980, II, §§ 27–29.

[63] Von Wright 1976, p. 38. See Habermas 1981.

[64] Von Wright 1979 a, p. 117.

[65] Von Wright 1981, p. 142.

[66] Von Wright 1976, p. 44.

[67] Von Wright 1980, III, § 34.

[68] Von Wrigfht 1979 a, p. 118.

[69] Von Wright 1980, III, § 39.

[70] *Ibidem*, §§ 31–34. See also 1981, pp. 134–36.

[71] *Ibidem*, §§ 35–38.

[72] Hempel 1965, p. 234.

[73] Von Wright 1980, III, § 34.

[74] Von Wright, 1976, p. 44; 1980, III, § 33.

[75] Von Wright 1980, III, § 34.

[76] Von Wright, 1976, p. 45; 1980, III, § 34.

[77] Von Wright 1980, § 48.

[78] Von Wright 1981, p. 133.

[79] Von Wright 1985, I, § 1.

[80] Von Wright 1988 a, p. 28.

[81] Von Wright 1985, I, § 5.

[82] *Ibidem*.

[83] See von Wright and Meggle 1989. See also von Wright 1985, 1985 a, 1985 b.

[84] Von Wright 1985, II, § 1.

[85] Even before the Seventies, von Wright's writings with a specific analytical commitment intersect with his essays on the humanistic argument. In the Sixties, for example, the volumes *The Varieties of Goodness, Norm and Action, The Logic of Preference*, published in 1963, find their counterparts in essays like "The Tree of Knowledge" and "Essay om naturen, människan och den vetenskapligt-tekniska revolutionen" (1960, 1963), which anticipate in many ways his reflections in the decades that followed.

[86] An expression of this phase are the texts in Swedish on W. Jäger's Paideia, on Spengler and Toynbee, Dostojevskij and Tolstoj.

[87] The writings of this period reflect his reawakened interest during those years in Hegel and Marx and the problems of the social and political *Weltbild*.

[88] The main writings to which we are referring, directly or indirectly, in our reconstruction of von Wright's philosophical humanism are the following: von Wright 1960, 1979 b, 1987, 1989, 1990, 1991 a, 1997 a.

[89] Tranøy 1974. This is the only work in English of which I know to date that has explicitly treated the subject of von Wright's philosophical humanism.

[90] Von Wright 1971, chap. I.

[91] See above the use of Kant as a source of inspiration for the compatibility thesis.

[92] Von Wright 1990, pp. 196–97.

[93] Schilpp and Hahn 1989, pp. 843–44.

[94] Von Wright 1980, Preface.

[95] See Section V below.

[96] See von Wright 1989 and 1991 a.

[97] Von Wright 1990, pp. 200–1.

[98] Von Wright 1979 c, p. 4.

[99] Von Wright 1988, 1988 a, 1994, 1998. Meriting particular attention is the *Auseindersetzung* with Malcolm, who defends, from the point of view of Wittgensteinian orthodoxy, a thesis with an "incompatibilist" flavor (Malcolm 1988).

[100] Von Wright 1999, p. 28.

[101] Von Wright 1985, II, § 8, p. 37.

[102] *Ibidem*, § 3, p. 31.

[103] *Ibidem*.

[104] Von Wright 1999, p. 31.

[105] Von Wright 1988 a, p. 26.

[106] *Ibidem*, p. 25.

[107] The involvement of "my body" in the understanding becomes clear in the case where I don't respond to the knock (*Ibidem*).

[108] Von Wright 1985, II, § 5, p. 34.

[109] See von Wright 1985 a, 1994.

[110] Von Wright 1988, p. 95; 1988 a, p. 32.

[111] Von Wright 1999, p. 30.

BIBLIOGRAPHY

Anscombe 1956
    Anscombe G. E. M.: "Aristotle and the Sea-Battle. De Interpretatione Chapter IX", *Mind*, 65, pp. 1–15.
Dorato 1995
    Dorato Mauro: *Time and Reality,* Clueb, Bologna.
Egidi 1999
    Egidi R.: "Grounds for Acting, Grounds for Knowing", in Meggle 1999, pp. 55–63.
Habermas 1981
    Habermas Jürgen: *Theorie des kommunikativen Handelns*, Bd. I. *Handlungsrationalität und gesellschaftliche Rationalisierung*, Suhrkamp, Frankfurt.
Hempel 1965
    Hempel Carl G.: *Aspects of Scientific Explanation and Other Essays in the Philosophy of Science*, Free Press, New York.
Hintikka 1973
    Hintikka Jakko: *Time and Necessity: Studies in Aristotle's Theory of Modality*, Clarendon Press, Oxford.
Le Poidevin 1991
    Le Poidevin Robin: *Change, Cause and Contradiction: a Defence of the Tenseless Theory of Time*, Macmillan, London.
Łukasiewicz 1920
    Lukasiewicz Jan: "On Determinism", in *Polish Logic 1920–1939*, ed. by S. McCall, Oxford University Press, Oxford, 1967, pp. 110–28. Reprinted in J. Łukasiewicz, *Selected Works*, ed. by J. Slupecki, North-Holland Publishing Co., 1970, pp. 152–78.
Malcolm 1988
    Malcolm Norman: "Mind and Action", in *Perspectives on Human Conduct*, ed. by L. Hertzberg and J. Pietarinen, E. J. Brill, Leiden-New York-Toronto, pp. 6–21.
Meggle 1999
    Actions, Norms, Values: Discussions with Georg Henrik von Wright, ed. by Georg Meggle, assisted by Andreas Wojcik, W. de Gruyter, Berlin-New York.
Moore 1912
    Moore Georg E.: *Ethics*, Oxford University Press, London.
Prior 1957
    Prior Arthur N.: *Time and Modality*, Clarendon Press, Oxford
Schilpp and Hahn 1989
    The Philosophy of G. H. von Wright, ed. by P. A. Schilpp and L. E. Hahn, Open Court, La Salle, Ill.
Smith 1993
    Smith Quentin: *Language and Time*, Oxford University Press, Oxford.
Smith and Oaklander 1995
    Smith Q. and L. Nathan Oaklander: *Time, Change and Freedom. An Introduction to Metaphysics*, Routledge, London and New York.
Stoutland 1982
    Stoutland Frederich: "Philosophy of Action. Davidson, von Wright and the Debate over Causation", in *Contemporary Philosophy. A New Survey*, ed. by G. Fløistad, Vol. 3, Nijhoff, The Hague, pp. 45–72.
Tranøy 1974
    Tranøy Knut Erik: "Von Wright's Humanism: His Critique of Culture and his Philosophy of Life", in Schilpp and Hahn 1989, pp. 489–516.
Von Wright 1960
    "Kunskapens träd" [The Tree of Knowledge] *Historiska och Litteraturhistoriska Studier*, 35, pp. 43–76. Reprinted with revisions in von Wright 1993, from which I quote.
Von Wright 1963
    Norm and Action. A Logical Inquiry, Routledge & Kegan Paul, London.

Von Wright 1963 a
The Logic of Preference, At the University Press, Edinburgh.
Von Wright 1963 b
Essay om naturen, människan och den vetenskapligt-tekniska revolutionen [Essay on Nature, Man, and the Scientific Revolution] Gleerups, Lund 1963, 25 pp.
Von Wright 1967
"The Logic of Action: a Sketch", in *The Logic of Decision and Action*, ed. by N. Rescher, Pittsburgh University Press, Pittsburgh, pp. 121–36.
Von Wright 1969
Time, Change, and Contradiction, Cambridge University Press, London, 32 pp. Reprinted in von Wright 1983 a, from which I quote.
Von Wright 1971
Explanation and Understanding, Routledge & Kegan Paul, London.
Von Wright 1974
Causality and Determinism, Columbia University Press, New York-London.
Von Wright 1974 a
"Determinismus, Wahrheit und Zeitlichkeit. Ein Beitrag zum Problem der zukünftigen kontingenten Wahrheiten, *Studia Leibnitiana*, 6, pp. 161–78.
Von Wright 1976
"Determinism and the Study of Man", in *Essays on Explanation and Understanding*, ed. by J. Manninen and R. Tuomela, Reidel, Dordrecht. Reprinted in von Wright 1983, from which I quote.
Von Wright 1977
"What is Humanism?", The Lindlay Lecture, University of Arkansas, Lawrence, Kansas, 25 pp.
Von Wright 1979
"Time, Truth, and Necessity", in *Intention and Intentionality. Essays in Honor of G. E. M. Anscombe*, The Harvester Press, Brighton.
Von Wright 1979 a
"The Determinants of Action", in *Reason, Action and Experience. Essays in Honor of R. Klibansky*, ed. by H. Kohlenberger, Meiner, Hamburg, pp. 107–19.
Von Wright 1979 b
"Humanism and the Humanities", in *Philosophy and Grammar*, ed. by S. Kanger and S. Öhman, Reidel, Dordrecht, pp. 1–16. Reprinted in von Wright 1993, from which I quote.
Von Wright 1980
Freedom and Determination, North-Holland Publishing Co., Amsterdam.
Von Wright 1981
"Explanation and Understanding of Action", *Revue Internationale de Philosophie*, 35, pp. 127–42. Reprinted in von Wright 1983.
Von Wright 1983
Practical Reason. Philosophical Papers, Vol. I, Blackwell, Oxford.
Von Wright 1983 a
Philosophical Logic. Philosophical Papers, Vol. II, Blackwell, Oxford.
Von Wright 1983 b
"A Pilgrim's Progress. Voyage d'un pélerin", in *Philosophes critiques d'eux-mêmes*, Vol. 12, ed. by A. Mercier and M. Svilar, Verlag P. Lang, Bern, pp. 257–94. Reprinted in von Wright 1993, from which I quote.
Von Wright 1984
Truth, Knowledge, and Modality. Philosophical Papers, Vol. III, Blackwell, Oxford.
Von Wright 1984 a
"Determinismus and Future Truth", in von Wright 1984.
Von Wright 1985
"Of Human Freedom", The Tanner Lectures on Human Values, Vol. VI, ed. by S. M. McMurrin, University of Utah Press, Salt Lake City, pp. 107–70. Reprinted in von Wright 1998, from which I quote.

Von Wright 1985 a
"Probleme des Erklärens und Verstehens von Handlungen", *Conceptus*, 18, pp. 3–19.

Von Wright 1985 b
"Sulla verità delle 'spiegazioni comprendenti'", in *Dilthey e il pensiero del Novecento*, ed. by F. Bianco, Angeli, Milano, pp. 127–35.

Von Wright 1987
"Wissenschaft und Vernunft", *Rechtstheorie*, 18, pp. 15–33. Translated into English in von Wright 1993, from which I quote.

Von Wright 1988
"An Essay on Door-Knocking", *Rechtstheorie*, 19, pp. 275–88. Reprinted in von Wright 1998, from which I quote.

Von Wright 1988 a
"Reflections on Psycho-Physical Parallelism", in *Perspectives on Human Conduct*, ed. by L. Hertzberg and J. Pietarinen, E. J. Brill, Leiden-New York-Toronto, pp. 22–32.

Von Wright 1989
"Science, Reason, and Value", *Documenta 49*, The Royal Swedish Academy of Sciences, Stockholm, pp. 7–28. Reprinted in von Wright 1993, from which I quote.

Von Wright 1990
"Dante between Ulysses and Faust", in *Knowledge and the Sciences in Medieval Philosophy*, ed. by M. Aszalos *et al.*, Helsinki, pp. 1–9. Reprinted in von Wright 1993, from which I quote.

Von Wright 1991
"Possibility, Plenitude and Determinism", in *Peter Geach: Philosophical Encounters*, ed. by H. A. Lewis, Kluwer, Dordrecht, pp. 83–98.

Von Wright 1991 a
"The Myth of Progress", in *Architecture and Cultural Values*, Lievestuore, pp. 66–89. Reprinted in von Wright 1993, from which I quote.

Von Wright 1993
The Tree of Knowledge and Other Essays, Brill, Leiden.

Von Wright 1994
"On Mind and Matter", *Journal of Theorethical Biology*, 171, pp. 101–10. Reprinted in von Wright 1998, from which I quote.

Von Wright 1997
"Progress: Fact and Fiction", in *The Idea of Progress*, ed. by A. Burgen, *et al.*, W. de Gruyter, Berlin, pp. 1–18.

Von Wright 1998
In the Shadow of Descartes: Essays in the Philosophy of Mind, Kluwer, Dordrecht.

Von Wright 1999
"Value, Norm, and Action in My Philosophical Writings. With a Cartesian Epilogue", in *Actions, Norms, Values. Discussions with G. H. von Wright*, W. de Gruyter, Berlin–New York.

Von Wright and Meggle 1989
Von Wright G. H. and Georg Meggle: "Das Verstehen von Handlungen", *Rechtstheorie*, 20, pp. 3–37.

WITTGENSTEIN AND TRADITION

1. I have chosen the theme of my talk in full awareness of its difficulties and complications. I am also conscious of the danger of being over-subjective in some of my judgements. But I find the challenge important for any attempt to "understand" Wittgenstein.

Wittgenstein grew up and was firmly rooted in an Austrian-Viennese cultural tradition. Any attempt to understand his personality must try to see him against this background. But Wittgenstein's work as a philosopher was accomplished almost entirely in environments the cultural traditions of which he did not share or even found highly uncongenial to himself.

It has therefore been suggested that Wittgenstein's philosophy, particularly that of the *Philosophische Untersuchungen*[1] simply *has* no background in tradition. This, I think, is right if understood to mean that Wittgenstein does not belong to or continue any particular movement, or trend or school in philosophy. But it is eminently false if taken to mean that Wittgenstein's thinking is unrelated to the great European tradition and can be understood and assessed in isolation from it. Wittgenstein's relation to tradition I shall here understand as an *anti-traditionalism, i.e.,* as a constant and relentless fight with patterns and ways of thinking which have been characteristic of Western philosophy and science at least since the late Renaissance and Baroque period. Simplifyingly, but I think also illuminatingly, one can identify this background as Cartesian. Wittgenstein is Descartes's great opposite in philosophy – roughly in the same sense in which Descartes himself may be regarded as an antipode to Aristotle.

It may sound strange to say that Wittgenstein is fighting Descartes in view of the fact that, as far as I have been able to detect, there is not a single mention by name of the great Frenchman in Wittgenstein's published or unpublished writings. Was he not aware then of what he was polemical against? Of course, he was. But his fight against a Cartesian legacy is not so much a criticism of particular doctrines as a fight against a certain climate of opinion in philosophy, an atmosphere of thought, to the creation of which no single philosopher has contributed more influentially than Descartes.

Did Wittgenstein see his own achievement as founding a new tradition in philosophy? Wittgenstein nowhere speaks at length of his own place on the historical map of the subject. But there is a passage in a paper which G. E. Moore later wrote on Wittgenstein's lectures at Cambridge in the early 1930s which suggests a conscious attitude on Wittgenstein's part to his place in history.[2] Moore reports Wittgenstein as having talked about a new way of doing philosophy, a "kink" in developments comparable to what took place in physics with Galileo or in chemistry with the abandonment of alchemy.[3] No further clue is given to how philosophy will develop

R. Egidi (ed.), In Search of a New Humanism, 35–46.
©1999 *Kluwer Academic Publishers. Printed in Great Britain.*

after the kink, but the turning point itself Wittgenstein saw as a break with a way of thinking to which he sometimes refers as "metaphysical".

I doubt whether Wittgenstein later would have taken this view of his position when seen in a historical perspective. Unfortunately, we miss a verbatim report of what he actually said in the lectures attended by Moore. Moore's account relates to the years which are now commonly distinguished as a "middle period" in the development of Wittgenstein's thought. This was a time when he was more engaged than in his later and lonelier years in what was "going on" in philosophy – in Austria and in England. What was "going on" was in a large measure due to the influence of the *Tractatus*.[4] But this was also the time when there took place the "kink" in his own thinking away from the *Tractatus* in the new direction which was to result in the *Untersuchungen*. And we have no evidence that he had thought of *it* as the dawn of a new tradition in philosophy.

2. I shall make no specific comments here on the Austrian background. Such comments were for a long time so completely absent from writings on Wittgenstein that an Italian author accused commentators in the Anglo-American orbit – to which Wittgenstein's influence was for a long time mainly confined – of portraying a "Wittgenstein aculturato". "Aculturato" should then be understood to mean, not uncultured, but detached from cultural traditions in his philosophy. Since then the picture of Wittgenstein's background has been amplified and completed: first by Janik and Toulmin in their book *Wittgenstein's Vienna*, later by his biographers McGuinness and Monk, by the perceptive Hungarian historian of ideas Christoph Nyíri, and by others.

I have myself written on Wittgenstein in relation to his times,[5] and Rudolf Haller and others have noted his Spenglerian attitude to Western civilization and to thinking about history generally. Like the Austrian legacy, these aspects of Wittgenstein probably pertain to his personality rather than to his philosophy. But I also think that the antitraditionalism characteristic of Wittgenstein's philosophy, particularly after the *Tractatus,* bears a significant relationship to his cultural pessimism and view of "the darkness of this time".[6] I shall not, however, here try to examine how Wittgenstein's "mood" is reflected in his purely philosophical writings – as distinct from the *obiter dicta* or "vermischte Bemerkungen" which he wrote down in many of his manuscripts. The task is interesting and I hope it will one day be taken up for intelligent scrutiny.

3. In the Preface to the *Tractatus* Wittgenstein says that he will not try to decide how far his efforts agree with those of other philosophers. Nor can anybody else do it for him, except in a conjectural way which I think is of little help to efforts to understand the book. There are reminiscences of early reading of Schopenhauer and Hertz and perhaps Kant, and there is a passing reference to Mauthner disclaiming association with the latter's *Sprachkritik*.[7] But Wittgenstein is anxious to mention that he owes "in large measure" the stimulation of his thoughts to "the great work" of Frege and the writings of his friend Bertrand Russell.

Frege's and Russell's concern with logic and its philosophical importance had been Wittgenstein's gateway to philosophy. But this does not mean that Wittgenstein in the *Tractatus* had continued their work. He did not join the logicist trend in the philosophy of mathematics, and he criticized, then and later, the idea that mathematics needs a foundation in pure logic. Nor did he accept Russellian type-theory as a means of coping with the paradoxes. It is a matter of dispute whether and to what extent he subscribed to the Frege-Russell ideal of a language "which obeys the rules of *logical grammar*",[8] but he credited Russell for having shown that the grammatical form of a proposition need not reflect its correct logical form.[9]

Just as it would be wrong to connect *Tractatus* with a specific tradition in the philosophy of logic and mathematics, it would also be a mistake to associate it closely with its influence on the logical positivist and later analytic movements in the philosophy of the century. This association, however, soon became current and still lingers on in some quarters. Yet to make it is to misunderstand the aim of the *Tractatus* and to be blind to the book's originality. Perhaps one could illuminate the connections here by saying that just as Frege and Russell had been the early Wittgenstein's main sources of inspiration, in a similar way *Tractatus* kindled the enthusiasm of the logical positivists but remained nevertheless to them an alien and little understood work.

The estrangement between *Tractatus* and logical positivism was, in fact, reciprocal. The positivists acknowledged that the book had been an immense influence. But they paid little attention to what was actually said in it. Apart from Ramsey's early review[10] there is, I should say, no serious study of the *Tractatus* from Wittgenstein's lifetime. It was only in the 1950s, when Wittgenstein's later work was becoming available to the reading public, that the *Tractatus* was "rediscovered" and a study of it for its own sake was inaugurated. Since then and up to the present, *Tractatus* scholarship has continued to flourish.

4. It is, as far as I can see, pure coincidence that, parallel with an reawakened interest in the *Tractatus,* there have occurred developments in linguistics and the philosophy of language which can be said to have given new actuality to Wittgenstein's early work. These developments are in origin connected with the name of Noam Chomsky and with the science of generative grammar and of psycholinguistics.

Chomsky regards his approach to language as heir to an earlier tradition which he calls "Cartesian linguistics"[11] thus recalling the very name of the philosopher with whom, above all, I am anxious to contrast Wittgenstein. Is there perhaps beside the contrast also a similarity? What is "Cartesian" about Chomsky's position is primarily his assumption of innate or *a priori* cognitive structures which count for the development of the linguistic ability of a child. In order to learn to speak the way it does, the child must be assumed already to have an inborn mental language, the grammatical structures of which it then recognizes in the natural language it is learning and which, recognition having taken place, the child can use for generating on its own new sentences of that language. The innate language has been called, by Jerry Fodor, *mentalese* or "the language of thought".

In a letter to Russell,[12] who had asked for explanations of some ideas in the *Tractatus* which puzzled him, Wittgenstein writes that the thoughts which he also calls the meaningful *(sinnvoll)* sentences (*Tractatus* 4.) are composed of mental units the configurations of which in the thoughts projectively picture possible states of affairs. This idea of Wittgenstein's which does not explicitly appear in the book may be regarded as an early anticipation of latter day psycholinguistics.

The structures of thought are the deep structures of which the sentences of a natural language present the surface structure. The deep structure is constitutive of the meaning *(Sinn)* hidden underneath and often badly distorted by the surface structure. The deep structures, one could say, warrant the *possibility of language*.

These ideas about language and meaning are certainly highly characteristic of Wittgenstein's position in the *Tractatus*.[13] So much so that one is tempted to call them "the fundamental thought" of the entire book.[14] To the extent that they can rightly be compared to "Cartesian linguistics", one can therefore say that *Tractatus is* a work in a Cartesian tradition although there is no acknowledgement and even no awareness of this by the author. Wittgenstein's later abandonment of what I propose to call his "two-level conception of meaning" and related doctrines of the *Tractatus* was freeing himself from a Cartesian load on his early thinking. These observations also throw light on some much debated questions how the Wittgenstein of the *Tractatus is* related to the Wittgenstein of the *Untersuchungen*.

5. With the *Untersuchungen* the absence of influences and tradition background is glaring. The only inspiration which the author acknowledges is from conversations with Ramsey and Sraffa. There is also an oblique reference in the Preface to Nicholas Bachtin, a philologist of Russian extraction who seems to have aided Wittgenstein to juxtapose and contrast his new way of thinking with his old one.

Ramsey's contributions to logic and philosophy have, deservedly, been the subject of research and re-evaluation in recent years. It is arguable whether Ramsey was not the originator of some ideas which, in the late 1920s, became prominent in Wittgenstein's writings.[15] Inspiration probably was mutual. A thought first suggested in conversation by Ramsey may have seemed to Wittgenstein novel and challenging, which in turn encouraged Ramsey to develop it further. The intellectual temper of the two men, however, was very different. This is reflected in the well known remark in *Vermischte Bemerkungen*[16] where Wittgenstein calls Ramsey a "bourgeois thinker", meaning that Ramsey was more interested in clarifying the foundations of existing structures than contemplating alternatives to them. (Like, *mutatis mutandis,* socialist to capitalist economy.)

Sraffa's influence was, I think, of a different nature. Sraffa had a rare and devastating critical acumen. I remember him once being introduced to a visiting economist at the Trinity College high table as "Der Geist der stets verneint". In the first instance Sraffa helped Wittgenstein to free himself from his earlier ideas. The story of the Napolitan gesture signifying contempt is well known. The gesture plays the role of a sentence. But this sentence has no analyzable form or structure. Wittgenstein told me that Sraffa acted on him like a gardener who is pruning a tree until it is quite bare in order that it may green again. Some time ago, incidentally, I found among Sraffa's papers in Trinity some brief and fragmentary notes which indicate that Sraffa was critical also of later ideas of Wittgenstein's. The notes in question are about the nature of philosophy.

6. What more than anything else has gained for Descartes the name "father of modern philosophy" is the sharp separation between body and mind, the material and mental, the physical and the psychical aspect of reality. True, Descartes was by no means the first to make the separation. His position has firm roots in a mediaeval tradition which has its ultimate ancestry with Plato. The novelty with Descartes was that he problematized the body-mind distinction in the setting of a new understanding – also forcefully promoted by him – of natural phenomena. Thereby he created a new problem situation in philosophy which did not exist before but which since has tormented Western thinking up to the present day.

How are body and mind related? The idea that body and mind interact causally is connected with notorious difficulties in view of the assumed causal closedness of the physical world- order. The alternative to interactionism seems to be reductionism of either the idealist or the materialist or the neutral monist type. They all belong within the Cartesian frame and none of them seems satisfactory.

There have of course been attempts to break away from the Cartesian tradition. They began, I would say, with Vico in the early eighteenth and Nietzsche in the nineteenth century – and have continued in our with Husserl and Heidegger, and Wittgenstein. But this "gigantomachia" has not ended and Western philosophy has not yet settled accounts with its Cartesian past. Quite to the contrary. In recent decades we have witnessed a remarkable – one is tempted to say surprising – revival not only of interest in Descartes's philosophy but of Cartesian thought generally. This has happened along different channels. One has been a renaissance of Descartes scholarship, both in the form of textual exegesis and in tracing the historic roots of Descartes's ideas in the scholastic mediaeval tradition. Another has been a resurgence of Cartesian metaphysical dualism – most notably in the joint work of Karl Popper and John Eccles. Of greater interest for our purposes are new developments with a Cartesian slant in science. We already mentioned Chomsky's generative grammar and its affinities with the ideas of the *Tractatus*. Here the innovator in linguistics was himself aware of his Cartesian ancestry. Another form of scientific neo-Cartesianism is less history-conscious. It is found in contemporary brain science and neurophysiology, and might itself be called a neuropsychology. It cannot claim affinity with the *Tractatus*. But it stands in strong implicit conflict with *Philosophische Untersuchungen* and Wittgenstein's work in the philosophy of mind. Finally, it should be mentioned that the now fashionable trend of *cognitive science,* of which neuropsychology may be considered an offshoot, represents an "intellectu-alism" in the study of mental phenomena which has an ultimate source in Descartes's view of mental phenomena as so many *cogitationes.* This approach too to psychological study is uncongenial to Wittgenstein. This holds eminently for his contributions to the philosophy of psychology after the completion of Part I of the

Untersuchungen which have been published in the four volumes with the title *Bemerkungen über die Philosophie der Psychologie*.[17] The fact that they have, so far, had very little influence either on empirical psychology or on contemporary philosophy of mind testifies to the tightness of the grip of the Cartesian tradition on Western thinking. But it would not surprise me if, in future, they will be regarded as the perhaps most lasting contribution of Wittgenstein's to philosophy.

7. It is one of Descartes's great merits as a scientist to have conceived of the brain and the nerves as *one* system within the human or animal body, and to have realized its basic importance to the mental phenomena which psychology studies. Descartes's vision of what happens in the brain and nervous system when we perceive and act, remember things, feel fear or anger, *etc.* is, however, pure speculation. It has practically no foundation at all in empirical facts. This, of course, is not the case with modern brain research, although it too remains strongly not to say violently speculative in its interpretation of the relevance of its findings for a philosophy of mind.

A difference between Descartes and some of his modern followers in the labyrinths of neuropsychology is that Descartes was no reductionist. He did not attempt to exorcize the concepts of our everyday talk of mental phenomena and replace them by their neurophysiological equivalents. This is what those moderns want to do who relegate the everyday concepts to what is contemptuously labelled Folk-Psychology. It is thought of as a false and obsolete *theory* of the causes of human behaviour and the nature of cognitive activity. The use of everyday psychological concepts such as belief, desire, fear, joy or pain to explain behaviour is compared to the phlogiston theory of combustion or the Ptolemean theory of planetary motion. To quote one of the protagonists of the new way of thinking: "When neuroscience has matured to the point where the poverty of our current conceptions is apparent to everyone, we shall then be able to set about reconceiving our internal states and activities within a truly adequate conceptual framework at last."[18]

These hyper-modern ideas were, of course, not known to Wittgenstein. But they should be mentioned here as the very antithesis to the way in which Wittgenstein conceived of the relation between the mind and the brain. Just as his later philosophy of language can be seen as the reversal of the meaning-constitutive rôles of the deep and the surface structures of sentences, similarly his philosophy of psychological concepts vindicates, one could say, the *primacy* of "Folk-Psychology", *i.e.,* our common sense conceptual framework, in relation to the neurophysiological findings and their hypothetical correlation with the states and processes we call mental. We must already have the concepts of belief or anger or fear *etc.* and know on which criteria we attribute them to a living being before we can ascertain what, if anything,[19] corresponds to them at the neural level. What they are, is open to view in our everyday experience and not something which is revealed to us by a study of processes beneath the surface of our conscious life. "Nothing is hidden".[20] This *primacy of the obvious* as I propose to call it, is one of the cornerstones of Wittgenstein's philosophy after the *Tractatus*.

8. Descartes is not only the source of the neuropsychological tradition in the philosophy of mind, tending ultimately to one form or other of what is nowadays called "eliminative materialism". He is also the founding father of the *introspectionist* tradition in empirical psychology. Its great classics are William James and Wilhelm Wundt. I have not found a single reference to Wundt in Wittgenstein's work. But James he knew and highly appreciated. In his early years he had been impressed by *The Varieties of Religious Experience*. Later he studied *The Principles of Psychology*. Taken with a grain of salt, one can say that the inspiration which Wittgenstein in his later thinking got from reading James is comparable to the one which the author of the *Tractatus* had received from Frege and Russell. But even stronger than in the case of the latter two, the inspiration was not so much for agreement and continuation, as for a critical *Abstandsnahme*.

The philosophical basis of introspectionism is the idea that mental phenomena are in a peculiar sense "subjective". They are accessible to direct inspection only by the person who *has* them – and not like physical phenomena open to intersubjective observation. Every subject individually has an inner world privately for himself of sensations, thoughts, emotions, and other mental things. All subjects collectively have in common an outer world of material bodies and physical events. Access to it, although possible for everyone, is mediated by the impressions which the mind receives from it. Descartes thought that the mind is better known to us than the body, *i. e.* the material world, since knowledge of the latter is mediated by the former. Can we be sure, however, that this mediating rôle of the mind gives us indubitable knowledge of the outer world? With this question Descartes made the quest for certainty and the removal of doubt central to his philosophy. Thereby he laid the foundation of an *epistemological* tradition which has been a *Leitmotiv* of European thought up to the present day.

Wittgenstein's attitude to this tradition can be characterized as a continued effort to dispel the web of mystification which philosophy has spun around the inner-outer cleavage of Cartesian dualism.

9. Wittgenstein's fight with Cartesian epistemology has two main forms or targets. One is a fight with *scepticism,* another with the idea of a *private language*. It testifies to the strength of the prevailing tradition that these two themes have been the most hotly debated ones relating to the later philosophy of Wittgenstein.

The debate on scepticism was recently given a new turn by Saul Kripke in his important book *Wittgenstein: On Rules and Private Language*. Kripke attributes to Wittgenstein a form of possible doubt also called "meaning-scepticism". It concerns, not the possibility of attaining indubitable knowledge about the things which are the objects of our talk, but the possibility of correctly understanding the meaning of this talk itself. This, in Kripke's words is "the most radical and original sceptical problem that philosophy has seen to date".[21]

I do not think that Kripke's observations, interesting as they are, reveal a hitherto unnoted abyss of doubt beneath the surface of words by which we make ourselves understood in ordinary discourse. Just as knowledge-scepticism is possible only within a frame of accepted certainties, similarly meaning-scepticism makes sense only within a commonly shared and unquestioned communication system. Thus what Wittgenstein – already in *Tractatus* (6.51) but more fully in his last work *Über Gewißheit*[22] – says about the senselessness of philosophical scepticism also applies, it seem to me, to the "new form of scepticism" discussed by Kripke.

Wittgenstein's refutation of scepticism as well as of the idea of a private language is deeply entrenched in his view of man as a social being and therewith of knowledge and language as phenomena presupposing life in a community of shared institutions and practices. Wittgenstein's philosophic anthropology is a radical break with the individualism and subjectivism of Western thought since Descartes. This break with tradition is, I think, a reason why Wittgenstein's thinking still remains so difficult to digest also for the present generation of philosophers. The difficulty can also be seen in the perspective of the excessive forms of narcissistic self-indulgence and libertarianism typical of late modern society. This is a facet of the "decline of the West" which Wittgenstein thought he was witnessing himself and which alienated him from his times.

10. I shall try to summarize Wittgenstein's view of the body-mind dualism as follows:

Body and mind are not "sharply distinct". But nor are they causally connected. Their connection is conceptual or logical. One could also call it, with caution, a *semantic* relationship. Behaviour are the physical signs of mental contents. Mental states and processes have behavioural criteria.[23]

It is instructive to compare Wittgenstein's view of the body-mind problem with that of Aristotle.[24] The latter called the soul the form of the body – and the body the matter of the soul. His terminology is strange to us. But it is not, I think, a distortion of Aristotle's thought to say that according to him the soul is those behavioural and functional features which are essential to a living being. In the individual case these features are the signs or criteria, on the basis of which we attribute mental states and events to the being.

Perhaps Wittgenstein's position could be called a revived version of Aristotle's. It was of course not intended to be this. But there is a noteworthy resemblance. It can be related to the fact that both Aristotle and Wittgenstein were great *logicians*. Descartes's frame of mind was different. He was no logician. And the breakthrough of Cartesianism in philosophy and science meant eradication from them of remnants of obsolete Aristotelianism. One could therefore say that Wittgenstein joins hands with Aristotle across three centuries of Cartesian domination on the philosophical stage.

11. The scientific revolution of the 17th and 18th centuries established mathematics and physics as the paradigm sciences setting a pattern which every science was supposed to conform to when it had freed itself from its metaphysical past and become a respectable member of the family. Chemistry in the late 18th, biology and the newly born sciences of sociology and psychology in the 19th century followed the set model – whether always with success is questionable. Philosophy remained a

more doubtful case. But it too has, particularly in our century, become increasingly imbued with the prevailing scientific spirit. Russell and after him Quine have been two forceful champions of the view that philosophy is "essentially one with science",[25] differing from the special sciences in the greater generality of its problems but agreeing with them as far as methods and truth- criteria are concerned.

Wittgenstein is one of the very few philosophers who have tried to articulate a view of what he as a philosopher was doing in explicit contrast to what scientists do. In the *Tractatus* he said (4.111 and 4.112) that "Die Philosophie ist keine der Naturwissenschaften" and that "Die Philosophie ist keine Lehre sondern eine Tätigkeit". In the chapter entitled "Philosophie" in the so called "Big Typescript" and in a more crystalline form in the *Untersuchungen* he professed essentially the same view.

It is therefore surprising that, although Wittgenstein's impact on the philosophy of the century has perhaps been greater than anybody else's, only relatively few have taken seriously his view of what philosophy is. The famous manifesto with which the Vienna Circle announced itself to the world, hailed Wittgenstein together with Russell and Einstein as leading proponents of a "wissenschaftliche Weltauffassung".[26] Few characterizations of him could be more *malplacé*.

I think there are several different conceptions implicit in what Wittgenstein said about philosophy. There is the idea that philosophical problems are inquietudes of the mind arising from failure to understand the logical grammar of language. The problems vanish when we free ourselves of "die Verhexung unseres Verstandes durch die Mittel unserer Sprache" (PU 109). This could be termed a *therapeutic* conception of philosophy. Philosophy is there to exorcize its problems, not to solve them.

Another conception is of philosophy as *descriptive* as opposed to theoretic and explicative. This aspect is characteristic above all of Wittgenstein's extensive treatment of psychological and also of mathematical concepts. It is related to a view of the language games as *Lebensformen,* forms of life, and the philosopher's comments on them as pertaining to the *Naturgeschichte des Menschen.*

In the preface to "Principia Philosophiae" Descartes compares the totality of human knowledge to a tree of which metaphysics is the root, physics the trunk and the other sciences the branches.[27] Metaphysics here stands for philosophy, – and Cartesian philosophy is above all epistemology although the term was not coined until much later. Descartes's simile illustrates a view of philosophy as a discipline which lays *the foundation* of the fabric of knowledge. Until this fabric can be proved to stand on a firm foundation, the results of the various sciences cannot be trusted, are not removed from doubt.

This view of philosophy as foundational is thoroughly opposed to Wittgenstein's. One could call him an anti-foundationalist, just as one calls him an antitraditionalist. His position on the issue, however, is not quite easy to understand and perhaps even more difficult to accept. It does not deny that philosophy is concerned with fundamental or basic concepts, such as *e.g.,* space and time, cause and free will, language and meaning. But the philosopher does not uncover their veiled essences or give to them a new foundation – like Frege and Russell who sought to found arithmetic in pure logic. Philosophy (PU 124) "leaves everything as it is" it leaves logic and mathematics to "take care of themselves" (another favourite phrase of Wittgenstein's). Instead of unveiling essences philosophy shows that there are no essences to be unveiled, only a multitude of linguistic usages to be described, the conflation of which confuses us and leads to a "metaphysical" use of misunderstood words. The philosopher's task is (PU 116) "to bring words back from their metaphysical to their everyday use" which can then be carried on undisturbed by linguistic storms. The philosopher is destructive rather than constructive. But what he destroys are only "Luftgebäude", castles of cards. (PU 118). I think it was this feature of the philosophic activity which Wittgenstein had in mind when he wrote the remark printed in the *Vermischte Bemerkungen* with a musical theme invented by him "I destroy, I destroy, I destroy".[28]

Wittgenstein's insistence that philosophy is not a science must not be mistaken for an anti-scientific attitude. It is true that Wittgenstein, particularly later in his life, came to take a very critical, not to say condemning, view of the repercussions on life of science and technology. But this is quite another concern of his.

Nor would Wittgenstein have denied that scientific questions which can be answered by ascertaining facts often fuse with philosophical questions of meaning or of interpreting the factual basis of scientific theorizing. Developments in science are among the most important sources of philosophical problems, *i.e.* conceptual confusions, – as witnessed by Bohr-Heisenberg quantum mechanics, Cantor's set theory, or Gödel's incompleteness proofs for formal systems.

12. Wittgenstein's "I destroy" reminds us of another great philosopher, whose figure has come to loom heavily over late Western thinking. He is Nietzsche. He called himself a philosopher "with the hammer". The prime target of his philosophical hammering was what he thought of as perverted values. Spengler's view of "the decline of the West" is another deconstructivist application of Nietzschean cultural criticism and relativism. And Spengler, as we know, Wittgenstein acknowledged as an influence on himself. Wittgenstein's apocalyptic vision of the world in the post-war years is indeed Spenglerian – though it is questionable whether this is not due to a similarity of intellectual temper rather than to an influence on Wittgenstein's thinking. (The thought-germs which Wittgenstein had picked up from reading Spengler relate, it seems, immediately to the idea of family-resemblance *[Familienähnlichkeit].*)

Wittgenstein is not alone to question the metaphysical inheritance of our philosophic past. The logical positivists did the same – partly under the impact of the *Tractatus.* A differently styled break with tradition is due to Heidegger. It is sometimes said that philosophy in our century has entered a *post-metaphysical* era. One can also relate the anti-traditionalism both of Heidegger and of Wittgenstein – though hardly that of the logical positivists – to the phenomena in contemporary culture which are heaped under the rubric *post-modern*. Characteristic of post-modernity is that certain beliefs and expectations – the French philosopher Lyotard calls them *grands récit* – have been abandoned as illusions and myths; for example the idea of continuous and necessary progress, the social utopias of communism and socialism, or the dream of an international world-order securing lasting peace and brotherhood of men. Wittgenstein certainly did not share any of these beliefs – with the reservation perhaps that he had an interest and maybe even a passing faith in the type of new society which had promised to emerge from the Russian revolution of 1917. Current "modernization" under the banners of Western liberal democracy is certainly not a political program which would have won his approval.

Wittgenstein's anti-foundationalism also matches the increased fragmentation now in progress of the scientific world-picture. This manifests itself, for example, in the apparent failure to achieve a contradiction-free and unified reconciliation of conflicting pictures of events in atomic dimensions, or in the limits to deterministic predictability among phenomena studied in so called chaos theory, or in the re-emergence of holistic and quasifinalistic arguments in the biological sciences. To this may be added an interest in non-classical systems of logic, counting Wittgenstein's position in *Bemerkungen über die Grundlagen der Mathematik*[29] as one of its progenitors. In these phenomena we witness the gradual eroding of patterns of rational thought characteristic of what I have here called the Cartesian tradition.

Perhaps such observations as I have made in this paper will help us locate Wittgenstein's place in the intellectual history of Europe. But whether his post-metaphysical and post-modern anti-traditionalism is the beginning of something new or only a sweeping the ground of the past must remain an open question. I would not hazard an answer to it. I am myself more inclined to look forward to continued erring in the wilderness of deconstruction and dissolution – perhaps for a long time to come – than to a continuation of the road Wittgenstein followed in philosophy. He said it himself: "Ich kann keine Schule gründen, weil ich eigentlich nicht nachgeahmt werden will"; "Es ist mir durchaus nicht klar, daß ich eine Fortsetzung meiner Arbeit durch andere mehr wünsche, als eine Veränderung der Lebensweise, die alle diese Fragen überflüssig macht."[30]

Academy of Finland, Helsinki

NOTES

[1] *Philosophische Untersuchungen. Philosophical Investigations* (henceforth PU), ed. by G. E. M. Anscombe and R. Rhees, Blackwell, Oxford 1953.
[2] G. E. Moore: "Wittgenstein's Lectures in 1930–33" Originally published in *Mind,* 63, 1954, and 64, 1955; reprinted in G. E. Moore: *Philosophical Papers,* Allen & Unwin, London 1959.
[3] G. E. Moore: *Philosophical Papers,* cit., p. 322.
[4] *Tractatus Logico-philosophicus* (henceforth *Tractatus*), ed. by D. F. Pears and B. F. McGuinness, Routledge & Kegan Paul, London 1961.
[5] "Wittgenstein in Relation to his Times", in *Wittgenstein and his Impact on Contemporary Thought,* ed. by Elisabeth Leinfellner *et al.,* Hölder-Pichler-Tempsky, Vienna 1978, pp. 73–8. Reprinted in my book *Wittgenstein,* Blackwell, Oxford 1982. Also "Wittgenstein and the Twentieth Century", in *Language, Knowledge and Intentionality: Perspectives on the Philosophy of Jaakko Hintikka,* ed. by Leila Haaparanta *et al., Acta Philosophica Fennica,* Vol. 49, Helsinki 1990.
[6] The words are from the Preface to *Philosophische Untersuchungen,* cit. ("Finsternis dieser Zeit".).
[7] *Tractatus,* cit., 4.0031. The reference is to Fritz Mauthner: *Beiträge zu einer Kritik der Sprache,* Cotta, Stuttgart 1901.

[8] *Tractatus*, cit., 3.325.

[9] *Ibidem*, 4.0031.

[10] Published in *Mind*, 33, 1923.

[11] Noam Chomsky: *Cartesian Linguistics*, Harper & Row, New York 1966.

[12] Of 19 August 1919. See *Ludwig Wittgenstein; Cambridge Letters*, ed. by Brian McGuinness and Georg Henrik von Wright, Blackwell, Oxford 1995, pp. 124–26.

[13] On the relationship between the *Tractatus* and contemporary psycholiguistics and theory of meaning see the book by Richard M. McDonough: *The Argument of the "Tractatus"*, State University of New York Press, Albany 1986, especially pp. 172–83.

[14] In contrast with Wittgenstein's saying in *Tractatus* 4.0312 about the "fundamental thought" (*Grundgedanke*) of the book. My remark should not be construed polemically.

[15] See the issue of *Theoria*, 57, Part 3, 1991 with contributions by Nils-Eric Sahlin and Rosaria Egidi, and others.

[16] *Vermischte Bemerkungen*, ed. by G. H. von Wright and H. Nyman, Neubearbeitung des Textes durch Alois Pichler, Frankfurt am Main, Suhrkamp, 1994, p. 53.

[17] *Bemerkungen über die Philosophie der Psychologie. Remarks on the Philosophy of Psychology*, Vol. I, ed. by G. E. M. Anscombe and G. H. von Wright, Blackwell, Oxford 1980; Vol. II, ed. by G. H. von Wright and H. Nyman, Blackwell, Oxford 1980; *Letzte Schriften über die Philosophie der Psychologie. Last Writings on the Philosophy of Psychology*, Vol. I: *Vorstudien zum zweiten Teil der "Philosophische Untersuchungen"*. *Preliminary Studies for the Part II of "Philosophical Investigations"*, ed. by G. H. von Wright and H. Nyman, Blackwell, Oxford 1982; Vol. II: *Das Innere und das Äussere 1949–1951. The Inner and the Outer 1949–1951*, ed. by G. H. von Wright and H. Nyman, Blackwell, Oxford 1992.

[18] Paul M. Churchland: *Scientific Realism and the Plasticity of Mind*, Cambridge University Press, Cambridge 1979, p. 44 ff.

[19] Cf. *Zettel*, ed. by G. E. M. Anscombe and G. H. von Wright, Blackwell, Oxford 1967, § 608.

[20] *Philosophische Untersuchungen*, cit., Pt. II, pp. 220–23. Norman Malcolm: *Nothing is Hidden*, Blackwell, Oxford 1986.

[21] Saul Kripke: *Wittgenstein on Rules and Private Language*, Blackwell, Oxford 1982, p. 60.

[22] *Über Gewißheit. On Certainty*, ed. by G. E. M. Anscombe and G. H. von Wright, Blackwell, Oxford 1969.

[23] *Philosophische Untersuchungen*, cit., § 580.

[24] In *De Anima*, especially Book 2.

[25] Bertrand Russell: *Sceptical Essays*, W. W. Norton & Co., New York 1928, p. 71.

[26] *Wissenschaftliche Weltauffassung, Der Wiener Kreis*, Arthur Wolf Verlag, Wien 1929, pp. 54–8.

[27] "Tota igitur Philosophia veluti arbor est, cujus radicaes Metaphysica, truncus Physica, & rami ex eodem pullulantes, omnes aliae Scientiae sunt, quae ad tres praecipuas recovantur, Medicinam scilicet, Mechanicam, atque Ethicam; altissimam autem & perfectissimam morum disciplinam intelligo; quae integram aliarum scientiarum cogitionem praesupponens, ultimus ac summus Sapientiae gradus est."

[28] *Vermischte Bemerkungen*, cit., p. 45.

[29] *Bemerkungen über die Grundlagen der Mathematik. Remarks on the Foundations of Mathematics*, ed. G. H. von Wright, R. Rhees , G. E. M. Anscombe, Blackwell, Oxford 1964.

[30] *Ibidem*, pp. 119, 121.

CARLO PENCO

WITTGENSTEIN IN RELATION TO OUR TIMES

1. A PROBLEM POSED BY VON WRIGHT

In "Wittgenstein in relation to his times" von Wright[1] poses a dilemma regarding the relationship between three Wittgensteinian tenets;

(i)   the view that individual's beliefs and thoughts are entrenched in accepted language games and socially sanctioned forms of life;

(ii)   the view that "philosophical problems are disquietudes of the mind caused by some malfunctioning in the language games, and hence in the way of life of the community";

(iii) the "rejection of the scientific-technological civilisation of industrialised societies".

The dilemma is the following: is Wittgenstein's rejection of technological civilisation strictly linked to his general view of philosophy? Or is it "only contingently – that is for historical and psychological reasons, connected with the other two in Wittgenstein's thought"?

Von Wright argues, even with some doubts, for a strong link between Wittgenstein's rejection of technological society and his general approach to philosophy; the argument is as follows: "because of the interlocking of language and ways of life, a disorder in the former reflects disorder in the latter. If philosophical problems are symptomatic of language, producing malignant outgrowths which obscure our thinking, then there must be a cancer in the *Lebensweise*, in the way of life itself" (p. 119).

The argument seems to be not compelling; among some of the main philosophical problems Wittgenstein is willing to "cure" there are misunderstandings lying in the history of our language some time before our technological civilisation (Wittgenstein refers to Augustine and Plato as suffering disorders of language). We should generalise the criticism to technological society to the effect of enclosing ancient Greece. In this way the criticism seems to loose all its polemical vein, becoming a generic criticism of the structures of Western thought since Greece. But probably this was the point Wittgenstein wanted to make in his criticism of the idea of progress and technological civilisation.

I will argue therefore for the second horn of the dilemma, relying on another kind of *de facto* argument: contemporary technological civilisation is embodying some of Wittgenstein's main ideas (we might also note that these ideas are among the

47

R. Egidi (ed.), In Search of a New Humanism, 47–53.
©1999 *Kluwer Academic Publishers. Printed in Great Britain.*

strongest points Wittgenstein gives against Greek classical tradition in philosophy). Therefore Wittgenstein's philosophy and modern civilisation seem really compatible, notwithstanding the distrust of modern civilisation which is apparent in Wittgenstein's personality.

2. MEETING BETWEEN WITTGENSTEIN'S IDEAS AND CONTEMPORARY TECHNOLOGICAL RESEARCH

I will briefly state three cases of strong affinities between the development of our technological civilisation and Wittgenstein's ideas.

The first case is the case of the idea of "frame" and "prototype" in A.I. and cognitive science. It was firstly established by Minsky 1975 where he developed his well known theory of frames, as concepts with defaul values which can be changed depending on new information. In stating his theory Minsky relied explicitly on Wittgenstein's idea of family resemblance predicates. The acceptance of this trend of thought has been widespread in different research environments, especially in the engineering environment with the construction of adequate formal tools (from semantic networks to default logics), and in cognitive science environments (starting with an analogous work on Wittgenstein's ideas developed by Eleanore Rosh on the concept of prototype).

The second case I want to offer has a deep similarity with Wittgenstein's idea of language-games. The case is the idea of toy-worlds. The idea behind the construction of toy worlds (one of the most famous is SHRDLU, by Terry Winograd 1972) can be expressed as the following: in order to simulate human language understanding you need to have a better mastery of the surrounding world, the background-knowledge and the actions which accompany the linguistic behaviour. But it is almost impossible to have a complete mastery of that; therefore you need to isolate some simple cases. In a toy-world very simple actions are performed, following simple orders, in a situation very similar to Wittgenstein's builders (PI, § 2). As in Wittgenstein's language games, the analysis of the working of language emerges from the analysis of very simple situations.[2]

The third case is the case of Contextual reasoning (see McCarthy 1993). Limited contexts of action are not only devised just in order to study the working of language; language itself is being now considered as a web of different contexts, where contexts are defined in a rich way as local theories of a limited aspect of the world. In some theories contexts, even if not organised in a hierarchic fashion, are connected with rules which permit passages from some contexts to some other contexts. Here we find a formal expression of the most characteristic feature of Wittgenstein's viewpoint on understanding: to understand an expression is to understand the language game in which it is at home, to master the particular technique of the language (game) in question (PI, § 199). If there is some truth in the idea that meaning is use in context, this trend in A.I. seems to be one of the most perspicuous representations of it.

3. A FIRST ANSWER: WITTGENSTEIN AGAINST SCIENTISM

An immediate reaction when commenting on these similarities might be: who cares? Wittgenstein didn't like Western technological civilisation; Western technological civilisation liked Wittgenstein. There is nothing more to say.

But, it seems to me, the evidence given above is related to a central core in Wittgenstein's philosophy: the idea of meaning as use, of the vagueness of our concepts and their being embedded in social practices and activities, together with the impossibility to give a straightforward theory of "the" language seem to be ideas which are so central to Wittgenstein's philosophy that it does not seem possible to detach them from the overall view of his philosophy. This assumption brings us back to von Wright's problem.

Let us give a more detailed look at Wittgenstein's rejection of the scientific-technological civilisation. The theme appears to be a constant in Wittgenstein's attitude, from the criticism of *Tractatus* against the blind belief of modernity in scientific laws, through the preface to *Philosophische Bemerkungen* where he express his distrust of Western civilisation to the last passages from the end of the forties quoted in *Vermischte Bemerkungen*: here he consider the "apocalyptic view of the world" and he asserts that it is "not nonsensical to believe that the age of science and technology is the beginning of the end of humanity" and that the idea of progress "is a delusion" and that mankind in seeking scientific knowledge "is falling into a trap" (VB, p. 56). A comment follows which may be is one of the strongest, but also somehow most naïve remarks of dissatisfaction with modern world: science and industry will "condense the world into a single unit", but it will be a world with no peace: "because science and industry do decide wars, or so it seems" (VB, p. 63).

Could we say that Wittgenstein was nostalgic in respect of better – or more honest – kinds of war fought in the past (included the one he was engaged with)? This is a question which will be remain unanswered, even if we may accept the suggestion given by von Wright, that Wittgentein's world view "has no vision for the future; rather it has a touch of nostalgia about the past" (p. 115). We may certainly assume at least that his attitude against Western civilisation is embittered by the war experience and strongly dependent on historical accident. But how much of this attitude is strictly tied with his philosophy?

Wittgenstein's apocalyptic remarks seem to be always mitigated by some critical attitude which compels him to take some distance in respect to the apocalyptic point of view: He asserts that "any speculation about a coming collapse of science and industry is, for the present and for a *long* time to come, nothing but a dream". And if we read carefully the passages, we note that "the apocalyptic view of the World" is not positively assumed but only considered as an hypothesis.

Did he ever adhere to the apocalyptic hypothesis? Explicitly he does not; he makes, in a few places, strong remarks on the negative sides of technology[3] (such as: "a technical development in film production does not correspond to a development in style"). But such kinds of assertions do not imply that a technical development cannot have a value for itself. In fact, this reaction against technology in art contrasts with the place the concept of "technique" has in his last writings. Beyond that, Wittgenstein's attitude to science has been always respectful: science is part of our representation of the world; it is accepted for such, it is part of our background (OC, §§ 600–604). This general recognition is also a result of his ever lasting appreciation for science and scientific endeavour (we cannot forget his great admiration for Boltzmann and Hertz), together with his admiration for any technical abilities and skill and his love for mathematical proof techniques (Kreisel speaks of his ability in diagonalisation games when he was teaching foundations of mathematics).

On the other hand he reacts against "popular semi-philosophical speculations" made by scientists, which "pander to people's curiosity to be titillated by the wonder of science without having to do any of the real hard work involved in understanding what science is about".[4] This is just one of many examples of his respect of sane scientific work, to be defended by superficiality and ideology. Appreciation of science runs against scientism.

A first answer to our dilemma therefore could be: Wittgenstein's philosophy is against scientism, but not against science and technology in principle. Plane scientific work is admired: science idolatry is feared. The constitutive role of science and technique in our thinking habits is well accepted and recognised, the role of the application of science and industry together (technology and the idea of progress) is considered dangerous. Both stances seem integral to his general attitude; but they are not clearly distinguished in his writings, where the second seems to involve a general disapproval of science which in not really involved. We might conclude: being against scientism is an integral part of Wittgenstein's philosophy and can be shared also by researches involved in our technological civilisation as a central attitude against any attempt to believe that science and technology may resolve the problems they have been responsible of.[5]

But this is not a good enough answer; even if we assume that Wittgenstein's reaction against technological civilisation is strictly depending on historical factor and not linked to his philosophical thought, there is still something of this antagonism with technological society which has a deep role in Wittgenstein's philosophy: the reaction against the influence of scientific way of thinking on philosophers, of which we have many testimonies in his life and in his writings.

4. A DEEPER DISSIMILARITY WITH WESTERN CULTURE?

We are therefore led to reconsider his distrust of the idea of progress as a symptom a deeper dissimilarity non only of his personality, but also of his philosophy, in respect to Western civilisation. Von Wright suggests that his idea of philosophy as a cure for the malfunctioning of language leads to the idea that "there must be a cancer in the way of life itself". If we assume that the cancer is the idea of scientific progress, we may be led to consider Wittgenstein's method in philosophy as an alternative to the scientific way of thinking. We could therefore consider his deeper mistrust in science as a desire to substitute science with some kind of new way of looking at things. Relying on contemporary literature on Wittgenstein,[6] we could label his method "anthropological method" or "morphological method": this method could be considered an alternative to scientific progress, a strategy to go deeper into the essence, instead of looking around for more and more data and results (just remember the preface to PB).

In this case his distrust towards scientific progress would remind us of the romantic Goethean attitude towards Newtonian physics, against which Goethe wanted a new kind of way of looking at the world. Wittgenstein's reference to Spengler gives a more determined impression of this general distrust against Western civilisation, and Waismann's disappointment against Wittgenstein in his last days is another sign of Wittgenstein distrust against science in general.

On the other hand, although he was certainly influenced by Spengler, Wittgenstein's remarks on him are critical; as far as Goethe is concerned, it is worth noting that Goethe is not mentioned among the main influences on his ideas: that could be a sign that Goethe was for him the greatest influence, so great to be not perceived as such, because too obviously part of his intellectual environment and therefore of his mental structure. But, although we may detect many great influences in Wittgenstein work, we are still facing a man who gave rise to the ideas of Wiener Kreis; and the respect for mathematics and science as a fundamental feature of human culture lurks behind any Wittgensteinian analysis; so in his last remarks on colour he reacts against Goethe's pretension to give a "theory", as an alternative to Newton's one:

Goethe's theory of the origin of the spectrum *isn't* a theory of its origin that has proved unsatisfactory; it is really not a theory at all. *Nothing* can be predicted by means of it. (BuF, III, 125; cfr. I, 70)

Goethe's work is a conceptual analysis, of the kind Wittgenstein wanted to pursue; to define his kind of analysis he has to be constantly aware of its difference from scientific analysis. But that does not mean to despise scientific analysis; we need to distinguish the two in order to avoid conceptual confusion, which happens when philosophers try to be scientific and scientists try to philosophise.

Even if it is clear that Wittgenstein strongly felt the danger of the invasion of scientific way of thinking inside philosophy, it seems that his own philosophy, free from this danger, is in the best position to interact with the scientific and technological culture of our times. Philosophy sometimes, even if this is not its aim, may prepare the way to science; it may deprive it of preconceptions and conceptual confusion. Once prejudices and misunderstandings are dissolved, the way is open for actual research on substantial problems. Wittgenstein anticipated many results, and certainly contributed to the building of many ideas which are essential in many sectors of our technological culture. Some of the ideas he was struggling for are now commonsense. But the kind of job he wanted philosophy to do is still to be pursued not against, but inside our civilisation.

CONCLUSION

We have to distinguish between an apocalyptic attitude and a criticism internal to our civilisation, which is permitted by its own development. As Wittgenstein realised, technological civilisation is going to unify the world in a single unit, whose cohesion is given by technology. A main core of this coherent unity is given, in technology and industry, by the new computational paradigm, which requires a detailed analysis of how language works. In such a work people are compelled to go deeper and deeper in the understanding of the subtleties of our natural language; and they are led to develop insights similar to Wittgenstein's or actually to pick up his ideas. Although Wittgenstein's personal remarks on civilisation can be taken over by apocalyptic thinkers, his overall philosophy can become an integral part of our technological civilisation and be a stimulus on one of the many different directions this civilisation may take.[7]

The strong passionate personality and the Jewish background have certainly given a great stress to the contrast between Wittgenstein's ethical attitude and the disaster of the apparent lack of values in the technological society as Wittgenstein felt it; but Wittgenstein's philosophy remains a contradictory tension which tries to hold together Jerusalem, Manchester and Athens, or, as he once said, Religion, Wissenschaft und Kunst (TB 8.1.1916, p. 79).

Università di Genova (Italy)

NOTES

[1] This paper was originally given at Wittgenstein Symposium in Kirchberg in 1977, where I had the occasion to listen to it; I quote here from the version which appeared in McGuinness 1982, p. 118.
[2] Differently from the frame theory, Toy Worlds have not been explicitly connected with Wittgenstein's ideas from the start. For a more explicit connection, see Penco 1999.
[3] Here "technology" may be defined, following von Wright 1989 "science plus industry"; but Wittgenstein never uses this term; he speaks only of "technique" and "technical".
[4] See the conversations of Wittgenstein with Drury, in Rhees 1981, p. 117.
[5] This belief is what characterises scientism in von Wright 1989, § 9. This belief can easily be connected with the desire to substitute science for philosophy and to overlap empirical problems with conceptual problems, which was one of the main concerns in Wittgenstein's criticism of the scientific point of view.
[6] It is enough here to refer to the results given in the paper by Andronico in this volume.
[7] As Wittgenstein said, when we think of the future, sometimes we forget the following: "dass sie [die Zukunft] nicht gerade läuft, sondern in einer Kurve, und ihre Richtung sich konstant ändern" (VB, p. 3).

BIBLIOGRAPHY

McCarthy 1993
McCarthy J.:"Notes on Formalizing Contexts", *International Joint Conference on Artificial Intelligence.*
McGuinness 1982
McGuinness B. (ed.): *Wittgenstein and his Times*, Blackwell, Oxford.
Minsky 1975
Minsky M.: "A Framework for Representing Knowledge", in P. Winston (ed): *The Psychology of Computer Vision*, New York, McGraw-Hill.
Penco 1999
Penco C.: "Holism in A.I.?", in M. L. Dalla Chiara *et al.* (eds.): *Language, Quantum, Music*, Kluwer, Dordrecht, 1999.

Rhees 1981
  Rhees R. (ed.): *L. Wittgenstein: Personal Recollections*, Oxford University Press, Oxford.
Von Wright 1978
  Von Wright G. H.: "Wittgenstein in Relation to his Times", in *Wittgenstein and his Impact on Contemporary Thought*, ed. by E. Leinfellner *et al.*, Hölder-Pichler-Tempsky, Wien. Reprinted in McGuinness 1982 and in von Wright 1982.
Von Wright 1982
  Von Wright G. H.: *Wittgenstein*, Blackwell, Oxford.
Von Wright 1989
  Von Wright G. H.: "Science, Reason, and Value", *Documenta 49*, The Royal Swedish Academy of Sciences, Stockholm, pp. 7–28.
Von Wright 1995
  Von Wright G. H.: "Wittgenstein and the Twentieth Century", in R. Egidi (ed.): *Wittgenstein, Mind and Language*, Kluwer, Dordrecht.
Winograd 1972
  Winograd T.: *Understanding Natural Language*, Academic Press, New York.
Wittgenstein 1953
  Wittgenstein L.: *Philosophische Untersuchungen. Philosophical Investigations*, ed. by G. E. M. Anscombe and R. Rhees, Blackwell, Oxford [PI]
Wittgenstein 1961
  Wittgenstein L.: *Tagebücher 1914–1916. Notebooks 1914–1916*, ed. by G. E. M. Anscombe and G. H. von Wright, Blackwell, Oxford [TB]
Wittgenstein 1964
  Wittgenstein L.: *Philosophische Bemerkungen. Philosophical Remarks*, ed. by R. Rhees, Blackwell, Oxford [PB]
Wittgenstein 1969
  Wittgenstein L.: *Über Gewißheit. On Certainty*, ed. by G. E. M. Anscombe and G. H. von Wright, Blackwell, Oxford [OC]
Wittgenstein 1977
  Wittgenstein L.: *Bemerkungen über die Farben. Remarks on Colour*, ed. by G. E. M. Anscombe, Blackwell, Oxford [BuF]
Wittgenstein 1980
  Wittgenstein L.: *Vermischte Bemerkungen. Culture and Value*, ed. by G. H. von Wright, in collaboration with H. Nyman, Blackwell, Oxford [VB]

CESARE COZZO

WHAT IS ANALYTICAL PHILOSOPHY?

Professor von Wright is a prominent analytical philosopher who has written about the very notion of analytical philosophy. Other analytical philosophers are present here and they have their ideas on this notion. As for me, I believe that it is not at all an obvious notion. Sometimes it seemed to me that analytical philosophy does not exist, or at least that there is no single common philosophical feature shared by all so-called analytical philosophers and only by them, though there are many family resemblances. Therefore I thought I might take the opportunity of this meeting in honour of Professor von Wright and propose as one of our themes for discussion, precisely the question: "what is analytical philosophy?". The natural start is Professor von Wright's description of analytical philosophy.

When Professor von Wright writes about analytical philosophy, for example in the first chapter of *Explanation and Understanding*, he remarks that

The logical positivism of the 1920's and 1930's was a main, though by no means the sole, tributary out of which grew the broader current of philosophical thought nowadays commonly known as analytical philosophy.[1]

But he immediately adds that

it would be quite wrong to label analytical philosophy as a whole brand of positivism.[2]

Indeed, Professor von Wright himself has clearly shown that analytical philosophers can develop philosophical positions which are opposed to fundamental tenets of the logical positivists, like methodological monism or the covering law theory of explanation. Although I have a direct experience of Italian non-analytical philosophers who still think that logical positivism and analytical philosophy are the same thing, I think nobody among us would deny that analytical philosophy encompasses a much wider philosophical area.

What then is analytical philosophy? In the recent essay "Wittgenstein and the Twentieth Century" von Wright writes:

In spite of the many tributaries which have, in the course of the years, emptied their waters into this river, I think it is right and illuminating to call analytical philosophy the mainstream of philosophic thinking in this century. In all its heterogeneity it retains the two features which I already mentioned as typical of its origin: the emphasis on logic and the alignment with science. It is, in short, the philosophy most characteristic of a culture dominated by scientific rationality.[3]

According to von Wright, analytical philosophy is the philosophical representative of Modernity in the twentieth century. It continues the tradition of the Enlightenment. The constant tenet of this tradition is that philosophy should be a rational enterprise and that natural science and mathematics are models of rationality. Sometimes this

R. Egidi (ed.), In Search of a New Humanism, 55–63.

leads to the idea that mathematics and natural sciences "set the pattern"[4] for philosophic thinking.

In this frame the development of *mathematical logic* as a tool for the foundation of mathematics provided a rigorous (mathematical) method which a philosopher can apply, as Professor von Wright did, beyond the philosophy of mathematics. Thus, to answer our question concerning analytical philosophy, we have to highlight the connection between analytical philosophy and philosophical logic. Von Wright describes philosophical logic as being, in his words,

the applications of the tools of formal logic to the analysis of concepts and conceptual structures in which philosophers traditionally have taken an interest.[5]

As Dag Prawitz pointed out in his talk to this meeting the very notions of logical consequence and logical truth are of great philosophical interest. Therefore the term "philosophical logic" would be misleading if it were taken to banish from the domain of philosophy those logics, like pure first or second order predicate logic, which focus upon logical consequence and logical truth, but were developed for a study of mathematical theories. Also these logics fully deserve the epithet "philosophical". On the other hand, logicians who deal with modal logic, temporal logic and other logics usually called "philosophical" nonetheless employ methods which are essentially the same mathematical methods of "mathematical" logic. Hence we ought to take the term "philosophical logic" (or simply: "logic") in a sufficiently wide sense.

Analytical philosophy might be conceived as the view that old philosophical theses and problems should take the form of theses and problems treated by logicians who study formal languages, formal systems and corresponding model theoretic structures. In this view, philosophical logic would be "ripe philosophy". A similar idea is advanced by the Swedish logician-philosopher Krister Segerberg in a paper where he deals with a topic of which von Wright, as Segerberg emphasizes, is the father: the logic of action.

Before the gold can be mined (the task of philosophical logic) prospectors must explore the terrain (the task of philosophy). [...] Philosophizing prepares the way for rigorous theorizing. [...] There is no difference of purview between philosophy of action and logic of action: the questions are the same, what differs is the technique.[6]

After the gold is found and the miners start working, prospectors become superfluous in a mine. Thus the metaphor of philosophers as prospectors and philosophical logicians as miners suggests that in any particular field (e.g. the philosophy of action) philosophical logic (e.g. the study of systems like dynamic logic) ought to replace old non-formal philosophy. I don't know whether this is what Segerberg really means. Anyway, I call it *strong philosophical logicism*. The idea that logical systems replace philosophical perplexities is to some extent also in the view of philosophy as "logical reconstruction" which, according to his "Intellectual Autobiography" (1972–73), von Wright adopted in his early work on induction and probability, and then abandoned:

the *end* of the philosophical inquiry was to silence a felt disquietude of the mind by making us realize that there was nothing to be uneasy about. The *means* to this end consisted in displaying clearly certain obscure logical structures. The result of the displaying or laying bare of structures was a piece of logic: a logic of demostrative induction, a logic of probability etc.[7]

Weak philosophical logicism might be the different view that, although philosophers should try to make rigorous their thinking by exploiting the methods of formal logic, and thus philosophical logic is an important part of the philosopher's work, still one never reaches a point where the non-formal and non-mathematical thinking about a key philosophical notion is fully replaced by a formal theory. On what grounds might one think that such a point will never be reached? Perhaps another quotation from one of von Wright's writings can help us:

A philosopher is concerned with fundamentals. [...] The basic concepts which he studies are mostly familiar to all of us. The words "time" or "truth" or "meaning" or "good", for example, belong to every man's vocabulary, and we learn to use them in childhood or early adolescence. It is only when we stop to reflect or are called upon to give an account of their meaning and use, that we feel puzzled.[8]

In the quoted essay "Time, Change and Contradiction" von Wright develops a formal theory of some temporal concepts. But the origin of a logic of time is, von Wright says, a notion (time) which is most familiar to all of us. The aim of philosophizing, and also of a logic of time, is a clarification of that pre-theoretic notion. The same would hold for a theory of proof, of truth, of meaning, of good, of justice, and so on. One can plausibly think that the non-formal reflection on these important familiar notions ought not to be only at the beginning of the formal enterprise; on the contrary it should constantly accompany the development of formal theories. Besides considering its internal simplicity and coherence, the principal way of *checking* whether a philosophical logic is on the right track is to compare its results with our common pretheoretical intuitions, judgments and well established practices which involve these familiar fundamental notions and precisely in this comparison there is always room for a non-formal philosophical reflection.

Without an agreement with *pretheoretical data* (as we may call such intuitions, judgments and practices) philosophical logic, or any kind of "rigorous theorizing", though rigorous, would be empty. Without a theory, on the other hand, pretheoretical data would be blind and unconnected. We need a theoretical clarification of philosophical fundamental notions in order to systematize pretheoretical data. Moreover, there are problematic occasions when we don't know how to apply those notions or we are unsure. In these cases a philosophical theory can guide us. Then the theory (differently from an empirical scientific theory) generates new data in agreement with itself, because in such problematic cases our judgments and practices are dictated by the theory. But this is not the only way in which a theory can generate new data. The theory can lead us to ask ourselves questions we had never previously thought of. Such questions can elicit refinements of our philosophical intuitions so that new intuitions, new judgements arise which the theory does not dictate to us (they may even contradict the theory), but which nevertheless are aroused by the theory. These new data are relevant for the theory, but they are not necessarily in agreement with it. For example, the development of a formal system for epistemic logic can lead us to ask ourselves for the first time whether the inference rule according to which "it is known that B" can be inferred from the two premises "it is known that if A, then B" and "it is known that A" is a correct rule or not. Our answer might be in the negative. Then we might conclude that the formal system in question is defective, but only through the development and the examination of that system would we have come to the non formal reflection and to the special intuitions concerning knowledge on which our conclusion is based. The proposal of a formal system would elicit new non formal data and new philosophical understanding on the basis of which we would reject the formal system. A theory generates new data and the new data require a new theory. When this process comes to an end, we have not replaced non-formal reflection with a formal theory, on the contrary: we have the non-formal ascertainment of a special balance between a theory (which does not necessarily coincide with a formal system, though it may contain one) and corresponding non-formal data.

Here I have in some way repeated an idea already defended in different contexts by Nelson Goodman,[9] John Rawls[10] and Dag Prawitz,[11] the idea that between philosophical theorizing on the one hand, and intuitions, judgments, and practices involving philosophical fundamental pre-theoretical notions on the other hand, there should be a *reflective equilibrium*. This is a conception of analytical philosophy which is very different, and, in my opinion, more plausible than the view which I called "strong philosophical logicism". It is a very wide conception of philosophy, because it involves only methodological requirements: the analytical philosopher ought to be rigorous, he/she ought to make clear and precise his/her theses and concepts and ought to give precise arguments to support them, possibly using formal logic as a tool in this effort to be rigorous, but also resorting to a non-formal consideration of pretheoretical data concerning fundamental philosophical notions. After all, in this sense, analytical philosophy is simply *rigorous philosophy aiming at reflective equilibrium*. Philosophical logic is an important aspect of rigorous philosophy, but one should be careful to avoid a too narrow notion of rigour. Also the notion of "logic" is changing.[12] Nowadays to think of rigorous theorizing and of logic only as the study of formal systems (meant as fixed sets of formal rules) or model-theoretic structures would be narrow-mindedness.

It seems to me that the view of philosophy as "*explication of conceptual intuitions*" which Professor von Wright defends in his "Intellectual Autobiography"[13] is similar to this conception of *rigorous philosophy aiming at reflective equilibrium*, especially when he writes:

To the concepts in which the philosopher takes an interest there normally answer words in ordinary language. The philosopher experiences their use as somehow unclear or in need of systematization [...] what the philosopher does in relation to language could, with due caution, be described as filling out gaps, or lacunas, in existing usage. This he cannot do by consulting usage – since there is none to be consulted. If he can be said to consult anything at all, this would be his own 'intuitions' about the concepts under discussion [...] But there exists a 'negative test'. This is afforded by what the language community, by and large, accepts or regards as correct usage. This the philosopher has no right to change. It defines, so to say, the borders of the gap which he tries to fill. Thereby it determines his very problem. The violation of usage would mean a distortion of the conceptual situation and be a sign that the philosopher, not language, has gone wrong.[14]

Philosophy as "explication of conceptual intuitions – von Wright maintains – can be distinguished from the activity of a logician or mathematician and also from the activity of a natural or social scientist.[15] On the latter point many analytical philosophers would not agree. In his paper on "Wittgenstein and the Twentieth Century" von Wright mentions Brentano as one of the near ancestors of analytical philosophy and quotes from his *Habilitationsschrift*: "vera philosophiae methodus nulla alia nisi scientiae naturalis est".[16]

Brentano's principle, which equates the methods of philosophy and natural science, makes the reader think of the revival of *naturalism* in American philosophy since Quine's "Epistemology Naturalized".[17] The naturalistic view which Quine defends "does not repudiate epistemology, but assimilates it to empirical psychology".[18] Today many philosophers who consider themselves analytical philosophers think of their own activity in accordance with such a naturalistic conception, and thus under the banner of cognitive science they run counter to the firm antipsyschologistic convictions of early analytical philosophers, like Frege, Wittgenstein and the logical positivists.[19] If *naturalized philosophy* is meant as *philosophy assimilated to natural science*, then it is different from philosophy aiming at reflective equilibrium. The latter might be called a quasi-empiric theorizing because it is confronted with data of our prephilosophical practice with which it ought to agree. Detecting such data is a very special kind of observation: for example the philosopher observes that people perform and accept deductive inferences with certain formal properties. But, if we take the view that philosophy aims at reflective equilibrium, philosophy and natural science differ at least in two respects, as far as the role of data is concerned. In the *first* place, the very notion of reflective equilibrium is introduced by contrasting reflective equilibrium with the relation between theory and data in natural science. Natural phenomena are never guided by the intention of conforming to the laws of physics even though they agree with such laws; phenomena can be *interpreted* in the light of a physical theory, but they are never *dictated* by the theory; on the contrary in problematic cases our judgements and acts involving a philosophical notion can be brought about by the intention of conforming to the principles of a philosophical theory. *Secondly*, it can be argued that the general non-normative and non-semantic nature of the relevant data in natural science is different from the normative and semantic nature of intuitions, judgments, and practices which count as philosophical data. Typical philosophical data are normative judgements according to which some act is right or wrong with respect to some philosophically relevant pre-theoretical notion of rightness. In this connection it is interesting to observe that in practice adherents to the naturalistic conception often also consider agreement with such normative and semantic data a criterion of adequacy for the views they put forward (for example, they deem it a test of a theory of reasoning to establish whether it agrees with the datum of common pretheoretic acceptance of a certain inference as correct or truth preserving); thus it seems that their philosophical *practice* is more in line with the metaphilosophical picture offered by the reflective-equilibrium view than with the naturalistic picture. (And if the naturalist replies that such normative and semantic data can be reduced to non-normative and non-semantic facts, it is difficult to dispel the suspicion that he/she is begging the question).

A different notion of analytical philosophy is proposed by Michael Dummett. According to Dummett, analytical philosophy is "post-Fregean philosophy".[20] In "Can Analytical Philosophy be Systematic, and Ought it to be?" (1975) he wrote that all practitioners of analytical philosophy share two views that – Dummett thinks – are at least implicit in Frege's philosophical method: 1) it is only by the analysis of language that we can analyse thought; 2) the philosophy of language is the foundation of all philosophy. More explicitly than the aforementioned conceptions of analytical philosophy, Dummett's characterization comes close to identifying analytical philosophy with the acceptance of specific philosophical tenets. I doubt that acceptance of thesis (1) is a necessary ingredient of analytical philosophy, but I agree with Dummett that (1) is true and I think that Dummett's justification of (1) is sound: it is essential to thoughts, that they can be communicated; thus, in order to understand how thoughts are possible, we have to understand how thoughts can be expressed, and to this aim it is necessary to understand how language functions. In more recent writings, while Dummett still maintains that (1) is a basic tenet of analytical philosophy, he acknowledges that "some recent work in the analytical tradition has reversed this priority, in the order of explanation, of language over thought".[21] The conclusion seems to me unavoidable that *now* (1) is not a thesis shared by all practitioners of analytical philosophy, and if we took acceptance of (1) as a defining feature of analytical philosophy, the resulting concept would be too narrow.[22] We might thus say that acceptance of (1) constitutes only a particular position within analytical philosophy: *language-centred philosophy*.

What about (2)? Does (2) follow from (1)? If it does, then perhaps Richard Rorty is right in describing such a *language-centred* analytical philosophy as *foundational philosophy*, that is

an armchair discipline capable of discovering the "formal" [...] characteristics of any area of human life, [which] enabled philosophy professors to see themselves as presiding over a tribunal of pure reason able to determine whether other disciplines were staying within the legal limits set by the "structure" of their subject matters[23]

Though Rorty's picture is caricatural, it is true that analytical philosophers have often thought that, on the basis of their theories of meaning (i.e. their accounts of the workings of language), they could detect the foundations of knowledge or morality and could decide whether given practices within different scientific and cultural areas were right or wrong, meaningful or meaningless, justifiable or unjustifiable, legitimate or illegitimate, objectively valid or simply expression of a subjective attitude. This is clearly true of Frege's logicism, of the conception of natural science advocated by the logical positivists, of Dummett's verificationist critique of classical mathematics, of Ayer's emotivist conception of ethical statements, etc.. Though naturalism is often opposed to foundationalism, naturalized philosophy also has this foundational attitude when it deals with disciplines which are outside the field of natural sciences. For example, I think it is not misleading to describe Hartry Field's[24] and Penelope Maddy's[25] work in the philosophy of mathematics as competing attempts at providing a naturalistic foundation of mathematics (they both start from naturalistic conceptions of reference which seem to undermine the value of mathematical knowledge). However, there are also analytical philosophers who criticize foundationalism, like Hilary Putnam.[26]

Dummett holds that the philosophy of thought can be approached only through the philosophy of language. Thus the philosophy of language has priority. Thesis (1) can be called *the language priority thesis*. But I don't think that (1) entails foundationalism. For example, according to the language priority thesis, the first problem that a philosopher of mathematics ought to solve concerns the meanings of mathematical sentences and the nature of our understanding of such sentences. But this is only the beginning of a philosophy of mathematics; there are other problems after that. To mention a few: what is the role of conjecture in mathematics? to what extent is mathematical justification holistic? what is the interplay between pure mathematics and applied mathematics? what makes a mathematical problem interesting? what is a rational change of language in mathematics? Acceptance of thesis (1) does not imply the view that a philosophical study of mathematics *coincides* with (or can be directly derived from) an analysis of the meanings of mathematical sentences. Neither does acceptance of thesis (1) imply that an analysis of the meanings of mathematical sentences yields any set of privileged (e.g. analytical) sentences or reasonings that can count as foundations of matematics. To say that a set of sentences or reasonings can count as foundations amounts to saying that such sentences or reasonings support all the rest of knowledge in a certain area and are not supported by it. But the language priority thesis (1) is fully compatible with the view that mathematics does not have and does not need foundations in this sense. It is possible to agree with Dummett on (1) and also on his further view that analytical philosophy ought to be *systematic* (because a satisfactory account of how language functions requires a systematic theory of meaning for an entire language) and at the same time to deny that the theory of meaning provides a *foundation* for the rest of philosophy or for any other discipline. To see that this is a consistent option, think of a theory of meaning which admits *epistemological* holism and denies that sentences (or inferences) can be true (or valid) only in virtue of meanings. According to the priority thesis, a theory of meaning should be the beginning of a philosophical investigation. But a beginning is not necessarily a foundation. The approach we adopt at the beginning is not a foundation if it can be called into question when it clashes with the results of another investigation or is endorsed only in so far as it agrees with such results. If we take the view that our theory of meaning is acceptable only if it harmonizes with certain pretheoretical data of our practice in everyday life, in science, and in other areas of culture, the theory of meaning will depend on philosophical or scientific investigations in specific areas concerning problems which are not immediately related to meaning. For example, it can be argued that a satisfactory study of mathematical knowledge ought to take into account the role of concepts that are paradoxical but fruitful, like the concepts of Newton's method of fluxions; on the basis of such an argument concerning mathematical practice, one can reject a theory of meaning according to which paradoxical fragments of language are meaningless.[27]

Very briefly and roughly I have listed at least six conceptions of philosophy: philosophical logicism, rigorous philosophy aiming at reflective equilibrium, philosophy as explication of conceptual intuitions, naturalized philosophy, language-centred philosophy, linguistic foundationalism in Rorty's sense. I am aware that my treatment of these views was little more than a cursory survey. Therefore I will not draw any conclusion, I simply put an end to this talk with two questions. Is there a characteristic feature which only these different conceptions of philosophy have in common? Please tell me: what is analytical philosophy?

Università di Roma "La Sapienza" (Italy)

NOTES

[1] G. H. von Wright: *Explanation and Understanding*, Routledge & Kegan Paul, London, 1971, p. 9. See also his later paper "Analytische Philosophie. Eine historisch-kritische Betrachtung", *Rechtstheorie"*, 23, 1992, pp. 3–25; reprinted in English translation in G. H. von Wright: *The Tree of Knowledge and Other Essays*, E. J. Brill, Leiden 1993.

[2] *Ibidem.*

[3] G. H. von Wright: "Wittgenstein and the Twentieth Century", in R. Egidi (ed.): *Wittgenstein: Mind and Language*, Kluwer, Dordrecht 1995.

[4] *Ibidem.*

[5] G. H. von Wright: Problems and Prospects in Deontic Logic. A Survey", in E. Agazzi (ed.): *Modern Logic,* Reidel, Dordrecht 1980, p. 399. Cfr. also "Intellectual Autobiography", in P. A. Schilpp and L. E. Hahn (eds..): *The Philosophy of G. H. von Wright*, Open Court, La Salle, Ill. 1989, p. 50.

[6] K. Segerberg: "Getting Started: Beginnings in the Logic of Action", in G. Corsi, C. Mangione, M. Mugnai (eds.): *Atti del Convegno Internazionale di Storia della Logica: Le teorie della modalità*, Clueb, Bologna 1989, p. 221.

[7] G. H. von Wright: "Intellectual Autobiography", cit., p. 46.

[8] G. H. von Wright: "Time, Change and Contradiction", in G. H. von Wright: *Philosophical Logic. Philosophical Papers*, Vol. II, Blackwell, Oxford 1983, p. 115.

[9] N. Goodman: *Fact, Fiction, and Forecast*, Bobbs Merrill, Indianapolis, New York-Kansas City, 1955, 1965[2].

[10] J. Rawls: *A Theory of Justice*, Oxford University Press, Oxford 1971.

[11] D. Prawitz: "Meaning and Proofs: on the Conflict between Classical and Intuitionistic Logic", *Theoria*, 43, 1977, pp. 1–40.

[12] Cfr. C. Cellucci: "From Closed to Open Systems", in J. Czermak (ed.): *Philosophy of Mathematics*, Hölder-Pichler-Tempsky, Wien 1993, pp. 206–20.

[13] Cfr. G. H. von Wright: "Intellectual Autobiography", cit., p. 49.

[14] *Ibidem.*

[15] *Ibidem*, p. 53.

[16] Quoted by R. Haller: "Wittgenstein and Austrian Philosophy", in J. C. Nyiri: *Austrian Philosophy: Studies and Texts*, Philosophia Verlag, München 1981.

[17] W. V. O. Quine: "Epistemology Naturalized", in W. V. O. Quine: *Ontological Relativity and Other Essays*, Columbia University Press, New York-London 1969, pp. 69–90.

[18] W. V. O. Quine: "Five Milestones of Empiricism", in W. V. O. Quine: *Theories and Things*, Harvard University Press, Cambridge, p. 72.

[19] Cfr. P. Kitcher: "The Naturalists Return", *Philosophical Review*, 101, 1992, pp. 53–114.

[20] M. Dummett: "Can Analytical Philosophy be Systematic, and Ought it to Be?", now in *Truth and Other Enigmas*, Duckworth, London 1978, p. 441.

[21] M. Dummett: *Origins of Analytical Philosophy*, Duckworth, London 1993, p. 4, cfr. M. Dummett: *The Logical Basis of Metaphysics*, Duckworth, London 1991, p. 3.

[22] [*Note added in November 1997*] One year after presenting this paper at the Rome *Colloquium* on Professor von Wright's philosophy I happened to read Fabrice Pataut's interesting "Interview with Michael Dummett" in *Philosophical Investigations*, 19, 1996, pp. 1–33, where Dummett (interviewed by Pataut in 1992) seems to come to a similar conclusion and thus seems to abandon the view that (1) is essential to analytical philosophy. In this interview Dummett emphasizes another characteristic feature of analytical philosophers, which persists even when they, like Gareth Evans or Cristopher Peacocke, deny the priority of language over thought: "I think the big difference between analytic philosophers and others is probably that all analytic philosophers assume something resembling the kind of semantics that underlies mathematical logic, *i.e.* Fregean semantics. Not necessarily in all the details, but they nevertheless assume some such structure, where the components of sentences or the components of thoughts [...] contribute to the semantic value of complete sentences or complete thoughts. The contribution is something that goes towards fixing their truth or assertibility" (*ibidem*, p. 18). Dummett acknowledges that this idea is "very vague and it might be difficult to apply it to some of the ordinary language philosophers".

[23] R. Rorty: *Philosophy and the Mirror of Nature*, Princeton University Press, Princeton 1979, p. 139.

[24] Cfr. H. Field: *Realism, Mathematics and Modality*, Blackwell, Oxford 1989.

[25] Cfr. P. Maddy: *Realism in Mathematics*, Clarendon Press, Oxford 1990.

[26] Cfr. H. Putnam: "Mathematics without Foundations", *The Journal of Philosophy*, 64, n. 1, 1967, pp. 5–22. Putnam criticizes also naturalized philosophy: cfr. "Why There Isn't a Ready Made World", *Synthese*, 51, n. 2, 1982, pp. 141–67 and "Why Reason Can't Be Naturalized", *Synthese*, 52, n. 1, 1982, pp. 3–23.

[27] If you are curious about non-foundational theories of meaning, you can find a detailed description of a systematic theory of this kind in my dissertation: cfr. C. Cozzo: *Meaning and Argument*, Almqvist & Wiksell, Stockholm 1994.

DAVID PEARS

"IN THE BEGINNING WAS THE DEED"
THE PRIVATE LANGUAGE ARGUMENT

My topic is Wittgenstein's critique of Phenomenal Foundationalism, which is usually abbreviated to "The Private Language Argument". The abbreviation is unfortunate because it suggests that there is a single compact argument to be found somewhere in the discussion that starts at *Philosophical Investigations* § 243.[1] The favourite candidate is, naturally, the argument presented at § 258: if there were no available connections between types of sensation and anything in the physical world, sensation-language would be impossible, because the words in its vocabulary would lack criteria of correct application.

This is an important argument and it has convinced many philosophers without any further reinforcement. However, it has been rejected by an equally large group who retorted that if the ability to recognize types of physical object can stand on its own feet, then so too can the ability to recognize types of sensation; and that, anyway, when a sensation-statement does need a check, it can perfectly well be provided by further sensations that occur in the context (phenomenalism).

The controversy about the validity of the "Private Language Argument" has gone on for a long time without any resolution. It is, therefore, a plausible conjecture that there is more to Wittgenstein's critique of Phenomenal Foundationalism that can be found in § 258. My suggestion will be that what should be added is his general account of the activity of applying words to things. (This was Kripke's leading idea, but my view of the account and its importance will differ from his.)

It would be rash to claim that the general investigation of linguistic activity is all that is needed by way of supplement, but there is a reason for the importance of action in Wittgenstein's critique: it is likely to serve as an antidote to the contemplative intellectualism of phenomenalism and other similar responses to the Argument from Illusion. The idea, that the whole world can be flattened on the screen of perception, begins to lose its plausibility when we add that the screen must be part of a person who is placed in the physical world and acts on the physical world. For there are familiar neo-Kantian arguments against the double reduction of person and physical world to which phenomenalism tries to constrain us. However, the question that I am addressing here is specific: What precise contribution to Wittgenstein's critique is made by his treatment of linguistic activity?

The first place to look for an answer is the general investigation of the application of words to things which precedes § 243 (rule-following). Such an application can often be justified, but

If I have exhausted the justifications, I have reached bedrock, and my spade is turned. Then I am inclined to say: "This is simply what I do" (PI, § 217)

R. Egidi (ed.), In Search of a New Humanism, 65–68.
© 1999 *Kluwer Academic Publishers. Printed in Great Britain.*

He adds that there are no "rails" to constrain what I do and that I do not even make a choice (so realism and conventionalism are both false). "I obey the rule *blindly*" (§§ 218–219). I have to do something, and I just do it.

This may seem to under-describe what it is like to apply a word, and it may also seem to under-state the effectiveness of my original training in its use. But the point is that I am making an unmediated connection between language and the world. (If there were no such connections, linguistic rules would "hang in the air" (PI, § 198)); and the effect of my earlier training is simply that it is now second nature for me to make that connection. I would feel the force of my training only if, for some reason, I was inclined to resist it.

One way to understand the second nature which is given us by training is to compare it with the natural patterns of action with which we are born. There are many similarities in spite of the difference in the way that they are acquired. E.g. if I say "I have a headache", my mouth functions as an essential element in the message received by my audience,[2] but I do not choose the mouth that utters the words.[3] This is, of course, stronger than the general thesis, that when I obey a rule I do not make a choice. For I was born without the ability to speak through any other mouth. But Wittgenstein is also making a deeper point when he says that I do not choose the mouth that speaks. In a discussion of the sentence "*I* see *this*" he explains that

it has no sense to ask "How do you know that it's *you* who sees it?," for I don't *know* that it's this person and not another one who sees before I point [sc. at myself] but one could, in certain cases, say I know *because* I point. This is what I meant by saying that I don't choose the mouth which says "I have toothache".[4]

In the passage in "The Blue Book" where he said this he distinguished two ways of locating a pain:

pointing to the painful spot without being led by the eye and on the other hand pointing to a scar on my body after looking for it.[5]

When training makes a pattern of action second nature for us, it is, of course, always one of many possible patterns, but it is important that our basic nature should ensure that the same training should produce the same effect on different people.

On the one hand we take as the criterion for meaning something which passes in our mind when we say it, or something to which we point to explain it. On the other hand, we take as the criterion the use we make of the word or sentence as time goes on.

[...] The connexion between these two criteria is that the picture in our minds is connected, in an overwhelming number of cases – for the overwhelming majority of human beings – with a particular use. For instance: you say to someone "This is red" (pointing); then you tell him" Fetch me a red book" – and he will behave in a particular way. This is an immensely important fact about us human beings. And it goes together with all sorts of other facts of equal importance, like the fact that in all the languages we know, the meanings of words don't change with the days of the week.[6]

In the special case of somatic sensations the vocabulary does not exploit the ways in which we naturally sort objects but is simply grafted onto a pre-existing pattern of expressive behaviour. That gives us a straightforward way of teaching a child the word "pain". The behaviour is naturally attached to the sensation-type, and the word then replaces the behaviour (PI, §§ 244–245). If the pain is someone else's, the pre-existing pattern of behaviour is sympathetic and helpful.

[...] it is a primitive reaction to tend, to treat, the part that hurts when someone else is in pain; and not merely when oneself is – and so to pay attention to other people's pain-behaviour, as one does *not* pay attention to one's own pain-behaviour.

But what is the word "primitive" meant to say here? Presumably that this sort of behaviour is *pre-linguistic*: that a language-game is based *on it*, that it is the prototype of a way of thinking and not the result of thought.[7]

When we read Wittgenstein's critique of Phenomenal Foundationalism, we tend to ignore his pervasive naturalism in our search for the punch-line, which, we suppose, must identify a criterion of correctness that is not available to the speaker of a private language (a necessarily unteachable language). Now it is not wrong to pick on § 258 and to take the criteria to be the agreement in judgements that is required if language is to be a means of communication between people (PI, § 242), and, more basically, the verification of predictions about the physical world. For it really is impossible to see how a sensation-language could ever get started if there were no connections between sensation-types and things in the physical world which produce effects, good or bad, on people's bodies without the mediation of perception.[8]

Now a phenomenalist would try to present the required connections as connections between sensations, but he would then face the formidable task of reducing the people who had the sensations and their movements in physical space to a purely sensory basis. But Wittgenstein does not pursue the controversy so far, and neo-Kantian objections to phenomenalism do not figure in his writings. Instead, he focusses on his adversaries' original position and takes their hypothesis to be, quite simply, that there are no available connections between sensations and the physical world. He does not credit them with the dubious advantages of re-writing the story of the physical world in sensory terms. In his view, they have simply inflicted an irreparable loss on themselves.

This view is a consequence of his naturalism and it is one of the points at which his critics have found his objections to Phenomenal Foundationalism inadequate. The move that he makes is really only the first move in a controversy whose next stage requires a second, more elaborate move against the phenomenalist's attempt to re-describe the original position in purely sensory terms. If his critics have expected too much of the move that he does make, his supporters have certainly done all that they could to create the excessive expectation.

But there is also another reason for the adverse verdict of his critics, a reason that I began to explain earlier in this paper. When people sift through his text hoping to find a single, compact argument, they usually pick on § 258. In the year after the publication of *Philosophical Investigations* its readers immediately rallied at this point to debate the validity of the appeal to verificationism. However § 258 is only a small part of the investigation which begins at § 243, and that, in its turn, is preceded by the general account of the application of words to things. If we must give a simple title to this whole sequence of remarks, a better one would be *The Foundations of Language: Nature and Training*.

No doubt, it is disturbing that the point of view from which Wittgenstein writes is human life rather than the artificial stage on which philosophers have usually taken their stand against the Argument from Illusion. But we must not let the familiarity of any of his conclusions blind us to the novelty of the way in which he reaches them. His method is to describe aspects of human life chosen for their relevance to the perennial problems of philosophy. The result is a kind of abstract, episodic rendering of anthropology: the truths are plain, but their selection and arrangement require a different kind of understanding.

I do not think there is any single key to the critique of Phenomenal Foundationalism that begins at § 243. I have chosen the theme of action because it is the one that is most forcefully opposed to the philosophy that he is rejecting. But the force is not applied at the point where its adversaries expect it. For, instead of fighting his way out of the egocentric predicament, he *starts* outside it with people already interacting. His concern with the isolated screen of consciousness is only to ask how philosophers ever hit on such a bizarre idea. He himself was convinced that language can develop only out of the natural reactions of people and their natural capacity to respond to training by taking on a second, much more elaborate nature. If we must find a "Private Language Argument", this is what it had better be.

The origin and the primitive form of the langage game is a reaction; only from this can more complicated forms develop.

Language – I want to say – is a refinement, 'in the beginning was the deed'.[9]

Christ Church, Oxford

NOTES

[1] *Philosophische Untersuchungen. Philosophical Investigations* (henceforth PI), ed. by G. E. M. Anscombe and R. Rhees, Blackwell, Oxford 1953.
[2] *Philosophische Bemerkungen. Philosophical Remarks*, ed. by R. Rhees, Blackwell, Oxford 1964, § 64.
[3] *The Blue and the Brown Books*, ed. and with a Preface by R. Rhees, Blackwell, Oxford 1958. See "The Blue Book", p. 68.
[4] "Notes for Lectures on 'Private Experience' and 'Sense-Data' ", *The Philosophical Review*, vol. 77, 1968, p. 310. Reprinted in L. Wittgenstein, *Philosophical Occasions 1912–1951*, ed. by J. C. Klagge and A. Nordmann, Hackett Publ. Co., Indianapolis & Cambridge 1993, pp. 274.
[5] *Ibidem.*
[6] *Lectures on the Foundations of Mathematics: Cambridge 1939*, ed. by C. Diamond, The University of Chicago Press, Chicago & London 1975, p. 182.
[7] *Zettel*, ed. by G. E. M. Anscombe and G. H. von Wright, Blackwell, Oxford 1967, §§ 540–541.
[8] See *Bemerkungen über die Philosophie der Psychologie. Remarks on the Philosophy of Psychology*, I, ed. by G. E. M. Anscombe and G. H. von Wright Blackwell, Oxford 1980, § 397.
[9] *Vermischte Bemerkungen. Culture and Value,* ed. by G. H. von Wright, Blackwell, Oxford 1980, p. 31, quoting Goethe, *Faust*, Part I.

MASSIMO DELL'UTRI

NATURALISM, WORLD AND TRUTH

1. In what follows I shall concentrate on Ludwig Wittgenstein's thought as it emerges from the essay by David Pears that appears in this volume. In addressing the Private Language Argument (henceforth PLA) Pears isolates two very important elements: the world and Wittgenstein's general naturalistic stance. Both elements contribute to form a coherent and powerful philosophy which, nevertheless, seems to have an Achilles' heel in its interpretation of truth. In other words, Wittgenstein's conceptions of the world and naturalism seem to lose their potential when conjoined with what is now called a *deflationary conception of truth* and, moreover, do not seem to need this at all. The next section is dedicated to a brief discussion of Pears' essay, whereas the other two to the connection of truth with, respectively, naturalism and world.

2. It is clear that the PLA is one of the chief points in Wittgenstein's writings which contain his central philosophical convictions. Moreover, there is widespread agreement among scholars that that argument does not exhaust itself in the small number of sections – those following § 243 – of *Philosophische Untersuchungen*,[1] but rather in a sense it appears at the very beginning of the book. Failure to see this initially led to the usage of the term "argument", as if – Pears complains – there were a brief, stringent and readily recognizable deduction of the impossibility of a private language.

According to Pears, since the best place to find such an argument is § 258, and since this section was far from definitively settling the issue, looking for another of Wittgenstein's theses which, combined with the thesis presented in § 258, be capable of defeating the antagonist, is unavoidable. This further thesis resides in the "general account of the activity of applying words to things", found before § 243 (the one in which Wittgenstein introduces the notion of a private language) and goes back as far as the first sections.

Pears presents the argument in § 258 as stating the necessity of "*available* connections between types of sensation and anything in the physical world" (my italics), the loss of which would render a language – all the more reason a sensation-language – impossible. Without those connections words "would lack criteria of correct application". Now, it is remarkable that nowhere in § 258 Wittgenstein does speak of *connections* among sensations and items in the world, let alone a *physical* world. He only argues the intrinsic impossibility for a person in isolation to connect in a stable and firm manner a sign (say, a word) to an inner sensation, because there is not the slightest ground for evaluating the correctness of that connection as time goes by: the stability of the connection must be ascertained at any time, and the only way to do this is to appeal to an *objective* criterion, i.e. the kind of criterion that the person,

R. Egidi (ed.), In Search of a New Humanism, 69–78.
© 1999 *Kluwer Academic Publishers. Printed in Great Britain.*

being as it were the arbiter of himself, cannot afford. So, it seems at first glance there is no question of the "world" in § 258.

Nevertheless, Pears is on the right track, since the world actually plays a central role in the argument against private language, as revealed by Wittgenstein's account preceding § 258 of applying words to things, an account which, according to Pears, should be added to that argument. This addition is of the utmost importance. Not only does it put the world in the foreground, but stresses the relevance of action for the entire question and in particular, linguistic action. This is why I find it appropriate to call *phenomenalism* – the position the PLA is aimed at defeating – a "contemplative intellectualism", as Pears does. The second term, "intellectualism", gives in some way the idea that by confining the philosophical weight of one's reflection in the intellect, one ends up *losing the world*, whereas the first term, "contemplative", in addition to this draws by contrast the attention to a possible antidote against the predicament, namely the appeal to the concept of *action* – the "deed". But why does the phenomenalist run the risk of "losing the world"?

Here "gaining" or "losing the world" are phrases referring to the capability a philosopher has to plausibly place the concept of the world in his system of thought. Given the centrality of the concept in epistemological and metaphysical matters, for a positive global evaluation of one's philosophy it is crucial to offer a plausible image of the world and the position of human beings within it. Take for instance a radical realistic philosophy according to which the world is completely independent of the human mind, so that the mind will never deliver a right description of the world, whatever its efforts. Or, on the contrary, take an idealistically oriented philosophy like phenomenalism, which tries to re-describe the world in terms of what is phenomenically grasped by the mind, so that the world amounts to a sort of logical construction out of the mind itself. The impossibility of saying how the world *in fact* is, in the former case, and failure to provide a complete and satisfactory translation of "thing-language" into "sense-datum" language, in the latter case, seem to characterize the discourse about the world developed by those philosophical positions as mere *façon de parler*. Hence, the loss I mention above.[2]

The core of Wittgenstein's argument is individuated by Pears in a "pervasive naturalism", a basic trait of Wittgenstein's philosophy which Pears justly stresses with the due force. We have seen how the entire question hinges upon the evaluation of the correct use of a sign by means of (objective) criteria; in the large majority of cases we are able to point to such criteria, moulded by the practices which gained a footing in our society, and therefore present good justification for those uses. However, justifications cannot continue unceasingly, but are fated to come to an end, the end where we get down to *bedrock*:[3] in case we do not for any reason content ourselves with a given set of justifications and try to reach a more profound depth, we find ourselves with the possibility of saying nothing other than "We do what we do!", or "We behave just as we do!". Why this is not pure anarchy? Why this does not license a Protagorean view of the "anything goes" type? Because those answers lie on an inner natural substratum: once we get down to bedrock, the only way to explain why we behave in a certain manner is by reference to our *nature*, a nature which in its turn warrants a sort of "uniformity" in the behaviour of people, whatever their culture.

Pears is quite explicit about the two levels in which our nature displays its effects: a fundamental one, the level of natural reactions in the strictest sense, those triggered by our innate response systems, like for example *yawning*; and a level of acquired responses, like those which derive from training we could be subjected to, like for example *writing with the right hand*. As will be clarified below, the interesting thing to note here is that, according to Wittgenstein, the first level points to a "pre-existing pattern of expressive behaviour" and, as far as linguistic reactions are concerned, to "prototypes" of ways of thinking and speaking.

To be sure, the Wittgensteinian naturalistic stance is not susceptible to a simple and uncontroversial interpretation.[4] Taken in its generality, naturalism is an epistemological position according to which every object of knowledge (belonging to whatever domain) is considered a *natural fact*, embedded in the spatiotemporal and causal orders, and thus susceptible to an analysis aimed at grasping its conformity to rules (its law-like behaviour) without any appeal to unverifiable elements, such as abstract entities or specific mental powers, intended as alleged explicative authorities.

To simplify a little, there are two possible ways of achieving that aim. The former amounts to making use of the scientific method and the language of natural sciences: using the scientific method as a tool for removing the veil of appearance and disclosing still deeper sections of reality; and the language of natural sciences as a tool for expressing the results obtained by means of the application of that method. It is along these lines that the programmes of reductionism and eliminativism – both pursued in the light of a more or less explicit physicalism – proceed.[5]

The latter way of displaying a naturalistic attitude consists of a denial of the appearance/reality dichotomy and (far from any methodological monism) in taking what *appears* as "all there is" and therefore as what one has to explain. When the demarcation between science and philosophy is sharpened[6] and "description" is substituted for "explanation", one gets a good approximation of Wittgenstein's position. The reason why it is just an "approximation" resides in the fact that in order to arrive at that position one has to add something else, namely the authentic sense of Wittgenstein's references to "nature", "natural history of human beings", "very general facts of nature", a sense which inherits his very convictions about the above-mentioned demarcation and description. According to Wittgenstein, philosophy has nothing to do with science so far as the latter aims at providing *theories*, i.e. hypothetical attempts at explaining governed by normative canons of correctness. Philosophy is not a matter of bold even if reasonable intellectual jumps with the hope of grasping truths and providing a monolithic foundation for our cognitive activity; it rather is an effort to describe the entire multifarious variety of the experience before our eyes, an experience primarily connected with what we *do* – not with what we *think* – and in relation to which the notions of truth, falsity, correctness, incorrectness and the like have no hold. It is simply *our* experience, something which characterises us from birth. A look at one of Wittgenstein's celebrated passages will help clarify this point. Wittgenstein responds to his interlocutor telling him that

... Our interest certainly includes the correspondence between concepts and very general facts of nature... But our interest does not fall back upon these possible causes of the formation of concepts; we are not doing natural science; nor yet natural history – since we can also invent fictitious natural history for our purposes...[7]

Here the author immediately places himself within a naturalistic outlook and claims that his real interest as a philosopher does not reside in the causal relation between general facts of nature and a definite conceptual system – that interest rather pertains to the conjectural inquiry of science. In fact, natural science (synchronically) investigates the causes of concepts by means of hypotheses, whereas natural history (diachronically) investigates a *particular* development of the natural world, under the hypothesis that that is the right development. What Wittgenstein is actually interested in is stressing the existence of a certain arbitrariness in the constitution of natural facts and the parallel absence of any necessity: far from being imposed on us by reality, those facts are deeply contingent, since they not only could have been different but also utterly invented. But, however arbitrarily they may be "caused", we have to take those facts for granted, and allow them to become *our* natural history, *our* bedrock. Thus, here there is nothing to explain, but something is in need of description, something which pulls philosophy before any discourse on truth and falsity, correctness and incorrectness – this discourse belongs to scientific analysis. So, according to Wittgenstein, "nature" does not play the role of a foundation. It is not something one can study like a scientist analyses the subatomic structure of reality. Actually it is not to be studied at all, but simply accepted as the secular heritage in which some rough dispositions to behaviour got inscribed, ready to elicit a constellation of *spontaneous* responses to verbal and non-verbal stimuli. All this is then combined with an anti-intellectualist view on the origin of language and concepts: "in the beginning was the deed".

To summarise: two main points arise from Pears' analysis of Wittgenstein's PLA. The first is the importance of the connection with the *world*; the second, the general attitude toward *naturalism*. Now, I would like to raise a question just on the background offered by Pears, a question which concerns the notion of *truth* – in particular, a sort of *incompatibility* between that background and the Wittgensteinian conception of truth.

3. The later Wittgenstein is known for having subscribed to what has been called the "redundancy theory of truth". It is a theory usually credited to Frank Plumpton Ramsey and endorsed, in a more or less similar way, by a number of philosophers, like Alfred Julius Ayer, Peter Frederick Strawson, Willard Van Orman Quine, Arthur Norman Prior, Dorothy Grover, Joseph Camp, Nuel Belnap and Paul Horwich.[8] The core element of the theory is the thesis according to which truth is an *empty* concept, with no use altogether in our theoretical explanations. The centuries of efforts to describe what truth is, the countless attempts to define the concept, and the laboriously worked over arguments meant to sustain particular definitions have all substantially failed to settle the question and gain general consent; and this shows that the concept does not actually need any analysis. Seeing things as they really are, these

theorists claim, one realizes that those efforts, attempts and arguments unduly inflated the concept with extraneous items.[9]

In particular, Wittgenstein's idea is that the appeal to the concept of truth as a tool designed to show how things *essentially* are – as opposed to how things apparently appear – is not any good, since there is nothing to discover, nothing to take off beneath the surface of language, and hence nothing one could apply any tool of that sort to. As we have already seen, all that is to be done is just *describe* how words and sentences are actually used by a community of speakers, and in this respect observe how truth manifests itself in linguistic usage. This draws the attention on the words "truth", "falsity", "true", "false", and puts in the foreground what has been called the *thesis of equivalence*,[10] namely the thesis according to which attributing truth to any sentence is equivalent to that sentence itself: in brief, if p is a sentence, "It is true that p if, and only if, p".[11]

Observance of the thesis by speakers seems to be *spontaneous* behaviour, a *natural* reaction when truth is at stake, showing a sort of instinctive way of using the word "true": each one of us would normally assert one horn of the equivalence having asserted the other, accepting for instance: "It is true that the rose is red" having accepted "The rose is red", and viceversa. Although Wittgenstein does not say this, we could say that the thesis of equivalence is part of that pre-existing pattern of expressive behaviour which constitutes the *two levels of our nature*,[12] as Pears puts it, so that its observance by speakers could be considered as *fact*, i.e. as having the same incontrovertible objective status of what we usually call a fact. One can find indirect proof of this by noting the pervasiveness of the thesis of equivalence in the reflection of several philosophers, which testifies to a widely acknowledged importance: as for analytical philosophy, since Gottlob Frege[13], who is credited the merit of having called attention on the thesis, every philosopher has based his discourse about truth on one form or other of the thesis.[14]

The character of fact assignable to the thesis of equivalence makes it assume a sort of *philosophical neutrality*, in the sense that it is not necessarily attached to a definite philosophical position: on the contrary, in virtue of its incontrovertibility it may appear in the writings of every philosopher, independent of his or her fundamental convictions.[15] Therefore, since basing one's proper truth-discourse on the thesis in order to express a peculiar position about truth does not suffice, something else should be added in order to qualify that position. As far as the redundancy theorists are concerned, what is to be added is the idea according to which the thesis of equivalence is all that can be said about truth, so that the *whole* discourse exhausts itself at just this point – it stops, as it were, just where it starts, and there is nothing else to say. Everything hinges upon the use of the word "true", upon its meaning, and the emptiness of the concept of truth leaves no room for any role of the concept in our linguistic activity, no room in particular in the act of *assertion*.

Wittgenstein's is precisely this position. His shift from the "picture theory" of the *Tractatus* to the redundancy theory of his later thought seems to be perfectly consequential. Denying the existence of a fixed correspondence between language and the world adds up to denying that the former be a means for the representation of the latter;[16] moreover, it adds up to denying the existence of something in common to all sensible language-parts, something describable as the *general form of propositions and of language*, as Wittgenstein puts it:[17] in particular, it amounts to saying that there is no common deep form such as, "This is how things are", nor equivalent forms such as, "This is a fact" or "This is true", i.e. forms which – being expressions of a picture theory – purport to show how the piece of language the "this" refers to directly refers to what is *external* to that piece itself, and able to legitimise it on an epistemological level. The relevant relations are not those between language and a mind-independent world, but between language-parts and other language-parts: far from having something in common, the various meaningful parts only show more or less close "family resemblances".[18]

The question could be asked: "Having thrown correspondence away and shifted the weight from the outside to the inside of language, why does Wittgenstein not subscribe to some form of the *coherence* or of the *pragmatist* theory of truth?" The answer is that in sticking to a correspondence theory he was aware of the intrinsic impossibility to describe and express in full terms what that correspondence amounted to, and thus how *truth* was to be accounted for. This is a conviction Wittgenstein never abandoned. Indeed, in turning to the position emerged by his later reflections he realized that not only was the nature of truth, interpreted as correspondence, indefinable, but that truth had no nature to define at all. In other words, he thought that the only truth there could be is correspondence, but given that there is no correspondence, there is no truth *tout court*; except as a useful linguistic device governed by the thesis of equivalence and the calculus of truth functions: i.e. something purely *formal*.[19]

It follows that the aforementioned phrases do not possess any privileged epistemological (and, for that matter, metaphysical) status and, therefore, the meaning that the correspondentist wants to assign to them: they merely derive the meaning of whatever sentence they are connected with.[20] In fact, according to Wittgenstein, since language does not represent anything, but is rather a means for gaining one's proper expressive and practical purposes, every bit of language has the meaning which it assumes in virtue of the *role* it plays in our life: in our case, the word "true" attached to a sentence appears as a tool for strengthening what that sentence says, or rendering its utterance aesthetically more telling, or expressing agreement, and the like,[21] but by itself has no distinctive meaning – and so the phrases belonging to the same family.

As they are, those phrases reveal themselves as propositional "schemata", empty frameworks devoid of a proper peculiar meaning but susceptible of being filled with the meaning of any sentence. It then does not make sense to ask whether they agree or not with reality, since they get employed as propositional variables. Hence the "semantic redundancy" of the phrases and the words they contain: to state that p is true (or to precede it with "It is a fact that") is simply to state p itself, whereas "It is true that" and "It is a fact that" do not add to or take anything from the meaning of p.

However, it seems there is a difference between Wittgenstein's and Ramsey's support of the redundancy theory. First of all, given that "true" has no peculiar meaning, Ramsey believes that it is possible to get rid of words like "true" and "false" from the language without any loss in expressive power, promoting thus a sort of "reconstruction" of natural language. Wittgenstein, on the contrary, thinks that language does not need any reconstruction at all, because it is in order just as it is.[22] Secondly, while Ramsey focuses his analysis on *assertion*,[23] thinking it has a special role in respect of truth, Wittgenstein does not single out any particular linguistic act, considering all linguistic acts on the same epistemological level.

As I have already stated, all of this seems perfectly consequential. But – I would observe – in so far as truth is concerned there is room to argue that the outcome of Wittgenstein's turn is not bound to be as it actually was. The criteria of correctness the PLA aims at (*agreement* in judgements and *verification* of predictions about the physical world, in Pears' wording) seem to be able to be characterised in terms of a *non-empty* concept of truth, i.e. a concept which possesses the very role Wittgenstein is not disposed to acknowledge, a role that could be roughly singled out as truth being the *aim* and at the same time the *possibility condition* of assertion.

Wittgenstein himself maintains that not *every* use comes off well: only uses which conform to socially acknowledged objective standards will do. As a consequence, if a speaker wants actually to communicate informations others can understand, then he cannot but take the *aim* to conform his assertions to those standards, so that such a conformity (ensuring the required agreement) makes the standards also a *condition of the possibility* of assertions: they indeed appear to be something without which one does not assert anything, but only utters senseless sounds, and neither does one agree upon anything – one merely discloses his or her own subjectivity.

To be sure, every person's aims are multifarious: they form a complex network shaped in hierarchical order. But, since the attainment of the majority of those aims involves the use of language, the aim to conform this use to the standards assumes a *fundamental* position (and, accordingly, importance): verbal communication will always have those standards of use[24] as a datum point. Even when, in following a major aim, one entertains the subsidiary aim to cheat, or lie, or conceal one's intention, the standards are still taken into account. Indeed, in those cases one will tend to reach one's aim loosening the observation of the standards proportionally to the pursued aim.

However, what is worth noting here is that observation of the standards of use seems to be a *natural* behaviour, something we spontaneously carry out, a sort of disposition somehow embedded in our intimate nature, be this taken in terms of genetic map or not. From this perspective, therefore, the efforts to conform to these standards show by full right to be part of the *pre-existing pattern of expressive behaviour* Wittgenstein points out.

Now, if we try to characterise the standards with just *one* concept, which other candidate fits better than the concept of truth itself? If that is so, then it is truth that warrants the *agreement* in judgements and the *verification* of predictions about the physical world, and it is a "presupposition" of truth of a substantial kind that forms part of our pre-existing pattern. An explanation of this is in order.

The complex and interwoven structure of linguistic and non-linguistic activities aim-directed and governed by the social standards was exactly the subject of

Wittgenstein's attention: Wittgenstein, following his maxim, "Don't think, but look",[25] managed so masterly to describe the structure he stressed as of *vital* importance for us – for our concrete life and knowledge. This structure is kneaded with *epistemicity*: it sights an actual *verification* of predictions, an agreement which is an agreement *for us*, connections between types of sensation and something in the world which are *available* – i.e. within the scope of the human cognitive faculties. From this point of view, all our activities (at least the more subtle ones) involve our knowledge, sensibility, intuitive capacity, values, sound judgment, and so on; in a word, our humanity, and reveal how the attempts to determine what is true an what is false, right or wrong, acceptable or blameable, beautiful and ugly are strictly intertwined. Being these attempts a craving for the relevant *facts of the matter*, we can take them as a single general great attempt to grasp *truth*.

Therefore if, as I was stating, we try to express by means of a sole notion the complex intertwining of concepts, we will find in our language no other more suitable word than "truth", so that far from being redundant, truth will then appear as a *substantial* notion that gains its substance from constituting a *coalescence* of notions like world, meaning, assertion, and justice, representing thereby the *beacon* of our verbal and non-verbal behaviour, a beacon "naturally" presupposed by our cognitive activity. Thus, it seems that Wittgenstein's naturalism appears less compatible with a redundancy view of truth than with a substantial concept of truth.

4. This paves the way for a few remarks about the second aspect of the background outlined by Pears, the world, and these remarks bear upon what could be seen as a consequence of the redundancy theory of truth.

A possible question prompted by the idea according to which Wittgenstein's naturalism would have better been conjoined with a substantial notion of truth could be something like the following: "Yes, but as a matter of fact Wittgenstein did not do that, and remained perfectly content with the redundancy theory. So, after all, what is wrong with this conception of truth?" It is the answer to this question that calls attention to the concept of world.

As far as Wittgenstein is concerned, Pears maintains that the mere fact of using a word like "dog" is sufficient to establish «an unmediated connection between language and the world». It is just here, he notes, that the power of the speaker's *deed* on the world resides. This sums up Wittgenstein's philosophy in a nutshell. His complex view of the human condition is far from the traditional conception based on a distinction between scheme and content,[26] which sooner or later faces the problem of developing a plausible explanation of how that content becomes a "representational" one, or viewing the matter from the other side, how the scheme applies to a non-conceptualised content. On the contrary, as I mentioned above, being that the Wittgensteinian finely intertwined complex structure of verbal and non-verbal actions and reactions among speakers and between speakers and world is essentially dropped within an epistemic framework, it directly depicts the world as a "world for us", i.e. in accordance with our cognitive capacities. It is in this epistemic framework that standards of correct usage emerge, where it is precisely a substantial notion of truth, which plunged in the aforementioned coalescence, informs the standards themselves, functioning as a *trait d'union* between language and the world, thus involving the world since the beginning.[27]

But things change when the redundancy theory enters the scene. Focusing the whole truth-discourse *only* on the thesis of equivalence, on the use of the word "true", does not seem *per se* to guarantee the wished for connection with the world, and strikes on the contrary as if the entire story took place on an intra-linguistic level.

So, denying the existence of a substantial concept of truth, a concept capable of functioning as a touchstone for assertions and conflicting theories about the world, and thereby determining *how the world is*, seems to have only the consequence we saw intellectualism run into, i.e. that of *losing the world*. If that is so, a thought close at hand is that within Wittgenstein's perspective the world cannot but end by becoming «flabby like a *gibus*».[28] And here we have to conclude is another aspect of the apparent incompatibility mentioned above.

Libera Università di Urbino (Italy)

NOTES

[1] L. Wittgenstein: *Philosophische Untersuchungen. Philosophical Investigations*, ed. by G. E. M. Anscombe and R. Rhees, trans. by G. E. M. Anscombe, Blackwell, Oxford 1953 (henceforth PI).

[2] In this connection the "moral twist" Hilary Putnam gives to the discussion of the danger of losing the world is interesting (cf. *Pragmatism. An Open Question*, Blackwell, Oxford 1995, ch. 3).

[3] PI, § 217, see also § 1.

[4] How that interpretation is far from being simple and uncontroversial is acknowledged by Pears himself: cf. his "Wittgenstein's Naturalism", in *The Monist*, 78, 1995, p. 412.

[5] This is also one of Howard Wettstein's contentions in his "Terra Firma", in *The Monist*, 78, 1995, p. 425.

[6] Pears himself, however, has called attention to the fact that the Wittgensteinian demarcation between science and philosophy is not quite that sharp: cf. his "Wittgenstein's Naturalism", cit., and "Wittgenstein on Philosophy and Science", in *Wittgenstein. Mind and Language*, ed. by R. Egidi, Kluwer, Dordrecht 1995, pp. 23–36.

[7] PI, II, section xii.

[8] F. P. Ramsey: "Facts and Propositions" [1927], in *The Foundations of Mathematics and Other Logical Essays*, ed. by R. B. Braithwaite, Routledge & Kegan Paul, London 1931, pp. 138–55; A. J. Ayer: *Language, Truth and Logic*, Gollantz, London 1936; P. F. Strawson: "Truth", in *Analysis*, 9, 1949, pp. 83–97; and "Truth" [1950], in G. Pitcher (ed.): *Truth*, Prentice-Hall, Englewood Cliffs N.J. 1964, pp. 32–53; W. V. O. Quine: *Philosophy of Logic*, Prentice-Hall, Englewood Cliffs, N.J. 1970; A. N. Prior: *Objects of Thought*, ed. by P. T. Geach and A. Kenny, Clarendon Press, Oxford 1971; D. L. Grover, J. L. Camp and N. D. Belnap: "A Prosentential Theory of Truth", *Philosophical Studies*, 27, 1975, pp. 73–125, now in D. L. Grover: *A Prosentential Theory of Truth*, Princeton University Press, Princeton 1992, pp. 70–120; P. Horwich: *Truth*, Blackwell, Oxford 1990.

[9] This is somewhat Horwich's presentation of the theory. In fact, it was Horwich who introduced the term "deflationist" to qualify the theory.

[10] M. Dummett: *Frege. Philosophy of Language*, Duckworth, London 1973, p. 445; and *Truth and Other Enigmas*, Harvard University Press, Cambridge, Mass. 1978, p. xx.

[11] Analogously, "It is false tha p if, and only if, not p".

[12] Not of course in the sense that the act of asserting the thesis is embedded in our *innate* behavioural system – since that would amount to saying that *all* languages contain the word "true" and the like, contrary to what actually is the case – but in the sense that the *disposition* to assert the thesis is so embedded.

[13] G. Frege: "Über Sinn und Bedeutung", *Zeitschrift für Philosophie und philosophische Kritik*, 100, 1892, pp. 25–50; "Meine grundlegenden logischen Einsichten" [1915], in G. Frege: *Nachgelassene Schriften und wissenschaftlicher Briefwechsel*, I, hrsg. von H. Hermes, F. Kambartel & F. Kaulbach, Meiner, Hamburg 1969; "Der Gedanke. Eine logische Untersuchung", *Beiträge zur Philosophie des deutschen Idealismus*, 1, 1918–19, pp. 58–77.

[14] Celebrated is Alfred Tarski's form, in virtue of which the thesis receives metalinguistic clothes and becomes " '*p*' is true if, and only if, *p*".

[15] In particular, the thesis is not necessarily attached to deflationism: Frege and Tarski, to name just them, are not deflationists about truth.

[16] At least as to what can be linguistically expressed, according to the *Tractatus*.

[17] Cf. PI, § 65.

[18] Cf. PI, § 67.

[19] Cf. PI, § 136.

[20] In particular, when used alone Wittgenstein claims they *stand for* the sentence in question (PI, § 134). This made Prior to individuate in Wittgenstein a forerunner of some ideas of his, later on developed by the prosentential theorists of truth (cf. Prior: *Objects of Thought*, cit., p. 38; and Grover, Camp and Belnap: "A Prosentential Theory of Truth", cit.).

[21] This is actually what other philosophers like Strawson, for instance, following Wittgenstein maintain, but what they say is contained, at least *in nuce*, in Wittgenstein's position.

[22] PI, § 98.

[23] "The problem with which I propose to deal is the logical analysis of what may be called by any of the terms judgment, belief, or assertion" is the opening sentence of Ramsey's "Facts and Propositions", cit.

[24] Standards of this kind may be grammatical, semantical, expressive, and the like: they may push on to state the right intonation in definite cases, or to coordinate verbal and non-verbal behaviour (by contrast compare saying "It's disgusting" and going on to eat with relish).

[25] PI, § 66.

[26] Or better, as John McDowell would have it, between "scheme and Given" (*Mind and World*, Harvard University Press, Cambridge, Mass. 1994, p. 4).

[27] For a similar interpretation of Wittgenstein's thought involving the concept of the world "from the start", see M. B. Hintikka & J. Hintikka: *Investigating Wittgenstein*, Basil Blackwell, Oxford 1986, esp. ch. 9; and H. Wettstein: "Terra Firma", cit.

[28] B. Russell: "On the Nature of Truth and Falsehood", in *Philosophical Essays*, Longmans-Green and Co., London 1910.

JOACHIM SCHULTE

WHAT WITTGENSTEIN WROTE

That we know what Wittgenstein wrote is in more than one respect largely due to the efforts of Georg Henrik von Wright. He is, as one of Wittgenstein's heirs as well as one of the editors or co-editors of several volumes containing Wittgenstein's writings, responsible for the format in which we read Wittgenstein. He has, as generous provider and observant keeper of what he himself modestly likes to call the "Wittgenstein Materials" at the Helsinki Department of Philosophy, helped many interested students and scholars to consult copies of Wittgenstein's writings and other materials relevant to understanding Wittgenstein's work. And he has, as the author of a catalogue of the Wittgenstein papers and several painstaking and at the same time eminently readable studies of the origins of the *Tractatus Logico-Philosophicus* and the *Philosophical Investigations*, made us familiar with the astonishing volume of Wittgenstein's literary *Nachlaß* and the background of the two books which made Wittgenstein's name famous.[1]

When looking through the list of manuscripts and typescripts left by Wittgenstein to Anscombe, Rhees and von Wright one wonders what they felt when they realized the amount of work which was awaiting them if they decided to let the educated world learn about some at least of the precious gems contained in the treasure bequeathed to them by their late teacher and friend. As we know, it was clear to them from the start that the book to be published under the title *Philosophical Investigations* had to be the first of any posthumous publications that were to be taken into consideration. What was also clear to them, and is only too easily forgotten nowadays, was that there had to be a companion volume containing Wittgenstein's later writings on the philosophy of mathematics.

Retrospectively, one may want to say that it was with these *Remarks on the Foundations of Mathematics* that some of the later trouble began. For many reasons it was deemed right that more than the typed and fairly polished writings on this topic should be brought out (and in those days "bringing out" involved, as a matter of course, translating it into English) while publication of anything approaching a full text was regarded as out of the question. Whereas publication of the *Philosophical Investigations* had generally been greeted with enthusiasm and ample praise to editors and translator for acquainting philosophers with this masterpiece, reactions to what was quite clearly intended as a *companion* volume were often cool or unfriendly.[2] Influential perusers of the book found reasons for their dissatisfaction – which, as has become clear, was simply due to their animosity against Wittgenstein's way of doing philosophy – first in the lack of thoroughness of Wittgenstein's arguments and later also in the selectiveness with which the editors had chosen the material to be published and translated.

R. Egidi (ed.), In Search of a New Humanism, 79–91.
©1999 *Kluwer Academic Publishers. Printed in Great Britain.*

In the years that followed Wittgenstein was still widely regarded as the author representative of modern (analytic) philosophy, and there continued to be a corresponding intellectual appetite for books bearing his name and containing yet more pages from his seemingly inexhaustible *Nachlaß*. Little by little people became aware of what was called Wittgenstein's "middle period", i.e. writings and conversation notes from the time between his return to Cambridge and philosophy in 1929 and his unsuccessful attempt at producing a German version of the Brown Book in 1936. Later it turned out that he had given a good deal of thought to questions of certainty and scepticism; that he had tried to cope with perplexing problems in the philosophy of psychology; and that he had dedicated his spare time to composing his own *Aphorismen zur Lebensweisheit*.

By the time these latter volumes had come out a veritable Wittgenstein industry had got under way and started to supply us with an all but stifling amount of secondary literature. That simply is the way of the academic world, and there is little to object to in this. Among those writing about Wittgenstein there were some who started to ask questions about the reliability of the published texts and the judiciousness of the choices made by their editors. Some of these questions could be answered by consulting a copy of the microfilm which had in the meantime been made of most of Wittgenstein's writings. But – apart from the fact that some who raised their voices in tune with the growing chorus of grumblers did so mainly because of their general hostility to Wittgenstein's philosophy – there really were reasons for grumbling inasmuch as no serious student of a philosophical work can be expected to turn to a microfilm-reading machine whenever he feels in doubt about whether his questions are due to the author's words or to his own incapacity of understanding them or to a faulty or incomplete transcription.[3]

That some of the bitter feelings arising from this situation were justified was understood by Wittgenstein's heirs, in my view especially by von Wright. He has taken ever more care and trouble to bring out dependable texts and to help those who have proposals for amending existing publications. Only someone who has himself tried to publish another man's writings without disfiguring it by a large number of errors can have an idea of what it means to produce a rightly so-called reliable text. At any rate, this is the state of affairs: there is a fair number of books representing Wittgenstein's life work as a philosophical author. It is likely that most of these books can be rendered more useful by correcting oversights and errors of transcription. What cannot in all cases be achieved, however, is a complete clarification of editorial policy and sufficient indication of choices and omissions without totally changing the character of the books hitherto published. To put it bluntly, one of the really serious questions is whether some of the books by Wittgenstein we know should be dropped from the canon, be it without replacement or be it with a different text superseding the old one.

Now, different people who have thought about this question have at different times come up with different answers to it. Presumably there is one book upon whose withdrawal from the canon and replacement by a very different version most scholars would agree, and that is the book edited by Rush Rhees under the title *Philosophische*

Grammatik. (Towards the end of this article I shall briefly come back to one aspect of this matter.) Similar feelings are, for similarly well-founded reasons, widespread regarding Geach's arrangement of *Zettel*, although in this case the choice among possible ways of remedying the situation is less obvious.

This, however, is by the way and may, in view of present or prospective editorial work, appear out of date. But the idea of a canon of Wittgenstein's works, which has just been alluded to, will play a major role in the considerations I here wish to put forward. I want to start by having a look at the general situation. As I said, there are a fair number of books of Wittgenstein's writings brought out by his heirs and friends Anscombe, Rhees and von Wright. These books are supplemented by various publications of lecture notes and letters, which in many cases are very helpful for understanding Wittgenstein's ideas and intentions. Evidently, these publications have mostly been published with the trustees' collaboration or approval.[4]

Then there are several volumes of the *Wiener Ausgabe*, which provides complete transcriptions of Wittgenstein's manuscripts of a certain period (1929–1933).[5] This edition will, under the terms of the trustees' permission, have reached its end after publication of another five volumes or so. And finally, there is the project of a Norwegian group led by Claus Huitfeldt of the University of Bergen to bring out a complete set of facsimile reproductions plus transcriptions-cum-search-software on CD-ROM. Partial realization of this project and a publication were announced for last year. It is to be hoped that we shall soon be able to see the fruit of so many people's labours.

But what shall we have if and when all these publications will be available? There can be no doubt that the transcriptions of the *Wiener Ausgabe* as well as the Norwegian facsimiles and transcriptions will be useful means of helping scholars with their work and that the Norwegian material will be the more helpful the more suitable the software developed by the Bergen group turns out to be. Of course, there will also be an extraordinary number of seminar papers, dissertations and higher-level articles and books basically reproducing results of word counts, stylistic comparisons, etc., facilitated by the Bergen software. But that cannot be helped, and no one except for the relevant examiners or reviewers will be obliged to read this material.

There is no respect, however, in which the availability of all these instruments will change our picture of Wittgenstein unless we at the same time decide to stop buying and reading the books available until now. This eventuality is not only unlikely; it is, as I wish to argue, undesirable. This is the real point of what I want to emphasize here. And it is a point variously connected with von Wright's work on Wittgenstein's papers: in many ways, I suspect, it is in agreement with his approach; in some respects, however, I shall focus on aspects he may want to judge differently.

The antecedents of the following remarks have a lot to do with a sentence near the end of von Wright's article "The Wittgenstein Papers". In the version printed in his book *Wittgenstein* it ran: "All the works of major interest have, in my view, now been published or are due to appear shortly." In what is at the time of writing this probably the most recent version of that article the sentence reads: "All the works of major interest have, in my view, now been published (save for the Big Typescript, perhaps)."

The crucial word here is of course the word "works". This notion of a work by Wittgenstein was taken up by me in a paper I wrote sometime in 1986. This paper was sent to von Wright, and we briefly discussed it shortly afterwards. We did not disagree much, nor did we agree completely. A version of my paper was given at a conference in Kirchberg am Wechsel where I tried to show that it was not unjustified to regard the unpublished typescript *Bemerkungen II* (TS 230) as a work by Wittgenstein.[6] (This typescript of 1945 or 1946 contains a reordering of a large number of the remarks in *Bemerkungen I* (TS 228), which in its turn was the main source for more than half of the paragraphs in the first part of the *Investigations*.) The argument of this contribution was partly based on three criteria, whose joint application seemed a good – but not necessarily a sufficient – reason for calling the manuscript or typescript in question a work. The argument as well as the three criteria were resorted to in the first chapter of my introduction to Wittgenstein to discuss various problems concerning the status of Wittgenstein's writings.[7] These three criteria (but, I am afraid, very little of the rest of my discussion) seem to have found their way into the literature, where they have been accepted or criticized, according to the standpoint of the author in question. Criteria like the ones proposed at the time as well as all kinds of informed discussion revolving around the idea of a "work" by Wittgenstein are relevant only if you think it right, commendable or mandatory to give some writings, and not other ones, pride of place. If you challenge the whole idea of separable texts of distinguishable rank and accordingly different status within the corpus of your author's writings, the notion of a work will be idle or anathema. Consequently, discussion and criticism of useful criteria of workhood are one thing; challenging the relevance of the notion of a work altogether is another.

That this notion is at best of limited value and applicability is implicit in an editorial procedure like the one favoured by the Bergen group. What is implicit in their policy has been turned into an explicit consequence by David Stern, who, in his undoubtedly competent and thoughtful article "The Availability of Wittgenstein's Philosophy" summarizes his view in the following words: "...we should consider his [Wittgenstein's] surviving papers as a family of works, connected by the constant process of reworking and rewriting that links the notebooks, manuscript volumes, manuscript rearrangements, typed selections from the manuscripts, and the subsequent typescripts".[8] Stern arrives at this view – which is almost entirely at variance with the conception I should like to defend – starting from a number of observations which are clearly reasonable and in many ways in agreement with my own impressions. Before coming to that, however, it will be useful to turn to another point of disagreement between Stern and myself because this is the point where all further differences of opinion have their roots. Stern writes that Schulte has

recently proposed that in order to count as a "finished work of Wittgenstein's", a piece of writing should satisfy the following conditions:

(1) the assessment by Wittgenstein himself that the text in question is an independent creation with a form suitable to its content; (2) a line of argument apparent to the reader, with theses, arguments, objections, underlying considerations, and examples, etc.; and (3) the formal stylistic polishing and formulation of the text which make it possible to call it "finished" and "complete".

Applying these standards to Wittgenstein's writings, Schulte eliminates all first draft writing, both in the notebooks and manuscript volumes, and selections from them that eliminate unwanted passages without rearranging the material into some more comprehensive order. However, Schulte acknowledges that "this clearly graduated picture is clouded somewhat by the fact that Wittgenstein was never quite satisfied with what he wrote" and this leads him to propose that one regard Wittgenstein's writings as "experiments" rather than something "finished and complete". (p. 457)

Unfortunately I shall have to begin by mentioning that I did not really say some of the things I am here quoted as having said. Setting the record straight will at the same time help to get the argument going.

First, I (in contrast to my translators) did not speak of criteria for "a finished work of Wittgenstein's". My text merely has "Kriterien für das, was man zu Recht ein Werk Wittgensteins nennen darf" (p. 52) – a *finished* work would be a different matter.[9] And, above all, if it really were "finished" (in any of the plausible senses of that word) we presumably should not need anything like my poor criteria to decide whether it actually was so.

Second, I did not really recommend regarding Wittgenstein's writings as "experiments", even though I do not totally dislike the idea. I merely said that Wittgenstein's most unfinished writings have the character of "Skizzen oder tastenden Versuchen". To be sure, the noun "Versuch" is ambiguous and *can* mean experiment; but here it was obviously intended in the sense of "attempt" or "first endeavour".

Now, however, we should talk about the criteria themselves. First of all, it must be remembered that they are *criteria*; they are neither necessary nor sufficient conditions but are intended as useful rules of thumb that can serve as general means helping us to come to a decision. Such criteria must be weighed against each other because they may (but need not) conflict. Furthermore, it is important to notice that the focus of the three criteria is deliberately different in each case. The first criterion regards the author; the second one concerns the reader; the third one is a matter of the form, or shape, of the text in question. That these criteria can be useful, specifically in application to Wittgenstein's writings, seems to me obvious and has been shown to be so by the examples mentioned in my original text.[10] Their usefulness does not imply the impossibility of better – and that means: more useful – formulations. What it does imply is that there is a (good) purpose they can serve. And at bottom it is *this* implication which is challenged by Stern and the tendency of his remarks.

Stern claims that these criteria are employed to "eliminate" "all first draft writing" etc. To "eliminate" them from what? Certainly not from Wittgenstein's writings, for his writings they are. Most (but probably not all) first draft writing by Wittgenstein does not satisfy my criteria. But that is exactly one of the purposes the criteria were designed for; if all the first drafts satisfied them, the criteria would be completely useless. But they were criteria to be used for deciding whether to count a certain writing as a *work* by Wittgenstein. If the result of applying them were that *all* writings by Wittgenstein are to be accepted as his works, then they would according to my lights be of no value, even misleading.

On the other hand, it is precisely this result which Stern wants to reach when he says that the entire body of Wittgenstein's literary *Nachlaß* should be regarded "as a family of works". And even though Stern emphasizes that the *Tractatus Logico-Philosophicus* and the *Philosophical Investigations* "cannot be treated on a par with the later posthumous publications", his insistence on every piece's by Wittgenstein being "internally related to other Wittgenstein texts" (p. 445) as well as on the "network" character of these texts shows that the stress is on the presumed (and in some cases undeniable) inadequacy of "the later posthumous publications" and not so much on the special status of the *Tractatus* and the *Investigations*.

The contrast between Stern's view and my own is not correctly described if one starts, as Stern does, from the impression that while he wants to take the entire *Nachlaß* into account, those who want to apply a more restrictive notion of a work wish to divide everything into two categories – good, i.e. publishable, pieces on the one hand and bad or inadequate pieces, which ought to be kept in a drawer, on the other. This claim is expressed when Stern writes that both von Wright and Schulte "take for granted that one must draw a line between the "finished" and the "unfinished", and that only the "finished" material is worthy of serious attention" (p. 457). This claim, however, is wide of the mark; and it fails to hit the nail on the head for several reasons. (Here, as before, I shall speak only for myself, even if I am sure that von Wright would agree with *some* of my points.)

First of all, there simply *is* a line between what is finished and what is unfinished. It is not always easy to recognize or draw, and it is often difficult to draw when you are dealing with manuscripts or typescripts evidently not regarded as completed by their authors. So the real problem is what to count as *more* or *less* finished, and as far as this question is concerned, there is a fair number of cases in which you can decide that manuscript B is more finished than manuscript A inasmuch as its remarks have been reshuffled in order to make certain lines of argument clearer and stylistic improvements have been indicated. In the case of Wittgenstein the situation is often complicated by the circumstance that besides manuscript B there exist manuscripts C and D, which are in a similar state as manuscript B but partially different from it. And the situation may be additionally complicated by the fact that we do not always know how to decide whether changes of wording really amount to stylistic *improvements* and whether they are purely stylistic or affect the content of what is being said. These are complications that face readers (and, in particular, editors) of such texts, and they are complications that readers somehow have to cope with. Contrary to an opinion which has recently gained immense popularity, readers do not normally find it helpful if all decisions are left to them. And while none of us are infallible, some of us – namely those with a good deal of experience and the necessary kind of sensibility – are quite adept at coping with such difficulties and helping less experienced and less sensitive readers by dint of editions, commentaries and detailed exegesis to understand certain general points as well as some of the nuances.

Second, I am sure that neither von Wright nor I have ever implied, let alone explicitly asserted, that only the finished material (or a certain part of the more finished material) "is worthy of serious attention". On the contrary, very few people can boast to have outdone von Wright or myself in point of paying and encouraging attention to the entire body of *Nachlaß* writings, regardless of their degree of finish.

But Stern does not quite mean what he says (or so I gather). He means that *equal* attention should be paid to all *Nachlaß* writings, irrespective of the degree of finish they display, and this equality should find expression in completely refraining from ranking those writings in one way or another.

With this claim we are back at our fundamental disagreement. Stern opts for the view that one should consider Wittgenstein's "surviving papers as a family of works, connected by the constant process of reworking and rewriting that links notebooks, manuscript volumes, manuscript rearrangements, typed selections from the manuscripts, and the subsequent typescripts". Stern feels that "the Wittgenstein *Nachlaß* is in certain respects poorly served by the linear arrangement of remarks of a traditional printed text"; and that "it is less a collection of texts than an hypertext, an interconnected network of remarks" (p. 462). Against this, I wish to defend the view that, if you want to do any kind of justice to Wittgenstein's *Nachlaß*, you need a notion of a work which does not comprise all his writings but serves to pick out some of them as being of different rank from – and I should not hesitate to say: higher rank than – other writings by the same author.

There are two main difficulties at the bottom of this whole debate, and these difficulties have been a constant cause of concern for Wittgenstein's editors and a lasting reason for dissatisfaction for his readers – scholars and laymen alike. The first difficulty is the obvious one that Wittgenstein himself never brought out a major philosophical publication except for his early *Logisch-philosophische Abhandlung* and did not leave any clear statement to the effect that certain of his papers were to count as "finished" or "more or less finished" works by him. Had Wittgenstein published two or three books after the *Tractatus Logico-Philosophicus* (as well he might have done), the situation would clearly have been a different one. In that case we should have Wittgenstein's own declaration that, at least at the time of publication, these were his ideas and these the words by means of which he wanted to get those ideas across. In the real world, however, things turned out differently and he published virtually nothing after his return to Cambridge (although one should remember that the mimeographing of the Blue and Brown Books and perhaps even his lending of certain typescripts to chosen friends constituted a form of publication).[11] Thus there is no direct statement by the author declaring that certain works represent his own considered views while other writings are to count as preliminary studies or mere drafts or false starts. Consequently there is no way of ranking the writings which could directly appeal to the authority of Wittgenstein himself to justify any choices made.

The second main difficulty is more intricate. Part of its nature can be inferred from Stern's shrewd observation that Wittgenstein's "characteristic unit of writing was not the essay or the book, but the "remark" (*Bemerkung*)" (p. 447). This is a shrewd, but not a completely judicious, thing to say. Even from the published writings, but considerably more so from the original manuscripts, does it transpire that Wittgenstein used a technique of writing which (at some stage) involved a certain amount of shifting around of individual remarks, which were generally short – often merely a few lines long and only in rare cases exceeding the space of a single page.

What is shrewd, but not judicious, in Stern's remark is the suggestion that this peculiar relevance of individual paragraphs or *Bemerkungen* stands in marked opposition to, or prevents, our author's writing an essay or a book at the same time. This is a delicate and an important matter, and I shall presently come back to it.

The late Rush Rhees liked to emphasize that the same, or nearly the same, remarks tended to occur in different manuscripts by Wittgenstein. He was also wont to make a lot of the fact that these changes of context affected the meaning of those remarks.[12] But is it a fact? I think it depends. Of course, in Wittgenstein's case there are plenty of remarks which occur in a number of different manuscripts or typescripts. And context can play a crucial role when the remark in question represents a step in the implicit or explicit argument developed or criticized at that point. In such cases we are dealing with groups of interconnected remarks, and it is clear that in these contexts withdrawal or insertion of individual remarks can affect the meaning of these remarks themselves as well as the meaning of surrounding remarks.

On this point there will be little disagreement. Equally little disagreement there should be on the point that there is a fairly large number of manuscripts and typescripts consisting, or containing groups, of unconnected or loosely connected or randomly connected remarks. This can (but need not) be the case with first drafts. But it is quite typical of one sort of manuscripts which excerpt earlier writings trying to retain only what still seems usable to the author at the time.[13] At early or fairly early manuscript stages, on the other hand, the order of remarks tends to follow a certain line of argument, presumably the line of thought the author was trying to follow or develop at that moment, but at a later stage of revising and reordering the earlier material this kind of line may be broken up completely as soon as Wittgenstein realizes that an entirely different arrangement would serve his purposes better. In this case the reordering may considerably affect the meaning of individual remarks, but it is also clear that the first, spontaneous, arrangement was a provisional one. This first arrangement may, retrospectively, explain how and why a certain idea came into Wittgenstein's mind, but that does not mean that it fully represents his considered views at any stage of his intellectual development.

Accordingly, we shall have to distinguish at least three types of occurrences of individual remarks: (1) occurrences in contexts where their meaning crucially depends on their place within a larger group of remarks; (2) occurrences in contexts where an individual remark's meaning is practically independent of, or indifferent to, the significance of any surrounding remarks; (3) occurrences in contexts where the meaning of individual remarks is influenced or coloured by their neighbours but is not radically changed, nor otherwise crucially affected, by insertion into a different context.

This admittedly rough but surely apposite distinction reflects a difference between types of manuscripts; and only the presence of a fair proportion of occurrences of type (1) would be characteristic of a *work*. To be sure, in more than one plausible sense can it be claimed that the *Bemerkung* is Wittgenstein's "unit of writing". But that must neither be taken to mean that he was the author of an enormous number of disconnected or at most slightly connected aphorisms nor must it be thought to imply that every time Wittgenstein changed the position of a remark he envisaged a new network of interrelated but in some sense independent *Bemerkungen*. In my opinion, this idea of a vast network or web is not only unrealistic but in some ways seriously misleading, especially insofar as it tends to make people overlook that Wittgenstein's manuscripts are of very different types and that the context-sensitivity of individual remarks can vary a great deal according to the different types of writing in which they can occur.

The idea of a network seems to rest on Stern's view that many of Wittgenstein's manuscripts, and in particular the large manuscript volumes, contain "a diary of Wittgenstein's work in progress" (p. 452) or, as he writes on another page of his article, "a record of the inner dialogue that was the driving force in the development of his philosophical work; they contain lengthy exchanges that are the starting point for a protracted struggle between conflicting intuitions, in which the final result is a telegraphic recapitulation of his earlier train of thought" (p. 453). This notion of a "diary" or a "record" of an inner dialogue can be correct only to the extent it would be true of practically anyone's drafts and preliminary sketches. But to the extent the description suggests that Wittgenstein, as a writer, was a kind of secretary taking down notes of what his conflicting inner voices told him, this description appears mistaken. It presents Wittgenstein's writings as a kind of *écriture automatique* dictated by "conflicting intuitions", and thus fails to do justice to what seem to me some of the most outstanding aspects of Wittgenstein's way of working, of which I want to underline only two: his ever-present will to give clear and deliberately, sometimes cunningly, organized form to his thought and his constant desire to lend persuasive expression to what he regards as a tempting but misguided counter-conception (which is a different matter from voicing a "conflicting intuition").

One may surely be confident that the inappropriateness of Stern's description can be demonstrated, but the point cannot possibly be argued here. For present purposes it must suffice to mention this description as one of the reasons for a competing view, a rival of what I still regard as the most convincing metaphor for Wittgenstein's writings, extracted from Wittgenstein's own last pages (*On Certainty*, §§ 97 ff.), the metaphor of a river and its bed: "...the deposits of sediment in the flow of the philosophical investigations of Wittgenstein, which with some justification can be called works, are at the same time also interruptions in the current; they are the points where Wittgenstein – probably because of his awareness of unsolved problems and unresolved difficulties – decided on an entirely new approach; they are the points at which the river seeks out a new riverbed."[14]

Now it is time to state the positive reasons, if any, for thinking that Wittgenstein's *Nachlaß* writings are to be regarded neither as a "family of works" nor as "an intricate network of multiple rearrangements and revisions" (pp. 462, 452). To begin with, there are a number of practical reasons connected with our capacities as readers of texts. A good case could be made for claiming that no one, or practically no one, would be *able* to read Wittgenstein in such a way that his impression of what he read was that of either a family of works (of equal or similar rank) or of an intricate network of multiple rearrangements etc. But all reasons connected with this issue will have to be left aside. Debates about the probable capacities of potential readers seem unfortunately to lead to no serious kind of argument conducive to persuasion and agreement or at least partial convergence of different standpoints. ("Unfortunate" it is because this situation has the consequence that readers' needs and wishes are too rarely taken into account.)

The decisive reason for thinking that neither the family-of-works nor the network conception are right is connected with the essential idea that in reading, interpreting, commenting on and editing an author's writing one should read, interpret, comment on and edit *what the author wrote*. Of course, this notion is not free from ambiguities. But these ambiguities can be cleared up as far as necessary.

Take the following example. When you sit down to write a letter and have just started, the right answer to the question "What are you writing?" is "I am writing a letter", even if in another sense of "write" you have only written down a few marks or words. When you have finished your letter or left it uncompleted, the correct answer to the question "What have you written" is "I have written a letter" or, perhaps, "I have tried to write a letter", even though it would not be wrong to describe what you have done as making a few marks on a sheet of paper. This is not the occasion to discuss the philosophical problems surrounding such a notion of "writing an x" but it may certainly be presumed that there is agreement on this: that the writer's intentions have a lot to do with, and will generally be decisive for, the way we shall classify the outcome of his activity.

It is not difficult to apply this type of consideration to the case of Wittgenstein's writings because there is no problem about knowing what he wrote. He was writing a book. His book. Even if he himself had not explicitly said so, the *Nachlaß* material shows beyond any reasonable doubt that Wittgenstein was writing a book. To be sure, among these papers there are some notes for lectures and some sketchy jottings whose nature is not quite clear, but the overwhelming bulk of these writings constitutes various stages of Wittgenstein's work on a book. And there can be equally little doubt that of this book he had different conceptions at different times.

If you want to understand an author's drafts of his letters, you will have to read them as drafts of his *letters*. If you want to understand an author's plans for, and drafts of, a comedy, you will have to read them as plans for, and drafts of, a *comedy*. If you want to understand an author's preliminary versions and drafts of a philosophical book, you will have to read them as preliminary versions and drafts of a *book*. If you do not, but instead proceed to treat them either as a series of fairly equal works or as consisting of networks of interrelated remarks, you are bound to understand little or to misunderstand entirely what the author was up to.

To differentiate between various degrees of distance from, or approximation to, a philosophical book or work by Wittgenstein you need to apply certain criteria; and the criteria I formulated at the time are of a kind that can help readers to decide on such degrees of distance or approximation. More useful or more complex criteria are no doubt conceivable. But in one way or another one will have to decide which texts come nearest to counting as works by Wittgenstein. A pocket notebook and many (parts) of his manuscript volumes are not works by Wittgenstein according to any defensible standards. They are first steps on the way towards a book and often clearly identifiable as such, among other things because Wittgenstein himself treated them as first steps by using various types of signs indicating changes intended to lead towards the production of a book. Typescripts collecting the author's selections of remarks from his manuscript volumes in the original order are still very far from being works; they are preliminary work done preparatory to arriving at a better arrangement to be further enriched by new remarks and clarified by cuts and corrections. Rearrangements of sifted and corrected remarks are obvious candidates for the status of work.

The idea that at bottom Wittgenstein was producing interrelated networks of remarks or writing non-linear hypertext is too ludicrous to be contemplated for a moment. What he wrote was books. Or a book; his book. But I hasten to add that non-linear representations or hypertext may turn out to be useful means of showing which manuscript stages led up to the most work-like versions he completed. What still needs to be demonstrated, however, is that these means will do a better job than a good facsimile. If they will not, they are superfluous or misleading. At any rate, they are not what Wittgenstein wrote.

The situation is clear, I think. If one has a fairly, but only fairly, restrictive notion of what constitutes a work by Wittgenstein in mind, one will come to the conclusion that not all the books published by Wittgenstein's heirs can really count as "works" in that sense. The *Remarks on the Philosophy of Psychology* or the two volumes of *Last Writings*, for example, all of them meticulously edited by Georg Henrik von Wright and Heikki Nyman, are for a variety of reasons excluded from really counting as "works". But that is as it should be. These publications represent a kind of in-between stage of Wittgenstein's writing which was never brought near completion and only found partially elaborated expression in what is known as Part II of the *Philosophical Investigations*. In some respects the situation will look even rosier as soon as good facsimiles and reliable transcriptions of the hitherto unpublished manuscripts of that period will be available. But this material will be useful only if we, as readers, understand that it is yet more remote from anything one might call a "work" by Wittgenstein than the above-mentioned volumes edited by von Wright and Nyman.

A further conclusion to be drawn is that not everything one may want to count as a work by Wittgenstein *has* been published. As has already been mentioned, a plausible case could here be made for *Bemerkungen II*. Other candidates are earlier versions of the *Philosophical Investigations*, but they will soon be taken care of by publication of von Wright's and Nyman's "Helsinki" edition of the *Philosophical Investigations* and its earlier versions, which is currently being completed at the Philosophy Department of the University of Bielefeld.

There is one work by Wittgenstein, however – and I am using the word "work" deliberately –, which is clearly and distressingly missing from the body of Wittgenstein's published writings, and hence from the canon of his works. This is the Big Typescript, and when I speak of the Big Typescript (TS 213), I mean the typescript in its naked form, without Wittgenstein's handwritten changes and instructions for further alterations.[15] That typescript constitutes a book, a work, which Wittgenstein had completed by 1933. He himself was dissatisfied with it and therefore started changing the text. But that does not affect the point that it was a book, a splendid book as a matter of fact. This does not mean that it would, if it were published, "with an explosion destroy all the other books in the world".[16] But it does mean that the philosophical world is a good deal poorer without it.[17] And it also means that our picture of Wittgenstein might be changed more profoundly by an appropriate edition of this work than by the publication of any other *Nachlaß* writings. With some hesitation and certain qualifications I thus agree with von Wright's judgement that "all the works of major interest have now been published (save for the Big Typescript, perhaps)". My quarrel is above all with that last "perhaps".

Universität Bielefeld (Germany)

NOTES

[1] Cf. "The Wittgenstein Papers", "The Origin of the Tractatus" and "The Origin and Composition of the *Philosophical Investigations*", all of them reprinted in von Wright's book *Wittgenstein*, Blackwell, Oxford 1982. In this context, it is also important to remember von Wright's edition of Wittgenstein's *Letters to C. K. Ogden* (Blackwell, Oxford 1973) and the enormous, and enormously valuable, work that went into Wittgenstein's *Cambridge Letters*, edited by McGuinness and von Wright (Blackwell, Oxford 1995). A more recent version of von Wright's article on the Wittgenstein papers can be found in *Philosophical Occasions: 1912–1951*, ed. by James Klagge and Alfred Nordmann, Hackett, Indianapolis, Indiana 1993.

[2] That the *Philosophical Investigations* and the *Remarks on the Foundations of Mathematics* were intended as companion volumes is borne out by the fact that on the back of early editions of these books the numbers "1" and "2" are printed in large type.

[3] Here there is also a practical point rightly stressed by Hintikka when he writes that reading Wittgenstein's "notebooks requires a constant series of comparisons between different pages of the same notebook and between different notebooks, which is agonizingly difficult on a microfilm machine" ("An Impatient Man and His Papers", *Synthese*, 87, 1991, p. 191.

[4] An exception appear to be the egregiously titled *Geheime Tagebücher*, Turia und Kant, Wien-Berlin 1991. This unfortunate pamphlet was clearly aimed at an audience keen on reading scandalous titbits from a famous thinker's private life. It is high time that Wittgenstein's notes be published where they belong, namely, alongside the text of *Notebooks 1914–1916*, whose title is, in view of the actual time of composition – 1914–1917 – also fairly odd.

[5] Cf. my review of the first two volumes of this edition in *Information Philosophie*, December 1995, pp. 54–60.

[6] There must be a certain irony in the fact that David Stern arrives at the conclusion that for me it should be an unwelcome result that *Bemerkungen II* might count as a "work" according to my criteria. Cf. Stern: "The Availability of Wittgenstein's Philosophy", in Hans Sluga and David Stern (eds.): *The Cambridge Companion to Wittgenstein*, Cambridge University Press, Cambridge 1996, pp. 442–76, in particular p. 458.

[7] Joachim Schulte: *Wittgenstein: Eine Einführung*, Reclam, Stuttgart 1989, American trans. by W. H. Brenner and J. F. Holley: *Wittgenstein: An Introduction*, State University of New York Press, Albany 1992.

[8] Stern: "The Availability of Wittgenstein's Philosophy", cit., p. 462. Further page references to this article will be given in brackets in the main text.

[9] Of course, one sees why the translators inserted that "finished". The English word "work" is a much wider term than the German word "Werk". In English the "countable/uncountable" difference is important: all the draft writings by Wittgenstein are his work, but it may well be that none of these writings constitutes *a* work by him.

[10] One author who seems to have found these criteria helpful is Oliver Scholz. Cf. his "Zum Status von Teil II der *Philosophischen Untersuchungen*", in Eike von Savigny and Oliver R. Scholz (eds.): *Wittgenstein über die Seele*, Suhrkamp, Frankfurt am Main 1995, pp. 24–40.

[11] That Wittgenstein planned to publish earlier versions of the *Philosophical Investigations* is described by von Wright in his "The Origin and Composition of the *Philosophical Investigations*", cit., pp. 120–22.

[12] Cf. the editor's note at the end of *Philosophische Bemerkungen*.

[13] Cf. *e.g.* parts of MS 116 and TSS 228, 229, 232.

[14] Schulte, p. 54; p. 35.

[15] Cf. Anthony Kenny: "From the Big Typescript to the *Philosophical Grammar*", in Jaakko Hintikka (ed.): *Essays on Wittgenstein in Honour of G. H. von Wright*, North-Holland Publishing Co., Amsterdam 1976, pp. 41–53. There Kenny draws what seems to be the only reasonable conclusion, viz. "that the most prudent editorial policy would have been to print the original Big Typescript as it stood rather than to seek for a definitive revision of it" (p. 52).

[16] As Wittgenstein says of the "book on Ethics which really was a book on Ethics", cf. "Lecture on Ethics", in *Philosophical Occasions*, cit., p. 40.

[17] Of course, a particularly sanguine reader might want to use the argument Wittgenstein himself applied to the case of the *Tractatus*: "Either my piece is a work of the highest rank, or it is not a work of the highest rank. In the latter (and more probable) case I myself am in favour of its not being printed. And in the former case it's a matter of indifference whether it's printed twenty or a hundred years sooner or later. After all, who asks whether the *Critique of Pure Reason*, for example, was written in 17x or y." (Letter to Russell, 6.5.20., trans. Brian McGuinness, *Cambridge Letters*, p. 154 f.) Presumably the fact the *Critique of Pure Reason* was avaible did make a difference to a few people living towards the end of the eighteenth century.

VON WRIGHT ON *ON CERTAINTY*

Wittgenstein's *On Certainty* was first published in 1969, and as all exegetes know, it was his last work,[1] the final seven entries being inserted into the manuscript only two days before he died. Professor von Wright's essay, "Wittgenstein on Certainty," was delivered at a conference in Helsinki in August of 1970, and as he later pointed out "it was at the time of its composition perhaps the fullest presentation of the newly published *Über Gewißheit* (*On Certainty*) containing Wittgenstein's latest philosophical writings."[2] As far as I know, it was also the first study of *On Certainty* to appear in print.

It is a remarkable paper. In fewer than seventeen pages von Wright accurately and deeply, and almost without any serious lacunae, describes the main themes in Wittgenstein's complex work. He says modestly that the expert will not find anything original in his study, though the uniniated may find it stimulating and useful as an introduction. He also states that he will neither evaluate *On Certainty* critically nor indicate the extent to which he agrees with Wittgenstein. His remarks are surely to be discounted. His discussion, read today, some twenty-five years later, provides a better account of both Moore and Wittgenstein than that of many a current "expert," and his criticisms of Moore, and a corresponding defense of Wittgenstein, are still worthy of consideration.

One of his most important contributions is to have seen, and emphasized, that Wittgenstein recognized that Moore's defense of the common sense view of the world, and of the existence of certainty, was original and philosophically significant. Some contemporary commentators, for example, Thomas Baldwin have dismissed Moore's epistemological work as a failure;[3] others have thought Moore was begging the question, and so forth. Von Wright's interpretation of Wittgenstein strongly suggests the opposite. If, as many of us believe, *On Certainty* is, as von Wright puts it, "a wonderful little book," it is so because, in effect, it deepens and corrects Moore's insights. Without Moore's pathbreaking reflections, *On Certainty* could never have been written.

What, then, was Wittgenstein's assessment of Moore's approach? According to von Wright, Wittgenstein appreciated Moore's defense of certitude, but felt that it was expressed in the wrong way: that it described this notion in epistemological terms, and that this was a serious mistake. As Wittgenstein says in *On Certainty*

Instead of "I know", couldn't Moore have said: "It stands fast for me that..." And further: "It stands fast for me and many others"...(§ 116).

The locution "standing fast" is, of course, just another epithet for certitude. As von Wright indicates, once a distinction between that which stands fast and knowledge is

R. Egidi (ed.), In Search of a New Humanism, 93–96.
©1999 *Kluwer Academic Publishers. Printed in Great Britain.*

drawn, it is clear that that which stands fast is not the sort of thing that can either be known or not known, be justified or not justified, be supported by evidence, be used to prove the existence of an external world, and so forth.

Wittgenstein's core idea in *On Certainty*, according to von Wright, is that "In every situation where a claim to knowledge is being established, or a doubt settled, or an item of linguistic communication (information, order, question) understood, a bulk of propositions already stand fast, are taken for granted. They form a kind of 'system'." (p. 171). The concept of knowledge does not itself apply to that which is presupposed in its use, that is, to the propositions which "stand fast," in any given knowledge situation. This is one reason why Moore's use of "I know" was out of place.

Von Wright also sees and brings out clearly that Wittgenstein is thus a kind of foundationalist, and according to him, is saying that if the foundation is something we have to accept before we can say anything is known or true, then the foundation itself is neither known nor true. As Wittgenstein puts it

If the true is what is grounded, then the ground is not true nor yet false. (*On Certainty*, § 205).

So on von Wright's interpretation, Wittgenstein is drawing a sharp distinction between foundational propositions, which Wittgenstein calls "hinge propositions," and those that occur in the language game. The language game in turn is just a name for the ordinary everyday practices we all engage in that include such activities as asserting, doubting, justifying, providing evidence for, and so on.

Wittgenstein's treatment of scepticism thus differs radically from Moore's. Moore thinks he can refute the sceptic's challenge that nobody can know anything by saying "But I, and many others, do." But as von Wright points out, Moore cannot attack the sceptics by assuring them that he knows this or that. "For one need not believe him [...] in order to vindicate a claim to knowledge, grounds must normally be provided, that is, we must be able to tell, how we know this." And Moore fails to provide such grounds. For Wittgenstein, in contrast, the problem of the existence of the external world is solved before it can be raised. In order to acquire the notion of an external world one must first acknowledge a huge number of facts that entail the existence of a world external to my mind. I can inquire whether this or that object is in the external world, or is perhaps only an illusion. But the grounds for my decision will be some facts which stand fast and which entail the existence of an external world. This explains why there is no procedure for investigating whether the external world itself exists. As von Wright affirms: "Its existence is so to speak, '*the logical receptacle*' within which all investigations concerning the mind-dependent existence of various objects are conducted."

This summary hardly does justice to the many other insightful things that von Wright says about Wittgenstein's ideas. My basic point is that his understanding of what Moore and Wittgenstein are doing is both deep and accurate. But, of course, his essay is very short; so it is natural to expect that some important things might have been ignored, minimized, or omitted, and that today, a quarter of a century later, he might wish to add to, to modify, or to abandon some things he said at that time. In the remaining part of my paper I will suggest three places for such reconsideration.

1. Wittgenstein states that it is generally required of one who advances a knowledge claim that one indicate how one knows that the claim is true. Von Wright reports this correctly, but then escalates what Wittgenstein says and affirms that "in a genuine knowledge situation there must be grounds for knowing," and that where grounds are lacking the situation is "spurious" (p.169). His use of "must" here is too strong. Wittgenstein says

"I know" often means: I have the proper grounds for my statement. (*On Certainty*, § 18).

His use of "often" is crucial in his approach. Moreover, there are counter-examples to von Wright's assertion. An idiot savant may correctly add a set of enormously long numbers without being able to say how he has arrived at the total. A person with perfect pitch can correctly identify any note but may not be able to say how he knows. He might say, "I just do. It is a gift I have." There is nothing spurious about these cases. The point is important. Wittgenstein stresses that how we are to assess what a person says will generally depend on the context in which the person says what he does. His objection to Moore is that Moore, in saying such things as "The earth exists," "I am a human being," or "Here is one hand," is neither a person with unusual gifts that he is now exercising, nor is the presumed context one that requires special gifts. It is thus as if Moore were to state, in response to the straightforward question, "Is Smith in the room?" that he knows that Smith is, but cannot say how he knows. And that response in a straightforward context would be senseless.

2. Von Wright correctly sees that the conceptual status of that which stands fast is different from anything which depends on it. I have suggested in my book, *Moore and Wittgenstein on Certainty*,[4] that because this is so the foundation cannot be any species of knowledge. Von Wright states that "one could say that every language game has a foundation which is a fragment of the player's pre-knowledge or *Vor-Wissen*" (pp. 172, 177). He recognizes that Wittgenstein does not use the term, "Vor-Wissen," yet his remark suggests, contrary to what he actually intends, that the foundation is a special kind of knowledge. I wonder if today von Wright would still wish to use the term *pre-knowledge* to describe the foundations?

3. At the end of his article there is a complex discussion in which Wittgenstein's views are assimilated to those of Thomas Kuhn. The suggestion is that Wittgenstein's reference to a framework is something like Kuhn's description of what he calls paradigms. I do not think the analogy is well taken. Kuhn is speaking of *theories*, such as the shift from a Ptolemaic to a Newtonian conception of the universe. It is clear that what Wittgenstein is describing as standing fast is not a theory, or a conceptual model. This becomes very clear when he states that

[...] the end is not certain propositions striking us immediately as true, i.e., it is not a kind of *seeing* on our part; it is our *acting* which lies at the bottom of the language game. (*On Certainty*, § 204).

Von Wright actually quotes this passage, and obviously understands it. I thus find it puzzling that he conflates Kuhn's and Wittgenstein's views in his essay.

Having said all this, I stand in awe at how good a paper he wrote in 1970.

University of California, San Diego (USA)

NOTES

[1] *Über Gewissheit. On Certainty*, ed. by G. E. M. Anscombe and G. H. von Wright, Blackwell, Oxford.
[2] In *Problems in the Theory of Knowledge*, ed. by G. H. von Wright, Nijhoff, The Hague 1972, pp. 47–60. Reprinted in G. H. von Wright, *Wittgenstein*, Blackwell, Oxford 1982.
[3] *G. E. Moore*, Routledge, London 1972.
[4] Oxford University Press, New York-Oxford 1994.

MARILENA ANDRONICO

MORPHOLOGY IN WITTGENSTEIN

1. When speaking about Spengler's impact on Wittgenstein's later philosophy, scholars usually refer to influence of two kinds:

(i)   One kind concerned Wittgenstein's general outlook toward his times, as underscored by von Wright in his paper "Wittgenstein in Relation to His Times" (1982);

(ii) Another kind affected the method Wittgenstein adopted in his later investigations on language, as stressed by Rudolf Haller in his paper "War Wittgenstein von Spengler beeinflusst?" (1988).

In both cases the suggestion that Spengler influenced Wittgenstein makes us uneasy. In the former case, we are shocked by Wittgenstein's extremely critical attitude towards scientific-technological civilization, an attitude that seems to be at odds with his interest in logical analysis. An expression of such shock can be found in Von Wright's paper, where the author wonders whether Wittgenstein's rejection of Western civilization should be regarded as a strict consequence of his general philosophy, or whether it should be brought back to mere historical contingencies.[1]

In the latter case, we are troubled by the very suggestion that Wittgenstein could have adopted Spengler's method of historical analysis – the morphological method – as a method for investigating the logical grammar of our ordinary language. As Rudolf Haller emphasized, Spengler's method was severely criticized by contemporaries such as Schlick and Neurath (Musil should be added) as confused and inaccurate (pp. 77, 80). How could Wittgenstein, the author of *Tractatus*, adopt such a method or find it fit for pursuing his old project of investigating the logic of language?

It seems to me that, if we can show that the adoption of the morphological method did not just depend on Wittgenstein's reading of Spengler's *Decline* but should rather be connected with the vicissitudes of the idea of philosophical analysis after the *Tractatus*, we will be less prone to regard Wittgenstein as a Spenglerian philosopher through and through, whose gloomy view of modern civilization is of a piece with his conception of philosophy, both being derived from the same source.

2. Wittgenstein saw the relevance of the morphological method to logical analysis in the late Twenties, while he was revising the "mistakes" (PI, Preface, p. viii) of *Tractatus*. For our purposes, it is important to bear in mind that when he was considering the adoption of the method he was thinking not just of Spengler's application of it in the *Decline*, but also – perhaps mostly – of Goethe's use of it in his naturalistic writings.[2]

97

R. Egidi (ed.), In Search of a New Humanism, 97–102.
© 1999 *Kluwer Academic Publishers. Printed in Great Britain.*

With Goethe, the method is a tool for a very peculiar treatment of the natural phenomena: one that rejects the distinction of surface and depth in the investigation of nature, while at the same time rejecting the customary idea that understanding natural phenomena amounts to causally explaining them. Morphology aims at *darstellen und nicht erklären.*[3] In his fight against Newtonian mechanism, Goethe was trying to invest the sciences with a new strategy: one that would look at nature in such a way that the phenomena of light, life, growth, and the metamorphosis of natural forms could become intelligible without being reduced to artificial constructs, i.e. to phenomena that can only be perceived under the very peculiar conditions of the scientist's laboratory.[4] In Goethe's conception nature reveals its forms to us of and by itself, in a sense, even though successful analysis always requires that the scientist be previously instructed to look at nature and its forms in the right way. He must learn to look at the surface of phenomena, seeing what is there open to the view (what is there under his eyes) and comparing the forms he sees with one another. Careful observation and comparison should allow him to reach an *overview* of the internal relations connecting the natural forms. To such a view each form would clearly display – exhibit – its function in relation to the other forms belonging to the natural series, revealing the logic of all transformations, be they real or possible.

What is really peculiar to such a method, however, is how the job of comparing natural forms is conceived. Goethe introduces the notion of the proto-phenomenon – *das Urphänomen* – to mean that the forms we experience in nature should be contrasted with a type-concept, a kind of entity that is conceived as both ideal and sensuous. The *Urphänomen* belongs to a natural series as one of its elements; but, on the other hand, it is an ideal construction, playing the role of a criterion for the organization of the natural phenomena into that same ordered series, in such a way that the network of relations among the elements of the series is brought out clearly.[5]

3. I would like to suggest that Goethe's idea of the morphological method provided Wittgenstein with the right stategy for dealing with two problems he encountered after the *Tractatus*:

(1)   The problem of how to preserve the old and basic idea that whatever belongs to the logical structure of language must show itself in language (cf.T 4.121, 4.122, 4.126, 6.12).

(2)   The probem of how to carry out the analysis of the logical structure of language, once the Tractarian notion of the essence of language had been criticized and relinquished, so that the dichotomy of depth and surface was no longer available: i.e. it was no longer possible to distinguish between a deep level of language, where logic is invariably at work, and a surface where misleading expressions may conceal such depth.

Wittgenstein criticizes the traditional notion of essence as an expression of the tendency (to which even the author of *Tractatus* had succumbed) to confuse the conceptual and the factual levels of an inquiry (Z 458), i.e. to regard a rule -a limit of sense- as sanctioning a factual limitation. In the *Tractatus* such a confusion makes the rules of logical syntax appear deeper (and harder) than the others, as if reflecting *a special kind of facts*, namely characteristic features of the world. In Wittgenstein's own words, we are so "impressed by the possibility of a comparison" that "we think we are perceiving *a state of affairs* of the highest generality" (PI 104, italics added). Such a view is illegitimate, for it implies that the philosopher must have a theory of language before he starts doing philosophy, contrary to Wittgenstein's characterization of philosophy as not a doctrine but an activity, aiming at the logical clarification of thought (T 4.112).

During the Thirties, Wittgenstein recognized that no rules can be thought of as deeper than others, and such that one could say that they mirror the features of the world, or of thought, better than others. On the contrary, *all rules are of the same kind* (LW 1930–32 p. 98). And they are all of them equally applied within ordinary language. It is therefore clear that philosophy should no longer be conceived as dealing with thoughts supposedly disguised by ordinary language: philosophy is now concerned with misleading pictures, expressing bad habits of thought (witness the very picture of the essence of language). In the new perspective, philosophy's critical task – its analytic function – does not disappear, even if it is so much harder to carry out as it clearly must be pursued within the one language we possess.

Wittgenstein adopted the morphological method because he saw in it a satisfactory strategy for dealing with the rules of language, one that would be faithful to his old (Tractarian) idea of the autonomy of logic.[6] With this method, in fact, the philosopher does not need a theory of language in order to analyze language (cfr. PI 109). The peculiarly comparative strategy makes it possible for him to analyze the logic without abandoning the terrain of the language he ordinarily employs. In the new perspective, the role of *Urphänomen* is played by the language games:[7] in fact, they are part of our common experience of language,[8] but on the other hand, they "are set up as *objects of comparison* which are meant to throw light on the facts of our language" (PI 130). They are set up as models, in the sense that they operate as measuring rods, not as "a preconceived idea to which reality *must* correspond" (PI 131). Like the *Urphänomene* in Goethean science, they help us build an order ("one out of many possible orders", PI 132) in our knowledge of the use of language, so that we can achieve a perspicuous representation of it. This is exactly the peculiar kind of understanding characteristic of morphological thought: understanding "which consists in 'seeing connexions' " (PI 122).

Another reason why the method would appeal to Wittgenstein is, that it made it possible for him to carry out the analysis of the rules of language according to an extended version of Frege's "context principle", i.e. according to the general idea that what belongs to logic *shows itself* in the *function* it plays in language. The principle is at work in the morphological notion of an *overview* of the forms of natural phenomena, and it is likewise operative in Wittgenstein's notion of an overview of the language games.[9] Describing linguistic contexts in such a way that we can clearly see how we use words, or constructing the series of linguistics contexts in such a way that we can notice their analogies and differences is all that the philosopher can legitimately do. This is the sense in which there are no discoveries in philosophy: "Philosophy simply puts everything before us, and neither explains nor deduces anything. – Since everything lies open to view there is nothing to explain" (PI 126). Philosophy's task consists in leading us to *recognize* the workings of our language "*in despite* of an urge to misunderstand them" (PI 109); it is not a matter of providing new information, but of "arranging what we have always known" (PI 109).

4. Thus, according to the view I am putting forward, Wittgenstein had reasons of his own to adopt the morphological method; the adoption did not depend on his reading of Spengler (or Goethe) in any simple way. This is also brought out by the fact that he did not straightforwardly adopt the method but modified it, by redefining its scope. Wittgenstein conceived of morphology as a method for exhibiting the rules of language: therefore, he only saw it fit *for dealing with concepts*, i.e. with the linguistic entities defined by such rules. Wittgenstein's philosophy, though clearly indebted to both Goethe and Spengler, is at the same time radically critical of their application of the morphological method: on Wittgenstein's view, both Goethe and Spengler misunderstood their own methodological intuition. Goethe was wrong in thinking that his morphological investigations of the phenomena of light would lead to an alternative *theory* of color, different from Newton's:

> Goethe's theory of the constitution of the colours of the spectrum has not proved to be an unsatisfactory theory, rather it really isn't a theory at all. Nothing can be predicted with it. (RC I, 70).

> Someone who agrees with Goethe believes that Goethe correctly recognized the *nature* of colour. And nature here is not what results from experiments, but it lies in the concept of colour. (RC I, 71).

Similarly, Spengler goes astray when he ascribes to the *object* of his inquiry, history, such features as are characteristic of the conceptual tools (the *Urphänomene*, the civilizations in his case) through which he analyzes it:

> Spengler could be better understood if he said: I am *comparing* different cultural epochs with the lives of families; [...] What I mean is: we have to be told the object of comparison, the object from which this way of viewing things is derived, otherwise the discussion will constantly be affected by distortions. Because willy-nilly we shall ascribe the properties of the prototype to the object we are viewing in its light; and we claim "it *must always* be ..." [...] But the prototype ought to be clearly presented for what it is (CV p. 14).

> But then how is a view like Spengler's related to mine? Distortion in Spengler: The ideal doesn't lose any of its dignity if it's presented as the principle determining the form of one's reflections. A sound measure. (CV p. 27).

Morphological analysis is only legitimate within conceptual research, i.e. within an investigation dealing with the sense of linguistic expressions.

To conclude: Wittgenstein did not adopt the morphological method simply because he had read Spengler. He adopted it because it made it possible for him to carry out logical analysis in the spirit of *Tractatus*, while avoiding some of the mistakes contained in that book. Radical criticism of the scientific and technological society is no necessary consequence of Wittgenstein's later conception of philosophy; it is rather to be brought back to historical and psychological contingencies.

Università di Torino (Italy)

NOTES

[1] "Particularly pertinent is the question whether the third aspect, the Spenglerian one, is only contingently, that is for historical and psychological reasons, connected with the other two [*i.e.* with "the view that the individual's beliefs, judgements, and thoughts are entrenched in unquestioningly accepted language-games and socially sanctioned forms of life" and with "the view that philosophical problems are disquietudes of the mind caused by some malfuncioning in the language-games and hence in the way of life of the community"] in Wittgenstein's thought. If the connection is only accidental or contingent, then one could say that Wittgenstein's attitude to his time is irrelevant to the understanding of his philosophy, even though it may be quite important to an understanding of his personality" (von Wright 1982, p. 118).

[2] In his introduction to the *Decline*, Spengler acknowledged his debt to Goethe as the source of the method adopted in the book (Spengler 1927, p. 7). Analyses of the Goethe-Wittgenstein relationship have been carried out by Schulte 1990 and Bouveresse 1996.

[3] *I.e.* at presenting, not explaining: Goethe 1795, HA XIII, 123.

[4] "What separated Goethe from the Newtonians was his refusal to reduce (except for explicit methodological reasons) the perceptibles qualities of objects – the so-called 'secondary qualities' – to 'primaries qualities' which have the (to Goethe mere methodological) advantage of being quantifiable" (Stephenson 1995, p. 26). My account of Goethe's morphological method in this paper is obviously sketchy and, in part, a simplification. More expanded presentations can be read in Amrine *et al.* 1987 and in Stephenson 1995.

[5] Stephenson 1995, pp. 13–15.

[6] "Logic must look after itself" (*T* 5.473); "Language must speak for itself" (PG 27c).

[7] "Our mistake is to look for an explanation where we ought to look at what happens as a 'proto-phenomenon' (*Urphänomen*). That is, where we ought to have said: *this language game in played.*" (PI 654).

[8] In the *Blue Book*, the language games are introduced as continuous with the linguistic reality we ordinarily experience: "These are ways of using signs simpler than those in which we use the signs of our highly complicated everyday language. Language games are the forms of language with which a child begins to make use of words" (BLB, p. 17).

[9] In his book *The Principles of Linguistic Philosophy* (partly based on conversations with Wittgenstein) Waismann has an enlightening account of this point. It is explicitly stated that the method adopted for the analysis of language is derived from ideas contained in Goethe's *Metamorphosis of Plants*. The method is said to involve a legitimate form of non-genetic, non-causal understanding of the natural phenomena. Goethe's conception of the original plant "implies no hypothesis about the temporal development of the vegetable kingdom such as that of Darwin. What then *is* the problem solved by this idea? It is the problem of synoptic presentation. Goethe's aphorism 'All the organs of plants are leaves transformed' offers us a plan in which we may group the organs of plants according to their similarities as if around some natural centre. We see the original form of the leaf changing into similar and cognate forms, into the leaves of the calyx, the leaves of the petal, into organs that are half petal, half stamens, and so on. We follow this sensuous transformation of the type by linking up the leaf through intermediate forms with the other organs of the plant. That is precisely what we are doing here. We are collating one form of language with its environment, or transforming it in imagination so as to gain a view of the whole of the space in which the structure of our language has its being" (Waismann 1965, pp. 80–1).

BIBLIOGRAPHY

Amrine *et al.* 1987
    Amrine F., Zucker F. J., Wheeler H. (eds.): *Goethe and the Sciences: a Reappraisal*, Reidel, Dordrecht.
Bouveresse 1996
    Bouveresse J.: *Wittgenstein et Goethe* [lecture unpubl.]
Goethe 1795
    Goethe J. W.: *Betrachtung über die Morphologie*, in Goethes *Werke*, Hamburger Ausgabe, Band XIII, hrsg. von E. Trunz, Wegner Verlag, Hamburg 1955.
Haller 1988
    Haller R.: *Questions on Wittgenstein*, Routledge, London.

Schulte 1990

  Schulte J.: *Chor und Gesetz. Zur "morphologischen Methode" bei Goethe und Wittgenstein*, Suhrkamp, Frankfurt am Main.

Spengler 1927

  Spengler O.: *Der Untergang des Abendlandes*, C. H. Beck'sche Verlagsbuchhandlung, München

Stephenson 1995

  Stephenson R. H.: *Goethe's Conception of Knowledge and Science*, Edinburgh Univ. Press, Edinburgh.

Von Wright 1982

  Wright, G. H. von: "Wittgenstein in Relation to His Times", in G. H. von Wright: *Wittgenstein,* Blackwell, Oxford.

Wittgenstein 1922

  Wittgenstein L.: *Tractatus Logico-Philosophicus* (T). Trans. by D. F. Pears and B. F. McGuinness, Routledge & Kegan Paul, London 1969.

Wittgenstein 1974

  Wittgenstein L.: *Philosophical Grammar* (PG), ed. R. Rhees. Trans. by A. J. P. Kenny, Blackwell, Oxford.

Wittgenstein 1958

  Wittgenstein L.: *The Blue and Brown Books* (BB), ed. by R. Rhees, Blackwell, Oxford 1969.[2]

Wittgenstein 1953

  Wittgenstein L.: *Philosophical Investigations* (PI), ed. by G. E. M. Anscombe and R. Rhees, Blackwell, Oxford, 1958[2]

Wittgenstein 1967

  Wittgenstein L.: *Zettel* (Z), ed. by G. E. M. Anscombe and G. H. von Wright. Trans. by G. E. M. Anscombe, Blackwell, Oxford, 1981.[2]

Wittgenstein 1977

  Wittgenstein L.: *Remarks on Colour* (RC), ed. G. E. M. Anscombe, Blackwell, Oxford.

Wittgenstein 1980 a

  Wittgenstein L.: *Vermischte Bemerkungen. Culture and Value* (CV), ed. by G. H. von Wright, with the assistance of H. Nyman, Blackwell, Oxford.

Wittgenstein 1980 b

  Wittgenstein L.: *Lectures: Cambridge 1930–1932* (LW 1930–32), ed. by D. Lee, Blackwell, Oxford.

Waismann 1965

  Waismann F.: *The Principles of Linguistic Philosophy*, ed. by R. Harré, Macmillan, London.

SANDRO NANNINI

THE LOGICAL CONNECTION ARGUMENT AGAIN

The positivist-historicist argument about the alleged or denied difference between the study of man and the study of nature began in Germany one century ago with *Einleitung in die Geisteswissenschaften* by W. Dilthey (1883) (discussion called by K.-O. Apel *Erklären/Verstehen-Kontroverse*).[1] It finds in *Explanation and Understanding*, published by G. H. von Wright 1971, its clearest contemporary formulation. An epistemological puzzle with strong metaphysical implications (like the distinction between mind and matter) becomes a problem that can be solved or at least clarified by common-language conceptual analysis.

Von Wright's *Explanation and Understanding* is at the crossroad of two lively discussions. The previously-mentioned discussion about the alleged difference between the logical structure of history, or the human and social sciences in general, on the one hand, and the logical structure of natural sciences, on the other, is combined by von Wright with the discussion (opened in 1957 by G. E. M. Anscombe in the booklet *Intention*) between the Neowittgensteinians who refuted the causal theory of action and their opponents (particularly D. Davidson 1963) who maintained it. At the core of von Wright's book is the idea that the Neowittgensteinian criticism of the causal theory of action prevents the study of man (history, the human and social sciences) from being of the same kind as the study of natural events.[2]

The study of man is different from the study of nature, according to von Wright, since at the core of historical, human and social sciences there exists a linguistic game very usual in common language but having nothing to do with the explanation of natural events by means of general laws: that is the intuitive perception of a conceptual link between an action and the intentions, motives, reasons and beliefs because of which it was done.

Von Wright says that an intentionalistic explanation is the inverse of a practical inference in which an action is derived from an intention and a belief.[3] For example: why does that man run? Because he wants to catch a train. In this case the *explanandum* is "That man runs" and the *explanans* is "That man has the intention to catch a train" and also "That man thinks that he can catch his train only if he runs."[4] What is the nature of the link between the *explanans* and the *explanandum* in such a situation? Three major answers have been given in the course of the discussion between the Neowittgensteinians and their opponents about action theories.

1. The link is a causal one, either according to a Humean analysis of causality (e.g. Hempel 1963) or in terms implying a description of cause and effect such that under that description their relation is covered by a general law (as it is according to

103

R. Egidi (ed.), In Search of a New Humanism, 103–112.
© 1999 *Kluwer Academic Publishers. Printed in Great Britain.*

Davidson [1963]).[5] Therefore intention and belief are logically independent from action in both cases.

Further, intentional explanations are in the first case explanation sketches (Hempel 1942), valid only if one tacitly adds folk psychology's *empirical* generalizations of the kind "If one wants to do x and he (or she) thinks he can do x only if he does y, then he sets himself to do y" (Churchland 1970).

But that hypothesis is refuted by the so-called Logical Connection Argument (Stoutland 1970) according to which the previous alleged generalization is not empirical, and, more generally, the tie between intentions and correspondent actions cannot be causal. There is a conceptual link between intentions plus beliefs and actions. Therefore, if one accepts the Humean principle that a cause must be logically independent from its effect the tie between the *explanans* and the *explanandum* of an intentionalistic explanation cannot be causal.

The proof that that link is conceptual and not causal is given by imagining a situation in which an intention (plus a belief) really does cause an action. In that case the very action is not any more intentional and the explanation is not any more intentionalistic.

Let us recall the famous example by Chisholm (1966) of the nephew who wants to kill his uncle in order to inherit his fortune. This desire agitates the nephew so severely that as he goes by car to his uncle's house to shoot him he drives excessively fast. Consequently he accidentally runs over and kills a pedestrian who, unknown to him, was none other than his uncle. It is true that in a certain sense (a causal sense) the nephew kills his uncle because of his intention of killing him, but this sense is not the sense of a normal intentionalistic (or teleological) explanation. The intention brings about its effect by virtue of provoking a state of excitement, not thanks to its content, that is, to its being an intention *of* killing his uncle.

Intentions (on a par with motives, desires, beliefs etc.) have contents, "intentions" in Brentano's sense. Intentions are distinguished from each other by having different contents. The intention of doing x is different form the intention of doing y only thanks to the difference between x and y. Intentions further explain (teleologically) actions in common language by their contents. My intention of opening a window explains why I opened a window just because it is *that* intention and not another, that is, because it is the intention *of opening a window*.

But in the example of the "killer nephew", although the intention of killing the uncle causes (and therefore causally explains) the death of the uncle, the explanation is not intentionalistic in any normal sense of the word. That is, the content of the intention (killing the uncle) is here inert, as it were; it does not guide the nephew's action. Any other intention or mental state that brought about excitement could have produced the same effect. The intention operates as cause independently of its content.

If the intention operates thanks to its content, as it does in common language explanations of human actions, there is a conceptual tie between the very intention and the action (*i.e.*, between the intention of doing x and x). In that case the independence between cause and effect required by Hume fails and the explanation cannot be causal.

If, instead, the intention operates independently of its content, as it does in the "killer nephew" example, the independence between cause and effect required by Hume is respected and the explanation is causal, but it is no more intentionalistic and does not match common language explanations of human actions by agents' goals.

The "killer nephew" example generated a long discussion about so-called wayward causal chains, that is, chains that causally link a certain intention and the correspondent action in a way that is unusual and different from the way that the agent thought to follow to realize the action. For example, the nephew did not intend to kill the uncle by means of his car. His action of running over a person is unintentional and he does not know that the pedestrian is his uncle. It is thought by some, therefore, that the wayward chains problem can be solved by adding the clause that in correct explanations of actions, intentions must not only bring about correspondent actions causally but they must also produce them in the way thought of by agents.

However, it is not so easy for "causalists" to free themselves from the wayward chains, as we can see by analysing another much-discussed example that I shall call the "killer alpinist" example.[6] An alpinist is climbing a mountain with a friend whom he hates so much for personal reasons that he has decided to kill him. The alpinist holds in his hands a rope that prevents the friend falling to his death at a difficult point. He is thinking that this is the right moment to realize his project and so decides to kill the friend by releasing the rope. But that decision (or intention) excites him so much that at the very instant he had set himself to intentionally release the rope, he unintentionally releases it. One cannot say in that case that the intention is linked to the action by a *wayward* chain because the alpinist kills the friend exactly at the moment and by the means which he had chosen. Is this therefore an example of an action's explanation that is both causal and intentionalistic? Does the alpinist's intention explain both causally and in the usual teleological way his action of killing his friend? Although the example is very strange and our intuitions waver when evaluating it, I think we have to say that the intention of killing the friend does cause his death but in such a way that the killer's action is not completely intentional. The intention operates like a simple "unintentional" (in Brentano's sense) state of excitement and not in virtue of its content (killing the friend), exactly as is the case in the "killer nephew" example.

Therefore, both examples (the "killer nephew" and the "killer alpinist") show that if one requires, like Hume, a complete logical independence of cause and effect, an intention cannot explain an action both causally and in the intentionalistic or common language sense.

2. The link between the *explanans* and the *explanandum* of an intentionalistic explanation is not causal, it is of logical necessity (see von Wright himself prior to *Explanation and Understanding*[7]; and see also Stoutland [1970]). If one does not do what one intended to do (provided of course that one knows how to do it, has the opportunity and the capability of doing it, etc.), that means either that in fact one did not intend to do so (e.g., one only wished to do so) or that one changed one's own mind.

However von Wright has convincingly refuted that hypothesis in *Explanation and Understanding*: see the example of the tyrannicide. A patriot wants to kill a tyrant. He can do so, the tyrant is sleeping in front of him, no one else is there, he has a loaded pistol and knows how to use it, etc. But he does not kill the tyrant. He does not, not because he changed his mind (that would be a change in the premises of the practical inference) but because he does nothing. A human being can be irrational, that is, it is possible that a human being does not act according to his or her intentions and beliefs although he or she has the possibility to do so.

Von Wright says however that, although the conclusion does not follow by logical necessity from its premises in a practical inference, there is a logically necessary tie between the *explanandum* and the *explanans* of its inverse, that is, an intentionalistic explanation. In other words, it is not logically necessary that the tyrannicide kill the tyrant if he intends to kill him (and knows how to kill him, has the possibility to do so, etc.). But if the tyrannicide really kills the tyrant you can say *after* the murder that his action followed necessarily from his intentions and beliefs. That necessity is logical but it exists only after the action: it is a *"ex post actu* necessity."* However, von Wright abandoned that difficult and strange concept[8] in later studies[9] in favour of the theory illustrated in point (3) below.

Those studies and the previous example of the tyrannicide show in any case that the theory of point (2), according to which there is a tie of logical necessity between intentions + beliefs and actions, is not plausible.

3. The link between the *explanans* and the *explanandum* of an intentionalistic explanation is neither causal nor logical. It is a third type of link which belongs to a particular linguistic game that allows in common language the explanation of an action by knowing an agent's intentions and beliefs. It cannot be a relation of true logical entailment because of the possibility (at least) of the tyrannicide example. But it is not causal either because of the Logical Connection Argument which von Wright accepts under a particular version that Nordenfelt (1974) called the Argument from Verification.

I can explain the man's running in our early example, for instance, by his wanting to catch a train. I see him running but I cannot see his intention; I cannot look into his brain. How can I be sure that he has that intention? Couldn't he be running to escape a robber? I can guess his intention and test my hypothesis only by watching the behaviour of the man and more particularly in certain crucial cases only by means of the action that is explained by that very intention (as seen in a certain context, of course). I infer that the man has the intention of catching a train by his running (to a station) and at the same time I explain his running by that intention. Therefore, there is a conceptual link between the *explanans* and the *explanandum* of an intentionalistic explanation because the verification of the obtaining of the intention is drawn by the obtaining of the action, whereas it is usually claimed that it is explicitly forbidden in a Humean causal explanation that the verification of the effect depends on the obtaining of the cause. That was (allegedly) made clear by Hempel and P. Oppenheim in *Studies in the Logic of Explanation* (1948).

Hempel and P. Oppenheim thought an explanation is valid if it satisfies the following conditions:

a) The *explanans* (a certain number of general laws L + a certain number of particular events' descriptions C [the determinant conditions or, briefly, the causes]) must entail the description of the *explanandum* E (another particular event). Let us say that L and C must entail E.

b) C and E must be logically independent (for example, the fact that Mary is tall and blond cannot explain the fact that she is tall).

c) The empirical verifications of C and E must be independent.

Point (c) is necessary because one can imagine examples of explanations that are false although they satisfy (a) and (b) and their premises and conclusion are true. For example, let us assume that L = "All metals are good conductors of heat", C = "if Ls (an example of L), then E", Ls = "If the Eiffel tower is metallic then it is a good conductor of heat" and E = "The summit of Mount Everest is snow capped". L is true (or, better, empirically well confirmed) and entails Ls; therefore Ls is true. But E also is true and therefore also C = "if Ls then E" is true (of course a conditional is true if both its antecedent and its subsequent are true). Therefore, firstly, if L entails Ls and it is true that C = "if Ls then E", then L and C together entail E. The condition (a) is satisfied. Secondly, C (= "If Ls then E") does not entail E without L. Therefore, also the condition (b) is satisfied. Thirdly, L, C and E are true. The explanation should be valid and true. But in fact it is absurd to explain the presence of snow on the summit of Mount Everest by the fact that metals are good conductors of heat and the Eiffel tower is metallic.

In order to avoid such absurdities, (c) must be introduced. In the previous example (c) is not satisfied because there is no other evidence of C's truth except the fact that E and L are true. The truth of C is not testable independently of the truth of E.

Let us return to the example of the man running to the station. Let us assume that we can guess his intention to catch a train only by his very running. That assumption is not true of course for all intentionalistic explanations of actions. As it is true that not all explanations of actions are intentionalistic, it is also true that on many occasions we know agents' intentions independently of their actions (the man could have said to me while he was running, "I want to catch a train in five minutes"). But *sometimes* we do guess agents' intentions only from their correspondent actions (sometimes I understand that the man wants to catch a train *only* by his very running). Those cases are crucial for von Wright's thesis because they seem to prove that at least some *plausible* intentionalistic explanations cannot satisfy condition (c) of Hempel's and Oppenheim's model and cannot be causal (in Humean sense).

Therefore, since intentionalistic explanations are at the core of the study of man, history or the human and social sciences cannot have the same logical structure as the natural sciences where Humean causal explanations are usual and perfectly acceptable.

If I understand von Wright correctly that third hypothesis is, on the whole, his position after *Explanation and Understanding*. I think that it is very stimulating but I do not think that the conclusion is completely acceptable. A fourth hypothesis seems possible; I think that *both* in the natural sciences and in history (together with the human and social sciences), valid explanations can be found where there is a conceptual link or, better, a "verification link" between the *explanans* and the *explanandum*.

In the natural sciences an event c can be the cause of another event e even if the obtaining of c can be verified only by the obtaining of e (provided that events of the type of e are caused by events of the type of c according to a well confirmed empirical law). An example drawn from Hempel (included in *Aspects of Scientific Explanation* [1965, p. 372], an essay following that previously quoted) can show more clearly what I mean.

Consider the dark lines of an absorption spectrum of a particular star. They are explained by saying that they are caused by the fact that the atmosphere of the star contains certain chemical elements. How can I verify that there are those elements in the atmosphere of the star? The very dark lines are the only evidence. The explanation is "self-evidencing" because the *explanandum* is the only evidence of the *explanans*.

Condition (c) of the 1948 essay has been violated but there is another way to distinguish valid explanations, such as dark lines, from invalid explanations, like that of Mount Everest. The explanation of dark lines is neither circular nor non-causal because it is supported by a well confirmed empirical theory in other contexts according to which certain chemical elements cause certain dark lines. It is true that in a particular case (the observation of stars) the presence of the cause (certain chemical elements) can be tested only by means of the effect (the dark lines of the absorption spectrum). But in many other cases (in a laboratory) that cause-effect relation can be tested in situations where the cause and the effect are independently observable or in any case empirically verifiable. That is not true in the case of Mount Everest. No one has ever observed any repeated relation whatsoever between snow on mountains and the physical properties of metals.

Therefore, we can substitute condition (c) with (c'): "The *type* of causal relation that exists between the cause and the effect must be testable in contexts where causes and effects are independently verifiable in an empirical way".

I think we can also apply this conclusion to the example of the running man. I can guess and verify his intention of catching a train only thanks to his running (in a certain context) but nevertheless I can explain his action thanks to his intention only because I can cover that intention and that action under some of the *empirical* generalizations of common sense that make up my knowledge of human beings. If I knew nothing about human beings, times of trains, etc., I could not understand the behaviour of that man.

Even if I see the man for the first time and do not know where he is going, etc., I can understand his action only because, firstly, I analyse it in different aspects or redescribe it in more general terms (e.g., running in order not to be late) and, secondly, I find in my large experience of human beings (of their psychology, preferences, needs, physical constraints, etc.) some empirical generalizations tested in many other cases and applicable to the present one. I have seen other human beings who ran, were late, wanted to catch trains etc.

A large part of that experience is gathered from myself, of course. But that belongs to the "context of discovery" and it is not sufficient to conclude that I can justify the truth of my explanations of other human beings' actions by empathy, that is, in a radically different way from the way I justify my explanations of natural events. I need some generalizations in both cases. Even the most obvious connection between an intention and an action that I find immediately true in myself must be tested in the behaviour of other people. As anthropogists know very well, what seems to be obvious to people belonging to the same culture can be absurd for others.

I need, for example, in order to explain the behaviour of the man who runs to a location where there is a station to know that there is a usual correlation between being late and running, that in stations there are trains and that trains (unlike taxis for example) have a time to start and therefore catching a train is something with regard to which one can be late, etc.

Further, I think that all that is *empirical* knowledge. Part of that knowledge can be embedded in the meaning of common language words of course. A railway station is by definition a place where there are trains. But that is true for all theoretical concepts in natural sciences. Forces (not themselves directly observable) are defined by laws (like $F = ma$) where they obtain. Does it mean that those laws are no longer empirical laws but definitions? Of course not!

I think therefore that the explanations of both human actions and natural events require empirical generalizations and follow the same logical structure: on the whole the covering laws model.

I have tried elsewhere (Nannini 1992, ch. III) to show how the covering laws model can also be applied to the explanations of human actions in common language. Some modifications must be introduced, of course. For example, human actions are usually covered not by deterministic laws but by empirical probabilistic generalizations or by "possibility laws" (empirical correlations whose probability is far from 1 and only approximately determined); *explanans* and *explanandum* must be described in "actionistic-intentionalistic terms" such that intensional contexts can arise, etc.

Therefore, I think that the Logical Connection Argument does not support the idea of a radical difference between the study of man and the study of nature.

One could object that even if the Logical Connection Argument does not support the classical difference between *Erklären* and *Verstehen* that difference nevertheless remains because scientists and historians for example work in a completely different way. The very "spirit" of their disciplines is different. Scientists try to isolate repeated empirical correlations in different contexts, historians try to understand singular events in the light of a wider context (von Wright 1980).

I am not sure that the distinction is completely true. I think that it is useful in epistemology to keep Reichenbach's distinction of "discovery and justification contexts". The undisputable differences in the methodological approach between the natural sciences and history or the human and social sciences belong to the "context of discovery". But if one wants to introduce norms that define the validity of explanations, I think the classical covering-laws model (if opportunely modified) fits very well for explanations of human actions.

Finally, a last objection. Even if methodological monism could be defended by distinguishing the two "contexts", what is the point of that thesis? How can a philosopher introduce norms of validity for both the natural and the human sciences when scientists and historians for example think that they do two different jobs?

I think that there is good reason nowadays to defend methodological monism from a philosophical point of view: the distinction between *Erklären* and *Verstehen* creates a barrier between the natural and the human or social sciences while the birth of cognitive sciences requires a cooperation. Philosophy of mind, for example, can no longer be developed only by means of conceptual analysis but requires the cooperation of human scientists with natural scientists. Philosophers, psychologists, linguists, cognitive anthropologists, etc., can no longer ignore the work of neuroscientists or artificial intelligence researchers. The necessary cooperation will be easier if philosophers show that the general criteria for theories' validity are just the same for all sciences.

Università di Siena (Italy)

NOTES

[1] Cf. Apel 1979 for a detailed historical introduction to that discussion (from Dilthey to contemporary philosophers including G. H. von Wright).

[2] Cf. Nannini 1992 for a reconstruction of both discussions in contemporary philosophy and for a more detailed reconstruction of von Wright's theories.

[3] Von Wright called those kinds of explanation teleological in *Explanation and Understanding*. Later he preferred to call them intentionalistic in order to avoid any confusion with "quasi-teleological" or funtionalistic explanations in biology (von Wright 1976 a).

[4] Von Wright adds many clauses to that simple formulation of (the inverse of) a practical inference in order to avoid obvious objections. But they do not touch the main point I am discussing here: that is, the nature of the link between the premises and the conclusion of a practical inference and of the correspondent explanation.

[5] A different possibility is given by Tuomela 1977 who introduces the concept of "purposive causality". A relation of purposive causality is not reducible to a relation of Humean or nomological causality but presupposes it.

[6] Cf. *e.g.* Davidson 1973, Brand 1984, p. 17 ff., Mele 1987 and Moya 1990, pp. 115–28.

[7] Cf. particularly von Wright 1963 a, 1963 b and 1968.

[8] I think that concept is strange because if *a* is a *logical* presupposition of *b* *a* entails necessarily *b* (at least in the classical sense of logic von Wright seems to speak of). Therefore if *a* and *b* are tied in such a way that *b* presupposes *a* and *a* does not imply *b* then it is better to say, as von Wright himself maintained after *Explanation and Understanding*, that the tie between *a* and *b* is conceptual but not properly logical.

[9] Cf. particularly von Wright 1972, 1976 a, 1976 b and 1980

BIBLIOGRAPHY

Anscombe 1957
    Anscombe G. E. M.: *Intention*, Blackwell, Oxford.
Apel 1979
    Apel Karl-Otto: *Die Erklären/Verstehen-Kontroverse in transzendental-pragmatischer Sicht*, Suhrkamp, Frankfurt a.M.

Brand 1984
Brand M.: *Intending and Acting. Toward a Naturalized Action Theory*, The MIT Press, Cambridge (Mass.)-London.

Chisholm 1966
Chisholm R. M.: "Freedom and Action", in K. Lehrer (ed.): *Freedom and Determinism*, Random House, New York, pp. 11–44.

Churchland 1970
Churchland Paul M.: "The Logical Character of Action-Explanations", *The Philosophical Review*, 79, 2, pp. 214–236.

Davidson 1963
Davidson Donald: "Actions, Reasons, and Causes", *Journal of Philosophy*, 60, pp. 685–700. Reprinted in D. Davidson: *Essays in Actions and Events*, Clarendon Press, Oxford, 1982.

Davidson 1973
Davidson Donald: "Freedom to Act", in T. Honderich (ed.): *Essays on Freedom and Action*, Routledge & Kegan Paul , London, pp. 139–56.

Dilthey 1883
Dilthey Wilhelm: *Einleitung in die Geisteswissenschaften*; in *Gesammelte Schriften*, I, Teubner and Vandenhoeck & Ruprecht, Stuttgart-Göttingen, 1966.

Hempel 1942
Hempel C. Gustav: "The Function of General Laws in History", in Hempel 1965.

Hempel 1963
Hempel Carl G.: "Reasons and Covering Laws in Historical Explanation", in S. Hook (ed.): *Philosophy and History. A Symposium*, New York University Press, New York, pp. 143–63.

Hempel 1965
Hempel Carl G.: *Aspects of Scientific Explanation and Other Essays in the Philosophy of Science*, The Free Press-MacMillan, New York-London.

Hempel 1948
Hempel C. G. and Oppenheim P.: "Studies in the Logic of Explanation," in Hempel 1965, pp. 245–95.

Manninen and Tuomela 1976
Manninen J. and Tuomela R. (eds.): *Essays on Explanation and Understanding*, Reidel, Dordrecht.

Mele 1987
Mele A. R.: "Intentional Action and Wayward Causal Chains: The Problem of Tertiary Waywardness", *Philosophical Studies*, 51, pp. 55–60.

Moya 1990
Moya C. J.: *The Philosophy of Action. An Introduction*, Polity Press, Cambridge.

Nannini 1992
Nannini S.: *Cause e ragioni. Modelli di spiegazione delle azioni umane nella filosofia analitica*, Editori Riuniti, Roma.

Nordenfelt 1974
Nordenfelt L.: *Explanation of Human Actions*, University of Uppsala, Uppsala.

Stoutland 1970
Stoutland F.: "The Logical Connection Argument", *American Philosophical Quarterly*, 4, pp 117–29.

Tuomela 1977
Tuomela R.: *Human Action and its Explication. A Study on the Philosophical Foundation of Psychology*, Reidel, Dordrecht.

Von Wright 1963 a
Wright G. H. von: *Norm and Action. A Logical Inquiry*, Routledge & Kegan Paul-The Humanities Press, London-New York.

Von Wright 1963 b
Wright G. H. von: "Practical Inference", *The Philosophical Review*, 72, pp.159–79. Reprinted in G. H. von Wright: *Practical Reason. Philosophical Papers*, Vol. I, Blackwell, Oxford 1983.

Von Wright 1968
  Wright G. H. von: "The Logic of Practical Discourse", in R. Klibansky (ed.), *Contemporary Philosophy. A Survey*, La Nuova Italia, Firenze, Vol. I, pp. 141–67.
Von Wright 1971
  Wright G. H. von: *Explanation and Understanding*, Cornell University Press, Ithaca, N.Y.
Von Wright 1972
  Wright G. H. von: "On so Called Practical Inference", *Acta Sociologica*, 15, pp. 46–72. Reprinted in G. H. von Wright: *Practical Reason. Philosophical Papers*, Vol. I, Blackwell, Oxford 1983.
Von Wright 1976 a
  Wright G. H. von: "Determinism and the Study of Man", in Manninen and Tuomela 1976, pp. 415–35.
Von Wright 1976 b
  Wright G. H. von: "Replies", in Manninen and Tuomela 1976, pp. 371–413.
Von Wright 1980
  Wright G. H. von: *Freedom and Determination*, North-Holland Publishing Co., Amsterdam.

SIMONE GOZZANO

ACTIONS, CAUSES, AND SUPERVENIENCE

The debate between "intentionalists" and "causalists" is still open. Its main points can be summarized in questions such as: are reasons causes? Can we conceive actions as effects of mental causes? According to "intentionalists" we should reply in the negative to both questions; "causalists", on the contrary, maintain that an affirmative answer is possible. Among the first group, Georg Henrik von Wright has argued that the link between reasons and actions is logical or conceptual; in the second group, Donald Davidson has defended the possibility of conceiving reasons as causes of actions. In this paper I present a critical argument concerning the identification of actions with physical (causal) events advanced by Davidson.

According to Davidson's action theory, what there is are just events, physical events. Some of these events, moreover, can be truly described in terms of what is intentionally done by agents: these are actions. Finally, some actions can be described by pointing out the intentional states that justify why the agent did what he did: these are intentional actions. Actions and intentional actions, however, do not form distinct classes; they are separated by the possible descriptions one may offer of events. So, actions are events. Events, in turn, are identified by theirs causes and effects (Davidson 1969, p. 179). Now, since Davidson maintains that reasons *are* causes, and actions (*qua* physical movements) *are* effects, actions should consequently be individuated by reasons and actions (*qua* physical movements).

In order to individuate the causes of an action one must look at the attitudes that *rationalize* that action. In particular, the rationalising attitudes are two states: a conative state, such as a want or a desire toward a certain action, and a belief state, such as that the action to be performed is of the type desired. These two states form the *primary reason* for the action (cf. Davidson 1963). Reasons and causes, however, go under quite different analyses: while reasons are intensional, because they are offered as, as it were, "interpretative" descriptions of events, causes are extensional, given that the substitution of coreferring expressions is possible *salva veritate*. Notwithstanding this difference, Davidson maintains that it is possible to identify reasons with causes. I wish to propose an argument with the aim to criticize this conclusion. Let me start by analysing the idea that an event is individuated by its causes and its effects.

Imagine a ball rolling on a pool table: its motion may have been caused by the hit of another ball or of a cue. What is significant for the ball to be rolling at that speed and in that direction is the force with which it has been hit and from what angle. Following this consideration, one might think that the notion of cause should be limited, in this case, to force and angle of hit. The cause, then, can have multiple, and different, realisations so that once the causing event has occurred, and the resulting event has

113

R. Egidi (ed.), In Search of a New Humanism, 113–118.
©1999 *Kluwer Academic Publishers. Printed in Great Britain.*

taken place, it is not possible to tell whether the cause was the hit of another ball or of a cue. What does matter is the force impressed on the rolling ball and the angle from which it was hit. One may say that the ball and the cue constitute different causes, even if they do not generate different effects. However, one could make the point in another way.

Suppose that in the actual situation the hitting ball is white, while in a counterfactual situation it is black. Because colours do not affect in any way the causal relation under analysis, should the two possible events be identified or not? Strictly speaking, if an event is individuated by its *relevant* causes and effects, then the events should be identified; if, on the contrary, an event is individuated by *all the causes that could be relevant in one situation or another* then we have two distinct events. However, how should we select which property could have causal powers in one situation or the other? Suppose that the colour of the hitting ball is crucial for the decision regarding the legitimacy of the shot, in the sense that its perception would cause some reaction in the players. Given the sameness of causal efficacy of the two situations, would the sameness of legitimacy follow? Obviously not. As for the decision about the legitimacy, then, we would count the two situations as quite distinct events. But in so doing, the individuation of events would depend, in an unspecified way, from other, and non-physical, notions and concepts, in this particular case the rules of pool game. Other possible relevant causal factors could be the brand of the balls, or the place the balls were stored last February, and so forth. So, the decision of choosing one property over another as a possible relevant cause seems entirely *ad hoc*. Davidson offers a possible way out from this: he can point out that events and individuals are interdependent so that we identify events by their causes and effects plus, at least, a demonstrative reference to an individual object (Davidson 1969, pp. 173–174). In the case of the pool we would say *"that* ball." An event is, then, individuated by its causes and effects with respect to one or more individuals. Having clarified this point, we can now move toward the relation between causes and reasons.

Consider the following situation. The coach of the local basketball team has a pupil. During one game, the pupil is unfairly hit by an adversary player. The player's name is Smith, and he has a nephew whose name is Joseph, but the coach does not have this information. The coach wants to punish the player who has hit his pupil, so he enters the field and hits him. To describe this action we may say: the coach hit the player to punish him. Alternatively, we may say: the coach raised his right arm, and with his fist hit the face of Smith, the uncle of Joseph. Following Davidson's theory of action, what we have is just a single action: it is by raising his arm and hitting the face of Smith, the uncle of Joseph, that the coach punished him; in a way, the punishment and the hitting coincide, and the hitting is nothing but the physical movements of the coach. As for the reasons for the action, they should be found in the coach's desire to punish whoever hit his pupil and in his belief that *that* particular player hit his pupil.

Let us now analyse the relation between the event of coming to know that *that* player unfairly hit the pupil and the event of hitting the player.[1] According to an extensional analysis, the first event caused the second independently from how we describe the two events. Whether we imagine that it is possible to encompass both events under a definite covering law or whether we rely on another interpretation of causality, one event being the cause of the other should be in no way affected by the way in which we describe them.[2] The two events can be described in many different ways. For instance, we may say that the coach retaliated on behalf of his pupil by hitting the player who hit him, or that he raised his fist and hit Smith, the uncle of Joseph, on his face, and so forth. If one of all the possible descriptions is intentional, then the event can be considered as an action. In particular, an action is intentional if it is done for a reason that rationalizes the action itself.

The coach coming to believe that *that* player unfairly hit the pupil explains, and according to Davidson causes, his hitting that player. In order to have a causal analysis, however, we should identify, in one way or another, the psychological level with the physical level. The event of acquiring a certain belief could be identified, for instance, with a neural event in the coach's brain (cf. Davidson 1963, p. 17). It is this event that causes the physical movements of the coach, that is, his hitting the player. The two events, then, can be characterised in an extensional context. A certain event in the coach's brain caused the rise of the coach's fist and his directing it toward the face of the adversary player, Smith, the uncle of Joseph.

Consider now a possible counterfactual situation. In this situation everything is identical with the actual situation; the only difference is that the player who hit the coach's pupil does not have a nephew, but a niece whose name is Josephine. As in the actual case, the coach does not know the name and the family relations of the player.[3] Now, from an individualistic point of view, the two situations are physically identical: the counterfactual neural event that causes the coach's action is type-identical with the neural event of the actual situation. Analogously, the reasons that rationalize the action are the same; however, we have two different actions: one is the hitting of Smith, the uncle of Joseph, the other is the hitting of Smith, the uncle of Josephine. Both in the actual and in the counterfactual situation, the causal relation between the neural event and the physical event is type-identical. However, that relation instantiates two different actions.

The analogy between the example of the pool table and of the coach is the following: since identity of causal relation does not imply identity of legitimacy, it is then possible that identity of causal relation does not imply identity of action.[4] In particular, the case of the coach shows that it is possible to have a type-identical causal relation that is not a type-identical action. Now, since actions cannot be identified with physical events, the identity of reasons with causes, being based on the first identity, collapses as well. Hence, reasons and causes can be identified only possibly, not necessarily. This means that the identity of reasons with causes cannot be maintained as a general thesis.

Davidson is well aware that the relation between the description of an event as a physical event and its description as an action is a crucial point. In analysing a similar objection on this question, he stresses that the physical identity between certain cases is only apparent, and that it is possible that the physical events can be redefined in such a way as to pinpoint various differences (Davidson 1973, p. 252). According to

Davidson it is possible to imagine two situations in which the intentional states are the same, everything physical is the same, and yet different actions are performed. "Thus a man might intend to keep a promise by going to the opera. Yet on one occasion his going to the opera with this intention might constitute the keeping of a promise, and on another occasion not (he might have forgotten the day)." (*ibidem*). However, *forgetting* is something physical, and this fact creates a difference between the two events. In my objection to this point, however, I relied on extrinsic properties, such as "being uncle", and not on intrinsic properties, such as "keeping a promise" or "forgetting to keep a promise", against which Davidson offered his reply. In the case I have presented, then, the counter-argument by Davidson does not apply.

However, the kind of counter-example I have been using is quite peculiar. It is based on the famous Twin-like cases, and these are based on the denial of the *supervenience* relation. What my argument shows, hence, is that Davidson's thesis of the identity of reasons with causes hinges on the acceptance of the supervenience relation between action events over physical events. In fact, in the two situations, the actual and the counterfactual, there is no identity of action events, even if there is identity of physical events. The supervenience relation, in the version explicitly endorsed by Davidson, holds that two mental events cannot differ unless there is a physical difference. In this case the relation has been extended so as to encompass action events. The example of the coach, as those by Putnam 1975 or Burge 1979, violates this constraint: it shows a case of action difference *without* physical difference (where the action event does not supervene on the mental event nor on the physical event).

In order to better appreciate the situation, the notion of supervenience needs to be clarified. How should we interpret the supervenience relation in this case? In one of his first papers on this problem, Davidson makes the point that the supervenience relation holds between individual events more than between *sorts* of events. In saying so, however, he says something more: "For what needs to be stressed is that it is the *descriptions* of individual psychological events, not sorts of events, that are supervenient on physical *descriptions*" (cf. Davidson 1973, p. 253, italics mine). That descriptions of events, and not events *per se*, are the subject of the supervenient relation is quite a natural consequence of Davidson's theory. In his view, psychological events *are identical to* physical events (*ibidem*, p. 248), and since the supervenience relation is asymmetrical, if the relation were applied to events *per se* we would have the contradiction of entities that both supervene and do not supervene on themselves. Hence, the supervenience relation holds between *descriptions* of events.

In the case of the coach, the physical descriptions of the two events are identical, while some possible action description is different. In one case we may say that the coach hit the uncle of Joseph, in the other we may say that the coach hit the uncle of Josephine. The supervenience relation, then, does not apply in the case I have been presenting.

At this point, a first tentative conclusion is possible: Davidson's thesis on the identity of reasons and causes relies on the idea that the descriptions of events *as* actions supervene on the descriptions of events *as* physical events. This thesis, then, does not take into account some of the most standard externalist arguments made against mental internalism. If one is willing to accept these arguments, and to not defend supervenience, then the identity between reasons and causes should be abandoned. If, on the contrary, one adhers to supervenience, the entire point is reduced to defending the supervenience relation against these critiques. Let me analyse, then, two of the defences of the supervenience relation that have been proposed.

In order to argue in favour of the supervenience of the mental over the physical, both Fodor (1987) and Searle (1983) have tried to show that causality should be relativized to worlds. Causal powers, Fodor urges, may vary from world to world, so it is not possible to compare the causal powers of a being on this Earth with the causal powers of a being on Twin Earth. On his part, Searle says that the fixation of intentional states depends on the causal relations between the subject and the world, and these relations are *token-reflexive*, in such a way that, for instance, the belief that there is a car in front of one is *essentially* caused by the car that is in front of one. Although I am not discussing here the interpretation of supervenience that emerges from these lines of thought, I want to point out that these defences do not affect in any way the argument I am making. Even if the supervenience relation is confined to a single world, it is always possible to make the point by means of the counterfactual analysis I have been putting forth. In particular, it is always possible to say: "Had Smith not been the uncle of Joseph, but of Josephine, the coach would have hit him anyway," and this description would correlate the same physical event, taking in one of the possible physical descriptions, with a different action description.

Finally, it should be noticed that the example of the coach cannot be taken apart by pointing out that for Davidson an event is individuated by its causes and its effects with respect to an individual. In fact, in this example, the causes and the effects are the same, and so are the individuals, unless one wants to say that being the uncle of Josephine, instead of being the uncle of Joseph, would affect Smith as an individual. Endorsing such a view would indicate that the fact that one becomes an uncle implies that he changes his identity. But if by becoming an uncle one changes his identity, how can we say that somebody has become an uncle?

What should be stressed, as a general conclusion, is that the logical or conceptual link advocated by von Wright as the one through which we should interpret the relation between reasons and actions, is completely independent from the acceptance of the supervenient relation. Whether one accepts this relation or not, it is always possible to maintain that reasons and actions are conceptually or logically linked. From this perspective, the "intentionalist" position endorsed by von Wright better faces the problem of giving an account of human action and, at the same time, offers a non-dualistic analysis of the relation between mind and body. Undoubtedly, a preferable position.

Università de L'Aquila (Italy)

ACKNOWLEDGEMENTS

This paper has been written thanks to a post-doctoral fellowship issued by the Università degli Studi Roma Tre. I wish to express my gratitude to this Institution and to my supervisor, prof. Rosaria Egidi.

NOTES

[1] I am transforming the belief state that *that* player irregularly hit the trainee, into the event of coming to believe that *that* player irregularly hit the trainee; similarly for wants and all the other intentional states. On this see Davidson 1993.

[2] It should be noticed that the point I am trying to make is independent from the intensionality of causal explanation (cf. Rainone 1996, p. 93).

[3] This example is along the lines of Burge's example about arthritis (cf. Burge 1979).

[4] I am not interpreting human action, and its rationalization, as a form of social convention in analogy with the conventional rules of a pool game, even if this is a possible interpretation

BIBLIOGRAPHY

Anscombe 1957

Anscombe G. E. M.: *Intention*, Blackwell, Oxford.

Burge 1979

Burge T.: "Individualism and the Mental", *Midwest Studies in Philosophy*, Vol. IV. *Studies in Metaphysics*, University of Minnesota Press, Minneapolis, pp. 73–121.

Davidson 1963

Davidson D.: "Actions, Reasons, and Causes", *Journal of Philosophy*, 60, pp. 685–700. Reprinted in D. Davidson: *Essays on Actions and Events*, Clarendon Press, Oxford 1980.

Davidson 1969

Davidson D. : "The Individuation of Events", in N. Rescher (ed.): *Essays in Honor of Carl G. Hempel*, Reidel, Dordrecht, pp. 216–34. Reprinted in D. Davidson: *Essays on Actions and Events*, cit.

Davidson 1973

Davidson D.: "The Material Mind", in P. Suppes et al. (eds.): *Proceedings of the Fourth International Congress for Logic, Methodology and Philosophy of Science*, Vol. IV, North-Holland Publishing Co., Amsterdam, pp. 709–22 Reprinted in D. Davidson: *Essays on Actions and Events*, cit.

Davidson 1993

Davidson D.: "Reply to Ralf Stoecker", in R. Stoecker (ed.): *Reflecting Davidson*, De Gruyter, Berlin-New York, pp. 287–90.

Putnam 1975

Putnam H.: "The Meaning of 'Meaning' ", in K. Gunderson (ed.): *Language, Mind and Knowledge*, University of Minnesota Press, Minneapolis, pp. 131–93. Reprinted in H. Putnam: *Mind, Language, and Reality*, Cambridge University Press, Cambridge.

Rainone 1996

Rainone A.: *Azione, causalità e razionalità in Donald Davidson*, ETS, Pisa.

Von Wright 1971

Wright G. H. von: *Explanation and Understanding*, Routledge & Kegan Paul, London.

GUIDO FRONGIA

JUSTICE, COOPERATION, AND THE "GOLDEN RULE"

In the last chapter of his book *The Varieties of Goodness*[1] dedicated to Justice, von Wright bases his analysis on the principle that he calls "The Golden Rule". He gives two somewhat different formulations of this principle (p. 201) which it is not possible to compare here. It will be sufficient for our purpose to refer to the first of those formulations which is also the better known: "Do to others what you want them to do to you, and do not do to others what you do not want them to do to you."

Let me try to summarize, in a necessarily imprecise manner, the connections that exist in von Wright's argument between the Golden Rule and the Principle of Justice. Here is how the latter is formulated: "No man shall have his share in the greater good of a community of which he is a member without paying his due." (p. 208). For von Wright that a man is "paying his due" means that he renounces "the smaller good" that he could derive from the harm done to other members of the community. As compensation he would expect to share, for a reasonable length of time, in the "greater good" of a community in which each member pays "his due." In the structure of this argument the Golden Rule becomes a principle which is needed primarily (but not only) to distinguish both what is good and what is harmful, for oneself and for others, on the basis of a criterion of "impartiality" that consists "in treating your neighbor as though his welfare were yours and your welfare his." (p. 209).

I will restrict myself here to making a few comments about some of the presuppositions that are necessary to make sense of the Golden Rule and to make it applicable to different types of communities, characterized by different rules of cooperation.

The most obvious and direct presupposition is one to which von Wright himself calls attention. In order for the Golden Rule to function in a society it must be assumed "that one man regards as wanted and unwanted roughly the same things as those which any other man regards as wanted and unwanted respectively" (p. 201). But this presupposition, von Wright points out, is not a "logical necessity" (*ibidem*). In saying this, I think he means that given the fact that certain individuals are members of the same community, it does not necessarily follow that they desire the same things and have the same preferences.

These passages bring to light some important aspects of the ethical theory of this author. The theory does not so much presuppose an equality (or quasi equality) in the material conditions in which the members of a community which make use of the Golden Rule might find themselves living. Examples of such material conditions might be those mentioned by many of the authors in the natural right and contractarian traditions, for example, when they refer to an original state of nature: a uniform availability of goods and of resources (equally distributed), but also similar physical

119

R. Egidi (ed.), In Search of a New Humanism, 119–122.
©1999 *Kluwer Academic Publishers. Printed in Great Britain.*

strength, conditions of health, manual skills, intelligence, and adaptability among the members of the community. Although von Wright sometimes makes reference to this complex of circumstances, he does not however consider them as a necessary condition. In this respect, his view separates itself from contractarian perspective. That perspective is based on reciprocity and exchange, where the requirement of an original equality of material conditions seems at least implicitly demanded for the constitution of a community founded on norms of conduct that are not arbitrary.

Instead, for von Wright, the appeal to the Golden Rule, requires a form of original equality that is much more difficult to define from a philosophical point of view: a uniformity (or quasi uniformity) in a vast gamut of faculties connected to sensibility, emotions, desire, expectations, and so forth. The community that has the most opportunities in its search for and pursuit of a common good is that in which the exercise of these faculties is more homogenous. Because of their commitment to the Golden Rule, the fact that its members would desire roughly the same things, does not become so much a source of conflict and of disaggregation. Rather it becomes a gluing together that favors communication among the members of the community, and therefore their cooperation in the pursuit of common objects, among which is also a common good.

However, as we have seen, if the presupposition of homogeneity is necessary to the functioning of the Golden Rule, it is not guaranteed by the simple existence of a community. Its status is empirical and not logical. In fact, there are communities in which this common feeling and desiring is more conspicuous than in others; at the furthest extreme, perhaps, there are also communities in which it is very weak or downright nonexistent. And that depends on variable or historical circumstances. It seems, for example, plausible to admit that this presupposition would be most easily realized in restricted communities. For these there are more easily definable criteria for membership in social groups. The presupposition would also exist for communities that are sufficiently homogenous to permit similar forms of value transmission among their members and among different generations; where, in consequence of that, there thrive customs and attitudes of life not too differentiated. Another fundamental demand, to which many authors in the contractarian tradition have called attention, is that those communities have to be sufficiently static or at least must have a regular or homogeneous development. Indeed, communities that do not undergo changes that are too rapid and radical are more apt to promote that reciprocal trust which favors the beginning and the continuing practice of an effective exchange of services and goods among its members. This exchange will have a better chance of resulting in a give and take, balanced relationship over time.

It is interesting to observe how all these requirements are more and more rarely satisfied in our contemporary societies. In them, the boundaries (not only geographical, but above all, human) tend to become always more extensive and difficult to define. A growing and uncontrollable mobility makes the ties that unite the members of these communities more and more differentiated, changeable and weak, and makes the expectations and the desires of their members less and less homogeneous. And above all, the increasingly rapid and unpredictable changes to which our societies are subject do not seem to favor confidence and expectation in a balanced exchange of goods and services, guaranteed over time. In sum, from the definitions that von Wright gives us, it seems natural to conclude that our contemporary communities continually less conform to that model that he calls the "moral community." Such communities are those most apt to respect the Golden Rule (even if only from motives of self interest) and therefore the rights of others. In other words, our societies seem to go in a wholly opposite direction to that which would carry us toward a community in which there would be general respect for the "Principle of Justice." Although von Wright, at least in the essay I am considering here, does not engage in this kind of speculation, it seems reasonable to conclude that his investigation is marked by a substantial pessimism about the actual conditions and the future of our communities.

I wish to add, however, that his perspective does not carry with it, at least not intentionally, a defense of localism. By this term, I refer here to that extreme form of ethical relativism that maintains that a system of norms of human conduct can be defined only in reference to a specific community. This community is characterized by specific bonds that unite its members, and consequently, by particular forms of cooperation that are possible and imaginable in it. One of the inevitable consequences (often undesired) of such localism is that the rules of conduct defined with reference to a given community cannot be exported (at least in principle) to other communities, not even those "sufficiently" similar. Systems of rules applied in different communities then become incommensurable.

Certainly, as has been seen, von Wright seems to regard the homogeneity of the communities as a property that might help their entrance into the realm of morality. However he is not locked into this point of view, but also forsees a way out of localism. In fact, he does not believe that there is only one possible form of morality, having an "heteronomous" origin, aimed at the maximization of one's own interest. On the contrary, mindful of Kantian teachings, he does not exclude the possibility that human choices could also derive (at least in some cases) from "moral motives," that is, from a "disinterested and impartial will to justice," which expresses itself in an "autonomous other-regarding duty" (p. 209). This possibility is in accord with that of the conceivability of an action guided by the Kantian norm that impels us "to treat our fellow humans as ends in themselves" (p. 211). And it is precisely this possibility that allows for a substantial enlargement of the boundaries of the idea of a community and, at least tendentially, its identification with the whole of humanity. Von Wright shows, in sum, his willingness not to exclude, at least in principle, that cosmopolitan view of morality that Kant has developed, first in his writings on the philosophy of the history of the decade of the 80's, and then, in a more systematic manner, in his much later work *On Perpetual Peace*.[2]

Certainly, differing from Kant, von Wright does not seem to believe that there are reasons in terms of which human beings ought to act solely following "moral motives," instead of their own interests, and those of their own communities. Therefore, there cannot be an argument that, in Kantian terms, could in itself induce action from a disinterested respect for moral norms. An appeal to a moral duty could be more efficacious for the purpose of inducing someone to conform his behavior to the Principle of Justice. And a "moral duty", unlike a "moral motive", is, according to the definition of von Wright, essentially heteronomous, *i.e.*, derived from considerations of interest.

As can be seen, the two paradigms of morality allowed by von Wright are not necessarily incompatible. This is openly recognized in the closing paragraph of his book: "we can make up a picture of society, in which justice and morality are kept going – even perfectly – through mere self-interest." (p. 209). And this choice of a double paradigm of norms of conduct offers him an undeniable advantage with respect to other contemporary ethical theories that have recourse to a form of "utilitarian justification" of morality (pp. 214–15). Indeed, von Wright's ethics allows for the theoretical possibility that if one starts from motives of interest one can arrive, even in the absence of heteronomous motivations, at the discovery of a cosmopolitan perspective of justice, no longer restricted to the interests of a specific community.

Università di Roma "Tor Vergata" (Italy)

NOTES

[1] Thoemmes Press, Bristol 1996 (Routledge & Kegan Paul, London 1963[1]).
[2] *Zum ewigen Frieden* (1795), in Kants Werke, Akademie-Textausgabe, Band VIII, W. de Gruyter, Berlin 1968.

MARIO DE CARO

VON WRIGHT ON THE MIND-BODY PROBLEM*

Materialism is the asymptote of psychology
G. Ch. Lichtenberg, *Aphorismen*

I. Looking at the development of Professor von Wright's philosophy, one could be surprised by the fact that, until very recently, he didn't appear interested in the mind-body problem. In his "Intellectual Autobiography", written in 1972–73, for example, von Wright writes – referring to his youthful interest in the mind-body problem and the other fundamental metaphysical questions about the nature of reality – that "strangely enough, this is an aerea in which, as an active philosopher I have (so far) done no work at all".[1]

It is not, of course, that every philosopher – not even one of the most influential analytical philosophers of the second half of the century – *must* be interested in this problem. The point instead is that very easily one could think that some of von Wright's theses in the theory of action and in the theory of explanation have important consequences with regard to the mind-body problem – at least if we take it in the following formulation: "What is the relation between our intentional attitudes and the physiological causes of our thinking and behaving?".

Von Wright's theses that, in my opinion, are relevant for the mind-body problem are his idea that the notion of cause itself is conceptually founded on the notion of action, and his view about the irreducibility of intentional explanations to the kind of explanations typical of the natural sciences (von Wright 1971, 1973). In any case, to understand the reason for which von Wright ignored that venerable question for such a long period, it is sufficient to consider what he eventually wrote about it: in the preface to the Italian translation of his *Freedom and Determinism* (von Wright 1984, p. 24), for example, he explicitly stated that the mind-body problem is a pseudo-problem. I would guess Professor von Wright still thinks this way.

II. Let's consider the argument that von Wright (1988 and 1994) recently proposed to prove that the celebrated mind-body problem is not a problem at all. His perspective is the one of the philosophy of action. We can think of acting as a three-levels process. First, there is the intentional level: the one according to which an agent acts *for a reason*. Secondly, there is the bodily level: the body's observable movements corresponding to actions. Thirdly, there is the correlated chain of events in the agent's neural system. What are the conceptual links between these levels?

The third level, the neural one, is still largely hypothetical, but there is no reason to think it will not one day be known in great detail. Many contemporary philosophers of mind think that the parallelism between the neural level and the intentional level is

R. Egidi (ed.), In Search of a New Humanism, 123–130.
©1999 *Kluwer Academic Publishers. Printed in Great Britain.*

philosophically fundamental, and to explain it they often resort to the so-called «mind-brain identity theories». On the contrary, according to von Wright the idea that *this* kind of parallelism is philosophically relevant depends just on a (very common) reductionist illusion.

First of all, there are the well-known arguments against the identity theories (it seems that there are not really acceptable criteria of identity between neural and intentional events, for example about their localizations).[2] Moreover, according to von Wright 1988, neurological observations and theories are not relevant for *our* system of psychological concepts. The intentional vocabulary is autonomous from (and cannot be reduced to) the physical vocabulary, and the intentional explanations cannot be replaced by those of natural sciences: a thesis on which von Wright has been dwelling for many years, and particularly in his influential *Explanation and Understanding* (von Wright 1971). What the neural bases of the mental are is just a *contingent* fact – extremely interesting from a scientific point of view, but philosophically irrelevant. Moreover to state that a specific neural phenomenon is the correlate of a certain mental phenomenon we need to have *already* identified that mental phenomenon: for this reason von Wright says that the mental has an *epistemic* priority over the neural.[3]

What can be said, however, is that the neural phenomena have *causal* priority over the behavioral phenomena on the basis of which we attribute intentional attitudes to the people: «the behavioural reactions which are the criteria of the mental are caused by things which happen in the neural system of the bodies under investigation» (von Wright 1994, p. 109). But it should be emphasized that, according to von Wright, the neural has *causal* priority over the behavioral only *as long as the latter is conceived as a physical phenomenon*. In *this* case, science – and only science – can explain that phenomenon, and its causal relationship with other phenomena:

[S]cience investigates facts about the material (physical) world and their causal interrelations. In the nexus of these facts and their connections the mental has no place. No "ghost in the machine" must be allowed to disturb the scientist's intellectual peace of the mind (von Wright 1994, p. 109).

III. Therefore, in principle, a causal explanations of actions can be given by science – but not by philosophy – at the neural level. On the contrary, the other two levels of explanations of actions (the intentional level and the level of bodily movements) are philosophically relevant. Von Wright thinks that these two levels of explanations have – as their respective *explananda* – two parallel "mechanisms" that go on when we act: the motivational mechanism of the action and the causal mechanism of the corresponding bodily movements. And *this* is a kind of philosophically relevant *parallelism* (whereas the neural-mental parallelism is not). The point, however, is that according to von Wright this parallelism is not problematic at all.

Let's imagine a person that hears a knock on the door and goes to open it: according to von Wright the motivational mechanism of his/her action and the causal mechanism of his/her bodily movements in executing it are both activated by *the same* event in the world. The same happens at the other end: «The agent's proceeding to opening the door would not be an action unless his body went through the appropriate movements» (von Wright 1988, p. 287).

The action and the bodily movements cannot collide, since they are two aspects of the same event in the world. The action is nothing more that *«the bodily movement viewed* (conceived, understood) *under the aspect of intentionality»* (von Wright 1994, p. 107; italics in the original). Between these two levels there is a *conceptual,* logically necessary connection – not an empirical, contingent one. Also, according to von Wright, since our attributions of mental attitudes to the people depend on behavioral criteria, there is a *semantic* priority of the behavioral over the mental.[4]

When we look at someone's behavior from the intentional point of view (that is, when we look at an *action*) we might explain *why* an agent did what he/she did, giving *the reasons* (beliefs, desires, intentions) for which that agent did that action. No physiological explanations can do perform this task, since what we are looking for at this level is just a *semantical* connection (not a *causal* one) between a reason and an action. But, on the other hand, according to von Wright, *no reason can cause the bodily movements*: they can be caused only by some prior physiological events.[5]

Summarizing: every time we act, two parallel chains go on. The first chain concerns only physical events (physiological phenomena and bodily movements): the links of this chain are causal in character. The other chain concerns mental events (reasons and intentional actions): the elements of this chain are connected only by semantic links. Nothing causal can affect the mental; no intentionality can intrude into the physical.

IV. From an ontological point of view von Wright is a monist (a physicalist or materialist monist), and for this reason he rejects interactionism.[6] But as regards the mental – we have just seen – he is not a reductionist at all (we could say he is a conceptual dualist or a dualist in relation to properties):

I agree with behaviourism, epiphenomenalism, and various form of materialism in rejecting the idea of mind-body *interactionism* as contrary to a scientific picture of the world.[7] I differ from behaviourism and materialism in that I cannot accept an *identification* of the mental with states of affairs in the material world. But at the same time I have a certain sympathy with this monistic view of the stuff that the world is made of (von Wright 1994, p. 109).

In this passage one thing should be noticed. Von Wright clearly states he agrees with «behaviourism, epiphenomenalism, and various forms of materialism» in sharply refusing interactionism; but immediately after he mentions the reasons for which he *does not* agree with behaviourism and materialism. What about epiphenomenalism, then? Should we think that von Wright is an epiphenomenalist?

I think we should. As we have seen above, von Wright explicitly states that a reason cannot cause any physical event. Still, something more should be said about this point. Let's read what else von Wright says about his own conception of the mind:

From the history of philosophy is known a position called epiphenomenalism. It regards consciousness (the mental) as a kind of "by-product" of underlying neural phenomena, as a world standing apart firm the physical world and neither having an influence on nor being influenced by it. My position has *some* resemblance with this. *Only I would reject the quasi-causalist idea of the mental as something "supervenient" on the material.* (von Wright 1994, p. 109; the latter italics are mine).

What von Wright is saying here is that he *would* consider himself an epiphenomenalist, *if it were not* for the "supervenience thesis".[8] Actually *de facto* the idea that the mental is not causally efficacious has been frequently associated with the supervenience thesis, and this association is surely important to understand the genesis of this conception;[9] still in my opinion the supervenience thesis is *not* an *essential* part of the definition of epiphenomenalism. There is *no conceptually necessary link* between epiphenomenalism and supervenience (I am pretty confident Professor von Wright would accept this). And, what is more important, often epiphenomenalism is defined without any reference to the supervenience thesis. So, for instance, according to Broad (1924, p. 472), epiphenomenalism may be defined in *two* ways. The first definition is the one, refused by von Wright, in which the causal inefficacy of the mental is connected with its supervenience on the physical. According to this definition,

certain events which have physiological characteristics have *also* mental characteristics, and that no events which lack physiological characteristics have mental characteristics. [...] And that an event that has mental characteristics never causes another event in virtue of its mental characteristics, but only in virtue of its physiological characteristics.

But there is also a second sense in which, according to Broad, epiphenomenalism can be defined. This second definition says that

no event has both mental and physiological characteristics; but that the complete cause of any event which has mental characteristics is an event or set of events which has physiological characteristics. And that no event which has mental characteristics is a cause-factor in the causation of any other event whatsoever, whether mental or physical.

In my opinion, von Wright's conception of mind fits perfectly with this definition. But if one is not convinced yet, he/she should consider this vivid illustration of the epiphenomenalist conception of the mind offered by Jaegwon Kim:

Think of a moving car and the series of *shadows* it casts as it moves: The shadows are caused by the moving car but have no effect on the car's motion. [...] The apparent regularities that we observe in mental events, the epiphenomenalist will argue, do not represent genuine causal connections; like the regularities of characterizing the moving shadows of a car or the successive symptoms of a disease, they are merely reflections of the real causal processes at a more fundamental level (Kim 1996, p. 129; italics are mine).

And now compare the last passage with this quotation from von Wright:

We have two sets of events in the world of space and time, and between them causal relationships. We also have, like a "*shadow*" accompanying the first set of events, a sequence of mental states and processes, semantically connected with it. In the picture of natural connections this set of mental phenomena plays no rôle (von Wright 1994, p. 109; italics are mine).[10]

Unhesitatingly von Wright uses the metaphor of the mental as a shadow: just the same metaphor used by Kim (and not just by him) in characterizing the epiphenomenalist conception! So, if this is the way in which the word "epiphenomenalism" is currently used in the philosophical debate, I think it should not be doubted that von Wright's conception is epiphenomenalistic.

But, to be fair with von Wright, something important has still to be said about this. As a matter of fact, to say nowadays that a certain conception of the mind is epiphenomenalistic it is not just a neutral way of *describing* or *explaining* that conception: it is a way of *attacking* it. The word "epiphenomenalism" is not normally intended to express *only* the thesis that reasons cannot be genuine causes; it is intended to say something more, something that makes this word a sort of philosophical insult. This «something more» depends on the scientistic dogma according to which the only legitimate explanations of a phenomenon can be offered by the sciences – the *natural* sciences. From this point of view, to hold – as von Wright holds – that the intentional concepts cannot be *reduced* to the concepts of the natural sciences *and* that they cannot be a part of the causal structure of the physical world is the same as to say that mental properties have no value at all, that they are just appearances or illusions. From *this* point of view, then, the charge of epiphenomenalism would be a really defamatory one.[11]

But we have to remember that von Wright does not share these scientistic assumptions. It is true, according to him, that reasons cannot be causes of physical events; but this *does not mean* that reasons have no value at all or that they are just illusions. According to von Wright, even if there is no ontological difference between the mental and the physical, they represent two different, but both indispensable, ways of looking at human beings:

[o]ne consists in relating overt behavioural reactions to intra-bodily causes and effects. The other consists in understanding what these reactions *mean*. The second way is characteristic of the study we call *psychology* (von Wright 1994, p. 110).

Therefore to say that von Wright's conception is a kind of epiphenomenalism is, on the one hand, tautological (he *explicitly* says that reasons cannot be causes of bodily movements). On the other hand, if this is intended to be a *charge* it misses the target, since for von Wright this is not a problem at all.

There is an important philosophical lesson in this story, I think. With coherence and courage, von Wright has recognized and accepted all the consequences that derive from the conjunction of two sets of widely held theses (even if some of these consequences, such as epiphenomenalism, can appear unpleasant to many). On one side von Wright shares many assumptions of physicalism (ontological monism; the idea that there is some kind of neurological correspondent of every mental event; the thesis that only physical properties can be involved in causation); on the other side, he refuses the reductionism and the eliminativism about the mental. Philosophers who do not like reductionism or eliminativism, but do not like von Wright's conclusions either (including epiphenomenalism) should, I think, give up some of the above mentioned physicalistic assumptions. This, however, would be equivalent to stepping beyond physicalism, a step that many people today may not be willing to take.

Some decades ago, however, a philosopher that Professor von Wright knows well – perhaps better than anyone – thought differently:

I saw this man many years ago: now I have seen him again, I recognize him, I remember his name. And why does there have to be a cause of this remembering in my nervous system? Why something or other, whatever it may be, be stored up there in any form? Why must a trace been left behind? Why should there not be a psychological regularity to which no physiological regularity corresponds? If this upsets our concept of causality then it is time it was upset. (Wittgenstein 1967, § 610).

Università de L'Aquila (Italy)

NOTES

* I am very grateful to Professor Rosaria Egidi, Professor Hilary Putnam and Professor G. H. von Wright who made very useful comments on a previous version of this paper.
This paper was written in the summer of 1998, while the author was benefiting from a Fulbright Fellowship, and from a Fellowship awarded by the Department of Philosophy of the University of Roma Tre.
[1] Cf. von Wright 1989, p. 5.

[2] As regards the relation that supposedly every mental state (for instance, a sensation of hearing) has with a brainstate, von Wright 1994, p. 105 wrote: «A brainstate exists in *space*. It is, in principle, open to inspection from "outside". A physiologist can register it on instruments. But the sensation, we think, is not "in space". So what the physiologist registers cannot be the sensation itself, only its accompaniment or correspondence in the brain. The *sensation* is registered only by the hearing subject. The subject, and the subject only, has it; it his/her "private property", hidden in the "mind" like a safe which is inaccessible to inspection by an outsider. Therefore it is absurd to identify the sensation with a bodily, material state». Probably some readers will not be satisfied with the "Cartesian" tone of this argument, evident in the picture of the mind like a "private theatre". At any rate, against the (types or tokens) identity theses also other, more philosophically neutral, arguments have been proposed: see, for example, Putnam 1994, p. 482 ff.

[3] It is interesting to notice that according to von Wright 1994, p. 104, the "something" in the brain that is *causally* responsible for a motoric reaction of the body is not necessarily a definite *region* of the brain: it could even be that it is the "total state" of the brain to be relevant (in any case this is just a matter of scientific, not philosophical, interest).

[4] This does not mean that von Wright accepts logical behaviorism: according to him, no finite combination of criteria for a certain mental phenomenon is either a (logically) *sufficient* or *necessary* condition for the presence of that mental phenomenon (von Wright 1994, p. 109).

[5] «The intentionality resides in the fact that the subject can, if challenged, account for the movement in the terms of some reason or reasons why she performed it. [...] This fact is responsible, I think, for the intuitive idea that in action something mental (traditionally referred as the "will") is a cause of some movements of the body. But this is a mistake. One call the reasons of an action the causes of the action. This is innocuous talk. But it does not make the reasons cause of the bodily movement. Its cause is *neural*» (von Wright 1994, p. 107).

[6] *Interactionism* is the thesis according to which the mental and physical are ontologically distinct, but still they can interact (Descartes, for example, was an interactionist).

[7] *Epiphenomenalism* states the mental events cannot have any mental efficacy. I will discuss this notion at length in a moment.

[8] The mind-body supervenience thesis (as it is presented in Kim 1996, p. 10) states that «[t]he mental supervenes on the physical in that any two things (objects, events, organisms, persons etc.) exactly alike in all physical properties cannot differ in respect of mental properties. That is physical indiscernibility entails psychological indiscernibility».

[9] This happened, for example, with T. H. Huxley 1901, ch. 5, who was the first defender of epiphenomenalism: he actually thought that mental events are effects of physiological processes going on in the nervous system. Nowadays Donald Davidson's influential *anomalous monism* (Davidson 1970) is often thought to be a form of epiphenomenalism (Kim 1992; Sosa 1992), even if Davidson 1992 himself strongly refuses this definition. At any rate Davidson was the first to introduce the notion of "supervenience of the mental on the physiological": so it is probable that von Wright is thinking about Davidson when he says he could accept epiphenomenalism if it were not for the supervenience thesis. Finally has to be noticed that Davidson, because of his adherence to semantic externalism (1988, 1990), has partially modified his view (cf. De Caro 1999).

[10] Actually in von Wright's conception, the "shadowy" character of the mental is even more evident that in other epiphenomenalistic views: for him it is not just that the mental events cannot cause physical events (as Huxley, for example thought); *they cannot not even be caused* by any physical events. At any rate,

some critics (for instance Kim 1992) think that also Davidson's anomalous monism presents this feature, since it does not leave to the mental *any* causal role (either active or passive).
[11] For example, Kim 1996, p. 129 ff. writes, in discussing Alexander 1920: «if epiphenomenalism is true, mentality has no work to do and hence is entirely useless, and this renders it pointless to recognize it as something real. Our beliefs and desires would have no role in causing our decisions and actions and would be powerless to explain them; our perception and knowledge would have nothing to do with our artistic creations and technological inventions. *Being real and having causal powers go hand in hand; to deprive mental of causal potency is in effect to deprive it of its reality*» (italics are in the original).

BIBLIOGRAPHY

Alexander 1920
    Alexander S.: *Space, Time, and Deity*, Macmillan, London.
Broad 1925
    Broad Ch. D.: *The Mind and Its Place in Nature*, Routledge & Kegan Paul, London.
Davidson 1967
    Davidson D.: "Causal Relations", *The Journal of Philosophy*, 64, pp. 691–703 . Reprinted in Davidson 1980 a, pp. 149–62.
Davidson 1980
    Davidson D.: "Mental Events", in L. Foster and J. W. Swanson (eds.): *Experience and Theory*, University of Massachussetts Press, Amherts, pp. 79–101. Reprinted in Davidson 1980 a, pp. 207–27.
Davidson 1980 a
    Davidson D.: *Essays on Actions and Events*, Clarendon Press, Oxford.
Davidson 1988
    Davidson D.: "The Myth of the Subjective", in M. Benedikt and R. Burger (eds.): *Bewußtsein, Sprache und die Kunst*, Verlag der österreichischen Staatsdruckerei, Wien, pp. 45–54.
Davidson 1991
    Davidson D.: "Epistemology Externalized", *Dialectica*, 45, 1991, pp. 191–202.
Davidson 1992
    Davidson D.: "Thinking Causes", in Heil and Mele 1992, pp. 3–17.
De Caro 1999
    De Caro M. (ed.): *Interpretations and Causes. New Pespectives on Donald Davidson's Philosophy*, Kluwer, Dordrecht.
Egidi 1998
    Egidi R.: "Grounds for Acting, Grounds for Knowing", in Meggle 1999, pp. 55–63.
Gjelsvik 1996
    Gjelsvik O.: "Von Wright on Mind and Matter", in Meggle 1999, pp. 65–78.
Heil and Mele 1992
    Heil J. and Mele A. (eds.): *Mental Causation*, Clarendon Press, Oxford.
Huxley 1901
    Huxley T. H.: *Methods and Results: Essays*, Appleton, New York.
Kim 1989
    Kim J.: "The Myth of Nonreductive Materialism", *Proceedings and Addresses of the American Philosophical Association*, 63, pp. 31–47. Reprinted in Kim 1993, pp. 265–84.
Kim 1992
    Kim J.: "Can Supervenience and «Non-Strict Laws» Save Anomalous Monism?", in Heil and Mele 1992, pp. 19–26.
Kim 1993
    Kim J.: *Supervenience and Mind*, Cambridge University Press, Cambridge.
Kim 1996
    Kim J.: *Philosophy of Mind*, Westview Press, Boulder.

McLaughlin 1994

McLaughlin B.: "Epiphenomenalism", in S. Guttenplan (ed.): *A Companion to the Philosophy of Mind*, Blackwell, Oxford, pp. 277–88.

Meggle 1999

Meggle G. (ed.): *Actions, Norms, Values: Discussions with G. H. von Wright*, W. de Gruyter, Berlin.

Putnam 1994

Putnam H.: "Sense, Nonsense, and the Senses: An Inquiry into the Powers of the Human Mind", *Journal of Philosophy*, 91, pp. 445–517.

Schilpp and Hahn 1989

Schilpp. P. A. and Hahn L. E.: *The Philosophy of George Henrik von Wright*, Open Court, La Salle, Ill.

Sosa 1992

Sosa E.: "Davidson's Thinking Causes, in Heil and Mele 1992, pp. 41–50.

Von Wright 1971

Von Wright G. H.: *Explanation and Understanding*, Routledge & Kegan Paul, London.

Von Wright 1973

Von Wright G. H.: *Causality and Determinism*, Columbia University Press, New York.

Von Wright 1984

Von Wright G. H.: Preface to *Libertà e determinazione*, Pratiche Editrice, Padova (Italian translation, by R. Simili, of *Freedom and Determination*, Acta Philosophica Fennica, Vol. 31, North-Holland Publishing Co., Amsterdam 1980.

Von Wright 1988

Von Wright G. H.: "An Essay on Door-Knocking", *Rechtstheorie*, 19, pp. 275–88. Reprinted in von Wright 1998.

Von Wright 1989.

Von Wright G. H.: "Intellectual Autobiography", in Schilpp and Hahn 1989, pp. 1–55.

Von Wright 1994

Von Wright G. H.: "On Mind and Matter", *Journal of Theoretical Biology*, 171, pp. 101–10. Reprinted in von Wright 1998.

Von Wright 1998

Von Wright G. H.: *In the Shadow of Descartes: Essays in the Philosophy of Mind*, Kluwer, Dordrecht.

Wittgenstein 1967

Wittgenstein L.: *Zettel*, ed. by G. E. M. Anscombe and G. H. von Wright, Blackwell, Oxford.

MAURO DORATO

THE CONFLICT BETWEEN THE STATIC AND THE DYNAMIC THEORY OF TIME IN ITS RELATION TO VON WRIGHT'S WORK AND TO HUMAN FREEDOM

1. TIME, CHANGE, CAUSATION AND FREEDOM

Von Wright's work has been characterized by an intense interest in the logic and the philosophy of time, dating back to his famous articles in the mid-sixties, "And Next" (1965), "And Then" (1966) and "Always" (1968), and to a paper that has been widely discussed in Italy, namely "Time, Change and Contradiction" (1969), which seemed to suggest the possibility of a formalization of dialectic logic in a moment in which Marxism held a strong grip on many Italian intellectuals. I think it is safe to assume that von Wright's interest in temporal logic was spurred both by his interest in modal logic – temporal and modal concepts have strong structural analogies and can be given a similar semantics – and by his concern for a theory of human action which could make room for a genuine notion of change and for our freedom (1980).

In what follows, I will discuss the view according to which the notion of change needed for free actions presupposes the human capacity of shaping and influencing the future, a future which then must be regarded as "open". "Open" here does not refer to some form of indeterminism, but simply means "(ontologically) unreal with respect to the past". Consequently, according to the view to be discussed – also known as the "dynamic theory of time" – *change is given by the becoming real in the present (alternatively, at time t) of previously unreal facts or events*. In one (*tenseless*) version of this theory, change can occur if and only if, for any time *t*, events or tenselessly conceived facts occurring *after t* are unreal, while events or facts *before t* (or simultaneous with *t*) are real (Broad 1923; Tooley 1997). In another (*tensed*) version, it is the absolute property of *presentness*, objectively and mind-independently possessed by facts or events, which separates a real past from an unreal future (Smith 1993). Such an ever-changing, monadic attribute of "being present" is allegedly possessed by all events successively, and the resulting ontological change is mirrored by the continuous shift in the truth-values of tensed sentences, a shift that has also been emphasized by von Wright's dynamic conception of truth and falsity (Simili 1984, p. 7). In both versions of the dynamic theory of time, the history of the universe is separated into a part which is already definite and one which isn't, and this condition is regarded as necessary for human freedom.

Having always been aware of the empirical component of the concept of time (von Wright 1969), von Wright would probably be sympathetic with the attempt at finding out whether such a theory of change is compatible with what we know about physical time. This task appears particularly pressing, because it is often said that the time of physics mandates an opposite, *static* theory of time, in which the future is as

R. Egidi (ed.), In Search of a New Humanism, 131–138.
©1999 *Kluwer Academic Publishers. Printed in Great Britain.*

real as the past, and the difference between past and future is merely mind-dependent. In such a temporally symmetric view, there is no *ontological* change from future, to present, to past, because they are all equally real. In the static theory of time, change amounts to difference of properties instantiated by an entity X at different instants of time: X changes if and only if it exemplifies two incompatible properties at two different instants of time.[1]

There is one neglected consequence of the static view of time on our understanding of causation that is highly relevant for our freedom: from the temporal viewpoint of a present cause, its future effect is real in the same sense in which we normally regard a past cause as determinate from the viewpoint of its present effect. Can we justify our capacity of influencing the future within a theory in which the future event which will occur as a consequence of our action is as definite as anything that occurred in the past? How could we "bring about" or "produce" a future event *via* our action if the causal relation is such that the "bringing about" or "producing" cannot have any ontological significance?

With the hope of offering a new standpoint from which the unity of von Wright's multifarious interests in the philosophy and logic of time and action could be better appreciated, in this paper I will try to establish whether the requirement of an open future is (i) compatible with the features of physical time and (ii) presupposed by a theory of human action that, like von Wright's, wants to make room for free will. With respect to these two issues, I will claim that, despite some arguments to the contrary, spacetime physics favors the static theory of time, and thereby forces us to regard the future as real as the past (i). However, I will also show that such a symmetric view of time does not jeopardize our ability to freely shape the future (ii). By relying on some previous works of mine, I will simply sketch the main argument for (i),[2] and give more emphasis to (ii), to be discussed in a framework which defends von Wright's "semi-compatibilist" stance (von Wright 1980). While the question of the compatibility of free will with determinism is one of the classic problems of metaphysics, the question whether a real, open future is necessary to our freedom has received less attention, at least within the context of the recent philosophy of time.

2. STATIC AND DYNAMIC THEORIES OF TIME AND THE TIME OF PHYSICS

As a matter of fact, if we are trying to establish whether a "temporally dynamic world" is compatible with physics, we have at our disposal some sophisticated and precise analysis provided by the analytic philosophy of time of our century. Such a philosophy can be correctly characterized as a battle-field divided into two camps, the so-called A and B theorists of time, who defend a *dynamic* and a *static* conception of the world respectively. The division between such two schools is usually represented as a division over the question whether the *tensed* distinction of "past", "present" and "future" is more fundamental than the *tenseless* relations of "before" and "after". "More fundamental" is, in its turn, usually interpreted as meaning "having truth conditions in terms of", so that the tensed theorist typically maintains that tensed sentences[3] have *tensed* truth conditions, while the tenseless theorist claims that tensed sentences have *tenseless* truth conditions.

Thanks to fundamental studies about the role of indexicals in ordinary language, nobody these days believes what the old tenseless theorist once took for granted, namely that each tensed sentence can be *translated* into a tenseless sentence without loss of meaning. If T stands for the tensed sentence "it is now 3:00 p.m." and S stands for the tenseless sentence: "the utterance T is simultaneous with the clock time 3:00 p.m.', obviously S does *not* mean the same as T. *The latter is true only at 3:00 p.m., and can therefore be used to give information about what time it is, while the former is always true if it ever true, and therefore cannot be used for the same purpose.* Since two sentences that don't have the same use cannot have the same meaning, T cannot be translated into S. This conclusion, however, is compatible with the tenseless theorist's claim that S can completely specify the conditions under which T is true.[4] For the tensed theorist instead, the truth conditions of sentences like T can only be given by using a tensed sentence.

Be that as it may, this conflict about the nature of the truth conditions of tensed sentence does not seem to be able to resolve the fundamental question about the nature of change that was broached before: do we live in a dynamic world in which the future is unreal, or should we consider the future as real as the past? As Tooley (1997) has recently pointed out, even if we were to establish that every tensed sentence has tenseless truth conditions, so that the tenseless facts are the only existing facts, we wouldn't have solved the problem whether the sum total of the tenseless facts varies (grows) from moment to moment, or whether tenseless facts are time-independent. As said above, the dynamic theorist thinks that the world and the truths literally "grow" by addition of facts, while the static theorist denies just this point.

In other words – even granting that the tensed properties of events (past, present and future) are mind-dependent, and that the only facts that we need to make tensed sentences true are *tenseless facts given by tenseless truth conditions* – it still remains open whether for any time t, facts *after t* are real or not. The only version of a theory of objective becoming that would be eliminated by accepting the thesis that all tensed sentences have tenseless truth conditions, is the *tensed* version. The tenseless version, with its related notion of change, would be left untouched, ready to be confronted with an "empirical test" coming from physical theories.[5]

If these semantic discussions do not seem decisive, and we want to face such a confrontation with physics, let us grant the static theorist that tenseless facts suffice to give the truth conditions of tensed sentence. In this respect, the elimination of the *tensed* version of change and becoming also seems in tune with the well-known argument by Grünbaum (1973) according to which physics does not need the notion of a flowing present moment, despite its momentous importance in the time of our conscious experience. Likewise, the asymmetry introduced by the flow of time does not seem to be reflected by the time reversal invariance of all fundamental physical laws.[6]

However, one immediate obstacle for the compatibility of *tenseless* becoming with physics would seem the relativity of simultaneity, a major conceptual consequence of the special theory of relativity. If the separation between the region of definiteness and the region of indefiniteness has to be *objective*, it must *independent* of the state of motion of the various inertial observers. But Einstein has taught us that any *global* separation of spacetime events induced by a surface of simultaneity depends on a particular choice of an inertial system. Different inertial frames will give us different global separations of real events (future) from unreal (past) ones: if event E can be *unreal* for us if it is in our future, but (relatively) past and therefore *real* for another inertial observer, one should conclude that all events in spacetime are real (Putnam 1967).

One way to overcome this difficulty is to relativize what is real to spacetime points rather than to inertial frames, by imposing a criterion of invariance for a primitive, binary relation of "being real with respect to". In this way, for any point p in Minkowski spacetime, all and only the events in the absolute past of p come out as real (i.e., those that are a possible cause of p), while all the other events would turn out to be unreal, including those that are simultaneous with p. This strategy of relativization of realities also seems relevant to von Wright's technical work in temporal logic, since for instance his temporal conjunction "and then" – or "and next" in the case of discrete time – can be regarded as a tenseless, binary relation of partial order R linking together two events or two elementary states of affairs happening at a certain time. One can then ask whether one can define such a relation "and then" in a special relativist setting, that is, whether a reflexive and transitive temporal relation "and then" can be defined in terms of the structure of Minkowski spacetime, and more specifically in terms of the relation of past causal connectibility C (this means that a is a possible past cause of b if and only if aCb).

By using a perfect formal analogy between "and then" and "being real as of" as defined by Stein (1991), one can prove that a is a past cause of b if and only if a is real with respect to b, if and only if a *and then* b holds.[7] In other, simpler words, one can prove that we can have a dynamic notion of causation also in Minkowski spacetime, provided one relativizes what is real to spacetime points, and drops the requirement of the objectivity of a world-wide present: what qualifies as now is not spatially extended, but is reduced to a point: "here" and "now" coincide. In this way, not only does one lay the foundations for a relativistic tense logic for the temporal relation "and then", but also proves that the requirement of an open future, that is deemed necessary for our free action, is compatible with the special theory of relativity.

Unfortunately, there are at least two difficulties for such an implementation of the dynamic view of time in Minkowski spacetime: (1) justifying an asymmetry for the causal relation – the relation of causal connectibility must only be future-directed and not past-directed – required by the asymmetry of von Wright's relation "and then"; (2) adjusting the reciprocal unreality of events in the same surface of simultaneity – a necessary consequence of objective becoming if one accept the hypotheses of Stein's theorem – with the outcome dependence of spacelike-separated measurement results as a result of the violation of Bell's inequalities in quantum field theory.

Here I will take for granted that both (1) and (2) make Stein's result look rather implausible, and that we should conclude that given the requirements of physical time, we should regard the future as real as the past.[8] Let it suffice to say that even if quantum non-locality did not involve some form of direct causation between the two measurement results, the possibility of one state being a partial cause of the other implies their reciprocal reality for any spacelike-separated events, a result which is incompatible with Stein's assumptions about objective becoming in special relativity, requiring that any two events in space be reciprocally unreal.

3. ONTOLOGICAL SYMMETRY OF PAST AND FUTURE AND HUMAN FREEDOM

Says von Wright in the *Logic of Action* (1967, p. 121) that "to act means to intentionally (willingly) provoke or prevent a change in the world (in nature)". Is it really necessary to assume that for our action to make sense, the future cannot be real as the past? If for reason of compatibility with physical theories, we must adopt the static theory of time, can we find a way to reconcile our intuition of being able to causally influence or change the future with a view of the causal relation in which the two *relata* are real, one from the temporal perspective of the other? In order to begin answering these questions, it is essential to clarify the meaning of "real future" or "real past", and the meaning of "provoking" or "preventing" a change in the future.

In one sense, we say that the past or the future is real, because any past – or future – tense proposition is definitively true or false now, in the present moment. Accepting bivalence about non-present-tense propositions commits us to say that also what is temporally non-present is real: that is, past and future events are now definitely real, even though we can know nothing about them.

This realistic position about the definiteness of truth value for future and past-tense propositions, obtained by separating truth from warranted assertibility, does not yet capture the whole story about what we intuitively take to be the essential difference between past and future events. Since this difference seems to concern our action, perhaps a better rendering of the intuitive sense in which the past is real but the future isn't is that we believe that *the past is unchangeable* and the *future*, at least in part, *depends on us and can be changed*. By acting or refusing to act, we make a difference in the future course of events. If physics requires us to abandon this intuitive difference between an immutable past and an open future, shouldn't we say that we must find a domain of reality which is totally independent from physics? Shouldn't we admit some kind of dualism to make room for our capacity to alter the future?

Luckily for those of us who are monists, this dualistic step does not seem necessary. There is a perfectly reasonable sense in which we are entitled to say that we can causally influence the future, even though, on closer analysis, *the future turns out to be as unchangeable as the past*. In this sense, one can restore the perfect ontological symmetry between past and future without having to accept the conclusion that we are puppets in the hands of fate. There is little doubt about the fact that the past cannot be altered; but likewise we cannot change what is going to happen, the actual future, even if what happens doesn't happen by way of necessity and is a consequence of our action.

An example will help. Suppose that this morning I pulled the brakes to avoid a car at a crossroad and that afterwards I proceeded safely in the left lane toward my office. By acting as I did, at the time of my action I have *avoided* a possible future accident and *provoked* the event given by my stopping. While the latter event, at the time of my pulling the brakes, is part of the actual future, the possible, non-actual event of the accident which I avoided is *not* part of the real future: in this trivial sense, literally I have *not changed* the actual future: I only *produced* it *causally*. By avoiding the accident, I only "eliminated" a possible, non-real event; consequently, I have not changed something which is part of reality, because *eliminating a possibility does not amount to a real change*. As a matter of fact, it is a mere *counterfactual* change. Since my pulling the brakes was causally necessary for the actual future to be the way it has been, we can express this fact in another way by saying that *without my action, the future would have been different. This counterfactual sentence expresses the only sense in which it is legitimate to say that we can "change" the future.* When we act, we *influence* or partially *produce* what will be the case, but we don't change it: I don't change the future course of events containing my stopping and my driving safely past the crossroad in the left lane, I make it happen the way it happens.

The ontological symmetry between past and future, when the "reality" of the future is interpreted either as bivalence or inalterability, does not seem to jeopardize our ability to influence (at least in part) the future, provided that the latter ability is not confused with the absurd thesis that we can change it: the future cannot be changed or altered exactly as the past. But if by "reality of the future" we rather refer to the fact that for any of my actions located at time t to have a later *effect*, at t there must be literally *nothing* that follows it, *then* we seem to run into troubles with the static view of time. On the basis of our intuition, we would want to claim that from the viewpoint of the cause, the effect cannot be real, since it is only the converse implication that holds: from the viewpoint of the present effect, the past cause must be real and definite, i.e., it must exist.

I will now argue that even this third sense of the "unreality of the future effect" is not in conflict with the perfect ontological symmetry between cause and effect that we must assume within the static theory of time mandated by physics.[9] The main point to realize is that in a tenseless theory of time, the claim that it is *always* (at any time) true to say that "event E occurs at t'", or that "E is before F'" does not entail that the *corresponding tenseless facts exist always or at any instants of time*. In other words, tenseless existence of facts or events does not amount to omnitemporal existence (at any instant). The *fact* that "E is before F", *qua* abstract, does not exist in time, and the concrete, physical fact to which it corresponds exists at best between E and F, extremes included (see Dorato 1997, ch. 3).

If event E occurs (tenselessly) at t' and it is now t, with t earlier than t', at t (i.e., now) the event E does not exist, both tensely and tenselessly (Oaklander 1997). It does not exist tensely because it does not exist now, but rather in the future; at t it does not exist tenselessly precisely because E exists only at t'. But the fact that at t the event *does not exist*, does not imply that at t it is not real. Its reality can be interpreted as being equivalent to the fact that the future event in question occupies a well-defined region of spacetime (i.e., it occurs somewhere and somewhen), but does not occupy the present region where we are now located. In fact, *there is a difference between tenseless existence and tenseless reality*: at *t*, it is possible to say *both* that the event occurring at *t'* does not exist *and* that it is real in the sense that it occupies a region of spacetime, in the same sense in which a past event is now real.

Consequently, by acting at *t*, we don't need to assume that the event that we bring about at *t'* exists beforehand; that would be absurd, because the action could not produce the desired state of affairs. Since at *t* the future event caused by our action exists neither tensely or tenselessly, we can safely assume that, as of the cause, the effect does not yet exist, and this is sufficient to make sense of our free action. At the same time, we can restore the temporal symmetry between past and future required by physics by admitting that there is a sense in which the future effect is real as of the cause because there is absolutely no physical reason to deny that event a well-defined position in the texture of spacetime.

Università di Roma Tre (Italy)

NOTES

[1] Notice that this is a mere change *in* time, rather than a change *of* time as in the dynamic theory.
[2] Dorato 1995, 1996, 1997.
[3] "Tensed" here means "that makes reference to the present moment".
[4] For this analysis, see Mellor 1981 and Faye 1989.
[5] The reason for facing such a confrontation is given by the methodologically reasonable injunction that any metaphysical claim which is in conflict with a well-confirmed physical theory should be amended or abandoned all together.
[6] With the possible exception of CP violations in weak interactions, entailing a temporal asymmetry for kaons decay.
[7] This extension of Stein's theorem to the relation "and then" holds provided the latter can be regarded as reflexive.
[8] See note 2.
[9] Such an ontological symmetry is not equivalent to a temporal symmetry between cause and effect.

BIBLIOGRAPHY

Broad 1923
    Broad C. D.: *Scientific Thought*, K. Paul, Trench, Trubner & Co., London.
Dorato 1996
    Dorato, M.: "On Becoming, Relativity and Nonseparability", *Philosophy of Science*, 63, 4, pp. 585–604.
Dorato 1995
    Dorato M.: *Time and Reality*, Clueb, Bologna.
Dorato 1997
    Dorato M.: *Futuro aperto e libertà. Un'introduzione alla filosofia del tempo*, Laterza, Roma-Bari.
Grünbaum 1973
    Grünbaum A.: *Philosophical Problems of Space and Time*, second enlarged edition, Reidel, Dordrecht
Faye 1989
    Faye J.: *The Reality of the Future*, Odense University Press, Odense.

Mellor 1981
    Mellor D. H.: *Real Time*, Cambridge University Press, Cambridge.
Putnam 1967
    Putnam H.: "Time and Physical Geometry", *Journal of Philosophy*, 64, pp. 240–47.
Oaklander 1997
    Oaklander N.: "Freedom and the New Theory of Time", in R. Le Poidevin (ed.): *Questions of Time and Tense*, Clarendon Press, Oxford.
Simili 1984
    Simili R. (ed.): Introduzione a G. H. von Wright: *Libertà e determinazione*, Pratiche Editrici, Parma, pp. 5–19.
Smith 1993
    Smith Q.: *Language and Time*, Oxford University Press, Oxford.
Stein 1991
    Stein H.: "On Relativity Theory and the Openness of the Future", *Philosophy of Science*, 58, pp. 247–67.
Tooley 1997
    Tooley M.: *Time, Tense and Causation*, Oxford University Press, Oxford.
Von Wright 1965
    Wright G. H. von: "And Next", *Acta Philosophica Fennica*, Vol. 18, Helsinki, pp. 293–304. Reprinted in von Wright 1983.
Von Wright 1966
    Wright G. H. von: "And Then", in *Societas Scientiarum Fennica. Commentationes Physico-Mathematicae*, vol. 32, n. 7. Reprinted in von Wright 1983.
Von Wright 1967
    Wright G. H. von: "The Logic of Action: A Sketch", in N. Rescher (ed.): *The Logic of Decision and Action*, Pittsburgh University Press, Pittsburgh, pp. 121–36.
Von Wright 1968
    Wright G. H. von: "Always" *Theoria*, 34, pp. 208–21.
Von Wright 1969
    Wright G. H. von: *Time, Change and Contradiction*, Cambridge University Press, London. Reprinted in von Wright 1983.
Von Wright 1980
    Wright G. H. von: *Freedom and Determination*, North-Holland Publishing Co., Amsterdam.
Von Wright 1983
    Wright G. H. von: *Philosophical Logic. Philosophical Papers*, Vol. II, Blackwell, Oxford.

ROSA M. CALCATERRA

W. JAMES' DEFENCE OF FREE WILL:
A STEP TOWARD A PARADIGM SHIFT

A prominent feature of von Wright's action theory is its study of the logical grammar of determinism. Its general outcome is the emancipation of the discussion about human freedom from traditional epistemological and ontological approaches. I would like to show here that William James's defence of free will reflects a similar aspect, notwithstanding the different theoretical and methodological frameworks of his own and von Wright's thought.

Leaving aside a specific comparative analysis, I will limit myself to pointing out that James' discussion of that topic is, on the one hand, an application of his anti-objectivistic representation of rationality, and on the other, a consequence of his refusal to reduce psychology to physiology, a point that clearly emerges in the *Principles of Psychology*.[1] In particular, my contention is that indeterminism is a precondition of the Jamesian experimental/pragmatical conception of both ethics and our knowledge of the physical world.

1. THE PRACTICAL FUNCTION OF RATIONALITY

The defence of free will is recurrent in James's works and is frequently considered as a mere personal option, with no other philosophical ground than the instance of taking into account emotional factors of human consciousness. This interpretation is reinforced by considering that the question is often linked, more or less explicitly, to the issue of religious faith, which, in turn, is not defended through traditional philosophical arguments, but again by means of a passionate emphasis on its deep roots in emotional life. For instance, the idea of individual freedom and the legitimation of religious faith are the same in *The Reflex Action and Theism* (1881) as well as in some passages of *The Sentiment of Rationality* (1879) and *The Dilemma of Determinism* (1884), representing the early expressions of James' "subjectivist" or "psychological" version of pragmatism. They were in fact later assembled in *The Will to Believe* (1897), one of his most castigated philosophical works, just because it is considered a defence of wishful thinking.[2] Actually James' purpose, as a whole, was not to provide an indiscriminate guarantee for believing attitudes, but rather to challenge both positivistic scientism and traditional metaphysics, bringing into play an anti-objectivistic description of rationality.

The rejection of the correspondence theory and, consequently, of any claim to "absolute" or "objective" truth, is indeed the framework of all the writings collected in *The Will to Believe*: a pivotal argument of the homonymous essay opening the volume is in fact the critique of the concept of "objective evidence" itself, which James describes as a "mere aspiration or *Grenzbegriff*, marking the infinitely remote

R. Egidi (ed.), In Search of a New Humanism, 139–146.
©1999 *Kluwer Academic Publishers. Printed in Great Britain.*

ideal of our thinking life" (WB, p. 23). Like several other beliefs which are embedded in our intellectual and practical life, it is rooted in our "passional nature." The idea that there is truth and that our minds are able to grasp it, is the fundamental belief on which our scientific efforts and social system is built upon. In particular James' thesis here is that adopting an unwarranted belief is fully legitimate whenever a question exceeding experimental criteria of knowledge, but of relevant ethical import, cannot be settled by cogent philosophical or scientific arguments.[3]

On the other hand, the substitution of the old metaphor of the knowing subject as the "spectator of reality" for that of the "agent of knowledge supports his earliest attempts to demonstrate the capacity of human individuals to accomplish more than a mechanical adaptation to their biological environment, thus elaborating Darwinism into a teleological theory of mind.[4] This aspect, later developed in the *Principles of Psychology*, is evident in *The Sentiment of Rationality*, whose essential outcome is the representation of cognitive processes as fundamentally practical activities, mostly directed to manage the uncertainties of human life. But a more striking version of James' anti-objectivism is represented by *The Dilemma of Determinism*, which, as a whole, exhibits the impossibility of grounding metaphysical-ontological discourse on "purely rational" arguments: the reconfiguration of the traditional discussions of determinism *versus* indeterminism in terms of a "personal choice", which he provides in this text, is actually a radical objection to metaphysical pretensions to catch the "true essence" of the natural and human world.

2. THE "EXPERIMENTAL" ACCOUNT OF HUMAN FREEDOM

In *The Dilemma of Determinism* (DD) the controversy between determinism and indeterminism is identified as a contrast between two metaphysical perspectives, respectively centred on the refusal or the acceptance of the ontological category of "possibility". But James argues that in spite of the claims by both indeterminists and determinists to ground their own position on "factual" considerations, they actually engage in mere speculation, depending on "different faiths or postulations of rationality":

To this man the world seems more rational with possibilities in it – to that man with possibilities excluded; and talk as we will about having to yield to evidence, what makes us monist or pluralist, determinist or indeterminist, is at the bottom always some sentiment like this. (DD, p. 119)

Apart from some terminological ambiguities, the subjectivist formulation of the issue turns out to be the fulcrum of a shift from the metaphysical-ontological perspective on the problem of the freedom or determination of human action to a phenomenological-pragmatical consideration of it. James' arguments in favour of free will appear in fact connected not to a defence of an indeterministic cosmology, but rather to the reduction of both deterministic and indeterministic metaphysics to the concept of fully unwarranted beliefs, of which James tries to value the actual meaning considering interpretations and descriptions of the human intellectual and practical experience they involve.

This strategy centres around the argument that determinism brings about a "dilemma", which forces us to consider moral judgements and attitudes as futile. The appraisal of human actions in terms of "good" and "evil" is actually a superfluity for a determinist or – we could say – a logical mistake. In his mind, each single occurrence is in fact supposed to be foredoomed from eternity and welded with the whole into an "absolute unity, an iron block". "Necessity" of what actually is and "impossibility" of any change in the future are his unique categories of the real (DD, pp. 117–18), so that, for example, acts of wanton cruelty, murders and treacheries, or – more generally – what is ordinarily called "sin or error", are justified as necessary parts of the world (DD, pp. 124–28).

In contrast, James maintains the impossibility of a theoretical explanation of evil and, using heavily ironical language about the optimistic version of determinism, such as that represented by Spencer's *Data of Ethics*, he emphasises the dramatic alternating of good and evil in individual and social human life, arguing for personal responsibility in giving an increasingly positive course to men's history (DD, pp. 129–31).

James insists that his reasons for defending indeterminism, and therefore free will and personal and social responsibility, are essentially "of a practical order" (DD, p. 132). But what really matters is that ethics itself is pictured as a "phenomenon" of human life, rather than as an "objective structure" of consciousness, metaphysically grounded. More specifically, ethics and the same concepts of free will or individual responsibility are detached from the hard contrast of determinism and indeterminism, which at the very end leads to a dogmatic negation of freedom or to a total assimilation of human behaviour to mere casualty. Thus James puts forward the idea of "relative ambiguity" of future developments of the natural and human world, rejecting the simple equivalence of "chance" "irrational" and "absurd": presuming the presence of "chance" in the world means nothing but accepting the uncertainty of the course of nature as well as of that of man's volitions, that is consenting to the category of "possibility" (DD, pp. 120–23; 137–38). According to his main argument, this is, in fact, the logical precondition of the essential distinction between bad and good actions, on which ethics and the same "willingness to act" depend; that is, ethics and the ordinary attitude of acting cannot be understood "without the admission of real genuine possibilities in the world" (DD, p. 135).

On the other hand, the category of "possibility" is the mark of the Jamesian anti-objectivistic account of rationality, which essentially includes the "experimental" nature of knowing processes, namely their essential link with human capacity to interact "pragmatically" with the natural world. This conception is summarised in an opening passage of *The Dilemma of Determinism,* where James makes clear his very intention of applying it to the moral field:

I myself believe that all the magnificent achievements of mathematical and physical science – our doctrines of evolution, of unity of law, and the rest – proceed from our indomitable desire to cast the world into a more rational shape in our minds than the shape into which it is thrown there by the crude order of our experience. The world has shown itself, to a great extend, plastic to this demand of ours for rationality. How much farther it will show itself plastic no one can say. Our only means of finding out is to try; and I, for one, feel as free to try a conception of moral as of mechanical or of logical rationality. (DD, p. 115)

3. JAMES' USE OF THE INTROSPECTIVE METHOD

In contrast to other "classics" of American pragmatism, James did not reject the value of introspective method,[5] and indeed he used it extensively in his *Principles of Psychology*, often with a phenomenological cast. However, despite his notorious statement that "Introspective observation is what we have to rely upon first and foremost and always" (PP, I, p. 185), he is quite aware of the inaccuracies of introspection. He points out, for instance, that the introspective method leads to the "psychologist's fallacy *par excellence*" – namely the tendency of the psychologist to ascribe his own inner experiences to the object he is analysing (PP, I, p. 196). This is because of "the misleading influence" of ordinary language on psychological vocabulary (PP, I, pp. 194–96), and, most important of all, because the psychologist's point of view is a peculiar one: he is, in fact a reporter of subjective as well as of objective facts (PP, I, pp. 184–85). But what are, for James, "objective facts"? The critical attitude toward the correspondence theory of truth is clearly expressed in several passages of this section of the *Principles*, where he questions both positivistic and "spiritualistic" assertions about introspection, coming to recognise, after all, its intrinsic fallibility:

Introspection is difficult and fallible; and that difficulty is simply that of all observations of whatever kind. (PP, I, p. 191)

Thus, considering that the subject matter of psychology is constituted by "the subjective data of which the psychologist treats, and their relations to their objects, to the brain, and to the rest of the world" and, moreover, that "introspection is no sure guide to the truth *about* our mental states" (PP, I, p. 197), James asserts the necessity to supplement it by "experimental" and "comparative" methods (PP, I, pp. 192–94). And actually, if we take a general view of James' applications of introspection in the *Principles*, they turn out to be not expressive of a methodological monism, but rather instrumental to his effort of overcoming any form of psychological reductionism.

From a historical point of view, a significant aspect of his *opus magnum* is in fact in the intention of keeping within certain boundaries physiological psychology, which at the time was acquiring strong credit in American universities , as well as to overcome the radically opposite stream, namely "transcendentalist" or "spiritualistic" psychology. Both physiologists and transcendentalists were, for James, too dogmatic: the former because of their radical tendency to restrict psychological research to the domain of brain-processes experiments; the latter because of metaphysical assumptions and total disregard of the "natural" conditions of mental processes, by which they were trying to salvage the "spiritual" side of human life. Therefore his intention was, on the one hand, to take into account a series of ordinary human feelings and thoughts, which the purely experimental approach of psychology was inclined to bracket; on the other hand, to provide new philosophical grounds for their description.

One of the most interesting philosophical implications of James's use of the introspective method is the rejection of a pivotal factor of traditional empiricism, namely the isolationistic conception of sensations, which he ruled out by his theory of the "stream of thought", developed in chapter IX of the *Principles*. It is worth observing that such a theory was in a way anticipated in an article of 1884, *On Some*

Omissions of Introspective Psychology,[6] where he questioned the traditional use of introspection, pointing out its typical connection to the concept of mind as a "metaphysical entity" or "substance". The replacement of this aspect with a picture of mind as "function" is indeed a specific feature of James' thought, and it is just in this way that he sets up the problem of will.

4. ATTENTION AND WILL: CRACKS IN THE ORGANICISTIC DESCRIPTION OF MIND

The representation of will in the *Principles* is strictly dependent on that of mind and consciousness as "selecting agencies", operating in consideration of behaviour. In a paradigmatic passage James describes the fundamental principle of his mind's theory: "Selection is the very keel on which our mental ship is built". Selectivity, in fact, is also indicated as the operative criterion of human sensorial organs, whose very function is, according to him, to pick up from the physical environment "those sensible qualities, which happen practically or aesethically to interest us" (PP, I, p. 285). With regard to the most elementary processes of senses, James apparently endorses identitism: selection depends here on "immediate attention", a basic psychophysical activity, which affects our perceptions, as well as our practical attitudes toward sensible objects (PP, I, pp. 434–47). But the organicistic explanation of attention seems to be not exhaustive for James, when he discusses the "active or voluntary" form of sensorial and intellectual attention. This circumstance is characterised as an act of attending to something whose interest is associated with something else (PP, I, pp. 416–18), ordinarily accompanied – he argues – by a "feeling of effort" to which "we are seriously tempted to ascribe spontaneous power": in short, in this case, we do tend to think that the effort is not a mere effect of pre-existent psychophysical factors, but rather a genuine cause of attention itself (PP, I, pp. 449–51).

James raises here the issue of free will, to which he clearly gives phenomenological import and which he is therefore reluctant to consider a pseudo-problem – as experimentalists tend to assert. Rather he thinks, as he will say in *Psychology: Briefer Course,*[7] that it is not an issue which can be put aside simply because it cannot be grasped by "scientific" criteria of verification (PBC, p. 392). Certainly, *qua* experimental psychologist, he thinks that to go beyond those criteria is impossible, but, *qua* critic of scientism, he suggests that psychology requires philosophical supplements. This attitude – quite evident in the treatment of several other topics – i.e. habits, "the Self", emotions, perception, and the mind-body problem – emerges clearly where he treats ironically the strictly "scientific" settlement of the question of the feeling of effort.

The feeling of effort certainly *may* be an inert accompaniment and not the active element which it seems (...) We *may* regard (voluntary) attention as a superfluity or a "Luxus", and dogmatize against its causal function with no feeling in our hearts but one pride that we are applying Occam's razor to an entity that has multiplied itself "beyond" necessity. (PP, I, pp. 452–53)

Apparently James is questioning the simple reduction of that mental event to brain processes: as he asserts more than once, neither introspection nor laboratory experiments supply safe data either for maintaining a strict causal connection between the body and mental activity, or for arguing that phenomena such as attention, thought, memory, feeling might contain purely mental factors (PP, I, 176–82; II, pp. 305, 570–71). In particular, he points out that both the "mechanical theory" – according to which the feeling of effort or, more generally the existence of the will, are mere illusions – and the "spiritual" point of view – according to which they are "genuine forces" – have "no facts definitely known to stand as arbiter between them" (PP, II, p. 454): in other words, both are "unwarranted beliefs", in the sense we formerly argued. And in fact James calls back the central argument of *The Dilemma of Determinism*:

Under these circumstances, one can leave the question open whilst waiting for light, or one can do what most speculative minds do, that is, look to one's general philosophy to incline the beam. The believers in mechanism do so without hesitation, and they ought not to refuse the same privilege to the believers in a spiritual force. I count myself among the latter, but as my reasons are ethical they are hardly suited for introduction to psychology. (PP, I, p. 454)

Nevertheless "ethical reasons" will be an essential part of the lengthy chapter on will, where he actually tries to ground pragmatically the idea of free choice. This concept is indeed presupposed in his own definition of psychology as "the science of Mental Life, both of its phenomena and their conditions", that opens the *Principles* (PP, I, p. 1), and in the further assessment that

The pursuance of future ends and the choice of means for their attainment are the mark and criterion of presence of mentality in a phenomenon. (PP, I, p. 8)

5. TOWARD A NON-CAUSALISTIC THEORY OF ACTION

The separation of mental activity from physical processes and the anti-mechanistic thrust of James's psychology represent the two main aspects of the treatment of the problem of volition, or acts of will, in chapter XXVI of the *Principles*.

Following Charles Renouvier – the author who notoriously influenced his "voluntarism – James ascribes volition exclusively to the field of ideas, qualifying it as "a psychical and moral act pure and simple" (PP, II, p. 560), consisting in the effort "to ATTEND to a difficult object and hold it fast before the mind" (PP, II, p. 561). The effort of attending to a specific idea and "feel the mind" with it, pushing aside all other contrasting thoughts, is indeed "the essential phenomenon of will". But, in arguing that this psychical state can be truly said to be an "act of will" only when there is "*consent* to the idea and to the fact which the idea represents" (PP, II, pp. 562; 564), he seems to suggest that voluntary heeding cannot be intended as a mere intellectual act, detached from concreteness. Rather, the element of "consent" covers the link between what James designates as the "will's true expressions" involving a personal choice and the awareness of the practical implications of what we are choosing. In other words, that feature recalls the interaction of subjective and objective or "factual" elements stated in the representation of rationality in *The Sentiment of Rationality,* as well as the pragmatist emphasis on the factual consequences of those elements, which is alive and well in the *Principles*.[8]

The pragmatist background emerges particularly in James passages about the role of "deliberation" in the field of behaviour, where he suggests that human ordinary actions – as distinct from bodily movements – rest on something quite similar to a successful conclusion of a voluntary heeding process. The "reinforcing" and "inhibiting" ideas involved in this process are here termed "*reasons* or *motives* by which the decision is brought about" (PP, II, p. 528). But it is also clear that he does not intend to ascribe a definite importance to reasoning, or, in other words, to consider mental processes as the "efficient cause" of behaviour. He points out, in fact, that unconscious and emotional factors are involved in practical deliberations, and suggests that human motivation can never be explained according to a unique criterion (PP, II, pp. 529–59). In a way, this perspective seems to be the framework of his entire discussion of the problem of will, and in particular of his defence of free will. From the very beginning, but especially after he endorsed the pragmatist conception of philosophy with increasing conviction, the issue appears in fact connected to the concept of belief. It is thus organised not in order to identify the ontological status of an assumed faculty or to provide an account of its definite function in man's life, by means of an appeal to strictly epistemological reasoning (PP, II, p. 822). In contrast, James' suggestion seems to be that the philosophical approach to the problem of human freedom essentially rises from a description of the way in which individuals can make reasonable choices, provided that they wish to live up to certain standards. Of course, here again the most difficult question is the choice of these standards; but then, these primarily regard what I would simply call the persistent interest of James – as a pragmatist – in a democratic way of life, which, in his mind, means a way of life suitable to protect social interests together with individual attitudes and perspectives.

Von Wright's clarification of the intermingling of social with individual factors of human behaviour – provided in the context of his "neowittgensteinian" theory of action – is an important, and I would say necessary, integration of the jamesian discussion of free will. In particular, his distinction between "internal and external determinants of action", i.e. between "volitative-cognitive factors working, so to say, 'from within' the agent" and "symbolic challenges put to him 'from without'",[9] represents an effective antidote against the risk that the notion of individual freedom – so dear to James – vanishes in a mere wishful thinking. Moreover, on the basis of that distinction, von Wright points out analogously to James "the *complexities* of human motivation" and "the equivocation of the term 'reason' (for an action)",[10] thus reinforcing the dynamic conception of rationality promoted by the pragmatists. But, above all, there is a paradigmatic passage by von Wright to which certainly James could have subscribed:

The "freedom" or "free will" of a man consists, in the *fact* that he acts, one could say. (...) To deny that an *agent* is *free* is to commit a contradiction in terms. The "mystery" of freedom, if there is one, is the "mystery" of the fact that there *are* agents and actions.[11]

Università del Piemonte Orientale (Italy)

NOTES

[1] W. James: *The Principles of Psychology* (henceforth PP), 2 vols., Holt, New York 1890; Dover, New York 1950; 3 vols., Harvard University Press, Cambridge, Mass. 1981. References and quotations in the text will be from the Dover edition.

[2] W. James: *The Will to Believe and Other Essays in Popular Philosophy* (henceforth WB), Longmans, Green & Co, New York 1897; Dover, New York 1956; Harvard University Press, Cambridge, Mass.-London 1979. References and quotations in the text will be from the latter edition.

[3] In these cases – James mantains – avoiding taking a decision and living open the question for the fear of incurring in error, is itself a "passional decision – just like deciding yes or no – and it is attended with the same risk of losing the truth" (WB, p. 20). The argument was intended to contrast a typical positivistic contention, namely that it is always wrong to believe anything upon insufficient evidence; however he clearly states that "*In concreto* the freedom to believe can only cover living options which the intellect of the individual cannot by itself resolve" (WB, pp. 29–33). Misinterpretations of the essays were probably due to the "luckless title which should have been 'Right to Believe' ", as James wrote to F. H. Bradley (cfr. R. B. Perry: *The Thought and Character of William James: Briefer Version*, Harvard University Press, Cambridge, Mass. 1948, p. 208).

[4] See for instance "Remarks on Spencers's *"Definition of Mind as Correspondence"* (1878); *"Brute and Human Intellect"* (1878); *"Are we Automata?"* (1879), in *Collected Essays and Reviews*, Longmans, Green & Co, New York 1920; Russell & Russell, New York 1969. It is also worth mentioning *Great Men, Great Thoughts and the Enviroment*, in WB, pp. 163–89, where he applies his elaboration of darwinism to historical-social field.

[5] On that topic Ch. S. Peirce's position is paradigmatic: he rejected very clearly the logical validity of introspection, but also the possibility of identifying, by introspective method, all those events we are accustomed to ascribe to the so called "inner world", including the assumed acts of will. We should also mention G. H. Mead, who described the entire dimension of "Self" as the result of social processes.

[6] *Mind*, n. 9, pp. 1–26. Reprinted in W. James: *Collected Essays and Reviews*, cit.

[7] W. James: *Psychology: Briefer Course* (henceforth PBC), Holt, New York 1892; Harvard University Press, Cambridge, Mass. 1984.

[8] Pragmatism was officially announced by James almost a decade after the publication of the *Principles*, but there is a general agreement about its unofficial presence throughout this work.

[9] G. H. von Wright, *Freedom and Determinism*, North-Holland Publishing Company, Amsterdam 1980, p. 67.

[10] Ivi, p. 62.

[11] Ivi, p. 79.

PAOLA DESSÌ

IS DETERMINISM IMPOSSIBLE?

After the publication of *Explanation and Understanding* in 1971 my main concern in philosophy came to centre round the idea of "determinism". It has been a tenet of that work that determinism in the sphere of natural events and the sphere of human actions differ radically from one another. In two subsequent books *Causality and Determinism* (1974) and *Freedom and Determination* (1980), I tried to clarify my thoughts on this difference. In the course of these efforts new questions constantly cropped up and many of them were oriented not so much towards the distinction between events and actions as towards the ideas of truth and knowledge and the modal notions of necessity and possibility.[1]

So wrote von Wright in the introduction to his book *Truth, Knowledge and Modality* (1984). In a difference from his previous works, in the essays in this book the problem of determinism is dealt with not by means of a contrast between causal explanation and teleological explanation, but rather through the examination of modal ideas. This plurality in the approach to determinism permits von Wright to be a point of reference (even if almost always implicit) both for those who discuss the determinism-freedom relationship in terms of intentions, ends, aims or preferences, and for those interested in establishing the logical possibility of a reconciliation between determinism and freedom.

In this essay I shall limit myself to examining the discussion raised by the writings of Peter van Inwagen on the logical impossibility of reconciling freedom and determinism.[2] Van Inwagen is convinced that a logical demonstration of the impossibility of exercising any sort of freedom in a completely determined world can be given.[3] In a deterministic world, everything is necessary and nothing is possible, or better yet, the possible is identified with the necessary and the necessary with the actual. In such a world we cannot make choices or decisions which could, even minimally, change it. Resorting to the terminology of the possible worlds, we can say, according to van Inwagen, that given the laws of nature and the state of the universe in a certain instant only one future possible world compatible with those conditions exists.

A non-formalised description of van Inwagen's argumentation is very simple, especially if we use an example that he himself suggests. Let us say that there is a judge (we can refer to him **J**) who can halt the execution of a death sentence simply by raising his hand at a certain instant represented by the letter **T**. In this scenario, our judge is under no pressure, and is not impeded physically (for example, he is not tied up, wounded or paralysed) or psychologically (he is not under the influence of drugs or hypnotised, and does not suffer from any mental disorder). When the **T** moment arrives, **J** does not raise his hand. According to van Inwagen, if determinism is true, **J** could not have raised his hand. In fact, he would have only been able to raise it if it were in his power to do one of the following things: either change the past, or change

147

R. Egidi (ed.), In Search of a New Humanism, 147–155.
© 1999 *Kluwer Academic Publishers. Printed in Great Britain.*

the laws of physics. Since both of these hypotheses are absurd, **J** could not have raised his hand when the **T** moment arrived. Therefore, van Inwagen can affirm that it is impossible to reconcile determinism and freedom.

Let us look at how van Inwagen makes this argument formally. Aside from the letters used over the course of the preceding narration, in the demonstration two others are used, the meaning of which will be presently explained. T_0 denotes an instant in time before the birth of **J**; P_0 denotes a proposition expressing the state of the world at T_0, **P** denotes a proposition expressing the state of the world at **T**; and **L** represents the conjunction of the laws of physics. The following is van Inwagen's passage in full:

The argument consists of seven statements, the seventh of which follows from the first six:
(1)   If determinism is true, then the conjunction of P_0 and **L** entails **P**.
(2)   If **J** had raised his hand at **T**, **P** would be false.
(3)   If (2) is true, then if **J** could have raised his hand at **T**, **J** could have rendered **P** false.
(4)   If **J** could have rendered **P** false, and if the conjunction of P_0 and **L** entails **P**, then **J** could have rendered the conjunction of P_0 and **L** false.
(5)   If **J** could have rendered the conjunction of P_0 and **L** false, then **J** could have rendered **L** false.
(6)   **J** could not have rendered **L** false.
(7)   If determinism is true, **J** could not have raised his hand at **T**.[4]

One observation is immediately apparent: van Inwagen, like Carl Ginet and James Lamb who have presented similar arguments, chooses a T_0 instant that happens even before the birth of our judge.[5] This choice is completely irrelevant to the argument. It responds to the rhetorical need to underline the inevitability of our choices rendering more dramatic the conclusion of the incompatibility between determinism and freedom. Even if the choice to make a reference to a condition which existed before the birth of the person who should exercise freedom is only a rhetorical device, it is fundamental to the fact that the present conditions are the result of a causal chain prior to the action. This is why some years later when Lehrer will show those who support compatibility a new path, substantially based on the semantics of the possible worlds elaborated by J. L. Pollock,[6] he will maintain that this is feasible only because one can exclusively make reference to present conditions and remain indifferent to the way in which these conditions were produced.[7] In this way, determinism would be a hypothesis, of which its taking place would not have any influence over our possibility to choose alternative actions. The compatibility between determinism and freedom can be established in an indirect way by demonstrating the irrelevance of determinism for the questions pertaining to freedom. This deals with a situation very similar to that which derives from the distinction placed by von Wright between "synchronic modality" and "diachronic modality". The propositions pertaining to the past are diachronically necessary, but this does not mean the propositions regarding the future are also diachronically necessary. Let us clarify this with the following example from von Wright:

A person is killed at t in an explosion. "Under the circumstances", we say, this was necessary–considering the strength of the explosion and that he happened to be near the exploding bomb. But he need not have been where he was at t. If at t' he had started to move away, which he could have done, he would not have been killed. But after t'' this was too late. Even if he had started to run then, he would have been killed. At t' (and before) it was possible that he would be saved. But at t'' (and after) this was no longer possible."[8]

Van Inwagen's reasoning has been criticised from varying points of view. For some, like Michael Slote and Tomis Kapitan, it would be formally correct only in the case in which the necessity and possibility we are dealing with were logical necessities and possibilities;[9] for others, like Jan Narveson, John Martin Fischer and David Lewis, his appearance of correctness is based on ambiguous terminology;[10] and for yet others, like Bernard Berofsky, the reasoning rises or falls according to the meaning attributed to the expression "natural laws".[11]

Let us examine the first objections. These have at their base the distinction between different kinds of necessity, i.e. *logical, physical* and *epistemological*. In correspondence with these different senses of the term *necessary* (and the related *possible* and *impossible* one) different systems of modal logic can be constructed. Not all of the principles which are valid for one type of modal logic are valid for the others. Regarding our discussion, there are two valid principles for modal logic that take on as the basic notion the idea of logical necessity (possibility and impossibility), which are not valid inside a modal system which has at its base the idea of physical or epistemic necessity (possibility, impossibility). These two principles are as follows:

(A)   closure under conjunction introduction;

(B)   closure under logical implication.

The principle (A) maintains that if the proposition **p** is necessary and the proposition **q** is necessary, then also necessary is the proposition that results from the conjunction of **p** and **q**. The principle (B) holds that if the proposition that maintains that **p** involves **q** is necessary, and the proposition **p** is necessary, then we have to conclude the necessity of **q**.

Slote offers examples of modality that do not obey these principles and then shows that the ideas in van Inwagen's reasoning are of the same type. In particular, to clarify how the principle (A) is not valid unless in cases dealing with logical necessity, Slote provides an example which to me best exemplifies the aim. Let us suppose that Jules and Jim are two friends who have not seen each other for many years and one morning they run into each other at the bank. Certainly we are talking about a random encounter. But yet, Jules had been going to the bank on that same day of the week at the same time for many years and Jim was there on explicit orders from his boss. We can, therefore, conclude that even though both Jules and Jim were not at the bank randomly their meeting each other was random. In other words, each of the two were in the bank as a consequence of a well-determined plan which called for them to be in the bank at that time; their meeting, nevertheless, was accidental in so far as it did not result from any sort of preordained plan. According to Slote, this serves to demonstrate that the necessity subtended by the concept of non-accidentality is relative, or like he says, it is selective in respect to a certain element, in this case the existence of a preordained plan. Even the (B) principle is not valid in this case. In fact, it could be said that it is necessary that the employee finds himself in the bank at a certain time with regard to the plan made by his boss, but it cannot be said that as being in the bank at that time means being alive at the time that the boss had planned that his employee would remain alive.

According to Slote, van Inwagen (like Carl Ginet, James Lamb and David Wiggins) employs, respectively, the two principles in premises (5) and (4) in which the necessity spoken of in the context of the discussion about the inevitability of the actions in a deterministic world is not logical necessity, but rather a selective kind of necessity similar to the one considered in the above-mentioned example. As a matter of fact, "certain past events will be necessary in the relevant sense (necessary in relation to the right sort of factor) and certain laws leading from them to an agent's later actions will also be necessary; but it will not follow that those actions are themselves necessary at some later time when the agent is considering whether to perform them. Of course, those actions will be determined by and presumably be predictable in terms of factors prior to the agent's desires and abilities. But those earlier factors, nonetheless, bring such actions about only by means of (causal chains involving) later desires (roughly coeval with the actions they help to bring about)."[12] Our future actions could vary according to our desires or our present capacity, even if these cannot have any influence on the past or on the laws. In other words, in respect to our desires and our present capacity that function as selective elements, the past and the laws will be inevitable; our future actions will not be.

A careful consideration shows that Slote finishes by discussing that the idea of determinism which must be focused on in the context regarding human freedom is Laplacean determinism embraced by van Inwagen. Certainly Slote is not the first to do this. In effect, from its earliest formulation, Laplace's determinism raised objections of this sort. Augustin Cournot, for example, tried to defend an alternative determinism to that of Laplace by using almost the same arguments as those Slote employed, and provided an example quite similar to Slote's two friends who met each other in the bank. Cournot spoke of two brothers at war on different fronts who fell in battle on the same day and for whom it is not valid to invoke fate. The death of each brother was necessary in the sense that it was the result of precise causal chains, but the fact that they had died on the same day was not the fruit of a superior necessity but rather the result of a random encounter of independent causal sequences.[13]

Significantly, even Jacques Monod, in his noted work *Le hasard et la nécessité*, uses a similar example to clarify the possibility of concomitance of "necessity" and "chance" in the evolutionary process.[14] Only in a Laplacean universe in which by definition every contingency is excluded can van Inwagen's reasoning have any foundation. Exclusively in the case in which the world is considered an integral unit and everything seen as the result of a single causal chain does it make sense to make physical necessity coincide with logical necessity.[15] The profound depth reached by Slote's analysis, thanks to the greater formal resources available today, should not allow one to lose sight of the persistence of themes which reveal the existence of problems that were never completely resolved.

Like Slote, other authors have negated the legitimacy of using in the argument the (A) and (B) principles held by van Inwagen. For example, for different reasons, Tomis Kapitan advanced the same criticism. In his opinion, ideas like those subtended by expressions, "being able to", "having the ability to", "being in control of", depend on the cognitive context in which they are connected. Let us imagine, for example, that a person called George was in prison and that his jailer – who could be considered a sort of nut case – once a month when everyone is asleep opened the doors of the cells and kept them open for an hour. Would it be accurate to say that, "Once a month George 'can' leave the prison, but he does not?" This would certainly be a strange way to describe the situation: poor George, being unaware of the bizarre behaviour of his jailer, does not see the real opportunity to escape.[16] Just like how it would not be right to say that a poor ignorant person "can" sue the local mayor, supposing that he had no idea of what a lawsuit is, or supposing that it was ignorant of how to raise a lawsuit.[17] To circumscribe the cases in which real possibilities open for the agent, Kapitan suggests that it could be said that an agent (S) is able to carry out a certain action (X) only when the following requisites are satisfied:

(i)   S has a concept of X;
(ii) S has some understanding of how to go about accomplishing X (i.e., which actions are needed to accomplish X);
(iii) S presumes that he/she is able to accomplish X.[18]

Being connected to the cognitive context, the modalities involved in van Inwagen's reasoning are epistemic ideas not subject to the principles of closure (A) and (B). Accordingly, the entire reasoning does not support any more. If then they would like to reformulate the two principles in such a way to take the epistemic component into consideration, it could be done, but it would have to be concluded that determinism constitutes a challenge only for omniscient beings and that, "for compatibilists resigned to finitude – if not to fate – there is no occasion for alarm".[19]

As has already been mentioned, van Inwagen's reasoning has also raised other objections. For example, there is no lack of criticism about the fact that its apparent correctness is based on an ambiguous use of language. This is the case of the expression "to render false" which recurs in propositions (3) and (4). When introducing the word "render" in the proposition (3), van Inwagen suggests that there is a certain causal connection between the fact that J raises his hand and the fact that P is false. Actually, Jan Narveson believes that the fact that the judge raised his hand does not render P false, but shows that P is false. This distinction applied to proposition (3) could be interpreted as a linguistic subtlety of little impact. However, we can see what happens when this same expression is used in the context of proposition (4). In this case it can be said that the fact that J can render P false means that it is in his power to change the state of the world in an instant preceding his birth, or change physical laws. In fact, the conjunction of P_0 and L is false when at least one of the two propositions is false. If instead we correctly interpret the expression "would have rendered false", what propositions (4) affirms is that if J had raised his hand he would have shown that the description of the state of the world expressed by proposition P_0 was wrong, or that the laws of physics expressed in proposition L were wrong. This affirmation no longer has the paradoxical flavour that it had in the prior formulation. Moreover, more importantly, in this new interpretation inferring proposition (7) which affirms the impossibility of reconciling determinism and freedom is no longer permitted.[20] The criticisms put forth by Fischer and Lewis are similar in content.[21]

As has been seen, Slote and Kapitan have contested the applicability of some principles of modal logic as being valid only for logical necessity. But there is another path which could be followed to refute arguments similar to van Inwagen's. What could be discussed is the conviction that there is any sense in which the laws of nature necessitate. Bernard Berofsky has been studying this since the 1970s. He maintains that the idea of "natural law" can be analysed without resorting to any modal idea. From a certain point of view, Berofsky's criticism is the most radical, as it does not concede to van Inwagen that necessity has any role in the concept of natural law, therefore undermining his reasoning at its roots. His writing could be summarised by saying that, in his opinion, it is possible to provide an interpretation of the laws of nature in terms of regularity which supports our intuition that they are inalterable and therefore place insurmountable limits on our choices but without implying that these are in any sense necessary. This means finding a kind of middle ground between necessity and chance: natural laws must be defined by requirements that are not so strong that they include just any kind of necessity, but strong enough to exclude chance. In both cases, in fact, a characteristic that is both necessary for exercising freedom and essential for ascribing responsibility would be missing. In the first case, we could never exercise any control over our actions because in some way we would be constrained by the laws we are subject to; and in the second case because the minimal sense of order which is essential for carrying out any conscious action would be lacking.

Berofsky certainly has not chosen calm waters to venture into. Everyone understands the difficulty Hume and others after him encountered when they tried to give a satisfying definition of natural law in terms of simple regularity. The biggest obstacle for Berofsky, and those who came before him is represented by the difficulty of distinguishing the laws of nature from other accidental generalisations without appealing to their supposed necessity.[22] It does not seem to me that this attempt, which Berofsky has dedicated himself to for more than twenty years, has been quite successful. In fact, the requirements he indicates for characterising natural laws encounter the same difficulty as authors like Nagel, Hempel and Goodman have faced on.[23] Von Wright himself has many times pointed out the limits of this perspective:

Why is this raven black?...What is required, if our search for an explanation is to be satisfied, is that the basis of the explanation be somehow more strongly related to the object of explanation than simply by the law stating the universal concomitance of the two characteristics ravenhood and blackness.[24]

Still today, philosophers of science are actively discussing the role of the laws of nature and causality all inside of scientific explanation and are far from finding a satisfying solution to these problems. Due to the inadequacy of a purely descriptive conception of scientific explanation, over the past few years an idea of the explanation has been posed again that has as its foundation a strong concept of cause, understood as individualisation of the hidden mechanisms of reality.[25] Understanding this difficulty can sufficiently explain why over recent decades no one has tried to fight van Inwagen's argument by appealing to the regularity of natural laws.[26] The re-emergence of themes and perspectives which already exist in non-recent philosophical traditions, even if concealed under the cover of a complex technical apparatus, confirms once again the viscosity of philosophic tradition which often finds itself going down the same road over and over again.

Università di Roma "Tor Vergata" (Italy)

NOTES

[1] Von Wright 1984, p. vii.
[2] For further philosophical discussions on this topic see Dessì 1997.
[3] References are to P. van Inwagen's formulation of the argument in van Inwagen 1975. For other formulations of the same argument see van Inwagen 1983.
[4] van Inwagen 1975, p. 191.
[5] Lamb 1977; Ginet 1980; but see also Wiggins 1973.
[6] See Pollock 1976.
[7] See Lehrer 1976; for a critic of Lehrer's analysis see Horgan 1977; for an account similar to Lehrer's see Brown 1988; Cross 1986.
[8] von Wright 1984, p. 99.
[9] Slote 1982; Kapitan 1991; but see also Horgan 1985.
[10] Narveson 1977; Fischer 1983; Lewis 1981.
[11] See Berofsky 1971 and 1987; but see also Vihvelin 1990.
[12] Slote 1982, pp. 19–20.
[13] See Cournot 1984 (1843), pp. 55–57.
[14] See Monod 1970, pp. 126–131.
[15] Doubts about assuming such a determinism are also expressed in Berofsky 1987, pp. 138–141.
[16] This example is by Dennett 1984, p. 116. As Dennett and Kapitan, Vihvelin also pointed out to epistemic aspects of the question: see Vihvelin 1988.
[17] This time the example is by Kapitan 1991, p. 235.
[18] Kapitan 1991, p. 235.
[19] Kapitan 1991, p. 241.
[20] See Narveson 1977, p. 85; but also Lehrer 1980, p. 199.
[21] See Fischer 1983 and Lewis 1983.
[22] See Berofsky 1971, ch. VI-VII; and 1987, ch. IX.
[23] Critics to Berofsky's proposal have been arised by Kim and by van Inwagen in theirs reviews to Berofsky 1971. See Kim 1973 and van Inwagen 1973.
[24] Von Wright 1971, p. 19.
[25] See, for example, Railton 1978 and Salmon 1984.
[26] Recently Vihvelin affirmed that what the argument for incompatibilism requires is "not just a non-Humean view of laws, but a particular kind of non-Humean view which entails that at deterministic worlds there are logical connections between facts about the world at one time and facts about the world at a later time". From Vihvelin's point of view what the incompatibilist needs is "an account of laws as relations between universals" (Vivhelin 1990, p. 372).

BIBLIOGRAPHY

Armstrong 1983
    Armstrong D. M.: *What is a Law of Nature?*, Cambridge University Press, Cambridge.
Berofsky 1971
    Berofsky B.: *Determinism*, Princeton University Press, Princeton.
Berofsky 1987
    Berofsky B.: *Freedom from Necessity. The Metaphysical Basis of Responsability*, Routledge & Kegan Paul, New York-London.
Brand-Walton 1976
    Brand M. and Walton D. (eds): *Action Theory*, Reidel, Dordrecht-Boston.
Brown 1988
    Brown M. A.: "On the Logic of Ability", *Journal of Philosophical Logic* , 17, pp. 1–26.
Cournot 1984 (1843[1])
    Cournot, A.: *Exposition de la théorie des chances et des probabilités*, in B.Bru (ed.): *Oeuvres Complètes vol. I*, Vrin, Paris.
Cross 1986
    Cross C. B.: " 'Can' and the Logic of Ability", *Philosophical Studies*, 50, pp. 53–64.
Dennett 1984
    Dennett D.: *Elbow Room. The Varieties of Free Will Worth Wanting*, Clarendon Press, Oxford.
Dessì 1997
    Dessì P.: *Le metamorfosi del determinismo*, Angeli, Milano.
Fischer 1983
    Fischer J. M.: "Incompatibilism", *Philosophical Studies*, 43, pp. 127–37.
Ginet 1980
    Ginet C.: "The Conditional Analysis of Freedom", in van Inwagen 1980, pp. 171–86.
Honderich 1973
    Honderich T. (ed.): *Essays on Freedom of Action*, Routledge & Kegan Paul, London.
Horgan 1977
    Horgan T.: "Lehrer on 'Could'-Statements", *Philosophical Studies*, 32, pp. 403–11.
Horgan 1985
    Horgan T.: "Compatibilism and the Consequence Argument", *Philosophical Studies*, 47, pp. 339–56.
Kapitan 1991
    Kapitan T.: "Ability and Cognition: A Defense of Compatibilism", *Philosophical Studies*, 63, pp. 231–43.
Kim 1973
    Kim, J.: "Review" of Berofsky 1971, *Journal of Philosophy* , 70, pp. 766–71.
Lamb 1977
    Lamb J.: "On A Proof of Incompatibilism", *Philosophical Review*, 86, pp. 20–35.
Lehrer 1976
    Lehrer K.: "Can in Theory and Practice: A Possible Worlds Analysis", in Brand-Walton 1976, pp. 241–70.
Lehrer 1980
    Lehrer K.: "Preferences, Conditionals and Freedom", in van Inwagen 1980, pp. 187–201.
Lewis 1981
    Lewis D.: "Are We Free to Break the Laws?", *Theoria*, 47, pp. 113–121. Reprinted in Lewis 1983, pp. 291–98.
Lewis 1983
    Lewis D.: *Philosophical Papers II*, Oxford University Press, Oxford
Monod 1970.
    Monod J.: *Le hasard et la nécessité*, Editions du Seuil, Paris.
Narveson 1977
    Narveson J.: "Compatibilism Defended", *Philosophical Studies*, 32, pp. 83–7.

Pollock 1976
  Pollock J. L.: *Subjective Reasoning*, Reidel, Dordrecht.
Railton 1978
  Railton P.: "A Deductive-Nomological Model of Probabilistic Explanation", *Philosophy of Science*, 45, pp. 206–26.
Salmon 1984
  Salmon W.C.: *Scientific Explanation and the Causal Structure of the World*, Princeton University Press, Princeton.
Slote 1982
  Slote M.: "Selective Necessity and the Free-Will Problem", *Journal of Philosophy*, 79, pp. 5–24.
Van Inwagen 1973
  Van Inwagen P.: "Review" of Berofsky 1971, *Philosophical Review*, 82, pp. 399–404.
Van Inwagen 1975
  Van Inwagen P.: "The Incompatibility of Free Will and Determinism", *Philosophical Studies*, 27, pp. 185–99.
Van Inwagen 1980
  Van Inwagen P. (ed.): *Time and Cause*, Reidel, Dordrecht.
Van Inwagen 1983
  Van Inwagen P.: *An Essay on Free Will*, Clarendon Press, Oxford.
Vihvelin 1988
  Vihvelin K.: "The Modal Argument for Incompatibilism", *Philosophical Studies*, 53, pp. 227–44.
Vihvelin 1990
  Vihvelin K.: "Freedom, Necessity and Laws of Nature as Relations between Universals", *Australasian Journal of Philosophy*, 68, pp. 371–81.
Von Wright 1971
  Von Wright G. H.: *Explanation and Understanding*, Routledge & Kegan Paul, London.
Von Wright 1974
  Von Wright G. H.: *Causality and Determinism*, Columbia University Press, New York-London.
Von Wright 1980
  Von Wright G. H: *Freedom and Determination*, North-Holland Publishing Co., Amsterdam.
Von Wright 1984
  Von Wright G. H: *Truth, Knowledge, and Modality. Philosophical Papers*, Vol. III, Blackwell, Oxford.
Wiggins 1973
  Wiggins D.: "Towards a Reasonable Libertarianism", in Honderich 1973, pp. 31–61.

THE SIGNIFICANCE OF PHILOSOPHICAL LOGIC

In the volume of *The Library of Living Philosophers*[1] devoted to his philosophy, von Wright writes that most of what he has written could perhaps be classified as "philosophical logic". However, when it comes to dividing different themes on which he has been writing, von Wright follows what I think is more or less the prevalent terminoly and puts under the heading "philosophical logic" themes such as logical truth, entailment, modal logic, the logic of time, deontic logic, preference logic, and counterfactual conditionals. I shall follow this terminology except that, for reasons that will soon become clear, I shall not count the theme of logical truth as particularly belonging to philosophical logic.

Von Wright has made many well-known contributions to Philosophical Logic. The list of topics just mentioned is impressively long. Many of the studies have been pioneering work that has initiated new branches of logic. Deontic logic is one case of many. In this paper there is no room to give a survey of all these many important contributions; I shall have to take them as already well known, or refer the reader to e.g. the already mentioned volume of *The Library of Living Philosophers*, where they are extensively discussed. Instead I want to take up a discussion concerning the philosophical significance of this whole field called Philosopical Logic.

First, however, a few words about the term "philosophical logic", which, in my opinion, is not a very happy one, having given rise to confusions about the character and significance of the field. The term was introduced as a counterpart to "mathematical logic". Historically, the latter term was first used for the new logic that so quickly became dominant in the beginning of our century, and, as a synonym to "symbolic logic", it was meant to emphasize what was seen as so characteristic of this logic, namely the use of mathematical and symbolic means. Against that background, "philosophical logic" is of course a misnomer: the branch of logic denoted by this name is clearly using mathematical and symbolic means to the same extent as mathematical logic.

However, in view of the fact that Mathematical Logic has been very successful in analyzing logical matters in mathematics but has left many notions outside of mathematics unanalyzed, it is true that the term "mathematical logic" has slowly also come to stand for logic that is particularly concerned with logical notions occuring in mathematics. It could then perhaps be suggested that Philosophical Logic is, in contrast, the branch of logic that deals with logical notions which are of special philosophical significance. Such a perspective would in my opinion be quite misleading. In particular, Mathematical Logic is of no less philosophical importance than Philosophical Logic, and the systems it studies are not alternatives but a prerequisite for systems studied by Philosophical Logic. The lattter point is one that

157

R. Egidi (ed.), In Search of a New Humanism, 157–161.
©1999 *Kluwer Academic Publishers. Printed in Great Britain.*

has also been stressed by von Wright. It is indeed one of his early important contributions that he saw various systems of modal logic and entailment not as an alternative logic, as was long common, but as systems built upon classical logic, "which Frege and Russell had placed on a firm footing" as von Wright writes.

The question to be discussed is thus the significance of these extra things that Philosophical Logic adds to Mathematical Logic. That there are significant additions to be made can not be doubted. In view of the fact that Mathematical Logic studies only a fragment of our deductive practice, there is obviously ample room for logical studies that go beyond traditional Mathematical Logic. Such studies are important if we want to understand how natural language works. For instance, anaphoric constructions exemplified in so-called donkey sentences,

> if he has a donkey, he treats it well,

play an important role in natural language, but it is not obvious how they are to be analyzed logically. One may ask for instance whether this way of letting "it" refer to "a donkey" can be represented within the frame of traditional Mathematical Logic or requires another kind of logic. There is here a rich field of study on the borderline between logic and linguistics, which is of interest in itself, and which has also important applications; for instance, when developing automatic devices for handling natural language such studies are absolutely essential. Few would claim a particular philosophical relevance of such a study, however, and what I want to discuss here is just the philosophical significance of Philosophical Logic.

To begin this discussion, let us briefly consider the following examples of Philosophical Logic to which von Wright has contributed: the logic of conditionals, modal logic and deontic logic. They differ in respects that are important for the discussion. Conditionals that cannot be analysed as material implications are essential in everyday language as well as in empirical sciences. They seem to be unavoidable ingredients in statements of how we conceive the world, and clearly, they demand philosophical attention. A theoretical study of them may require some explications that may give rise to changes in their use, but since we are interested in their actual use, we do not want to allow a very great deviation. The philosophical study of them may thus go hand in hand with a study of how they are actually used in natural language. In other words, a philosophical and a linguistic interest may merge here.

In contrast, modal notions such as necessity and possibility are important first of all in certain philosophical theories. Although modal expressions certainly occur also in everyday contexts, they seem seldom be used there in their philosophical sense, and one cannot expect that their uncertain and fluctuating everyday use can throw much light upon their philosophical meaning.

Deontic notions seem to have an intermediate position: they are of course frequent and important in everyday language as well as in legal contexts, and they are also key concepts in moral philosophy. One may hope that their uses in these different contexts are interrelated and influence each other.

How are we then to evaluate these three rapidly expanding branches of Philosophical Logic with respect to the task of clarifying the admittedly very important philosophical notions which they are about? It seems to me that this task has unfortunately not been much forwarded by Philosophical Logic. This is dissappointing, but after all one should perhaps not expect that philosophically important notions are best approached by studying their logic.

The primary task in the study of conditionals is, I think, to understand their pragmatics: under what conditions can one rightly assert a conditional, and what can be rightly inferred from such assertions? When such questions are settled, one may be able to give a good answer to what they really mean, what their truth amounts to, and what logical laws they comply with. It seems to me that we are still far from such goals.

In the case of modal notions we do have a number of different logical systems, and they have turned out to have many fruitful and unexpected applications outside of modal and philosophical contexts. But the great number of different modal systems is precisely what is so philosophically embarassing, because one cannot say that there has been any attempt to match different systems of modal logic with different philosophical notions of necessity and possibility. The systems of modal logic and the philosophical theorizing about modal notions seem to be divorced from each other. Modal logic has therefore not brought us much closer to an understanding of what is meant by necessity and possibility, and consequently, we seem as far as ever from knowing even what logical laws govern philosophical necessity and possibility.

The situation seems to be similar in the case of deontic logic. In this field there is the curious situation that to every proposed law there is also a counter-example or paradox suggesting the unvalidity of the law proposed. For instance, it may seem obvious that if A and B are two states or actions such that the state or action "A & B" is obligatory, then both A and B are obligatory, too. For instance, from it being the case that I ought to tell the truth and keep my promises it seems to follow both that I ought to tell the truth and that I ought to keep my promises. Letting "O" stand for "it is obligatory that" we may write the proposed law in the form

$$O(A \& B) \rightarrow OA \& OB$$

But from an utilitarian point of view, this law is after all not so obvious: A & B may have the best consequences of all available alternatives and ought then to be done, but A and B alone may not have the best consequences, and neither of them should then be done. The law thus seems to be sensitive to what moral theory we have about moral obligations.

The proposed law is the dual to the law that says that if A and B are two states or actions such that one is permissable, then the state or action "A or B" is also permissable. If "P" stands for "it is permissible that", this dual law may be written

$$PA \lor PB \rightarrow P(A \lor B)$$

and is thus equivalent with the one given above, assuming classical logic and the usual definitions of P and O in terms of each other. But aginst this later law, there is a well-known counter-example, the so-called Ross' paradox: it may be permissible to mail a letter but not permissible to either post the letter or burn it.

When evaluating the situation in deontic logic, one should keep in mind that counter-examples could easily be given also to basic laws in classical propositional logic. For instance, "and" is often used in everyday language in such a way that the law of commutativity does not hold: "A and B" does not imply "B and A" when there is a connotation of temporal order in the use of "and". This does not disturb classical logic, because its logical constants have a clear meaning, which makes it irrelevant that corresponding expressions in natural language may sometimes be used with a different meaning. The success of classical logic depends on the fact that one has isolated an interesting and important use of some logical expessions in natural language. In this way one has been able to fix certain concepts and to study their logical properties.

The moral of this seems to be that one cannot expect a philosophically interesting development in logic, if one is not able to demarcate in some way a definite and significant meaning of the notions studied. How this is to be achieved may vary. In the case of conditionals, what seems to be lacking is first of all knowledge of the pragmatics of these expressions, the identification of various uses of conditionals in serious contexts. In the case of modal and deontic notions, it seems to be the philosophical theories about these notions that need to be developed. Philosophical logic could have a role to play in a project of clarifying central philosophical notions, but this requires that logical study and conceptual analysis join together and do not go their own ways, which is now most often the case.

There is also another aspect of the significance of philosophical logic to which I want to draw attention. To my mind, logic is a branch of philosophy not primarily because of a specifically philosophical nature of the notions occuring in various logical systems, but because the very phenomena of logical consequence and logical truth are of outermost philosophical interest. I think that von Wright shares this view concerning the philosophical essence of logic. In his autobiography that is published in the volume of *The Library of Living Philosophers* devoted to his philosophy, von Wright tells us that it was the notion of logical truth which attracted his attention at an early stage, and he describes how his attempt to approach it via the distributive normal form led him into Philosophical Logic and, in particular, gave rise to *An Essay in Modal Logic*.[2]

One can roughly distinguish two different approaches to the notions of logical consequence and logical truth. One starts with a notion of logical possibility, and conceives the content of a sentence to consist in its division of all possible worlds into those with which it is compatible and those with which it is incompatible. It then takes a sentence to be logically true when it is compatible with everyting, or, in other words, when it leaves all possibilities open and therefore has no content. This was the line taken by Wittgenstein in *Tractatus*, and it is the line also followed by von Wright when he explains logical truths as tautologies by appeal to the distributive normal form. The other approach is a constructive one, which is closer to the later Wittgenstein, and which rejects the first approach as one approriate only for an omniscient being, who can survey all existing logical possibilities. Not being able to attach any meaning to such a notion, the constructive approach starts instead from how we make inferences and what we count as establishing a truth. It conceives the content of a sentence to be reflected in what counts as verifying the sentence. Normally the establishing of a truth requires extra-linguistic evidence, i.e. it is not enough to know only what it is to verify the sentence in question. But there is the extreme case when a truth is established by just appealing to what counts as verifying it without the use of any extra-linguistic evidence. Logical truth is understood as a truth that can be established in this way; logical truth becomes then again a kind of degenerated truth, obtained as a limit, but now in a different way.

These two approaches to logical truth were first worked out for predicate logic. The philosophical interest of Mathematical Logic derives above all from the fact that it has isolated and developed a sufficiently interesting and broad class of logical inferences, which has enabled it to approach fruitfully the concepts of logical consequence and logical truth. From this point of view one can say that the philosophical significance of Philosophical Logical is primarily that it has broaden the scene and provided further material for philosophical reflections on logical consequence and logical truth.

In his pioneering work *An Essay in Modal Logic*, von Wright gave further support to the first approach to logical truth by extending the notion of tautology and the use of distributive normal form from propositional logic to several new systems of Philosophical Logic that he developed in this work. The debate between the two approaches was in this way enriched but not decided since Philosophical Logic also yields strong arguments in favour of the second approach. From a constructive point of view one may object to the idea of linking the content of a sentence to its distributive normal form on the ground that even in the case of classical predicate logic, we cannot effectively transform an arbitrary sentence into distributive normal form. A much more radical criticism of that approach to logical truth is forthcoming if one doubts that there is a definite truth value attached to each sentence. Such doubts are raised by the intuitionists already in connection with the quantifiers of predicate logic, but it seems to me that they are strongly reinforced given the broader scene of Philosophical Logic. In particular, there seem to be good reasons to doubt that the conditionals can be analysed in such a way that a definite truth value is always attached to them. If this is right, the first approach to logical truth is blocked, and the second approach seems to be what remains.

Regardless of what position one takes with regard to these questions, they illustrate my point that the philosophical significance of Philosophical Logic is above all that it enriches the discussion of the phenomena of logical consequence and logical truth, which I take to be what logic as a philosophical discipline is primarily concerned with.

Stockholm University (Sweden)

NOTES

[1] *The Philosophy of Georg Henrik von Wright*, ed. by P. A. Schilpp and L. E. Hahn, Open Court, La Salle, Ill. 1989.
[2] North-Holland Publishing Co., Amsterdam 1951.

MIRELLA CAPOZZI*

A REMARK ABOUT THE PRINCIPLE "OUGHT ENTAILS CAN": VON WRIGHT AND KANT†

In *Norm and Action* von Wright discusses the principle "Ought entails Can". He also points out that this principle is associated chiefly with the ethics of Kant, but he makes it clear that he is interested in giving his own point of view on the subject, rather than investigating "what Kant meant by it" (*NA* 108). I believe however that von Wright's point of view is interesting also with respect to giving an insight into Kant's theory.

I. According to von Wright the principle "Ought entails Can" affirms a relation of logical (not causal) entailment between a premise "to the effect that there is a norm of such and such a character and content" and a conclusion "to the effect that the enjoined or permitted thing, which is the content of the norm, can be done" (*NA* 110). This means that the "existence of a norm" depends logically on "facts about ability" (*NA* 110). Therefore the principle under discussion can be formulated, for norms which are prescriptions (i. e. commands, permissions, and prohibitions given by a norm-authority to some norm-subject(s), (*NA* 7), in the following way: "*That there is a prescription which enjoins or permits a certain thing, presupposes that the subject(s) of the prescription can do the enjoined or permitted thing*" (*NA* 111).

But what does it mean that the subjects of a prescription *can do* the enjoined or permitted thing? Von Wright distinguishes two meanings of *can do*: 1) *can do* as an *ability* to do "the *kind* of thing which the norm enjoins or permits" (*generic ability*); 2) *can do* as *success* "in each individual case" (*NA* 111). Von Wright maintains that the meaning of *can do* involved in his formulation of the principle "Ought entails Can" is only the first one. In order to exclude the second meaning he considers the case of a person who has been commanded to do a certain thing on a certain occasion, but fails. If *can do* were meant as success in each individual case, the fact that this person *cannot do* on that occasion the thing he or she is commanded to do would entail, *modo tollente*, that "there is *not* a duty to do this thing" (*NA* 110). Failure to obey the norm in a individual case would annihilate the norm, and this is not acceptable. On the contrary, if the subjects of a prescription do not have generic ability to do the prescribed thing, "it is natural to say" that they "cannot 'receive' " "the order at all" (*NA* 122).

II. Kant does not have a fully fledged theory of norms. He has, however, a general theory of goal-oriented willing and within this theory he also considers actions done in obedience to a prescription. This is not surprising for it is Kant's view that human beings always act for the sake of an end (Korsgaard 1996 176), and this obviously also applies to actions done because one ought to do them.

R. Egidi (ed.), In Search of a New Humanism, 163–170.
©1999 *Kluwer Academic Publishers. Printed in Great Britain.*

Kant's theory of rational goal-oriented willing is governed by a general law: *Who wills the end, wills (so far as reason has decisive influence on his actions) also the means which are indispensably necessary and in his power* (*Gr* IV 417). This law – which for Kant is analytically true – is formulated for agents endowed with a perfectly rational will. This is not the case with human beings who have to be constrained by imperatives: what a perfectly rational will (a holy will) necessarily *would* do is what imperfectly rational agents *ought* to do (*Gr* IV 413–4). Therefore Kant formulates the general law of rational goal-oriented willing as follows: *Whoever wills an end, ought to will the means*. This law can also be expressed in a hypothetical form: *If you will a certain end you ought do a certain act*. The latter sentence is a hypothetical imperative which obligates the agent to an action on condition that the agent has a *desire* for something that the action would bring about.[1]

Formulated as a hypothetical imperative the general law of goal-oriented willing takes into account the above mentioned peculiarity of human actions, i. e. that they are all purposive, so that, as Kant maintains, "I ought to do something because I will something else [*Ich soll etwas thun darum, weil ich etwas anders will*]" (*Gr* IV 441). The purposive nature of human actions is essential to compensate for the imperfection of human will and characterises human beings as rational. According to Kant, when acting rationally human beings follow a kind of three-step procedure: 1) before they do a certain act *x*, they look out for the result of doing *x*; 2) in case they approve of that result, they assume it *as an end* worth obtaining; 3) since it is analytically true that whoever wills an end ought to will the means, they consider the act *x*, which is the means to obtain the assumed end, as something they ought to do in order to obtain that end (*Rel* VI 7 note). This is a rational procedure because only rational beings (though imperfect as to their will) are "capable of projecting ends, acting on the basis of self-imposed general principles (maxims) and in the light of objectively valid rational norms" (Allison 1996, 126).

Goal-oriented willing is governed also by the moral law: *A perfectly rational will acts only through maxims which it could also will to be universal laws*. For beings who have an imperfect rational will this law too – which for Kant is not analytic – must be given the form of an imperative. This time, however, the imperative is categorical: *Act only according to that maxim through which you can at the same time will that it should become a universal law* (*Gr* IV 421. Cf. Schneewind 1992 319–20).

III. Kant would agree to a very large extent with von Wright's analysis of the principle "Ought entails Can". On the one hand, hypothetical imperatives, which can be considered as prescriptions in so far as they have a kind of self-imposed normative character subordinated to an end (*NA* 11), presuppose generic ability. Indeed the general law of goal-oriented willing itself says that "Who wills the end, wills [...] also the means which are [...] *in his power* [my italics]". On the other hand, and *a fortiori*, generic ability is presupposed by the categorical imperative which is patently a prescription: how could we act as if the maxim of our action were to become, through our will, a *universal law of nature* unless *every* human agent was supposed to be *able* to perform that kind of action? Kant leaves no doubt on this point: "duty [...] commands us [...] nothing but what we can do [*Pflicht* [...] *gebietet uns* [...] *nichts, als was uns thunlich ist*]" (*Rel* VI). The fact that the categorical imperative operates mostly through vetoes is not an impediment here. As von Wright has shown, "ought to" and "must not" are interdefinable (*NA* 83-5), therefore the principle that "Ought entails Can" applies to vetoes as well.

In my opinion Kant would also agree with von Wright in saying that if someone, having generic ability to do what a norm prescribes, fails to do it on an individual occasion, the norm is not thereby annihilated. This is particularly obvious for the categorical imperative: our failures in obeying it are far from annihilating it.

IV. However in Kant's conception the ability presupposed by a prescription is more than generic ability. This will become apparent if we refer to von Wright's analysis of the "classical" theory of norms which applies primarily to prescriptions, and which he calls "the *will-theory* of norms" (*NA* 120). According to this theory, "norms are the expressions or manifestations of the will of some norm-authority with regard to the conduct of some norm subject(s)" (*NA* 121). Von Wright – who judges this theory "substantially correct" as a theory of the ontological status of prescriptions generally – maintains that the will of which commands are manifestations is "seldom a will to make do or forbear 'for its own sake', but has some ulterior end in view" (*NA* 121).

Given that for Kant actions done in obedience to a prescription also fall within his theory of rational goal-oriented willing, a human being has to ask: "if I do what I ought to do, what will be the result thereof?" This question can hardly concern the content of the prescription. If an authority prescribes: "Open the door", the subject of the prescription knows that the result of his or her obedience will be that a closed door will be open. When the subject asks: "what will be the result of my doing the prescribed act?", the subject wants to know what, in von Wright's terms, the ulterior end is that the authority has in view. But this means that the subject expects that *there is such an end* (which definitively proves that Kant adopts the will-theory of norms). Kant is absolutely clear on this point: it is a natural property of human beings that in all their actions they must conceive "a further end, beyond the law [*außer dem Gesetz noch einen Zweck*]" (*Rel* VI 7 note).

But human beings not only expect that there is an end "beyond the law". Given the purposive character Kant ascribes to all their actions, they have to approve of the ulterior end beyond the law and make it their own, so as to try to attain it by doing what the law prescribes. This means that they expect that, by doing what the law prescribes, *they will be able to attain, at least in principle, the ulterior end beyond the law*. Therefore from the point of view of an agent who cannot but act purposively the principle "Ought entails Can" not only affirms that the subjects of a prescription can receive it only if they are generically able to do the content of the prescription. It also affirms that the subjects of a prescription can receive it only if they also judge that they, *at least in principle, are able to attain* the end beyond the prescription, on the presupposition that there is one.

V. This reading of the principle "Ought entails Can" can be clarified if we consider the motives of subjects of a prescription who, though able to do the prescribed thing, decide not to do it. In *NA* von Wright considers only motives for disobedience and seems to restrict them to the opposition of the subjects of a prescription either to the content or to the ulterior end of that prescription.

However it is possible to consider the case of a subject of a prescription who is able to do the content of the prescription and who does not oppose it. As human beings always do, this subject asks the "Kantian" question about the ulterior end of the prescription. There are two answers to this question that can constitute motives for not doing the content of the prescription. Case 1) The subject sees that the prescription is *pointless*, i. e. it has no ulterior end. Case 2) The subject sees that the prescription has an ulterior end, agrees with it and is willing to obtain it by doing the prescribed thing. Nonetheless this subject realises that he or she *is in principle not able to attain the ulterior end of the prescription*.

These are motives for not receiving a prescription rather than for disobeying it. Those who disobey receive the prescription, i. e. recognise it as existent, in as much as they admit that they can do what they ought to do, where "can do" means that they have generic ability to do the prescribed thing and are also able to attain the ulterior end of the prescription. But, since they actively oppose the content and/or the ulterior end of the prescription, they decide to disobey. Those who would consider themselves justified in not receiving a prescription whose content they are able to do, acknowledge the prescription as existent only in so far as they possess the required generic ability. But they consider either the prescription pointless or themselves in principle not able to attain the ulterior end of the prescription. In a Kantian perspective, according to which human beings must conceive of an end beyond the law, a prescription that lacks an ulterior end, or whose ulterior end cannot be attained in principle by those who are asked to obey, is seriously defective. Therefore, just as von Wright argues that if the subjects of a prescription cannot (have no generic ability to) do the prescribed thing, then "there is *not* a duty to do this thing" (*NA* 110), why should this argument not apply also to subjects who have generic ability to do the prescribed thing, but cannot attain the end beyond the prescription, either because there is none or because it is in principle unattainable for them?

In discussing disobedience von Wright makes a very interesting observation: a prescription can be obeyed just for fear of punishment. Indeed fear of sanction (threat of punishment) is "a motive for obedience to the norm in the absence of other motives for obedience and in the presence of motives for disobedience" (*NA* 126). Obviously also subjects who would feel justified in disregarding a prescription for the reasons discussed above could consider fear a motive for doing the content of a pointless prescription or of a prescription whose ulterior end they cannot attain. But it is important to stress, as von Wright does (*NA* 127–8), that fear of sanction can function as a motive of obedience only if the norm-authority issuing the prescription is strong enough to guarantee that transgressors will be punished.

VI. All this is important if we are to appreciate Kant's treatment of the moral law. This law, as we have seen, presupposes generic ability on our part: "duty [...] commands us [...] nothing but what we can do" (*Rel* VI 47). What duty commands must be "*thunlich*", "doable", i. e. must be "something which can be achieved through human action" (von Wright 1998 6). Indeed the moral law would seem to presuppose only our generic ability for, as a formal principle, it commands absolutely, whatever the result might be [*es mag auch der Erfolg* [...] *sein, welcher er wolle*]" (*Rel* VI 7 note; *Gr* IV 416), i. e. independently of the objects of our faculty of desiring (the matter of the will), therefore "independently of any end [*unangesehen* [...] *irgend eines Zwecks*]" (*KdU* §91 note V 471).

But precisely this is the problem. Human beings do not simply do (as they should) what pure reason prescribes them in the law: they have to compensate for their imperfect will with rationality. Thus they look out for the result even of acts that ought to be done in obedience to the moral law (*Rel* VI 7–8 note). The control of rationality over imperfect will ensures that human beings cannot obey blindly. Therefore they cannot but ask: "what is to result from this right conduct of ours [*was* [...] *aus diesem unserm Rechthandeln herauskomme*]"? (*Rel* VI 5).[2] As I have pointed out referring to prescriptions in general, this question does not concern the content of the moral law, but its ulterior end.

Does the moral law have an ulterior end? Surely the moral law is not pointless: we are not in the situation of the subject of a prescription described in Case 1) above. Indeed the ulterior end of the moral law is so important as to be the "final end [*Endzweck*] of all rational beings" (*KdU* §91 note V 471). This *Endzweck* is the highest good (*summum bonum*) which functions as a point of connection [*Beziehungspunkt*] for the unification of all ends (*Rel* VI 5), and is the desirable objective outcome of all moral and historical efforts of mankind. But then: can we, at least in principle, attain the highest good? This depends on *what* the highest good is.

VII. Kant gives different definitions of the highest good in different contexts (Cf. Yovel 1980 48 ff.). For the present discussion we can refer to his definition of the highest good as "happiness in as much as it is possible in accordance with duty" (*KdU* §91 note V 471), i. e. as the agreement between our pursuit of the "satisfaction of all our desires" (*KrV* A806/B834) and the duty moral laws impose on us.

Now when we are confronted with the moral law we find ourselves in the same situation as the subject of a prescription described above in Case 2). Though we are able to do what the moral law prescribes, though we recognise that there is an end beyond the law and approve of it, though we are ready to make it our own end so as to attain it by obeying the law, our speculative reason cannot help seeing that to expect from nature alone (in us and outside us) the achievement of the *summum bonum* thanks to our good conduct is "a groundless and vain, though well meant, expectation" (*KdU* §91 note V 471). This puts us in a difficult position. For the final end is a duty "in as much as it is attainable [*sofern er erreichbar ist*]", and vice versa – which definitely confirms our reading of the Kantian sense of the principle "Ought entails Can" – "if it is a duty it must also be attainable [*wenn er Pflicht ist, auch erreichbar sein muß*]"(*EF* VIII 418).

Notice that for Kant obedience to the categorical imperative makes us worthy to be happy. But this is not enough. We still want to know: if we so act as to be worthy of happiness, can we hope to partake of it? (*KrV* A 809/B837). To this question there is no certain answer. Indeed, for all we can see, there is no certainty of a reward for the virtuous (nor of punishment for the vicious). If the moral law were on a par with any other prescription, the inaccessibility of the final end, which would be the only appropriate reward for our good conduct (as well as the uncertainty of punishment for the disobedient), would make us feel justified in not receiving it.

But the categorical imperative can never be annihilated. Kant's well known way out of this *impasse* is oddly reminiscent of von Wright's analysis of the need of a strong authority threatening punishments when motives for obeying a prescription are lacking. In fact – putting the emphasis on reward rather than on punishment – Kant maintains: "if the most rigorous observance of moral laws must be thought of as cause of the bringing about of the highest good (as end) [*als Ursache der Herbeiführung des höchsten Guts (als Zwecks)*], then – because the capacity of men is not sufficient to bring it about that happiness in the world be in accordance with worthiness to be happy – an omnipotent moral being as lord of the world must be assumed, under whose providence this accordance takes place, that is it must be assumed that morality inevitably leads to religion" (*Rel* VI 7–8 note). In this way Kant reverses von Wright's observation that if we know that there exists a strong authority threatening punishments we (sometimes) obey a prescription which we would otherwise disobey, or which we would not receive because it is defective. Kant fundamentally agrees with this observation where ordinary prescriptions are concerned. But in the case of the moral law he argues the other way round: since this law appears defective because we cannot attain its ulterior end in this life, we must assume a providential intelligence, sufficiently strong to be omnipotent, which can *promise* that in another life we shall attain, as the reward for our good conduct, the end beyond the moral law.[3] Briefly: we need to believe (since we cannot prove) in a super-human authority and in the immortality of our souls as a condition for obeying the moral law and, *ex converso*, this belief is justified because we have to obey a law which cannot be annihilated although we are not able to attain its ulterior end in this life (Cf. Korsgaard 1996 172). Only thus – says Kant – is it that "I know that he who behaves well, is worthy of happiness, and I believe that he will partake of it" (*Reflexion* 2491 XVI 92). For Kant this extraordinary situation has positive aspects: 1) it does not appeal to a kind of irrational faith, but is based on an analysis of rational action (and indeed it is a "rational moral faith", *L* IX 72 note); 2) it makes our moral conduct meritorious, for if we knew that God exists and our souls are immortal, our moral conduct would be only a wise consequence of such knowledge. Therefore "free faith in God is meritorious, apodictic certainty and constrictive faith born out of fear is not" (*Reflexion* 5495 XVIII 198–199), and this is why "we are given only so much light [*ist uns nur so viel Licht gegeben*]" (*ibidem*).

VIII. To conclude, von Wright's claim that the principle "Ought entails Can" affirms that the subjects of a prescription are supposed to have generic ability to do the content of the prescription, but are nor supposed to succeed on every single occasion, can be perfectly adapted to Kant's philosophy. However it seems to me that for Kant, due to his thesis that all human rational actions are purposive, and to his endorsing what von Wright calls the will-theory of norms, the subjects of a prescription are also supposed to be able in principle to attain the prescription's ulterior end. Consequently, the fact that we "ought" to obey a prescription entails that we "can" both do the content of the prescription and attain its ulterior end. In case we cannot attain the ulterior end of the prescription we should be justified in not receiving it, just as if we had no generic ability to obey. But when it comes to the moral law we find that, although we cannot attain this law's ulterior end, it is impossible not to receive it. Therefore, whereas von Wright points out that the existence of an authority capable of punishing transgressors can be a motive for obeying an ordinary prescription whose (immediate or ulterior) end we oppose (or whose ulterior end seems impossible to attain), Kant argues that, because there exists a law which cannot be annihilated, despite the fact that its ulterior end cannot be attained in this life, we must necessarily assume the existence of a divine authority capable of guaranteeing that our obedience will be rewarded with the attainment of that ulterior end in a life beyond our biological existence.

Università di Siena (Italy)

NOTES

* I wish to thank Prof. B. F. McGuinness for helpful philosophical and linguistic suggestions concerning this paper.
† Research for this paper has been supported by 60% MURST funds.
[1] According to lecture-notes taken by students of one of Kant's pre-critical courses on logic, Kant commented on the odd status of judgements which are imperatives but lack necessity: "A judgement is expressed practically if it enunciates a possibly necessary action. This probably seems to be contradictory, that something is *possibly necessary*. But here it is completely correct, for the action is always necessary, to be sure, namely if I want to bring the thing about; but the case is not necessary, but merely possible" (*Logik Blomberg* XXIV, p. 278).
[2] Cf. Yovel 1980, pp. 40–1: "The pure principle of morality demands that man act without regard of consequences. He ought to do his duty regardless of circumstances, even if he has good reason to believe that the consequences of his act will be lost in a hostile and indifferent nature. As far as the formal law is concerned, a man can act in a vacuum, without contributing to any real change in the world. However Kant regards such a situation as incompatible with human nature [...] even when he [man] acts from duty, disregarding his self-interest and thus becoming *subjectively* moral, he still wants objective results that contribute to the implementation of a moral project in the world. Man is naturally incapable of intending to perform futile [...] deeds but constantly demands to know "what is to result from this right conduct of ours".
[3] Cf. *KrV* A633-4/B 661-2: "Now since there are practical laws which are absolutely necessary, that is the moral laws, it must follow that if these necessarily presuppose the existence of any being [*irgend ein Dasein*] as the condition of the possibility of their *obligatory* power, this existence must be *postulated*; and this for the sufficient reason that the conditioned, from which the inference is drawn to this determinate condition, is itself known *a priori* to be absolutely necessary".

BIBLIOGRAPHY

Quotations from Kant are from *Kant's Gesammelte Schriften*, hrsg. von der Königlich Preussischen Akademie der Wissenschaften zu Berlin und Nachfolgern, 1902– . Citations are located by an abbreviation, followed by the number of the volume (roman numerals) and page of the *Akademie* edition, except for quotations from the *Kritik der reinen Vernunft* which are located by the pagination of the first edition of 1781 (A) and of the second edition of 1787 (B).

Allison 1996
  Allison H. E.: *Idealism and Freedom. Essays on Kant's Theoretical and Practical Philosophy*, Cambridge University Press, Cambridge.
Kant 1796
  Kant I. (*EF*): *Verkündigung des nahen Abschlusses eines Tractats zum ewigen Frieden in der Philosophie*.
Kant 1785
  Kant I. (*Gr*): *Grundlegung zur Metaphysik der Sitten*.
Kant 1800
  Kant I. (*L*): *Logik. Ein Handbuch zu Vorlesungen*.
Kant 1790
  Kant I. (*KdU*): *Kritik der Urtheilskraft*.
Kant 1781
  Kant I. (*KrV*) *Kritik der reinen Vernunft* (1787²).
Kant 1793
  Kant I. (*Rel*): *Die Religion innerhalb der Grenzen der bloßen Vernunft*.
Korsgaard 1996
  Korsgaard C. M.: *Creating the Kingdom of Ends*, Cambridge University Press, Cambridge.
Schneewind 1992
  Schneewind J. B.: "Autonomy, Obligation and Virtue: An Overview of Kant's Moral Philosophy", in P. Guyer (ed.): *The Cambridge Companion to Kant*, Cambridge University Press, Cambridge.
Von Wright 1963
  Von Wright G. H. (*NA*): *Norm and Action. A Logical Enquiry*, Routledge & Kegan Paul-The Humanities Press, London-New York.
Von Wright 1999
  Von Wright G. H.: "Deontic Logic – as I See It", in *Norms, Logics, and Information Studies. New Studies in Deontic Logic*, ed. by P. McNamara and H. Prakken, IOS Press, Amsterdam.
Yovel 1980
  Yovel Y.: *Kant and the Philosophy of History*, Princeton University Press, Princeton.

CARLO CELLUCCI

THE DECIDABILITY OF SYLLOGISM

Aristotle is often blamed for developing the theory of syllogism instead of writing a Greek version of Frege's *Begriffsschrift*. With hindsight, however, one must admit that he had a good reason for doing so: syllogism, and more generally monadic logic, is decidable whereas polyadic and even dyadic logic is undecidable. As van Heijenoort [10] points out, in that respect Aristotle's theory of syllogism was a lucky strike because Aristotle hit into a part of logic where quantifiers are inessential: monadic logic can be translated into a quantifier-free calculus. In another respect, however, Aristotle's restriction to the theory of syllogism was unjustified: monadic logic is decidable only in principle, not in practice. All known decision procedures for it are too complex to be feasible.

That does not mean that there is no difference between alternative decision procedures. For example, the decision procedure for monadic logic of Bernays-Schönfinkel [3] presented in current textbooks – such as Hilbert-Bernays [8], Church [4], Hunter [7], Boolos-Jeffrey [2] – is somewhat cumbersome. The alternative decision procedure of Behmann [1], Quine [9] and von Wright [11] is simpler. It consists in first reducing every sentence of monadic logic to Herbrand normal form [6], then moving quantifiers to the innermost possible place inside the sentence and finally applying the truth-table decision procedure.

Strangely enough the Behmann-Quine-von Wright procedure is generally neglected in current textbooks. This is rather unfortunate because under several respects it is more agreeable than the current Bernays-Schönfinkel procedure. In this paper we present a version of the Behmann-Quine-von Wright procedure reduced to its bare essentials.

Definition 1. In what follows we assume that all notions and notations not explicitly explained are defined like in Enderton [5]. By $\mathfrak{L}$ we designate a first-order language without equality all of whose non-logical symbols are one-place predicate symbols.

Definition 2. By an *elementary quantification* we mean a formula of $\mathfrak{L}$ of the form $\exists x \bigwedge_{i=1}^{n} \varphi_i$ where each φ_i is either Px or $\neg Px$ for some one-place predicate symbol P.

Definition 3. We say that a formula φ of $\mathfrak{L}$ is in *Herbrand normal form* if it satisfies the following conditions:

(i) φ is a truth-functional combination of elementary quantifications;
(ii)   all elementary quantifications in φ contain the same one-place predicate symbols, occurring once each.

171

R. Egidi (ed.), In Search of a New Humanism, 171–174.

Theorem 4. For any sentence φ of $\mathfrak{L}$ there is a sentence φ' of $\mathfrak{L}$ in Herbrand normal form such that $\models \varphi \leftrightarrow \varphi'$.

Proof. Let φ be a sentence of $\mathfrak{L}$. By the Prenex Normal Form Theorem there is a prenex formula $Q_1 x_1 ... Q_n x_n \varphi'$, where Q_i is $\exists$ or $\forall$, such that

(1) $\models \varphi \leftrightarrow Q_1 x_1 ... Q_n x_n \varphi'$.

Let $P_1, ..., P_k$ be the one-place predicate symbols occurring in φ'. We may assume without loss of generality that $Q_n \equiv \exists$. [For, if $Q_n \equiv \forall$, then replace $Q_n x_n$ by $\neg \exists x_n \neg$ and apply the procedure described below to $\exists x_n \neg \varphi'$ rather than to $\exists x_n \varphi'$].

By the Disjunctive Normal Form Theorem there is a formula $\bigvee_{i=1}^{m} \tau_i$ of $\mathfrak{L}$ in disjunctive normal form such that

(2) $\models \varphi' \leftrightarrow \bigvee_{i=1}^{m} \tau_i$ where τ_i is a finite conjunction of atomic formulas or negations of atomic formulas.

Let ρ_i be the conjunction of the conjuncts of τ_i in which x_n does not occur, and σ_i the conjunction of the conjuncts of τ_i in which x_n occurs. Then $\models \exists x_n \varphi' \leftrightarrow \exists x_n \bigvee_{i=1}^{m} \tau_i$ [by (2)] $\leftrightarrow \bigvee_{i=1}^{m} \exists x_n \tau_i \leftrightarrow \bigvee_{i=1}^{m} (\rho_i \wedge \exists x_n \sigma_i)$ [for, $\models \exists x_n \tau_i \leftrightarrow \exists x_n (\rho_i \wedge \sigma_i) \leftrightarrow \rho_i \wedge \exists x_n \sigma_i$ since x_n does not occur in ρ_i], so

(3) $\models \exists x_n \varphi' \leftrightarrow \bigvee_{i=1}^{m} (\rho_i \wedge \exists x_n \sigma_i)$.

We can assume without loss of generality that every elementary quantification $\exists x_n \sigma_i$ in $\bigvee_{i=1}^{m} (\rho_i \wedge \exists x_n \sigma_i)$ contains all of $P_1, ..., P_k$, occurring once each. To show that we distinguish two cases.

Case 1: $\exists x_n \sigma_i$ does not contain P_j. Then replace $\exists x_n \sigma_i$ by the formula $\exists x_n (P_j x_n \wedge \sigma_i) \vee \exists x_n (\neg P_j x_n \wedge \sigma_i)$ [for, $\models \exists x_n (P_j x_n \wedge \sigma_i) \vee \exists x_n (\neg P_j x_n \wedge \sigma_i) \leftrightarrow \exists x_n ((P_j x_n \wedge \sigma_i) \vee (\neg P_j x_n \wedge \sigma_i)) \leftrightarrow \exists x_n \sigma_i$].

Case 2: $\exists x_n \sigma_i$ contains some P_j twice.

Subcase 2.1: $\exists x_n \sigma_i$ contains the conjunct $P_j x_n$ twice. Then drop one of the two conjuncts $P_j x_n$ [for, $\models P_j x_n \wedge P_j x_n \leftrightarrow P_j x_n$].

Subcase 2.2: $\exists x_n \sigma_i$ contains the conjunct $\neg P_j x_n$ twice. Then drop one of the two conjuncts $\neg P_j x_n$ [for, $\models \neg P_j x_n \wedge \neg P_j x_n \leftrightarrow \neg P_j x_n$].

Subcase 2.3: $\exists x_n \sigma_i$ contains both the conjunct $P_j x_n$ and the conjunct $\neg P_j x_n$. Then drop the whole disjunct $\rho_i \wedge \exists x_n \sigma_i$ [for, in such case $\models \neg(\rho_i \wedge \exists x_n \sigma_i)$, so $\models \chi \vee (\rho_i \wedge \exists x_n \sigma_i) \leftrightarrow \chi$].

Now $\models \varphi \leftrightarrow Q_1 x_1 ... Q_{n-1} x_{n-1} \bigvee_{i=1}^{m} (\rho_i \wedge \exists x_n \sigma_i)$ [by (1) and (3)], so $Q_n (\equiv \exists)$ can be moved to the innermost possible place inside φ. Applying the same procedure successively to $Q_{n-1}, ..., Q_1$ we finally obtain a sentence φ' with the required properties.

Definition 5. We say that two elementary quantifications are *essentially identical* if they differ at most with respect to their variables and the order of their conjuncts; *essentially different* if they are not essentially identical.

Definition 6. Let φ be a sentence of $\mathfrak{L}$ in Herbrand normal form, let $\rho_1, ..., \rho_m$ be the elementary quantifications and $P_1, ..., P_k$ the one-place predicate symbols contained in φ. Let h be a truth-assignment for $\mathfrak{L}$. We say that h is *good* for φ if one of the following conditions is satisfied: either

(i) $\rho_1, ..., \rho_m$ are all possible essentially different elementary quantifications containing $P_1, ..., P_k$, and $h(\rho_i) = 1$ for some i, $1 \leq i \leq n$; or

(ii) $\rho_1, ..., \rho_m$ are not all possible essentially different elementary quantifications containing $P_1, ..., P_k$.

Theorem 7. Let φ be a sentence of $\mathfrak{L}$ in Herbrand normal form, let $\rho_1, ..., \rho_m$ be the elementary quantifications and $P_1, ..., P_k$ the one-place predicate symbols contained in φ. Then, for every truth-assignment h that is good for φ, $\models \varphi \Leftrightarrow h(\varphi) = 1$.

Proof. $\Rightarrow$. Assume $\models \varphi$. Let h be any truth-assignment good for φ. Let $\rho_{i_1}, ..., \rho_{i_n}$ be those among $\rho_1, ..., \rho_m$ such that $h(\rho_{i_1}) = ... = h(\rho_{i_n}) = 1$. Let $\mathfrak{A}$ be the structure for $\mathfrak{L}$ defined by:

$|\mathfrak{A}| = \{1, ..., n\}$,

$P_i^{\mathfrak{A}} = \{j : \rho_{i_j}$ contains a conjunct of the form $P_i x$, for $1 \leq j \leq n\}$.

[So, if ρ_{i_j} contains some conjunct of the form $P_i x$, then $j \in P_i^{\mathfrak{A}}$; if ρ_{i_j} contains some conjunct of the form $\neg P_i x$, then it does not contain the conjunct $P_i x$, so $j \notin P_i^{\mathfrak{A}}$].

Let s be any assignment in $\mathfrak{A}$. Then clearly $\models_{\mathfrak{A}} \rho_{i_1}[s], ..., \models_{\mathfrak{A}} \rho_{i_n}[s]$ and $\not\models_{\mathfrak{A}} \rho_i[s]$ for $i \neq i_1, ..., i_n$, $1 \leq i \leq m$. So for $1 \leq i \leq m$,

(1) $\models_{\mathfrak{A}} \rho_i[s] \Leftrightarrow h(\rho_i) = 1$.

It can be easily shown by induction on φ using (1) that

(2) $\models_{\mathfrak{A}} \varphi[s] \Leftrightarrow h(\varphi) = 1$.

Since $\models \varphi$ we have $\models_{\mathfrak{A}} \varphi[s]$, so $h(\varphi) = 1$ [by (2)], as required.

$\Leftarrow$. Suppose that $h(\varphi) = 1$ for every truth-assignment h good for φ. Let $\mathfrak{A}$ be any structure for $\mathfrak{L}$ and s any assignment in $\mathfrak{A}$. Let h be a truth-assignment for $\mathfrak{L}$ such that for $1 \leq i \leq m$,

$h(\rho_i) = 1 \Leftrightarrow \models_{\mathfrak{A}} \rho_i[s]$.

It can be easily shown by induction on φ that

(3) $h(\varphi) = 1 \Leftrightarrow \models_{\mathfrak{A}} \varphi[s]$.

It can also be shown that h is good for φ. We distinguish two cases.

Case 1: $\rho_1, ..., \rho_m$ are all possible essentially different elementary quantifications containing $P_1, ..., P_k$. Then clearly for some i, $1 \leq i \leq m$, $\models_{\mathfrak{A}} \rho_i[s]$, so by the choice of h we have $h(\rho_i) = 1$. Therefore h is good for φ.

Case 2: $\rho_1, ..., \rho_m$ are not all possible essentially different elementary quantifications containing $P_1, ..., P_k$. Then h is good for φ.

Since h is good for φ, by our hypothesis $h(\varphi) = 1$, so $\models_{\mathfrak{A}} \varphi[s]$ [by (3)]. Since $\mathfrak{A}$ and s are arbitrary we conclude that $\models \varphi$.

Example 8. Let $\varphi \equiv \neg \exists x \neg P x \rightarrow \exists x P x$. Then $\exists x \neg P x$ and $\exists x P x$ are the only prime constituents of φ. We write in rows all possible truth-assignments h over the prime constituents of φ, together with the corresponding $h(\varphi)$'s:

$\exists x \neg Px$	$\exists x Px$	$\neg \exists x \neg Px$	$\rightarrow$	$\exists x Px$
0	0	1	0	0
0	1	1	1	1
1	0	0	1	0
1	1	0	1	1

Disregarding the first row that is not good for φ, all the remaining rows yield $h(\varphi) = 1$, so $\models \varphi$ [by Theorem 7].

Theorem 9   (*Decidability of Monadic Logic*). The set of all logically valid sentences of $\mathfrak{L}$ is decidable.

Proof.   Let $Pr_{\mathfrak{L}}$ be the set of all logically valid sentences of $\mathfrak{L}$. Let $Pr'_{\mathfrak{L}}$ be the set of all logically valid sentences of $\mathfrak{L}$ in Herbrand normal form. By Theorem 7 the set $Pr'_{\mathfrak{L}}$ is decidable. By inspection of the proof of Theorem 4 there is an algorithm that converts every sentence of $\mathfrak{L}$ into a sentence of $\mathfrak{L}$ in Herbrand normal form. So, since $Pr'_{\mathfrak{L}}$ is decidable, such is $Pr_{\mathfrak{L}}$.

Università di Roma 'La Sapienza' (Italy)

BIBLIOGRAPHY

[1] H. Behmann, 'Beiträge zur Algebra der Logik', *Mathematische Annalen* 86 (1922), pp. 163–229.

[2] G. S. Boolos-R.C. Jeffrey, *Computability and Logic*, Cambridge University Press, London 1980.[3]

[3] P. Bernays-M. Schönfinkel, 'Zum Entscheidungsproblem der mathematischen Logik', *Mathematische Annalen* 99 (1928), pp. 342–372.

[4] A. Church, *Introduction to Mathematical Logic*, Princeton University Press, Princeton 1956.

[5] H. B. Enderton, *A Mathematical Introduction to Logic*, Academic Press, New York 1972.

[6] J. Herbrand, 'Investigations in proof theory', in *Logical Writings* (W. Goldfarb ed.), Reidel, Dordrecht 1971.

[7] G. Hunter, *Metalogic. An Introduction to the Metatheory of Standard First-Order Logic*, Macmillan, London 1971.

[8] D. Hilbert-P. Bernays, *Grundlagen der Mathematik I*, Springer-Verlag, Berlin 1968[2].

[9] W. V. Quine, 'On the logic of quantification', *Journal of Symbolic Logic* 10 (1945), pp. 1–12.

[10] J. van Heijenoort, 'Subject and predicate in Western logic', in *Selected Essays*, Bibliopolis, Naples 1985, pp. 17–34.

[11] G. H. von Wright, 'On the idea of logical truth (I)', in *Logical Studies*, Routledge & Kegan Paul, London 1957, pp. 22–43.

MARIA LUISA DALLA CHIARA AND ROBERTO GIUNTINI

DYNAMIC IDEAS IN QUANTUM LOGIC

1. INTRODUCTION

An abstract investigation about quantum histories naturally meets ideas that have been developed in the framework of *dynamic logic* [5], where possible relations between *truths* and *actions* are studied. The aim of this paper is to investigate a general semantic framework that admits of a number of possible applications. A particular case will be represented by quantum histories ([6], [4]).

2. HISTORICAL STRUCTURES

The basic concept of our semantics is that of historical structure.

Definition 2.1   A *historical structure* is structure

$$\mathcal{M} = \langle T, S, Ev, Histev, Op, \mathcal{D} \rangle,$$

where

1) T is a linearly ordered set of times. In the following a time-sequence $\langle t_1, \ldots, t_n \rangle$ will be always written according to the order $\leq$.

2) S is a function that assigns to each $t \in T$ a set S_t of *possible states* at time t. For simplicity all S_t are supposed to be (ontologically distinct) copies of a fixed (timeless) S^*.

   From an intuitive point of view, states can be regarded as *possible worlds* of a Kripke-style semantics: pieces of information about possible states of affairs (or fragments of reality).

   In the physical examples: S^* will (naturally) contain the possible states of the physical system under investigation. For instance: in classical mechanics (CM), the pure and/or the mixed states of an appropriate phase space Ω. In quantum theory (QT), the class of all density operators of an appropriate Hilbert space $\mathcal{H}$.

3) Ev is a function that assigns to each $t \in T$ a set $\mathcal{E}v_t$ of *events* at time t. For simplicity, all $\mathcal{E}v_t$ are supposed to be (ontologically distinct) copies of a fixed (timeless) $\mathcal{E}v^*$.

   In the physical examples: $\mathcal{E}v^*$ will contain the possible physical properties of the physical system. In CM: measurable subsets of the phase space Ω. In QT: either *projections* or more generally *effect operators* in the appropriate Hilbert space $\mathcal{H}$. From an intuitive point of view projections represent *sharp properties* generally expressing that the value of a given quantity lies within a certain exact

175

R. Egidi (ed.), In Search of a New Humanism, 175–182.
©1999 *Kluwer Academic Publishers. Printed in Great Britain.*

Borel set. Effects, instead, may represent also *fuzzy properties*, that may be disturbed by a certain noise (mathematically, an effect is defined as a linear bounded operator between the null (0) and the identity (1I) operator on $\mathcal{H}$). Any timeless state s will assign to any timeless event α a value in the interval [0, 1]:

$$s(\alpha) \in [0, 1].$$

A state s is said to *verify* an event α ($s \models \alpha$) iff $s(\alpha) = 1$. Similarly for all states in S_t and all events in $\mathcal{E}v_t$.

The set $\mathcal{E}v^*$ of the timeless events has a structure (for simplicity all $\mathcal{E}v_t$ are assumed to be isomorphic to $\mathcal{E}v^*$). The minimal structure that seems to be necessary for QT is an *effect algebra* (called also an *unsharp orthoalgebra* [1]):

$$\langle \mathcal{E}v^*, \oplus, \mathbf{1}, \mathbf{0} \rangle,$$

where $\oplus$ is a partial operation that represents an *exclusive disjunction* (*aut*), whereas $\mathbf{1}, \mathbf{0}$ are the *certain* and the *impossible* event, respectively.

In this framework one can define a *partial order relation* $\sqsubseteq$ between events that can be thought of as an implication relation:

$$\alpha \sqsubseteq \beta \Longleftrightarrow \exists \gamma [a \oplus \gamma = \beta].$$

In a classical situation it will be natural to require that $\mathcal{E}v^*$ is a Boolean algebra. We will call *historical sequence* a sequence of events $\langle \alpha_{t_1}, \ldots, \alpha_{t_n} \rangle$, where each α_{t_i} is in $\mathcal{E}v_{t_i}$. Of course, the algebraic structure of each $\mathcal{E}v_{t_k}$ can be naturally transferred to the set of all historical sequences ($\prod_{i=1}^{n} \mathcal{E}v_{t_i}$). We will call *temporal support* ([6]) of the historical sequence $\langle \alpha_{t_1}, \ldots, \alpha_{t_n} \rangle$, the time-sequence $\langle t_1, \ldots, t_n \rangle$. Composition between temporal supports and historical sequences with disjoint temporal supports is defined in the expected way.

4) *Histev* is a function that assigns to each time-sequence $\langle t_1, \ldots, t_n \rangle$ the set of the historical events $Histev^{\langle t_1, \ldots, t_n \rangle}$ at time $\langle t_1, \ldots, t_n \rangle$. This set is equipped with a structure (at least an effect algebra).

Physical examples:

In CM: $Histev^{\langle t_1, \ldots, t_n \rangle}$ is a σ-field of subsets of the *cartesian product*

$$S_{t_1} \times \ldots \times S_{t_n}.$$

In other words, a historical event (at time $\langle t_1, \ldots, t_n \rangle$) is a set of sequences $\langle s_{t_1}, \ldots, s_{t_n} \rangle$, where any s_{t_i} is a pure state of the system at time t_i.

In QT: $Histev^{\langle t_1, \ldots, t_n \rangle}$ can be identified either with the set of the projections or with the set of the effects of the *tensor product*

$$\mathcal{H}_{t_1} \otimes \ldots \otimes \mathcal{H}_{t_n},$$

where each $\mathcal{H}_{t_i}$ represents the Hilbert space of the system at time t_i.

Any historical sequence of events must be represented by a historical event. However, not all historical events will represent historical sequences. For instance, in QT the sequence $\langle \alpha_{t_1}, \ldots, \alpha_{t_n} \rangle$ (where each α_{t_i} is a projection) will be represented by the tensor product $\alpha_{t_1} \otimes \ldots \otimes \alpha_{t_n}$ of the projections $\alpha_{t_1}, \ldots, \alpha_{t_n}$. Such a product is a projection in the tensor-product space $\mathcal{H}_{t_1} \otimes \ldots \otimes \mathcal{H}_{t_n}$. Of course, not all the projections in the tensor-product space will have this factorized form. For instance, the orthocomplement of a factorized historical event $\alpha_{t_1} \otimes \ldots \otimes \alpha_{t_n}$ will not generally correspond to any historical sequence of events. Our physical examples naturally suggest to require the following general conditions:

(4.1)   For any time t_k and any time-sequence $\langle t_1, \ldots, t_k, \ldots, t_n \rangle$, there exists a function f that maps $\mathcal{E}v_{t_k}$ into $Histev^{\langle t_1, \ldots, t_n \rangle}$:

$$f : \mathcal{E}v_{t_k} \rightarrow Histev^{\langle t_1, \ldots, t_n \rangle}.$$

Further, such f is an embedding that preserves the algebraic structure of $\mathcal{E}v_{t_k}$.

This guarantees that any event at time t_k is represented by a historical event in any longer time-interval. For instance, in the projection-case, $f(\alpha_{t_k})$ will be $1\!\mathrm{I}_{t_1} \otimes \ldots \otimes \alpha_{t_k} \otimes \ldots \otimes 1\!\mathrm{I}_{t_n}$.

(4.2)   For any time sequence $\langle t_1, \ldots, t_n \rangle$, there is a function g that transforms any historical sequence $\langle \alpha_{t_1}, \ldots, \alpha_{t_n} \rangle$ of events into a historical event $\eta^{\langle t_1, \ldots, t_n \rangle}$ of $Histev^{\langle t_1, \ldots, t_n \rangle}$:

$$g \langle \alpha_{t_1}, \ldots, \alpha_{t_n} \rangle \mapsto \eta^{\langle t_1, \ldots, t_n \rangle}.$$

Further, such g is a homomorphism of $\prod_{i=1}^{n} \mathcal{E}v_{t_i}$ into $Histev^{\langle t_1, \ldots, t_n \rangle}$ 1.

Definition 2.2   Two historical sequences $\langle \alpha_{t_1}, \ldots, \alpha_{t_n} \rangle$ and $\langle \beta_{t_1}, \ldots, \beta_{t_n} \rangle$ are called *equivalent* ($\langle \alpha_{t_1}, \ldots, \alpha_{t_n} \rangle \approx \langle \beta_{t_1}, \ldots, \beta_{t_n} \rangle$) iff $g(\langle \alpha_{t_1}, \ldots, \alpha_{t_n} \rangle) = g(\langle \beta_{t_1}, \ldots, \beta_{t_n} \rangle)$. Since g is a homomorphism, the equivalence relation $\approx$ turns out to be a congruence on the algebraic structure induced on $\prod_{i=1}^{n} \mathcal{E}v_{t_i}$. Further, the relation $\approx$ is required to satisfy the following condition:

let $\langle t_m, \ldots, t_n \rangle$ and $\langle t_i, \ldots, t_j \rangle$ be two disjoint temporal supports: if $\langle \alpha_{t_m}, \ldots, \alpha_{t_n} \rangle \approx \langle \alpha'_{t_m}, \ldots, \alpha'_{t_n} \rangle$ and $\langle \beta_{t_i}, \ldots, \beta_{t_j} \rangle \approx \langle \beta'_{t_i}, \ldots, \beta'_{t_j} \rangle$, then $\langle \alpha_{t_m}, \ldots, \alpha_{t_n} \rangle \circ \langle \beta_{t_i}, \ldots, \beta_{t_j} \rangle \approx \langle \alpha'_{t_m}, \ldots, \alpha'_{t_n} \rangle \circ \langle \beta'_{t_i}, \ldots, \beta'_{t_j} \rangle$.

In other words, the relation $\approx$ is preserved under composition ($\circ$) of historical sequences.

Any historical event $\eta^{\langle t_1, \ldots, t_n \rangle}$ that represents (via g) a historical sequence will be called a *history*[2]. We will indicate by $Hist^{\langle t_1, \ldots, t_n \rangle}$ the subset of $Histev^{\langle t_1, \ldots, t_n \rangle}$ that contains all the histories. Instead of $g(\langle \alpha_{t_1}, \ldots, \alpha_{t_n} \rangle)$ we will simply write: $\eta^{\langle \alpha_{t_1}, \ldots, \alpha_{t_n} \rangle}$.

On this basis one can naturally define a notion of *historical truth*. This is a semantic notion that may hold between a sequence of states and a historical event. Let us first consider the case where both the state-sequence and the historical event refer to the same temporal support $\langle t_1, \ldots, t_n \rangle$.

Definition 2.3   *Restricted definition of historical truth*
$(\langle s_{t_1}, \ldots, s_{t_n} \rangle$ *verifies* η: $\langle s_{t_1}, \ldots, s_{t_n} \rangle \models \eta)$
We will distinguish the case of histories from that of historical events that do not represent histories.

a) Let η be the history $\eta^{\langle \alpha_{t_1}, \ldots, \alpha_{t_n} \rangle}$. Then:
$\langle s_1, \ldots, s_n \rangle \models \eta$ iff for any sequence $\langle \alpha_{t_1}, \ldots, \alpha_{t_n} \rangle$ s.t. $g(\langle \alpha_{t_1}, \ldots, \alpha_{t_n} \rangle) = \eta$: $s_{t_i} \models \alpha_{t_i}$, for any s_{t_i} and α_{t_i} $(1 \leq i \leq n)$.
b) Let η be a historical event (belonging to $Histev^{\langle t_1, \ldots, t_n \rangle}$) that is not a history. Then:
$\langle s_{t_1}, \ldots, s_{t_n} \rangle \models \eta$ iff for at least one history $\delta^{\langle \alpha_{t_1}, \ldots, \alpha_{t_n} \rangle}$:
i) $\delta^{\langle \alpha_{t_1}, \ldots, \alpha_{t_n} \rangle} \sqsubseteq \eta$;
ii) $\langle s_{t_1}, \ldots, s_{t_n} \rangle \models \delta^{\langle \alpha_{t_1}, \ldots, \alpha_{t_n} \rangle}$.

Our truth definition can be naturally extended also to the case where a state-sequence and a historical event refer to different time-sequences. Let us first introduce a procedure that permits to normalize any history to a given time-sequence.

Definition 2.4   *Normalization of a historical-sequence to a given time sequence*
Let $\langle \alpha_{t_m}, \ldots, \alpha_{t_n} \rangle$ be a historical sequence and let $\langle t_i, \ldots, t_j \rangle$ be any time-sequence. The *normalization* of $\langle \alpha_{t_m}, \ldots, \alpha_{t_n} \rangle$ to $\langle t_i, \ldots, t_j \rangle$ is the following historical sequence:

$$\lceil \langle \alpha_{t_m}, \ldots, \alpha_{t_n} \rangle \rceil^{\langle t_i, \ldots, t_j \rangle} := \langle \beta_{t_i}, \ldots, \beta_{t_j} \rangle,$$

where

$$\beta_{t_k} = \begin{cases} \alpha_{t_k}, & \text{if } t_k \text{ is in } \langle t_1, \ldots, t_n \rangle; \\ \mathbf{1}_{t_k} & \text{otherwise} \end{cases}$$

($\mathbf{1}_{t_k}$ is the certain event at time t_k). Accordingly, the normalization of a history will be automatically determined (via g):

Definition 2.5   *Normalization of a history to a given time-sequence*
Let $\eta^{\langle \alpha_{t_m}, \ldots, \alpha_{t_n} \rangle}$ be a history and $\langle t_i, \ldots, t_j \rangle$ be a time-sequence. The *normalization* of $\eta^{\langle \alpha_{t_m}, \ldots, \alpha_{t_n} \rangle}$ to $\langle t_i, \ldots, t_j \rangle$ is the history

$$\lceil \eta^{\langle \alpha_{t_m}, \ldots, \alpha_{t_n} \rangle} \rceil^{\langle t_i, \ldots, t_j \rangle}$$

that is univocally determined by the historical sequence $\lceil \langle \alpha_{t_m}, \ldots, \alpha_{t_n} \rangle \rceil^{\langle t_i, \ldots, t_j \rangle}$. One can easily prove that Definition 2.5 is a good definition since it is independent from the choice of the representative.
On this basis we can define a general notion of historical truth:

Definition 2.6   *General definition of historical truth*
($\langle s_{t_1}, \ldots, s_{t_n} \rangle$ *verifies* $\eta^{\langle t_i, \ldots, t_j \rangle}$: $\langle s_{t_1}, \ldots, s_{t_n} \rangle \models \eta^{\langle t_i, \ldots, t_j \rangle}$)
Let $\eta^{\langle t_i, \ldots, t_j \rangle}$ be a historical event.
$\langle s_{t_1}, \ldots, s_{t_n} \rangle \models \eta^{\langle t_i, \ldots, t_j \rangle}$ iff there is a history $\delta^{\langle t_i, \ldots, t_j \rangle}$ s.t.:

i) $\delta^{\langle t_i, \ldots, t_j \rangle} \sqsubseteq \eta^{\langle t_i, \ldots, t_j \rangle}$;

ii) $\langle s_{t_1}, \ldots, s_{t_n} \rangle \models \lceil \delta^{\langle t_i, \ldots, t_j \rangle} \rceil^{\langle t_1, \ldots, t_n \rangle}$.

A historical sequence will be called *normal* when all historical events can be normalized to any time sequence.

It turns out that any historical structure where all $Histev^{\langle t_1, \ldots, t_n \rangle}$ are structured as complete lattices is trivially normal.

5) *Op*, the *operation function*, is a function that associates to any pair of time t_i, t_j a set of *operations* $\mathcal{O}_{t_i}^{t_j}$

$$Op : \langle t_i, t_j \rangle \mapsto \mathcal{O}_{t_i}^{t_j},$$

where $\mathcal{O}_{t_i}^{t_j}$ is a subset of a set of admissible operations $\mathcal{O} \subseteq \{f \mid \overline{S^*} \to S^*\}$ ($\overline{S^*} \subseteq S^*$). In other words, admissible operations transform states into states. As an example let us think of some natural quantum operations.

(1) *A Schrödinger evolution operation*
   $f_{\mathcal{U}}$.
   Let $\mathcal{U}$ be a function associating to each pair of time $\langle t_i, t_j \rangle$ a unitary operation $\mathcal{U}_{t_i}^{t_j}$ in the appropriate Hilbert space $\mathcal{H}$. Then

$$f_{\mathcal{U}_{t_i}^{t_j}}(s) := \mathcal{U}_{t_i}^{t_j} s \mathcal{U}_{t_i}^{t_j*}$$

(where $\mathcal{U}_{t_i}^{t_j*}$ is the adjoint of $\mathcal{U}_{t_i}^{t_j}$). From an intuitive point of view $f_{\mathcal{U}_{t_i}^{t_j}}$ represents a spontaneous evolution of the system (governed by Schrödinger equation) in the time interval $[t_i, t_j]$, where s represents the initial state.

(2) *A von Neumann-Lüders collapse operation*
   Let α be any effect.

$$f^{\alpha}(s) := \frac{\alpha^{\frac{1}{2}} s \alpha^{\frac{1}{2}}}{Tr(s\alpha)} \qquad (Tr(s\alpha) \neq 0)$$

Intuitively, $f^{\alpha}(s)$ represents the transformation of state s induced by a measurement that has been performed in order to check whether the system in state s satisfies property α (provided the result was positive). On this basis, $\mathcal{O}$ can be identified with

$$\{f_{\mathcal{U}} \mid \mathcal{U} \text{ is a unitary operator}\} \cup \{f^{\alpha} \mid \alpha \text{ is an effect}\}.$$

Also in our general semantics, some operations in $\mathcal{O}_{t_i}^{t_j}$ may represent spontaneous evolutions whereas other operations may represent state transformations induced by an action. A typical action is a test performed in order to check whether a certain property α holds.[3]

On this basis a class of *accessibility relations* can be naturally defined in terms of our operations (differently from Kripke semantics, where accessibility relations are usually dealt with as primitive). Let s, u represent timeless states.

States s and u are called *accessible in the time interval* $[t_i, t_j]$ (we will write $Acc_{t_i}^{t_j}(s, u)$) iff there exists an operation $f \in \mathcal{O}_{t_i}^{t_j}$ s.t.

$$u = f(s).$$

States s and u are *absolutely accessible* ($Acc(s, u)$) iff for at least two times t_i, t_j:

$$Acc_{t_i}^{t_j}(s, u).$$

Let α be an event. The states s, u are *α-accessible* ($Acc^{\alpha}(s, u)$) iff there exists an operation f^{α} s.t.

$$u = f^{\alpha}(s).$$

Since all S_t are copies of S^* our accessibility relations are automatically transferred to pairs of states that may belong to different S_t.

6) $\mathcal{D}$ is a (possibly empty) set of *decoherence functionals* d ([6]). From the intuitive point of view, $d(\eta, \delta)$ measures the degree of interference between the historical events η and δ.

In this framework one can naturally define the notions of *consistent history* and of *consistent and exhaustive set of histories*.

3. DYNAMIC AND TEMPORAL OPERATORS

Different logical operators that have a temporal or a dynamic meaning can be naturally defined in our semantics.

Definition 3.1   *The temporal conjunction* and then $\sqcap\nearrow$
Let $\eta^{\langle t_m, \dots, t_n \rangle}$, $\delta^{\langle t_i, \dots, t_j \rangle}$ be two historical events. Generally $\sqcap\nearrow$ is a partial operation that turns out to be always defined in the particular case of a normal historical structure where any $Histev^{\langle t_1, \dots, t_n \rangle}$ gives rise to a lattice.

$$
\eta^{\langle t_m, \dots, t_n \rangle} \sqcap\nearrow \delta^{\langle t_i, \dots, t_j \rangle} := \begin{cases} \mathbf{0}^{\langle t_m, \dots, t_n \rangle \circ \langle t_i, \dots, t_j \rangle}, \text{ if } \langle t_m, \dots, t_n \rangle \text{ does not preceed} \\ \qquad\qquad \langle t_i, \dots, t_j \rangle \text{ w.r.t the order } \leq; \\ \lceil \eta \rceil^{\langle t_m, \dots, t_n \rangle \circ \langle t_i, \dots, t_j \rangle} \sqcap \lceil \delta \rceil^{\langle t_m, \dots, t_n \rangle \circ \langle t_i, \dots, t_j \rangle}, \text{ if this inf} \\ \qquad\qquad \text{exists in } Histev^{\langle t_m, \dots, t_n \rangle \circ \langle t_i, \dots, t_j \rangle}; \\ \text{undefined,} \qquad\quad \text{otherwise.} \end{cases}
$$

As an example, suppose two histories $\eta^{\langle \alpha_{t_1}, \alpha_{t_2}\rangle}$, $\delta^{\langle \beta_{t_3}, \beta_{t_4}\rangle}$ $(t_1 < t_2 < t_3 < t_4)$.
    According to our definition we will have:

$$\eta^{\langle \alpha_{t_1}, \alpha_{t_2}\rangle} \sqcap \!\!\nearrow \delta^{\langle \beta_{t_3}, \ldots, \beta_{t_4}\rangle} = \eta^{\langle \alpha_{t_1}, \alpha_{t_2}, 1_{t_3}, 1_{t_4}\rangle} \sqcap \delta^{\langle 1_{t_1}, 1_{t_2}, \beta_{t_3}, \beta_{t_4}\rangle}$$

$$= \gamma^{\langle \alpha_{t_1} \sqcap 1_{t_1}, \alpha_{t_2} \sqcap 1 t_2, 1_{t_3} \sqcap \beta_{t_3}, 1_{t_4} \sqcap \beta_{t_4}\rangle}$$

$$= \gamma^{\langle \alpha_{t_1}, \alpha_{t_2}, \beta_{t_3}, \beta_{t_4}\rangle}.$$

We obtain in this way the expected meaning of a temporal conjunction: $\eta^{\langle \alpha_{t_1}, \alpha_{t_2}\rangle}$ *and then* $\delta^{\langle \beta_{t_3}, \beta_{t_4}\rangle}$ is the history determined by the historical sequence $\langle \alpha_{t_1}, \alpha_{t_2}, \beta_{t_3}, \beta_{t_4}\rangle$.

A dynamic implication
Let us refer to to set $\mathcal{E}v^*$ of all timeless events and to the set S^* of all timeless states. Let $\alpha \in \mathcal{E}v^*$. We define first a function $\boxed{\boxed{\alpha}}$ that assign to each $\beta \in Ev^*$ a set of timeless states:

$$\boxed{\boxed{\alpha}} : \mathcal{E}v^* \to \mathcal{P}(S^*) \qquad \text{(where } \mathcal{P}(S^*) \text{ is the power-set of } S^*\text{)}$$

satisfying the condition:

$$s \in \boxed{\boxed{\alpha}}\beta \quad \text{iff} \quad \forall u [Acc^\alpha(s, u) \Rightarrow u \models \beta].$$

From the intuitive point of view, $s \in \boxed{\boxed{\alpha}}\beta$ has the following meaning: suppose we test α on a state s and we obtain a positive result; then, any state into which s is transformed after such a test verifies β. Of course, $\boxed{\boxed{\alpha}}\beta$ does not necessarily determine an event. In the case where $\mathcal{E}v^*$ has the structure of a complete lattice, one can easily define the following total operation:

$$\boxed{\alpha} : \mathcal{E}v^* \to \mathcal{E}v^*,$$

where

$$\boxed{\alpha}\, \beta := \sqcap\{\delta \mid \forall u \in \boxed{\boxed{\alpha}}\beta : u \models \delta\}$$

Otherwise, $\boxed{\alpha}$ will represent a partial operation.
    In the particular case of standard quantum logic the dynamic implication is always defined and corresponds to the *Sasaki implication*. For, one can easily show that for projections α, β:

$$\boxed{\alpha}\, \beta = \alpha \to \beta := \alpha' \sqcup (\alpha \sqcap \beta),$$

where α' is the orthocomplement of α. This shows that the standard logical implication admits a natural dynamic interpretation.

M. L. Dalla Chiara – Università di Firenze (Italy)
R. Giuntini – Università di Cagliari (Italy)

NOTES

[1] If the *algebraic tensor product* of the effect algebras $\mathcal{E}v_{t_1}, \ldots \mathcal{E}v_{t_i}$ exists ([3]), then $Histev^{\langle t_1, \ldots, t_n \rangle}$ can be identified with such a product. The function g turns out to be an n-morphism of $\prod_{i=1}^{n} \mathcal{E}v_{t_i}$ into $Histev^{\langle t_1, \ldots, t_n \rangle}$.

[2] In [6], historical sequences are called *history-filters*, while historical events are called *history-propositions*.

[3] See von Wright [13].

BIBLIOGRAPHY

[1] M. L. Dalla Chiara and R. Giuntini, "Unsharp quantum logics", *Foundations of Physics*, 24 (1994), 1161–1177.
[2] M. L. Dalla Chiara and R. Giuntini, "A fuzzy dynamic semantics for quantum histories", preprint.
[3] A. Dvurečenskij, "Tensor product of difference posets", *Transactions of the American Mathematical Society*, 347 (1995), 1043–1057.
[4] M. Gell-Mann and J. Hartle, "Alternative decohering histories in quantum mechanics", in K. K. Phua and Y. Yamaguchi (eds.), *Proceedings of the 25th International Conference on High Energy Physics*, World Scientific, Singapore, 1990.
[5] D. Harel, "Dynamic logic", in D. Gabbay and F. Guenthner (eds.), *Handbook of Philosophical Logic*, III, Kluwer, Dordrecht, 1984.
[6] C. J. Isham, "Quantum logic and the histories approach to quantum theory", *Journal of Mathematical Physics*, 35 (1994), 2157–2185.
[7] C. J. Isham and N. Linden, "Quantum temporal logic and decoherence functionals in the histories approach to generalized quantum theory", *Journal of Mathematical Physics*, 35 (1994), 5452–5475.
[8] P. Mittelstaedt, "Relativistic quantum logic", *International Journal of Theoretical Physics*, 22 (1983), 293–314.
[9] P. Mittelstaedt and E. W. Stachow, "Analysis of the EPR-experiment by relativistic quantum logic", *International Journal of Theoretical Physics*, 22 (1983), 517–540.
[10] R. Omnès, *The Interpretation of Quantum Mechanics*, Princeton University Press, 1994.
[11] B. Penther, "A dynamic logic of action", *Journal of Logic, Language, and Information*, 3 (1994), 169–210.
[12] S. Pulmannová, "Difference posets and the histories approach to quantum theories", preprint.
[13] G. von Wright, "The logic of action", in N. Rescher (ed.), *The Logic of Action and Decision*, University of Pittsburgh Press, 1967.

EUGENIO BULYGIN

TRUE OR FALSE STATEMENTS IN NORMATIVE DISCOURSE

I. My purpose in this paper is to investigate the different kinds of true or false statements that occur in normative discourse. As a *Leitfaden* for this investigation, I will take the work of Georg Henrik von Wright.

By normative discourse, I will understand a discourse containing typical normative terms like "ought", "ought not", "may", "obligatory", "prohibited", "permissible", etc. Sentences in which such normative or deontic terms occur von Wright calls *"deontic sentences"*. Deontic sentences are frequently used for formulating norms, i. e., as *norm-formulations*. But norms can also be formulated by means of other linguistic devices (as, for instance, traffic lights, sentences in the imperative mood, and even sentences in the indicative). In *Norm and Action*,[1] von Wright introduces the distinction between norms and norm-formulations, saying that "The norm-formulation is the sign or symbol (the words) used in enunciating (formulating) a norm" (N&A, p. 93). This seems to imply that norm-formulations are the linguistic counterpart of norms. But later he adds that deontic sentences can also be used for making *normative statements*. When a norm-formulation is used *prescriptively*, it expresses a norm. Norms as prescriptions have no truth value: they are neither true nor false. But the same norm-formulation can also be used *descriptively*, in which case it expresses a normative statement that is true or false. It is a characteristic feature of deontic sentences that "the very same words may [...] be used to enunciate a norm (give a prescription) and to make a normative statement" (N&A, p. 105).

In *Norm and Action* (as well as in some later publications, like "The Foundation of Norms and Normative Statements",[2] von Wright seems to distinguish four different entities: norm-formulations, norms, normative statements, and norm-propositions. A norm-formulation is a linguistic entity, and as such it is characteristically ambiguous, since it can be used either prescriptively or descriptively. If used prescriptively, it expresses a norm, which has no truth value; if used descriptively, it can give rise either to a normative statement, or to a norm-proposition, both of which have a truth value. Thus, we have two kinds of entities that can be true or false. But it is not clear what a normative statement is, and how it is related to norm-propositions.

A normative statement, schematically speaking, is a statement to the effect that something or other ought to or may or must not be done (by some agent or agents, on some occasion or generally, unconditionally or provided certain conditions are satisfied). The term "statement" is here used in that which I propose to call its "strict" sense. A statement in the strict sense is either true or false. (The sentence which is used in making a statement expresses a proposition.) (N&A, p. 105)

R. Egidi (ed.), In Search of a New Humanism, 183–191.
©1999 *Kluwer Academic Publishers. Printed in Great Britain.*

On the other hand, a norm-proposition is defined as a proposition to the effect that a norm exists ("The proposition that such and such a norm exists, I shall call a *norm-proposition*"; N&A, p. 106).

These quotations suggest the following distinction: A sentence used (descriptively) to say that some action is obligatory, prohibited, or permitted (i. e., that something ought to, or must not, or may be done) expresses a normative statement, whereas a sentence used to say that a norm to such and such effect exists expresses a norm-proposition. To use a (slightly modified) example of von Wright: If in reply to a question I say "You must not park your car in front of my house", and what I am doing is not issuing a prohibition, but giving the questioner information concerning the regulations for parking a car, then my sentence is descriptive and the statement I make is a normative statement. If, instead, I say "There is a norm that prohibits parking in this place", then my sentence expresses a norm-proposition.

But that suggestion does not seem acceptable. What is the difference between informing about the existing regulation and saying that there is a norm prohibiting to park a car in this place? How could I inform someone about the existing regulation other than by saying that there is a norm that prohibits parking here? If my information is true, then there is in fact a norm to the effect that parking is prohibited; and if there is no such norm, then my normative statement is false. Appearances notwithstanding, both sentences say exactly the same thing. In other words, even if the normative statement saying that parking is prohibited seems to refer to the action of parking, and the norm-proposition seems to refer to the existence of a norm, both have exactly the same truth conditions and, moreover, they have the same meaning. Von Wright's assertion that a normative statement expresses a proposition can now be completed by saying that the proposition expressed by a normative statement is a norm-proposition.

But then, there are not three but only two (non-linguistic) entities: norms and norm-propositions. What von Wright calls normative statements are norm-propositions in disguise. The sentences

(1)   You must not park here

and

(2)   There is a norm that prohibits parking here

have the same meaning, (2) being an expanded form of (1). A sentence like (2), expressing a norm-proposition in its expanded form, has the advantage of no longer being ambiguous: it could not possibly be used for issuing a prohibition, for it is clearly descriptive, while sentence (1) is characteristically ambiguous, as it can be used to formulate a norm or to express a norm-proposition.

This interpretation is supported by the fact that in later publications von Wright himself no longer uses the term "normative statement" and speaks only of norms and norm-propositions. In "Norms, Truth and Logic" (1982, included in PR), he says: "In *Norm and Action* (1963) I made a tripartite distinction which I think is useful between norms, norm-formulations and norm-propositions" (PR, p. 131), without even mentioning normative statements.

But, on the other hand, if normative statements are just an elliptic form of norm-propositions, then the whole talk about the foundation of normative statements loses its point. Von Wright already mentions this topic in *Norm and Action*: "By the *truth-ground* of a given normative statement I understand a truthful answer to the question *why* the thing in question ought to or may or must not be done" (N&A, p. 105), and he develops it in "The Foundation of Norms and Normative Statements" (1965, included in PR).

Now, if the proposition a normative statement expresses is nothing but a norm-proposition, the question of "Why?" seems out of place. One does not actually ask "Why?" in front of descriptive propositions. For instance, if I say "Snow is white" and somebody asks me "Why?", I would certainly feel perplexed: I would not know what to say. The answer "Because it is" does not seem very illuminating, and the same is true for other possible answers like "Because that's what nature is like", or "Because God created things that way". And yet, von Wright emphatically says:

> *One* important type of answer to the question "Why ought (may, must not) this or that be done?" is the following: *There is a norm* to the effect that this thing ought (may, must not) be done. The existence of the norm is here the foundation or truth-ground of the normative statement. (PR, p. 68)

I am unable to see why such an answer should be important, because what it amounts to is only a repetition, in expanded form, of the same norm-proposition already expressed by the normative statement. It seems to me that in this case von Wright has fallen victim to the systematic ambiguity of deontic sentences which he so emphatically denounces. Because the question "Why?" and the answer "Because there is a norm to the effect that..." make sense only when the deontic sentence is used prescriptively, in order to formulate or express a norm. In that case, it is perfectly reasonable to answer "You ought to do *p*, because there is a norm enjoining or prescribing *p*", although even then this answer is not quite satisfactory, for it does not give a conclusive reason for doing *p*, unless one adds "... and you ought to obey this norm" (which is often tacitly assumed in such an answer).

If I am right, then there is no such thing as "the philosophic *problem of the foundation* of normative statements" (PR, p. 67). We can, of course, ask for the truth-ground of a normative statement, and the answer would be that the truth-ground of the normative statement (or the norm-proposition) is the fact that there is such-and-such a norm, just as the fact (or the proposition) that snow is white is the truth-ground of the sentence "Snow is white". This shows, by the way, that one should not equate the truth-ground, as von Wright does, with the foundation of a normative statement.

II. If we accept that (so far) there is only one kind of true or false normative sentences, namely, those expressing norm-propositions (either in what I have called the elliptic or in the expanded form), the question may be asked what the truth conditions of such norm-propositions are, and even whether such truth conditions exist at all. A powerful attack on the notion of a norm-proposition as a bearer of truth has been launched by Tecla Mazzarese in her essay " 'Norm proposition'. Epistemic and Semantic Queries".[3]

Mazzarese argues that norm-propositions cannot be regarded as purely descriptive (true or false) propositions. Contrary to the widespread view that assumes a norm-proposition to be the meaning of a single, simple statement describing a single, simple entity, Mazzarese maintains that a norm-proposition is the meaning of a conjunction of two different statements: an *interpretative statement* (of the form "Norm-formulation *NF* expresses norm *N*") purporting to describe what a given norm requires, and a *validity statement* (of the form "*NF* belongs to the sources of the law") purporting to describe the fact that this norm is valid. Now, Mazzarese's main contention is that at least interpretative statements are not really descriptive, but *ascriptive* in character, and, therefore, are neither true nor false. Hence, norm-propositions, being a conjunction of two components, one of which is neither true nor false, also lack truth value. (In fact, Mazzarese argues that it is also doubtful that validity statements are purely descriptive and have a definite truth value. But I shall disregard that part of her argument.)

Mazzarese's claim that interpretative statements are not descriptive, but ascriptive is based on the (certainly correct) insight that the widespread view of "legal interpretation as an activity by means of which the meaning of a norm formulation may be discovered and/or clarified" (*ibidem*, p. 48) is wrong. She rightly points out that this view presupposes that a norm-formulation always expresses only one norm, and restricts the activity of the interpreter to the identification of that norm. This view is certainly false; thus far, we agree. Her next step, however, is less convincing. She argues that to every norm-formulation (as a linguistic entity) there corresponds a plurality of norms, because norms are the meanings of norm-formulations, and there is always a plurality of meanings that can be ascribed to a linguistic expression. Therefore, the interpreter is always faced with a plurality of possible norms, and there are no logical criteria for determining which of them is the "right" one. Thus, the interpreter's task is to evaluate these possible meanings, or norms, in the light of certain assumed values, choose one of them on the basis of that evaluation, and ascribe it to the norm-formulation in question. He does this by means of interpretative statements. Therefore, interpretative statements are not descriptive, but ascriptive and, hence, neither true nor false.

There are several reasons for considering Mazzarese's argument to be "less convincing". In the first place, she takes a logically unwarranted step: From the negation of the sentence "A norm-formulation always expresses one single norm", Mazzarese jumps to the conclusion that "A norm-formulation always expresses a plurality of norms". But this conclusion does not follow from the premises. All we can infer is that a norm-formulation *sometimes* expresses a plurality of norms, but not that it always does so. In other words, from the negation of the proposition that all norm-formulations are univocal, it does not follow that all norm-formulations are ambiguous. Thus, Mazzarese's assertion that there is (always) a plurality of norms corresponding to a norm-formulation stands in need of an independent argument. The only argument Mazzarese offers in support of her contention regarding the plurality of norms is based on the fact that there are different methods of interpretation which usually lead to different results. She examines some of these methods or criteria, like the criterion that focuses on the wording of a norm-formulation, the criterion based on the so-called *ratio legis*, the one focussing on the systemic view, and the method of *analogia juris*. All of them do "not lead in many cases to a unique and undoubtful interpretative statement" (p. 49). That is true, but from this it does not follow that those criteria *never* lead to one clear and uncontroversial result. And it is that latter assertion which Mazzarese needs in order to support her claim. Her conclusion of the discussion of different methods or criteria of interpretation is:

In fact to acknowledge that according to and because of the different criteria of legal interpretation a norm formulation can be taken to express more than one norm amounts to doubting both that an interpretative statement is descriptive, and that an interpretative statement can be conceived as true or false.

Well, sometimes – but not always. I have the impression that Mazzarese has a tendency to commit a mistake which may be called the "fallacy of illegitimate generalization" and that consists in inferring a universally quantified sentence from an existential one. Here are several illustrations of that fallacy:

(1)   If in some cases a norm-formulation expresses a plurality of norms, then in all cases a norm-formulation expresses a plurality of norms.

(2)   If in some cases different criteria of interpretation lead to more than one norm, then different criteria of interpretation always lead to more than one norm.

(3)   If in some cases it is doubtful whether a norm-formulation belongs to the sources of the law, then it is always doubtful whether a norm-formulation belongs to the sources of the law.

(4)   If in some cases it is doubtful whether a given norm is valid, then it is always doubtful, regarding all norms, whether they are valid.

In the second place, the contention that all norm-formulations are ambiguous is untenable, because if it were true we could have no norms at all. This can be easily shown. Let us assume then that all norm-formulations are always ambiguous. Suppose we are confronted with a norm-formulation p_1; according to our hypothesis, p_1 is ambiguous, i. e., it has several meanings and so it expresses several possible norms. After careful inspection and after evaluating the different alternatives, we decide to pick one of them in order to ascribe it to our norm-formulation. But as there is no access to meanings other than through language, we must produce a new norm-formulation that should depict the meaning (or the norm) we chose. Let us call it p_2. According to our hypothesis, however, p_2 also is ambiguous and therefore has several meanings. So, again, we must choose one of them, and this we can do only by producing a third norm-formulation, which also will be ambiguous, and so on, *ad infinitum*. Thus, if there are no univocal norm-formulations, all we will have is pluralities of possible norms, but we will never be confronted with one definite norm.

This is a particular case of a more general problem: It is an essential feature of language that at least some of its expressions must be univocal. A language that does not meet this condition is useless as a tool of communication.

In the third place, I think it is misleading to define a norm-proposition "as a proposition to the effect that a given norm is valid, or as a proposition describing a valid norm" (*ibidem*, p. 39). It is true that Mazzarese does not regard this definition as satisfactory and that it is only a starting point for her discussion. Moreover, she rightly doubts that there can be such a thing as a description of the validity of a norm (*ibidem*, p. 41). I agree that it is difficult to see what is meant by the description of the validity of a norm, unless by "validity" we understand that the norm belongs to, or is a member of, a set or system of norms. The fact that a norm belongs to a given system of norms can certainly be described. Nevertheless, it is dangerous to start from a misleading characterization of norm-propositions.

I have already remarked that norm propositions usually take one of two forms. In their elliptic form, they state that a given action (or state of affairs resulting from an action) is prohibited (obligatory, permitted). The elliptic form is what Carnap has called the *transposed mode of speech*:

By a transposed mode of speech we mean one in which, in order to assert something about an object *a*, something corresponding is asserted about an object *b* which stands in a certain relation to the object *a*.[4]

In the expanded form a norm-proposition states that there is (in a given normative system) a norm prohibiting (enjoining, permitting) a certain action. So in order to say that in a given normative system there is a norm (object *a*) prohibiting action *p*, we say that *p* (object *b*) is prohibited.

In both cases, norm-propositions are *relative* to a norm or rather to a set of norms (a normative system), although the reference is often not spelled out, but only tacitly assumed. I have argued that both forms are synonymous, because an action has the property of being prohibited (obligatory, permitted) if and only if there is a norm (in the corresponding normative system) prohibiting (enjoining, permitting) it. But neither in the elliptic form nor in the expanded form does a norm-proposition describe a valid norm; rather, it describes the fact that a norm belongs to a certain system. So norm-propositions are not about norm-formulations, but about norms, i. e. about interpreted norm-formulations. This fact presupposes that we already know which norm is expressed by the norm-formulation in question. If a norm formulation is not ambiguous, no interpretative statement is needed in order to know what norm is expressed by it. If it is ambiguous, we must first assign one of the possible meanings to it. So norm-propositions (sometimes) presuppose interpretation, but they do not contain interpretative statements. In my view, Mazzarese's contention that they are a conjunction of interpretative statements and validity statements is wrong, because norm-propositions state a relationship between a *norm (not a mere norm-formulation)* and a normative system, and as long as both terms of this relationship are not determined, there is no norm-proposition.

Now, I see no reason for doubting that a norm-proposition has a definite truth value (*i.e.*, that it is true) if the norm in question belongs to (is a member of) the corresponding normative system. Only if there were no norms at all could it be maintained that norm-propositions have no truth value.

It could be argued that even in cases when a norm-formulation is univocal, situations may arise in which the norm is neither clearly applicable nor clearly inapplicable. This is true, but it only shows that the norm in question is vague and that the case fall within its area of penumbra. Vagueness, however, must not be confused with ambiguity. If the norm-formulation is ambiguous, then there are several norms expressed by it. This situation calls for a decision about which of the possible norms we will choose to ascribe to the norm-formulation. But a norm-formulation may be at the same time perfectly univocal, so that we know which norm is expressed by it, and vague. This means that in front of an atypical case we do not know whether the norm is applicable to it. This is what has been called a *gap of recognition*.[5] But the fact that norms are vague (or, rather, that they contain vague concepts) does not entitle us to deny that norm-propositions are true or false. They are true if the norm they refer to belongs to the system in question, and they are false if this is not the case, even if in some situations we may not be able to ascertain whether they are true or false. But the fact that they are true (or false) in clear cases is enough to maintain that they have truth values.

III. In what is, for the time being, his latest paper on deontic logic, "Ought to be – ought to do",[6] von Wright introduces another category of true or false normative sentences: socalled *sentences of practical necessity*. Although such sentences are mentioned in his earlier work, it is in this paper where von Wright assigns them a major role in normative discourse:

> Another service to the subject that the distinction [between norms and practical necessities] does is that it assigns to the notion of truth a much greater role in normative contexts than some philosophers, including myself, used to think in the past. Not only the existential propositions ("norm-propositions") to the effect that such and such norms exist (have been given) are true or false, but also the statements about what must or may be done in order to follow their rule. (p. 70)

To begin with, it seems to me an exaggeration to say that "The *Tun-Sollen/Dürfen* is descriptive, the *Sein-Sollen/Dürfen* alone is prescriptive" (p. 69). It is not difficult to find examples of norms of the "Tun-Sollen" type. Commands like "Jump into the water!", "Climb that tree!", "All members of the club must go to the meeting" are clearly norms of the "Tun-Sollen" type. They impose the obligation to do something, that is, to perform a certain action. What they prescribe is an action, not a state of affairs. So it is certainly not true that "Sein-Sollen" alone is prescriptive: there are genuine norms of both types.

In the second place, it is not always easy to distinguish between a norm imposing an obligation to perform an action and a norm imposing an obligation to produce (or to sustain, as the case may be) a state of affairs. The command given to my wife "Please, prepare dinner before 8 p. m.!" can be viewed as a norm of the "ought-to-be" type (according to that norm, my wife is under the obligation to see to it that dinner is ready before 8 p. m.), or as a norm of the "ought-to-do" type (in which case my wife has the obligation to perform the action of preparing dinner before 8 p. m.). To prepare dinner is a complex action which requires the performance of many other actions, but a complex action is still an action and not a state of affairs. There seems to be no clear criterion for distinguishing between norms whose content is an action, and norms whose content is a state of affairs.

In the third place, it is far from clear what the criterion is for distinguishing between what one ought to do and what one must or has to do in order to obey or satisfy a norm, that is, between genuine obligations and practical necessities. Linguistic usage, as von Wright rightly observes, is rather vacillating, for expressions like "ought", "must" or "has to" are used in both contexts: the normative and the practical one. Suppose A has been commanded to open a certain window; A is sitting, and unless he gets up he cannot open the window. His action of rising is a necessary condition for his action of opening the window. Shall we say that he ought to get up (obligation), or that he must get up (practical necessity in order to comply with the norm)? I am inclined to say that he is not under an obligation to get up, but if he wants to fulfil his obligation of opening the window, then he must get up. It would, thus, be a case of practical necessity, and the sentence "A must get up" is true in relation to the command.

Suppose now that the condition is not only necessary on empirical grounds, but is logically necessary. Consider the case of A who has been commanded to play the piano, and there is also a prohibition to smoke in the room where he is to play. Is he then under an obligation to play the piano without smoking? I feel inclined to answer this question in the affirmative. Obviously, he has to play the piano without smoking. But shall we say that this is his obligation, because of the two norms, or that it is a practical necessity for him to do both things (i.e., to play the piano, and to refrain from smoking) if he wants to obey both norms? It sounds rather strange to say that he must play the piano without smoking, but that he has no obligation to act this way. Moreover, according to von Wright's criterion, the norms Op and Oq entail the norm $O(p.q)$, for the set of the first two norms becomes inconsistent if we add to it the negation norm of $O(p.q)$, which is $P\text{-}(p.q)$. The set $\{Op, Oq, P\text{-}(p.q)\}$ is inconsistent because the conjunction $p.q.\text{-}(p.q)$ is not doable, since it is a contradiction. And if the norm $O(p.q)$ is entailed by the norms Op and Oq, then the action of A consisting in playing the piano without smoking is a genuine obligation and not a mere practical necessity. A generalization of this example would lead us to what may be called the *Principle of Obligatoriness*: It is obligatory (according to a given set of norms) to perform all actions that are logically necessary in order to satisfy all obligations established by the norms of this set. This result is rather strange: If an action is empirically necessary, then there is no obligation, but only a practical necessity. But if it is logically necessary, then there is a genuine obligation. I think we need an explanation for this difference.

Universidad de Buenos Aires (Argentina)

NOTES

[1] Routledge & Kegan Paul, London 1963 (henceforth, N&A).

[2] In *The Foundations of Statements and Decisions. Proceedings of the International Colloquium on Methodology of Science*, ed. by K. Ajdukiewicz, Warsaw 1961, pp. 351–67. Reprinted in G. H. von Wright, *Practical Reason. Philosophical Papers*, Vol. I, Blackwell, Oxford 1983. Henceforth PR.

[3] *Rechtstheorie*, 22, 1991, pp. 39–70.

[4] R. Carnap, *The Logical Syntax of Sprache*, Kegan Paul Trench, Trubner & Co., London, 1937, § 80; 1959, p. 308 ff.

[5] Cf. C. E. Alchourrón and E. Bulygin, *Normative Systems*, Springer Verlag, Wien 1971, pp. 31–4.

[6] In G. H. von Wright, *Six Essays in Philosophical Logic*, Societas Philosophica Finnica, Helsinki 1996, pp. 62–7.

"NORM PROPOSITION"
A TENTATIVE DEFENSE OF A SCEPTICAL VIEW

0. INTRODUCTION

The main concern of this paper is to provide a tentative defense of what might be labelled "a sceptical view" on the notion of norm proposition.

Despite the appearance, such an attempt is not confined to the search of a convincing reply to Bulygin's critical remarks,[1] but also aims at furthering a dialogue with von Wright who has given the notion a key position in depicting a logic of norms in 1963 with *Norm and Action*, and since then, from time to time, in some later works till his 1996 *Ought to Be-Ought to Do*.[2]

The point of departure of such a tentative defense will be a sketchy survey of (rather than a properly analitically developed inquiry into) the basic reasons why the notion of norm proposition can be maintained to be perplexing (§ 1). Afterwards, in order to supply a new, sharper, statement of the terms on which the sceptical view on norm propositions is grounded, Bulygin's critical remarks will be recalled.

1. THREE MAIN CONTENTIONS OF A SCEPTICAL VIEW

The term "norm proposition", though not also the notion it denotes, is probably first used by von Wright.[3]

Leaving aside the variety of ways it has been termed and/or characterized, the notion at issue can be roughly defined as a proposition to the effect that a given norm is valid, or as a proposition describing a valid norm.

The notion of norm proposition has been (and still is) acknowledged a great significance in depicting a logic of (legal) norms, and in grounding a theory of legal cognition because of its allegedly descriptive function, and because of its allegedly true/false qualification of the entity it denotes.

Now, first, the notion of norm proposition, rather than being the meaning-content of one single statement (i.e., the meaning-content of a norm formulation expressing a valid norm), cannot but be the result of a disguised conjunction of at least two different statements, namely: (a) an interpretative statement, and (b) a validity statement.

Secondly, neither interpretative nor validity statements can be conceived of as descriptive statements.

Thirdly, neither interpretative nor validity statements can be conceived of as true / false statements.

Thus far, the starting point, and the very kernel of the sceptical reading of the notion of norm proposition, as suggested in my 1991 paper referred to by Bulygin.

193

R. Egidi (ed.), In Search of a New Humanism, 193–204.
©1999 *Kluwer Academic Publishers. Printed in Great Britain.*

None of these three contentions seems to me to be rejected. Though they surely may need to be improved resorting to a more accurate formulation and/or to a richer argumentation, nonetheless each of them holds good.

That is the way it is with the first contention. Intimate as their connection can be maintained to be, interpretative and validity statements are neither to be confused with each other, nor with the notion of norm proposition (§ 1.1.).

That is the way it is also with the second and third contention, respectively, because of fuzziness (in its twofold semantic and pragmatic dimension) being a distinguishing feature of the language of law.[4]

Namely, fuzziness of the language of law in its *semantic* dimension (i.e., the sort of fuzziness due to the very wording of the norm formulations of a legal system) affects interpretative statements both insofar as their allegedly descriptive function, and their allegedly property of being true/false are concerned (§ 1.2.).

Likewise, fuzziness of the language of law in its pragmatic dimension (*i.e.*, the sort of fuzziness due to the complex net of relationships holding among the norms expressed by the norm formulations of a legal system) affects validity statements both insofar as their allegedly descriptive function, and their allegedly property of being true/false are concerned (§ 1.3.).

1.1. NORM PROPOSITIONS AS DISGUISED CONJUNCTIONS OF INTERPRETATIVE AND VALIDITY STATEMENTS

According to the first contention of the sceptical view on norm propositions:

A statement of the form "The norm n is valid" is a disguised conjunction of at least two statements:

(1) "The norm formulation NF expresses the norm n"
(2) "NF belongs to the sources of law".

[...] If a further requirement for a norm to be valid is added to its being a meaning of a norm formulation that belongs to the sources of law, then the statements (1) and (2) are no longer sufficient to uncover correctly the disguised conjunction of statements hidden in "The norm n is valid". In this case, another statement concerning the fulfilment of the further requirement at issue has to be added.[5]

Before focusing on Bulygin's criticisms to such a contention, a preliminary remark is in order.

According to Mendonca's reading,[6] the wording of the validity statement (i.e., "NF belongs to the sources of law") amounts to maintaining that validity applies to norm formulations, not to norms.[7] Now, unhappy as this wording of validity statements can be taken to be, Mendonca's suggested reading has no steady ground. Namely, neither has a steady ground when the context is confined to the bare definition of the notion of norm proposition, the query at issue being the very meaning-content of the statement: "The norm n is valid". Nor has any justification of a sort, when the context is widened to the variety of arguments supporting the sceptical view on norm propositons, the common kernel of the different arguments being the very query to identify what can be taken to count as a valid norm.

Where Mendonca's remark mainly touches upon a matter of formulation of the contention at issue, Bulygin's criticisms claim a plain refusal of its very idea. To be sure, Bulygin sharply contests its radical statement along with the sceptical view on norm propositions.[8] Moreover, though the connection between the two criticisms is not declared, he challenges as well what can be taken to be a sort of loose, implicit assumption of a similar tenet occurring in some works of von Wright's. In either case, the little attention Bulygin is inclined to devote to interpretative concerns is the common source of his critical remarks.

That is the way it is, first, when Bulygin challenges the distinction von Wright draws between the notions of normative statement (i.e., "A statement to the effect that something or other ought to or may or must not be done (by some agent or agents, on some occasion or generally, unconditionally or provided certain conditions are satisfied)"[9]), and norm proposition (i.e., "The proposition that such and such a norm exists"[10]).[11] Bulygin doubts the soundness of the distiction ultimately because he does not take seriously any interpretative concern in finding out what a valid norm is about; i.e., what is required by a valid norm. To be sure, the way he lays down his critical remarks to von Wright's distinction actually does not ignore the very reason which grounds it: i.e., that any (purported) description of a valid norm cannot but be about an interpretative as well as a validity component. What Bulygin does disregard is the autonomous relevance the interpretative one does carry. That is why he states:

What is the difference between informing about the existing regulations and saying that there is a norm prohibiting parking cars in this place? How can I inform about existing regulations but saying that there is a norm prohibiting to park? If my information is true, then there is a norm to the effect that parking is prohibited and if there is no such a norm, then my normative statement is false. In spite of the appearances, both sentences say exactly the same.[12]

The little attention Bulygin is inclined to devote to interpretative issues affects also his second, direct criticism against the contention conceiving of any norm proposition as the result of a disguised conjunction of an interpretative statement and a validity statement. To be sure such a contention cannot be rejected, as Bulygin seems to suggest, resorting to the view according to which interpretation occurs only when the obscurity of the text requires it; in Bulygin's words:

If a norm formulation is not ambiguous no interpretative statement is needed in order to know what norm is expressed by it. If it is ambiguous, we must first assign to it one of the possible meanings. So norm propositions (sometimes) presuppose interpretation, but they do not contain interpretative statements.[13]

Now, rather than supplying a counter-argument, this assertion of Bulygin's actually amounts to a concealed juxtaposition of two different views on the notion of interpretation, namely: (a) the one according to which *in claris non fit interpretatio*, and (b) the one according to which the meaning of any text is a matter of interpretation, regardless of its being liable just of a singular, rather than a plurality of readings.

1.2. INTERPRETATIVE STATEMENTS AND SEMANTIC FUZZINESS OF THE LANGUAGE OF LAW

Interpretative statements (i.e., the first main term of the disguised conjunction a norm proposition amounts to) cannot be maintained to be either descriptive or true/false both because of fuzziness being a distinguishing feature of the language of law, and because of the variety of criteria of legal interpretation.

First. Fuzziness of the language of law in its semantic dimension is a primary hindrance in the way to drawing a one to one correspondence between norm formulations, on the one hand, and the norms interpretative statements pretend they express, on the other. Semantic fuzziness is very difficult to prevent and/or to get rid of. As a matter of fact several terms occurring in norm formulations, though on different grounds, are far from being sharply defined (or definable), and from allowing the interpreter to face what the "exact meaning" of a norm formulation can be taken to be. That is so not only because of the use of *e.g.* common language terms, evaluative terms, psychological terms, legal terms which might carry divergent meanings in reason of different legal definitions they have been given. That is so, further, because of the widespread employment of the so-called standards or general clauses [in German: *Generalklausen*, in Italian: *clausole generali*] and/or common sense notions [in German: *Erfahrungssätze*, in Italian: *massime d'esperienza*].[14]

Second. Far from confining the scope of differing interpretative statements any norm formulation can give rise to, the variety of interpretative criteria – both those which might be required by different legal systems, and those which might be recommended by different legal cultures – confirm, when not widen, the number of norms a norm formulation can be taken to express. Seldom sharply fixed, not only different criteria of legal interpretation, but usually one and the same criterion can ground divergent interpretative results.[15] Far from being a minor or secondary remark, the plurality of interpretative results any norm formulation can give rise to because of the variety and indeterminacy of the interpretative criteria, is by itself a sufficient reason to doubt both the descriptive function and the true/false qualification of interpretative statements.[16] Further, as noticed by Merkl, since varying the interpretative tool the interpretative result varies as well, one could even state that there are as many legal systems as interpretative criteria.[17]

In a word, the semantic fuzziness of the language of law and the fuzziness of the most usual interpretative criteria lead to interpretative results which are fuzzy not because of any uncertainty in the formulations they are given, but because there is no one way to decide which is the right one. Despite the sharp and peremptory wording they happen to be addressed, there is no objective way to find out the very norm a norm formulation expresses; rather, there are different subjective reasons claiming in favour of the one, or the other.

1.3. VALIDITY STATEMENTS AND PRAGMATIC FUZZINESS OF THE LANGUAGE OF LAW

Validity statements (*i.e.*, the second main term of the disguised conjunction a norm proposition amounts to) cannot be maintained to be either descriptive or true/false. That is primarily so because of the pragmatic fuzziness of the language of law; *i.e.*, the sort of fuzziness due to, and stemming from, the complex network of relations which hold (or can be assumed to hold) among different norms expressed by the norm formulations whose totality constitutes a given legal system.

To begin with, that is so as a consequence of the fuzziness of norm formulations themselves. Because of its fuzziness, any norm formulation leads to different interpretative statements which – being fuzzy in their turn – point out to a greater or lesser degree of correctness which *norms* the norm formulation is taken to express. That is to say that each interpretative statement points out – to a certain degree of correctness – which is the *valid* norm expressed by the norm formulation. Thus, insofar as statutory legal systems are concerned, any interpretative statement of a given norm formulation conveys a validity statement on the norm it asserts to be expressed by the norm formulation.[18] Now, since any interpretative statement of a given norm formulation is fuzzy, the validity statement which it conveys cannot but be fuzzy in its turn. This is not obviously to maintain that a norm can be more or less valid.[19] This is simply to point out that the question as to whether a given norm is valid can be open to debate, and hence that the norm at issue can lead to different fuzzy validity statements; *i.e.*, statements which, alike interpretative statements, are "true" only to a certain extent, depending on the differing (legal) criteria their assessment is grounded on.

Further, fuzziness of validity statements is due to the network of relations which might be drawn among the norms constituting a given legal system. In particular, at least three main sources of such a sort of fuzziness of validity statements can be singled out.

First. The validity criteria of a legal norm can give rise to doubts on the legality of a given norm (that is the case of a putative unconstitutional norm as well as of a putative void or voidable contract).[20]

Second. The so-called defects of a legal system – namely: gaps,[21] normative conflicts,[22] and redundancy – can give rise to doubts on the validity of the norms (expressed by the norm formulations) which happen to be the subject matter of such defects.

Third. Derogation – both in its implicit and in its explicit form – can give rise to doubts on the validity of the derogated norms (*i.e.*, on the norms whose validity is to be taken to have been repealed).[23]

2. A NEW STATEMENT OF THE SCEPTICAL VIEW

Thus far, I have partly iterated, partly restated three basic contentions on which the sceptical view of the notion of norm proposition is grounded.

Hence, the main criticism such a view meets is still to be given an answer. What is still in need of a reply is that (though acknowledged to have taken a start from some sound feature of legal phenomena and language, nonetheless) such a view is accused to fail because commits what Bulygin labels the "fallacy of illegitimate general-ization"; *i.e.*, because is conceived of as faulty of what more rudely logicians usually call "wild induction".

Now, the very way Bulygin denounces the "fallacy of illegitimate generalization" actually suggests, at least partly, what a reply such a denounce could be given.

According to Bulygin:

From the negation of the sentence "A norm formulation expresses always one single norm". Mazzarese jumps to the conclusion that "A norm formulation expresses always a plurality of norms". This conclusion does not follow from the premises. All we can infer is that a norm formulation sometimes expresses a plurality of norms, but not that it always does so. To put in other words: from the negation that all norm formulations are univocal, it does not follow that all norm formulations are ambiguous.[24]

Now, I will leave aside the temptation to reply that the "fallacy of illegitimate generalization" is actually committed by those who, defining the notion of norm proposition, gave for granted, and purported a one to one correspondence between the norms of a legal system and the (homonymous) statements describing them. To be sure, from the allegedly possibility to get such a correspondence in some case, would not follow (because of the very logical mistake which Bulygin reminds us) that the one to one correspondence can be taken to hold good for every norm of the system.

Though sound and grounded, such an answer would not take us very far. Thus, following Bulygin's argumentation I will attempt to providing a further answer, which contrary to what I actually did in my 1991 paper,[25] clearly states that *any* norm formulation can be given different readings with regard to the norms it can be taken to express, and different evaluations with regard to the validity of these norms.

Such a further answer takes a start from Bulygin's juxtaposing and mixing two critics which are not equivalent, namely: (a) to acknowledge that *sometimes* a norm formulation can be given different readings does not mean that it can *always* be given different readings, and (b) to acknowledge that *some* norm formulation can be given different readings does not mean that *all* norm formulations can be given different readings.[26]

The two critics are not equivalent. They actually range over two different sets of variables, namely: the one concerns a so to say dyachronic view on the interpretative queries any norm formulation can give rise to, whereas the other concerns a synchronic (*rectius*: an atemporal) view on which norm formulations give rise and which norm formulations do not give rise to interpretative queries.[27]

Now, the second criticism, i.e., the one focusing on the distinction between norm formulations which can, and norm formulations which can not and / or need not be given different readings, is ideologically biased and linguistically unwarrented. When, and how to draw the borderline between the two sorts of norm formulation depends upon, and varies along, with the interpreter's choices and evaluations.

Thus, contrary to his intended warning, Bulygin is simply right when stating:

If there are no univocal norm formulations, all we have are pluralities of possible norms, but [...] never [...] a definite norm.[28]

That is actually just the way it is because what a norm formulation can be taken to express is never given once for good. The other way round, as it is with *any* linguistic expression, the meaning of a norm formulation cannot but be context dependent, i.e. cannot be confined to its allegedly literal domain, because it cannot but vary along with a number of variables, differing as the case may happen to be. Now, though surely preventing the possibility to drawing any sharp borderline between univocal and not univocal linguistic formulations (be they norm formulations or not), the context dependent nature of meaning, far from condemning us to be left with a language which is a usless tool of communication,[29] simply calls our attention to the plurality of variables (be they semantic, synthactic, pragmatic or else not even *stricto sensu* linguistic in nature) which may happen to take part in determining what a meaning a linguistic expression can be taken to be about.

Strange as it may sound, a concession to such a view, not its refusal, is provided by Niiniluoto's own way to phrase the distinction between univocal and not univocal norm formulations. To be sure, norm formulations whose wording consist only of "common terms which have (at least currently) a well established meaning",[30] contrary to what Niiniluoto purports, do not ground any true norm-proposition. What they can be taken to ground are, at most, interpretative statelments highly convincing because of the widely shared opinion they rely on, within a given (prominent) legal culture.

Quite differently from the previously so to say ideologically biased and linguistically unwarrented distinction, the first criticism of Bulygin's touches upon a different issue, namely that one and the same norm formulation can be given different readings, as the case may be. If this (and not the one stemming from distinction between univocal and not univocal norm formulations) is the way it is, then here it is the decisive point leading to a new statement of the sceptical view on norm propositions.

That is so since to acknowledge that the possibility of differing readings of a norm formulation is not given once for good, is not but a different way to state that any norm formulation is fuzzy, and, further, that its degree of fuzziness (both in the semantic and the pragmatic dimension) may (and does) vary along with different contexts.[31]

That is to say, for what and to what an extent a norm formulation can be taken to be fuzzy (a) because of the variety of norms it can be taken to express, and (b) because of the possible differing views on the validity of the norms it is taken to express depends on, and varies along with, different contexts; i.e., is the result of a complex and mutable set of variables.

No sentence, no expression, simple and plain as it may be taken to be, is actually free from the possibility of differing readings and understandings, if just one starts to worry about its "real" meaning. Not to resort to the boring everyday legal practice (where on any matter there are always at least two different competing views which the decision-maker is asked to settle), J. R. R. Tolkein will help us in providing an example of the context dependent different degrees of fuzziness of the apparent semantically plain expression, "Good morning":

All that the unsuspecting Bilbo saw that morning was an old man with a staff. [...]

"Good morning!" said Bilbo, and he meant it. The sun was shining, and the grass was very green. But Gandalf looked at him from under long bushy eyebrows that stuck out further than the brim of his shady hat.

"What do you mean?" he said. "Do you wish me a good morning whether I want it or not; or that you feel good this morning; or that it is a morning to be good on?"

"All of them at once" said Bilbo. "And a very fine morning for a pipe of tobacco out of doors, into the bargain. [...]

"Very pretty" said Gandalf. "But I have no time to blow smoke-rings this morning. I am looking for someone to share in an adventure that I am arranging, and it's very difficult to find anyone."

"I should think so – in these parts. We are plain quiet folk and have no use for adventures. Nasty disturbing uncomfortable things. Make you late for dinner! [...]" He had decided that he was not quite his sort, and wanted him to go away. But the old man did not move. [...]

"Good morning!" he said at last. "We don't want any adventures here, thank you! [...]". By this he meant that the conversation was at an end.

"What a lot of things you do use *Good morning* for!" said Gandalf. "Now you mean that you want to get rid of me, and that it won't be good till I move off." [J. R. R. Tolkein, *The Hobbit or There and Back Again*, 1937]

Università di Pavia (Italy)

NOTES

[1] Reference is to the critical remarks Bulygin's contribution to the present volume "True and False Statements in Normative Discourse", directly addresses to my 1991 paper " 'Norm Proposition': Epistemic and Semantic Queries".

[2] To be sure von Wright's standpoint is given due attention in featuring the so to say "sceptical view" on norm propositions, both in my 1991 paper and, though in a somewhat different perspective, in a previous work of mine (namely, Mazzarese 1989, pp. 135–67). Further, in my 1991 paper (first discussed in one of the Research Seminars held by von Wright at the Philosophy Department of Helsinki) much attention is also paid to the contentions maintained by Aarnio and Niiniluoto, two Finnish scholars whose analyses on the topic are undeniably influenced by von Wright.

[3] Cf. von Wright 1963.

[4] On fuzziness as a distinguishing feature of the language of law (or law-maker language) as well as of the language of legal dogmatics (or jurist language) and the language of adjudication (or judicial-maker language), cf. Mazzarese 1996, pp. 171–91 and Mazzarese [in print]. For a stimulating introduction to the logico-linguistic category of fuzziness, together with a rich overview of some of its actual and potential applications, cf. Kosko 1994.

[5] Mazzarese 1991, pp. 42–3 A further requirement for a norm to be valid, beside its being meaning of a norm formulation belonging to the sources of law, can be taken to be its acceptance, mentioned e.g. by I. Niiniluoto 1981 b. On Niiniluto's further requirement for a norm to be valid, and hence on the need to add one more statement concerning the fulfilment of this requirement, cf. Mazzarese 1991, p. 45.

[6] Cf. Mendonca1 997, p. 37.

[7] Undoubtedly perplexing as Mendonca correctly stresses, the tenet according to which validity applies to norm formulations has actually been maintained, though not along with the sceptical view on norm propositions. That is obviously the case when, though on different theoretical grounds, norms are conceived of as their linguistic formulations, as e.g. by Scarpelli 1959; Alchourrón and Bulygin 1971; Opalek 1972; Hernandez Marín 1984. That is the case, further, with some authors which maintain that validity can apply to norm formulations as well as to norms. Cf. e.g. Conte 1988, pp. 446–52; Guastini 1987, pp. 18–9.

[8] The other way round, no challenge on the point occurs in the critical survey Niiniluoto 1991 supplies of the sceptical view. That is probably so because of the attention he himself devotes to both validity and interpretative statements, rispectively, though in two distinct works on the notion of norm proposition, namely Niiniluoto 1981 a and 1981 b.

[9] Von Wright 1963, p. 105.

[10] *Ibidem*, p. 106. The same characterization formulated in 1963 occurs in the very recent von Wright 1996, pp. 64–5.

[11] A distinction analogous to von Wright's one is drawn by Aarnio 1981, pp. 425–26 between interpretative statements and norm statements (a norm statement being conceived of as "a statement which says something about the content of a valid norm").

[12] See "True and False Statements in Normative Discourse", in this volume, p. 184.

[13] *Ibidem*, p. 188.

[14] On fuzziness and general clauses it is worth quoting what Wróblewski 1983, p. 326 maintains: "It is not so, that the law-maker for the certainty of law and effectiveness of channelling the behavior avoids

indeterminacy of rules he formulates or he refers to – on the contrary, he can use fuzzy language of general clauses for imposing the burden of decision on the decision-maker and wait for the results having always several means of his own intervention, if needed. In this way he enables both individualized decisions and the adaptability of enacted law to changing situation without modifying the text of valid legal rules".

[15] Such a contention holds good with regard to the most usual criteria of legal interpretation, and, contrary to what is stated in Mazzarese 1991, p. 49, mainly with regard to the allegedly literal criterion. Not to mention the differing readings such a criterion has (and still is) given, that is obviously so because of the very doubtful and problematic notion of "literal meaning" such a criterion relies on. To this point cf. Mazzarese, *Literal Interpretation: Jurists and Linguists Confronted* [ms.]

[16] A similar remark occurs also in Wróblewski 1992, p. 122: "The expression "rule R has meaning M' can be true or false in a determined language of legal discourse if it is relativised to the directives of interpretation and to evaluations, and if this relativisation fulfils certain conditions. This relativisation, however, does not eliminate the problem of choice of these directives and evaluations. [...] Accordingly, one ought to treat the expression "rule R has meaning M' as a decision of operative interpretation and demand not its truth or falsity, but rather its best or most adequate justification".

[17] Cf. Merkl 1916. Though less radical in its formulation, a similar contention occurs in Bulygin 1992, p. 27: " 'E' chiaro che un mutamento nella interpretazione di una norma giuridica equivale ad una modificazione di tale norma, e quindi ad un cambiamento nel sistema. [...] Ma non vi è alcun cambiamento nella formulazione ufficiale della norma".

[18] A similar remark occurs in Aarnio 1981, p. 426: "Interpretative statements and norm statements are only two sides of the same coin", where "norm statement" is used to term "a statement which says something about the content of a valid norm" [*ibidem*, p. 425]. Significant as well the point made by Twining and Miers 1976, 1982,[2] p. 163: "Questions of interpretation may be part of a process of determining the validity of a rule".

[19] The tenet that a norm can be valid to a greater or lesser degree is maintained by Ross 1958, p. 45: "According to the traditional view the validity [...] of a particular norm is derived from the superior norm in conformity with which it has come into being [...]. On such premises, obviously, the concept of validity must be absolute – either a rule of law is valid or it is not. [...] In fact the assertion that a rule is valid law is highly relative. It can also be said that a rule can be valid law to a greater or lesser degree varying with the degree of probability with which it can be predicted that the rule will be applied".

[20] A similar remark is made by Twining and Miers 1976, 1982[2], pp. 150–51: "Doubts about the very existence of a legal rule may be relatively rare; but disputes about the validity of a rule are frequent, for example in respect of delegated legislation under the *ultra vires* doctrine, or in determining the constitutionality of acts of state legislatures in the United States and like jurisdictions. Doubts about the identity of an alleged rule or principle are [...] commonplace in the context of case law". Insofar as unconstitutional norms are concerned, the soundness of the tenet at issue seems to be denied by Bulygin 1991, p. 267, and at least to be conceived as open to debate by Moreso 1993.

[21] Gaps and reasoning by analogy are a prominent source of fuzziness in the language of law. To the point cf. e.g. Reisinger 1975, 1982; Atienza 1986, pp. 155–77 and Philipps 1990.

[22] Normative conflicts are mentioned as a possible source of fuzziness of the language of law by Wróblewski 1983, p. 328. A similar remark occurs in Peczenik and Wróblewski 1985, pp. 30–1. Remarks on normative conflicts as a source of uncertainty and/or indeterminacy of legal systems – though without any explicit reference to fuzziness – are provided e.g. by Mazzarese 1987 a, pp. 351–53.

[23] Derogation is mentioned as a possible source of fuzziness of the language of law by Wróblewski 1983, p. 328. A similar remark occurs in Peczenik and Wróblewski 1985, pp. 30–1. Remarks on derogation as a source of uncertainty and/or indeterminacy of legal systems – though without any explicit reference to fuzziness – occur *e.g.* in Bulygin and Alchourrón 1977; Alchourrón and Bulygin 1978; Bulygin 1982; Luzzati 1987; Mazzarese 1987 b, pp. 83–7.

[24] See *"True and False Statements in Normative Discourse"*, in this volume, p. 186. A similar remark occurs also in Niiniluoto 1991, p. 369: "It is not enough to prove that *some*, many, or most norm formulations are uncertain or indefinite with respect to their validity or interpretations [...] and, hence, it can be disproved by showing that there are at least some cases where a norm with definite content definitely belongs to the legal order".

[25] Such an hesitation is denounced by Niiniluoto 1991, p. 369.

[26] Clearly distinct, rather than overlapping with each other, the two critics occur also in Niiniluoto 1991, pp. 369–70: (a) "sometimes there is no uncertainty whatsoever about the status of a norm formulation NF: The sentence NF may be a statute printed, e.g., in the text of Criminal Law in Finland. Moreover, such a sentence may happen to contain only common terms which have (at least currently) a well-established

meaning. [...] In such cases [...] we do have the possibility of making a true norm-description about the Finnish order"; (b) "A valid norm formulation NF (of the form 'given cases of type p, it ought to be the case that q') may allow for several, even an unlimited number of interpretations [...]. However, there may be special cases p_o which clearly fall under the description p. [...] Then the derived norm formulation 'If p_o then Oq' expresses a norm which serves as a *partial* characterization of the meaning of NF".

[27] Differently phrased, a similar distinction is drawn by Guastini 1997, pp. 282–83, and p. 290 in criticizing the so-called open texture theory of legal interpretation.

[28] Bulygin, *"True and False Statements in Normative Discourse"*, in this volume, p. 187.

[29] In Bulygin's words: "It is an essential feature of language that at least some of its expression must be univocal. A language that does not meet this condition is usless as a tool of communication".

[30] Niiniluoto 1991, p. 369.

[31] Such an answer holds good also when the criticism at issue is phrased resorting to the distiction between hard and easy cases, as in Mendonca 1997, pp. 30–1.

BIBLIOGRAPHY

Aarnio 1981

    Aarnio Aulis: "On Truth and Validity of Interpretative Statements in Legal Dogmatics", Third part of A. Aarnio, R. Alexy, A. Peczenik: "The Foundation of Legal Reasoning", *Rechtstheorie*, 12, pp. 423–48.

Alchourrón and Bulygin 1971

    Alchourrón Carlos Eduardo and Bulygin Eugenio: *Normative Systems*. Springer-Verlag, Wien.

Alchourrón and Bulygin 1978

    Alchourrón Carlos Eduardo and Bulygin Eugenio: "Un modello per la dinamica dei sistemi normativi", in A. Martino (ed.): *Logica, informatica diritto*, Le Monnier, Firenze, vol. I, pp. 133–43.

Atienza 1986

    Atienza Manuel: *Sobre la analogía en el derecho. Ensayo de análisis de un razonamiento jurídico*, Civitas, Madrid.

Bulygin 1982

    Bulygin Eugenio: "Time and Validity", in A. Martino (ed.): *Deontic Logic, Computational Linguistics and Legal Information Systems*, North-Holland Publishing Co., Amsterdam, vol. II, pp. 65–81.

Bulygin 1991

    Bulygin Eugenio: "Algunas consideraciones acerca de los sistema jurídicos, *Doxa*, 9, pp. 257–79.

Bulygin 1992

    Bulygin Eugenio: "Sull'interpretazione giuridica", in P. Comanducci and R. Guatini (eds.): *Analisi e diritto 1992. Ricerche di giurisprudenza analitica*, Giappichelli, Torino, pp. 11–30

Bulygin and Alchourrón 1977

    Bulygin Eugenio and Alchourrón Carlos Eduardo: "Unvollständigkeit, Widersprüchlichkeit und Unbestimmtheit der Normenordunungen", in A. G. Conte, R. Hilpinen, G. H. von Wright (eds.): *Deontische Logik und Semantik*, Athenaion, Wiesbaden, pp. 20–32.

Conte 1988

    Conte Amedeo G.: "Minima deontica", *Rivista internazionale di filosofia del diritto*, 65, pp. 425–75.

Guastini 1987

    Guastini Riccardo: "In tema di abrogazione", in C. Luzzati (ed.): *L'abrogazione delle leggi. Un dibattito analitico*, Giuffrè, Milano, pp. 3–31.

Guastini 1997

    Guastini Riccardo: "Interpretive Statements", in E. Garzón Valdés, W. Krawietz, G. H. von Wright, R. Zimmerling (eds.): *Normative Systems in Legal and Moral Theory. Festschrift for Carlos E. Alchourrón and Eugenio Bulygin*, Duncker und Humblot, Berlin, pp. 279–92.

Hernández Marín 1984

    Hernández Marín Rafel: *El derecho como dogma*, Tecnos, Madrid.

Kosko 1994

    Kosko Bart: *Fuzzy Thinking*, Flamingo, London.

Luzzati 1987
Luzzati Claudio: "Abrogazione ed indeterminatezza nell'ordinamento giuridico", in C. Luzzati (ed.): *L'abrogazione delle leggi. Un dibattito analitico*, Giuffrè, Milano, pp. 65–75.

Mazzarese 1987 a
Mazzarese Tecla: "Antinomia", in: *Digesto IV edizione. Sezione Civile*, Vol. I, UTET, Torino, pp. 347–53.

Mazzarese 1987 b
Mazzarese Tecla: "Variazioni in tema d'abrogazione", in C. Luzzati (ed.): *L'abrogazione delle leggi. Un dibattito analitico*, Giuffrè, Milano, pp. 77–91.

Mazzarese 1989
Mazzarese Tecla: *Logica deontica e linguaggio giuridico*. Padova, Cedam.

Mazzarese 1991
Mazzarese Tecla: " 'Norm Proposition': Epistemic and Semantic Queries", *Rechtstheorie*, 22, pp. 39–70.

Mazzarese 1996
Mazzarese Tecla [1996]: *Forme di razionalità delle decisioni giudiziali*, Giappichelli, Torino.

Mazzarese [in print]
Mazzarese Tecla, "Semantic and Pragmatic Fuzziness of Legal Language", *Archivum Iuridicum Cracoviense* [in print].

Mazzarese [manuscript]
Mazzarese Tecla: "Literal Interpretation: Jurists and Linguists Confronted. Report to the *IVR 18th World Congress*", La Plata/Buenos Aires.

Mendonca 1997
Mendonca Daniel: *Interpretación y aplicación del derecho*, Universidad de Almería, Almería.

Merkl 1916
Merkl Adolf: "Zum Interpretationsproblem", *Grünhutsche Zeitschrift für das Privatrecht und öffentliche Recht der Gegenwart*, 42, pp. 535–56.

Moreso 1993
Moreso José Juan: "Sobre normas inconstitucionales", *Doxa*, 11, pp. 247–62.

Niiniluoto 1981 a
Niiniluoto Ilkka: "On Truth and Argumentation in Legal Dogmatics", in A. Aarnio, I. Niiniluoto, J. Uusitalo (eds.): *Methodologie und Erkenntnistheorie der juristischen Argumentation*, Duncker und Humblot, Berlin, pp. 53–76.

Niiniluoto 1981 b
Niiniluoto Ilkka: "On Truth of Norm Propositions", in I. Tammelo, A. Aarnio (eds.): *On the Advancement of Theory and Tecnique in Law and Ethics*, Duncker und Humblot, Berlin, pp. 171–80.

Niiniluoto 1991
Niiniluoto Ilkka: "Norm Propositions Defended", *Ratio Juris*, 4, pp. 367–73.

Opalek 1972
Opalek Kazimierz: "Les normes, les énoncés sur les normes et les propositions déontiques", *Archives de philosophie du droit*, 17, pp. 355–72.

Peczenik and Wróblewski 1985
Peczenik Aleksander and Wróblewski Jerzy: "Fuzziness and Transformation: Towards Explaining Legal Reasoning", *Theoria*, 51, pp. 24–44.

Philipps 1990
Philipps Lothar: "Naheliegende Anwendungen neuronaler Netze in der Rechtswissenschaft", *Iur PC*, 11–12, pp. 820–27.

Reisinger 1975
Reisinger Leo: "Über die Anwendungsmöglichkeiten der Theorie unscharfer Mengen (Fuzzy Set Theory) im Recht", *Datenverarbeitung im Recht*, 4, pp. 19–157.

Risinger 1982
Reisinger Leo: "Legal Reasoning by Analogy. A Model Applying Fuzzy Set Theory", in C. Ciampi (ed.): *Artificial Intelligence and Legal Information Systems*, North-Holland Publishing Co., Amsterdam, vol. I, pp. 151–63.

Ross 1958
    Ross Alf: *On Law and Justice*, Stevens, London.
Scarpelli 1959
    Scarpelli Uberto: "Contributo alla semantica del linguaggio normativo", Torino, Memoria dell'Accademia delle scienze di Torino. Reprint ed. by A. Pintore, Giuffrè, Milano, 1985.
Twining and Miers 1976
    Twining William and Miers David: *How to Do Things with Rules*, Weidenfeld and Nicolson, London.
Von Wright 1963
    Von Wright Georg Henrik: *Norm and Action. A Logical Inquiry*, Routledge & Kegan Paul, London.
Von Wright 1996
    Von Wright Georg Henrik: "Ought to Be-Ought to Do", in G. H. von Wright: *Six Essays in Philosophical Logic*, Acta Philosophica Fennica, Helsinki, pp. 63–70.
Wróblewski 1983
    Wróblewski Jerzy: "Fuzziness of Legal System", in U. Kangas (ed.): *Essays in Legal Theory in Honor of Kaarle Makkonen*. Monographic issue of *Oikeustiede*, 16, pp. 311–30.
Wróblewski 1992
    Wróblewski Jerzy: *The Judicial Application of Law*, ed. by Z. Bankowski and N. MacCormick, Reidel, Dordrecht.

AMEDEO G. CONTE

THREE LEVELS OF DEONTICS

Ἀπλοῦς ο τῆς ἀληθείας μῦθος ἔφυ.
The language of truth is simple.
Euripides

"Alle Wahrheit ist einfach." —
Ist das nicht zwiefach eine Lüge? —
"Every truth is simple." —
Is this not a twofold lie? —
Friedrich Wihelm Nietzsche

0. LOGIC OF *DEONTIC TRUTHS*, LOGIC OF *DEONTIC SENTENCES*, LOGIC OF *DEONTIC VALIDITY*

0.1. Truth is *simple*. But deontics is *threefold*. Within deontics I have distinguished *three* logically independent questions.

0.2. The logical independence of these three questions can be formulated with a sentence from Ludwig Wittgenstein's *Tractatus logico-philosophicus*. I will quote Wittgenstein's sentence in German, in the English translation by David F. Pears and Brian McGuinness, in the Swedish translation by Anders Wedberg (Swedish is the mothertongue of Georg Henrik von Wright), and in the Finnish translation by Heikki Nyman:

Eines kann der Fall sein oder nicht der Fall sein und alles übrige gleich bleiben.

Each item can be the case or not the case while everything else remains the same.

Ett kan vara fallet eller icke vara fallet och allt det övriga förbli sig likt.

Jokin seikka voi olla niin tai näin tai olla niin olematta, vaikka kaikki muu pysyy samana.[1]

0.3. The three logically independent questions of deontics are as follows.

(i)   The first question concerns *deontic truths*. Are there *deontic formulas* which are *logically true* in virtue of the meaning of the *deontic* terms occurring in them? (In other words: Are there *deontic-logical* truths?)
The first question will be discussed in § 1..

(ii) The second question does not concern deontic truths, but *deontic sentences*. Can *deontic sentences* be terms of logical *entailment-relationships*? (In other words: Are there logical *entailment-relationships* between deontic sentences?). Within the second question I distinguished two sub-questions, *viz.*:

205

R. Egidi (ed.), In Search of a New Humanism, 205–214.
©1999 *Kluwer Academic Publishers. Printed in Great Britain.*

(ii.i)   Can deontic sentences *entail* deontic sentences?

(ii.ii) Can deontic sentences *be entailed* by deontic sentences?

The second question will be discussed in § 2..

(iii)   The third question concerns neither deontic truths, nor deontic sentences, but *deontic validity*. Are there logical *entailment-relationships* at the level of deontic validity? (In other words: Can there be logical *entailment-relationships* between the deontic *validity* of one deontic sentence and the deontic *validity* of another?) Within the third question I have distinguished two sub-questions, *viz.*:

   (iii.i)   Can the deontic validity of one deontic sentence *entail* the deontic validity of another deontic sentence?

   (iii.ii) Can the deontic *validity* of one deontic sentence *be entailed* by the deontic *validity* of another deontic sentence?

The third question will be discussed in § 3..

1. THE LOGIC OF DEONTIC TRUTHS

1.0. Introduction

The first question concerns (the existence of) *deontic truths*: Are there *deontic formulas* which are *logically true* in virtue of the meaning of the *deontic* terms occurring in them? (In other words: Are there *deontic-logical truths*?)

1.1. A negative answer to the first question: Ernst Mally's deontics

1.1.1. The existence of *deontic truths* was acknowledged by the Austrian philosopher and logician Ernst Mally (1879–1944) in his book *Grundgesetze des Sollens. Elemente der Logik des Willens*, 1926. Mally is the inventor of the German noun *"Deontik"* (in English: "deontics") and of the German adjective *"deontisch"* (in English: "deontic"). Both *"Deontik"* and *"deontisch"* derive from the Greek participle τὸ δέον *"tò déon"*, which means "that which is obligatory", "that which ought to be done".[2]

1.1.2. Mally's deontics is a theory of *deontic truths*: but, according to Mally, *deontic truths* do *not* belong to *logic*.

1.1.2.1. *Deontic* truths are not *logical* truths since *logic* is the logic of (theoretical) thinking [*Logik des Denkens*],[3] the logic of (theoretical) judgement [*Logik des Urteils*],[4] while *deontics* is the logic of the (atheoretical) will, the logic of (atheoretical) volition [*Logik des Willens*],[5] *i.e. bouletic* logic. (The Greek noun βούλησις *"boúlesis"* means "will", "volition".)

1.1.2.2. Mally's deontics is a *counterpart* of logic, not a *part* of it.[6]

1.1.3. Two philological remarks.

(i)   The *French* equivalent of Mally's German phrase "*Logik des Willens*" ["logic of the will", "logic of volition", "bouletic logic"], *i.e.* "*logique de la volonté*", occurs in the title of the book: Paul Lapie (1869–1927), *Logique de la volonté*, 1902.

(ii)   The *Finnish* equivalent of "*Logik des Willens*", *i.e.* "*tahto-logiikka*" (the Finnish noun "*logiikka*" corresponds to the German noun "*Logik*" and to the English noun "logic"; the Finnish noun "*tahto*" corresponds to the German noun "*Wille*" and to the English noun "logic") occurs in a Finnish book published two years before Mally's *Grundgesetze des Sollens*: Elieser Kaila (1885–1938), *Oikeuslogiikka* [*Logic of Law*], 1924.[7]

1.2. The affirmative answer to the first question: G. H. von Wright's deontic logic

1.2.1. Mally's deontics is *parallel* to logic, not a *part* of it.

Georg Henrik von Wright was the first to acknowledge that *deontic truths* belong to *logic*: in particular, to the new part of logic which he calls *deontic logic* (*deontisk logik* in Swedish, von Wright's mothertongue; *deonttinen logiikka* in Finnish).[8] Deontic logic is (according to von Wright) the (logical) theory of *logical* truths which are specifically *deontic-logical* truths. In other words: Deontic logic deals with *logical* truths which are such in virtue of the semantics (of the *intension*) of *deontic* terms.

1.2.2. According to von Wright there are *two* types of deontic formulas expressing *logical truths*.[9]

(i)   The deontic formulas of the *first type* express *truths of logic* for reasons which have nothing to do with the *specific* character of the *deontic* terms occurring in them. For instance:

$$(Pp \supset Pq) \supset (\neg Pq \supset \neg Pp).$$

This is a *logical truth* (a *truth of logic*), but not a *deontic-logical truth*: it is just an application of a variant of the scheme called *modus tollens*, which is valid for *any* sentence, whether deontic or not.

Another deontic formula expressing a *truth of logic* for reasons independent of the *specific* character of the *deontic* terms occurring in it is:

$$(Op \wedge (Op \supset Oq)) \supset (Oq).$$

This is a *logical truth*, but not a *deontic-logical truth*: it is just an application of the scheme called *modus ponens*, which is valid for *any* sentence, whether deontic or not.

(ii)   The deontic formulas of the *second type* express *truths of logic* for reasons which depend upon the *specific* character of the *deontic* terms occurring in them.[10] For instance:

$$(Op \wedge O(p \supset q)) \supset (Oq).$$

In von Wright's own words:

If doing what we ought to do commits us to do something else, then this new act is also something which we ought to do.[11]

In other words:

If p is obligatory and if doing p commits us to do q, then q is obligatory too.

This *truth of logic* is *not* an application of any scheme which is valid for *any* sentence, whether deontic or not.

1.2.3. The deontic formula:

$$(Op \wedge O(p \supset q)) \supset Oq$$

must of course be distinguished from the deontic formula:

$$(Op \wedge (Op \supset Oq)) \supset Oq.$$

(i)   The *first* formula, *i.e.*:

$$(Op \wedge O(p \supset q)) \supset Oq$$

expresses a *logical truth* for reasons which depend upon the *specific* character of the *deontic* terms occurring in it.

(ii)   The *second* formula, *i. e.*:

$$(Op \wedge (Op \supset Oq)) \supset Oq$$

expresses a *logical* truth for reasons which do *not* depend upon the *specific* character of the *deontic* terms occurring in it.

1.2.4. The deontic formula:

$$(Op \wedge O(p \supset q)) \supset Oq$$

is a nice instance of *deontic* truth. Here are four further examples of *deontic* truths.

(i)   First example:

$$Op \supset Pp.[12]$$

(ii)   Second example:

$$(\neg Pq \wedge O(p \supset q)) \supset \neg Pp.$$

In von Wright's own words:

If doing something commits us to do the forbidden, then we are forbidden to do the first thing.[13]

(iii) Third example:

$$Op \supset OOp.[14]$$

(iv)   Fourth example:

$$O(Op \supset p).^{15}$$

The deontic-logical truth:

$$O(Op \supset p)$$

belongs to *logic*. Its counterpart in *pragmatics* is a "grammatical sentence" [*grammatischer Satz*] of Ludwig Wittgenstein:

Der Befehl befiehlt seine Befolgung.
An order orders its own execution.[16]

2. THE LOGIC OF *DEONTIC SENTENCES*

2.0. Introduction

In § 1. I have analyzed the *first question* of deontics (Are there *deontic-logical* truths? Are there *deontic* formulas which are *logically* true in virtue of the *intension* of the *deontic* terms occurring in them?).

The *second question* of deontics concerns not (the logic of) *deontic truths*, but (the logic of) *deontic sentences*. Can *deontic sentences* be terms of logical *entailment-relationships*? (In other words: Are there logical *entailment-relationships* between deontic sentences?)

In particular:

(i)   Can deontic sentences *entail* deontic sentences?

(ii)   Can deontic sentences *be entailed* by deontic sentences?

2.1. The negative answer to the second question

2.1.1. The answer to the second question will necessarily be negative if we make the following two assumptions:

(i)   Logical entailment-relationships can only exist between *apophantic* sentences (*i.e.* between sentences which are true-or-false);

(ii)   Deontic sentences are *anapophantic* (*i.e.*: not-apophantic) sentences.

2.1.2. The negative answer to the second question is the thesis of *inferential opacity in deontic contexts*. (My phrase "*inferential* opacity in deontic contexts" is a variation on the phrase "*referential* opacity in deontic contexts".)[17]

2.1.3. A prefiguration of the thesis of *inferential opacity* in deontic contexts occurs in a work of the Danish philosopher and logician Jørgen Jørgensen (1894–1969), *Imperativer og Logik*, 1938. (The object of Jørgensen's inquiry is not *deontic* sentences, but *imperative* sentences [in Danish: *imperativer, imperativiske sætninger*].[18]) I will quote Jørgensen's relevant passages in Danish and in English:

(i)   Imperativer kan ikke [...] indgaa som *konklusioner* i logiske slutninger.
      Imperatives cannot be *conclusions* of logical inferences.

(ii) Imperativer kan ikke [...] indgaa som *præmisser* i logiske slutninger.
      Imperatives cannot be *premises* of logical inferences.

2.2. The affirmative answer to the second question

2.2.1. A little-known Polish philosopher, Jerzy Sztykgold, shares the two assumptions which lead to the *negative* answer to the second question,[19] but paradoxically he answers it in the *affirmative*. Sztykgold rejects the thesis of *inferential opacity* in deontic contexts: according to him, *deontic sentences* can be terms of logical *entailment-relationships*.[20]

2.2.2. The reason for Sztykgold's affirmative answer to the second question lies is his semantics of deontic sentences.

2.2.2.1. According to Sztykgold's semantics of deontic sentences, the predicate which applies to deontic sentences is not *truth* [in Polish: *prawda*], but *rightness* [in Polish: *słuszność*]. Rightness is the deontic counterpart (the deontic analogue) of truth.

2.2.2.2. How are *rightness* and *truth* related? Rightness [*słuszność*] is distinct from truth, but does "strictly correspond" to it. Rightness has the same logical behaviour as truth. (By the same token: unrightness [*niesłuszność*] is distinct from falsity [*fałsz*], but does "strictly correspond" to it. Unrightness has the same logical behaviour as falsity.)

2.2.2.3. In virtue of this *analogy* between rightness [*słuszność*] and truth [*prawda*], deontic sentences can be terms of logical *entailment-relationships*. In particular:

(i)   Deontic sentences can *entail* deontic sentences;

(ii) Deontic sentences can *be entailed* by deontic sentences.

2.2.3. Here are the relevant passages (in Polish and in English) of Jerzy Sztykgold's paper *Negacja normy*, 1936:

(i)   Do norm mają zastosowanie kryterja słuszności i niesłuszności, odpowiadające ściśle kryterjom prawdy i fałszu.
      To norms apply the criteria of rightness [*słuszność*] and unrightness [*niesłuszność*]. These criteria (rightness and unrightness) strictly correspond to the criteria of truth [*prawda*] and falsity [*fałsz*].

(ii) Wszystkie tezy rachunku zdań mają zatem zastosowanie także i do norm.
Therefore, all theses of propositional calculus [*rachunek zdań*] also apply to
norms.[21]

3. THE LOGIC OF *DEONTIC VALIDITY*

3.1. Logic vs. ontology in deontics

3.1.1. I distinguished three questions of deontics.

The *first question* was: Are there *deontic-logical* truths? The *first question* was
discussed in § 1..

The *second question* was: Are there logical entailment-relationships between
deontic sentences? The *second question* was discussed in § 2..

The *third question* is: Are there logical entailment-relationships between the
deontic validity of one deontic sentence and the *deontic validity* of another? (In other
words: Are there logical entailment-relationships at the level of *deontic validity*?) The
third question will be discussed here in § 3..

3.1.2. In four earlier papers I suggested that the answer to the third question depends
on the sense we give to the phrase "deontic validity" ["*Sollgeltung*",
"*Sollensgeltung*"].[22] If deontic validity is defined as *existence* in a normative
system,[23] then the answer to the third question (Are there entailment-relationships at
the level of deontic validity?) will necessarily be *negative*. What logic applies to is
truth, not *existence*. Therefore, there are *no* entailment-relationships at the level of
deontic validity. *Logical* relationships are not *ontological* relationships.

3.2. Logical relationships vs. ontological relationships in von Wright's philosophical deontics

3.2.1. The insight that *logical* relationships are not *ontological* relationships can be
found in two important essays by von Wright: *Norms, Truth, and Logic*, 1983, and *Is
There a Logic of Norms?*, 1991.

(i) In *Norms, Truth, and Logic* von Wright *implicitly* denies that *normative
entailment-relationships* are *existential relationships*.

It is an *illusion* to think there is a *logical* problem here. The illusion originates from thinking that
normative entailment is an *existential relationship* between norms.[24]

(ii) In *Is There a Logic of Norms?* von Wright *explicitly* denies that *normative
entailment-relationships* are *existential relationships*.

That one norm *entails* another norm does *not* mean that if the first "*exists*", then the second "*exists*"
too.[25]

3.2.2. *Logical* relationships are not *ontological* relationships: entailment-relationship
belongs to *logic*, not to *ontology*.

Università di Pavia (Italy)

NOTES

[1] Wittgenstein 1961, 1.21.

[2] Incidentally: τὸ δέον "*tò déon*" is not etymologically related to the verb δέω "*déo*" which means "to bind".

[3] Cf. Mally 1926. Reprinted in Mally 1971, p. 232.

[4] *Ibidem.*

[5] *Ibidem*, pp. 229 and 232.

[6] The term "counterpart" is the English counterpart of Mally's German term "*Gegenstück*".

[7] Elieser Kaila is not to be confused with Eino Kaila (1890–1958), von Wright's teacher in Helsinki.

[8] Cf. von Wright 1951 a, p. 1; 1951 b; 1964, p. 261.

[9] Cf. von Wright 1951 a, p. 5; 1957, p. 62.

[10] Cf. von Wright 1951 a, pp. 5 and 12; 1957, pp. 63 and 72.

[11] Cf. von Wright 1951 a, p. 12; 1951 b, p. 39; 1957, p. 72.

[12] The sense of the deontic-logical truth: $Op \supset Pp$ is discussed by von Wright in von Wright 1983 b, p. 191 and von Wright 1984, p. 453. Cf. Azzoni 1991, p. 116.

[13] Cf. von Wright 1951 b, p. 39.

[14] The sense of the deontic-logical truth: $Op \supset OOp$ is discussed in von Wright 1983 a, p. 146.

[15] Cf. Prior (1914–1969) 1955. The deontic-logical truth: $O\ (Op \supset p)$ is discussed in von Wright 1983 a, p. 146.

[16] Cf. Wittgenstein 1953, I, § 468, p. 133. Wittgenstein's sentence is discussed in Conte 1983, § 2.3.2. pp. 72–5. Reprinted in Conte 1995, pp. 302–5.

[17] *Referential* opacity in deontic contexts is investigated in Conte 1976, § 1.1., pp. 14–5. Reprinted in Conte 1989, pp. 150–51 and in Conte 1978, § 1.2.2.2., pp. 223–24. Reprinted in Conte 1989, pp. 201–2.

[18] Cf. Jørgensen 1938; Conte 1996.

[19] The two assumptions which lead to the negative answer to the second question are: (i) logical entailment-relationships can only exist between *apophantic* sentences (*i.e.* between sentences which are true-or-false); (ii) deontic sentences are *anapophantic* (*i.e.* not-apophantic) sentences.

[20] Sztykgold 1936.

[21] The key-word in Sztykgold's deontics is "*słuszność*". Sztykgold himself does not define this term. Paolo di Lucia and Giuseppe Lorini have found two works on *słuszność*: Pietka 1930 and Soldenhoff 1966.

[22] Cf. Conte 1965; Conte 1967; Conte 1968; Conte 1986.

[23] Deontic validity is defined as existence in a normative system, for instance, by Hans Kelsen (1881–1973). Cf. in particular Kelsen 1960, p. 9: "Mit dem Worte "Geltung" bezeichnen wir die spezifische *Existenz* einer Norm" (By the word "validity" we will designate the specific *existence* of a norm).

[24] Cf. von Wright 1983 a, p. 158.

[25] Cf. von Wright 1991, p. 277.

BIBLIOGRAPHY

Alarcón Cabrera, Conte 1995
  Alarcón Cabrera, Carlos and Conte, Amedeo G.: *Deóntica de la validez*, Tecnos, Madrid.
Azzoni 1991
  Azzoni, Giampaolo M.: *Cognitivo e normativo*, Angeli, Milano.
Conte 1965
  Conte, Amedeo G.: *Logique et normes*, Torino [unpublished.]
Conte 1967
  Conte, Amedeo G.: "In margine all'ultimo Kelsen", *Studia ghisleriana*, serie I, 4, pp. 113–25. Reprinted in Conte 1989, pp. 17–30; Conte 1997, pp. 391–411. English translation: *Hans Kelsen's Deontics*, in Stanley L. Paulson (ed.): *Normativity and Norms*, Clarendon Press, Oxford 1998, pp. 331–341.
Conte 1968
  Conte, Amedeo G.: "Primi argomenti per una critica del normativismo", Tipografia del libro, Pavia. Reprinted in Conte 1997, pp. 413–80.
Conte 1976
  Conte, Amedeo G.: "Codici deontici", in *Intorno al "codice". Atti del terzo convegno della AISS* (Pavia, 1975), La Nuova Italia, Firenze, pp. 13–25. Reprinted in Conte 1989, pp. 147–61.

Conte 1978
Conte, Amedeo G.: "Parerga leibnitiana", in A. A. Martino *et alii* (eds.): *Logica, informatica, diritto*, Le Monnier, Firenze, pp. 217–55. Reprinted in Conte 1989, pp. 193–233.
Conte 1983
Conte, Amedeo G.: "Paradigmi d'analisi della regola in Wittgenstein", in R. Egidi (ed.): *Wittgenstein. Momenti di una critica del sapere*, Guida, Napoli, pp. 37–82. Reprinted in Conte 1995, pp. 262–312.
Conte 1986
Conte, Amedeo G.: "Deontico vs. dianoetico", *Materiali per una storia della cultura giuridica*, 16, pp. 489-94. Reprinted in Conte 1995, pp. 347–54.
Conte 1989
Conte, Amedeo G.: *Filosofia del linguaggio normativo*, I, Giappichelli, Torino (1995^2).
Conte 1995
Conte, Amedeo G.: *Filosofia del linguaggio normativo*, II, Giappichelli, Torino.
Conte 1996
Conte, Amedeo G.: "Imperativernas semantik hos Jørgen Jørgensen". Paper delivered at the University of Uppsala, Sweden [unpublished.]
Conte 1997
Conte, Amedeo G.: *Filosofia dell'ordinamento normativo*, Giappichelli, Torino.
Conte 1998
Conte, Amedeo G.: "Nomothética. La lógica deóntica como praxeología de la legislación". Paper delivered at the University of Seville, Spain [unpublished.]
di Lucia 1992
di Lucia Paolo: *Deontica in von Wright*, Giuffrè, Milano.
Jørgensen 1938
Jørgensen, Jørgen: "Imperativer og Logik", *Theoria*, 4, pp. 183–90.
Kelsen 1960
Kelsen, Hans: *Reine Rechtslehre*, F. Deuticke, Wien.
Mally 1926
Mally, Ernst: *Grundgesetze des Sollens. Elemente der Logik des Willens*, Leuschner und Lubensky, Graz. Reprinted in Mally 1971, pp. 227–324.
Mally 1971
Mally, Ernst: *Logische Schriften*, Reidel, Dordrecht.
Pietka 1930
Pietka, Henryk: *Słuszność w teorji i praktyce*, Instytut Wydawniczy Kasy im. Miankowskiego, Warszawa.
Prior 1955
Prior, Arthur Norman: *Formal Logic*, Clarendon Press, Oxford.
Soldenhoff 1966
Soldenhoff, Stanisław: "Słuszność i obowiązek w systemie etyki W. D. Rossa", *Etyka*, 1, pp. 221–65.
Sztykgold 1936
Sztykgold, Jerzy: "Negacja normy", *Przegląd filozoficzny*, 39, pp. 492–94. Italian translation by J. Wróblewski and A. G. Conte: "Negazione di norme", *Rivista internazionale di filosofia del diritto*, 69, 1992, pp. 490–97.
von Wright 1951 a
von Wright, Georg Henrik: "Deontic Logic", *Mind*, 60, pp. 1–15.
von Wright 1951 b
von Wright, Georg Henrik: *An Essay in Modal Logic*, North-Holland Publishing Co., Amsterdam.
von Wright 1957
von Wright, Georg Henrik: *Logical Studies*, Routledge & Kegan Paul, London.
von Wright 1964
von Wright, Georg Henrik: "Normit ja logiikka", *Ajatus*, 26, pp. 255–76.

von Wright 1983 a
  von Wright, Georg Henrik: "Norms, Truth, and Logic", in G. H. von Wright: *Practical Reason. Philosophical Papers*, Blackwell, Oxford, 1953, pp. 130–209.
von Wright 1983 b
  von Wright, Georg Henrik: "Proposizioni normative condizionali", *Epistemologia*, 6, pp. 187–200.
von Wright 1984
  von Wright, Georg Henrik: "Bedingungsnormen: ein Prüfstein für die Normenlogik", in W. Krawietz *et alii* (eds.): *Theorie der Normen. Festgabe für Ota Weinberger zum 65. Geburtstag*, Duncker und Humblot, Berlin, pp. 447–56.
von Wright 1991
  von Wright, Georg Henrik: "Is There a Logic of Norms?", *Ratio Juris*, 4, pp. 265–83.
Wittgenstein 1961
  Wittgenstein, Ludwig: *Tractatus logico-philosophicus* [1921[1]]. New edition with English translation, ed. by D. F. Pears and B. F. McGuinness, Routledge & Kegan Paul, London.
Wittgenstein 1953
  Wittgenstein, Ludwig: *Philosophische Untersuchungen. Philosophical Investigations*, ed. by G. E. M. Anscombe and R. Rhees, Blackwell, Oxford.

PAOLO DI LUCIA

SOLLEN BETWEEN SEMANTICS AND PRAGMATICS

Das Sollen ist ein Denkmodus
wie das Futurum und das Präteritum,
oder wie der Konjunktiv und der Optativ [...]
Georg Simmel

0. AMBIGUITY OF DEONTIC SENTENCES VS. AMBIGUITY OF DEONTIC LINGUISTIC FORMS

0.1. The pragmatic ambiguity (or better pragmatic ambivalence) of deontic *sentences* is a very well-known phenomenon. This phenomenon has been isolated by the German logician Christoph Sigwart (1830–1905). Deontic sentences (ought-sentences) are subject to a double interpretation: they may be used to *prescribe* norms (*prescriptive* deontic sentences) or they may be used to *describe* norms (*descriptive* deontic sentences).[1]

0.2. The thesis of the pragmatic ambiguity (or ambivalence) of a deontic sentence is developed independently of Sigwart by the Swedish philosopher Ingemar Hedenius (1941), whose distinction between "*äkta rättssatser*" ("authentic legal sentences") and "*oäkta rättssatser*" ("non-authentic legal sentences") is the starting point of Georg Henrik von Wright's interpretation of deontic logic (1963).[2]

0.3. At a different level, a similar phenomenon of ambiguity (or ambivalence) in deontic language is to be found in many deontic *linguistic forms*. That is to say, that many *prima facie* deontic linguistic forms are subject to a double interpretation.

This pragmatic ambiguity (or ambivalence) of *prima facie* deontic linguistic forms has been deeply explored by the German philosopher Herbert Spiegelberg (1904–1990) in his deontic trilogy.[3] He seems to limit himself to analyzing the ambivalence of deontic *linguistic forms* rather than considering the ambivalence of whole sentences. One might say that he remains below the threshold of the sentences.

The subject of my paper is the pragmatic ambivalence of *prima facie* deontic *linguistic forms*. In particular, the first part of the paper deals with the *thetic* function of four *prima facie* deontic linguistic forms; the second part deals with the *nomothetic* function of Kelsenian "*sollen*" ("*ought*").

1. THE THETIC FUNCTION OF *PRIMA FACIE* DEONTIC LINGUISTIC FORMS

Spiegelberg has contributed to semantics and pragmatics by singling out four *prima facie* deontic linguistic forms, which are pragmatically ambivalent:

215

R. Egidi (ed.), In Search of a New Humanism, 215–220.
©1999 *Kluwer Academic Publishers. Printed in Great Britain.*

(i)   the German modal verb "*sollen*";

(ii)   the English modal verb "*shall*"

(iii) the Latin imperative mood;

(iv)   the Latin subjunctive mood.

According to Spiegelberg, these four *prima facie* deontic linguistic forms can have not only a *deontic* sense, but also a *thetic* function,[4] *i.e.* they can be used *to constitute, to pose, to create* a non-pre-existing state of affairs.

1.1. The Thetic Function of the German Modal Verb "Sollen"

According to Spiegelberg, the German modal verb "*sollen*" (which occurs in terms like "*Sollnorm*", "*Sollsatz*", "*Sollsatzlogik*", "*Sollgeltung*", "*Sollverhalt*", "*Soll-sachverhalt*") has not only a *deontic* sense, but also a *thetic* function (sense is a semantic notion, function is a pragmatic one). For instance, in sentences like:

(1)   Buchstabe "*S*" soll das Satzsubjekt bedeuten.[5]

the verbal form "*soll*" has the function of constituting ("zum bestehen bringen") a state of affairs:

"soll" hat die Funktion, einen Sachverhalt zum Bestehen zu bringen." (Die Zeitwort "soll" hat hier die Funktion einer nochgar nicht bestehenden Sachverhalt aufzusetzen.)"[6]

Among sentences in which "*sollen*" is used in a thetic function:

(2)   Zwei Aussageformen A und B *sollen* äquivalent heißen, wenn A ↔ B allgemeingültig ist.[7]

(3)   Spiegel der sachsen *sol* diz buch sin genant.[8]

(4)   Das soll jetzt ein Haus sein.[9]

Sentences in which "*sollen*" is used in a thetic function have a semantic peculiarity: they are non-apophantic sentences. Spiegelberg writes:

der ausgedrückte Gedanke erhebt keinen Anspruch auf Wahrheit, auf Deckung des behaupteten mit einem tatsächlichen Sachverhalt.[10]

According to Spiegelberg, the paradigm case of sentences in which *sollen* has a thetic function is the *legislative sentences*. In his own words:

Noch klarer ist der Fall der normativen Festsetzung, besonders in der Form eines statuierenden Gesetz. Denn eine solche Festsetzung entwirft nicht nur einen eigenartigen Sachverhalt, eine Ordnung oder Anordnung, sondern sie erteilt ihm zugleich eine eigentümliche Festigkeit, eine Seinsart die häufig auch als Geltung bezeichnet wird.[11]

1.2. The Thetic Function of Other Prima Facie Deontic Linguistic Forms

The phenomenon of the pragmatic ambivalence occurs in the case of other linguistic forms which are *prima facie* deontic. In particular: the English modal verb "*shall*" has not only a *deontic* sense, but also a *thetic* function. It has a deontic sense in sentences like:

(5)   Thou shalt not kill,

whereas it has a thetic function in sentences like:

(6)   All legislative powers shall be invested in Congress.

The idea of the thetic function of the English verb "shall" was formulated by Spiegelberg. He writes:

The shall-sentence, characteristic of all statutory regulations, sets forth an order in which the referents of the subject and predicate are put into a new relationship, not yet determined by their natures: it takes the "shall" to bring it about. It fixes it by bestowing on it a certain artificial stability. [...] Without such an establishment this relation does not exist. It is the special act of ordering that establishes such an order.[12]

The semiotic status of shall-sentences is discussed in jurisprudence by Elmer A. Driedger. Let us consider the sentence:

(7)   There *shall be* a corporation.

According to Driedger, the shall-sentence is a paradigm case of a "creative shall", in which "shall" is used as a "non-obligatory auxiliary". In his own words:

This kind of provision does not have continuing operation, and the present tense is therefore not suitable. It operates to create something the moment the words are spoken, and its force is then spent.[13]

Moreover, according to Spiegelberg, the Latin future imperative mood has not only a *deontic* sense in sentences like:

(8)   Estote parati;

but also a *thetic* function in sentences (from the ancient Roman Twelve Tables Code) like:

(9)   Uti lingua nuncupassit, ita jus esto;

(10) Sacer esto;

(11) Dis sacer esto;

and in sentences (from wills) like:

(12) Heres esto.

According to Spiegelberg, latin future imperative, which is used in legislative text, has two semantic peculiarities: non-*deonticity* and *non-agentivity*. In his own words:

Vgl. z. B. die Zwölftafelgesetze ("uti lingua nuncupassit, ita jus esto", "dis sacer esto", "se fraude esto" oder "heres esto" in Testamenten; man beachte auch, daß in diesen Beispielen unmittelbar keinerlei Verhaltenspflichten festgesetzt werden; schon deswegen kann es hier nicht um Befehle handeln.[14]

Finally, according to Spiegelberg, the Latin subjunctive mood has not only a *deontic* sense ("conjunctivus cohortativus") in sentences like:

(13) Gaudeamus igitur;

(14) Alterius non sit qui suus esse potest;

but also a *thetic* function ("conjunctivus constitutivus") in sentences like:

(15) Anathema sit;

(16) Fiat lux.

2. FROM *THETIC* TO *NOMOTHETIC* FUNCTION OF '*SOLLEN*' IN HANS KELSEN'S DEONTICS

2.1. The idea of the thetic function of deontic forms is not only relevant for semantics and pragmatics of deontic language, but is a conceptual tool for the interpretation of one of the most debated concepts in contemporary legal philosophy: the Kelsenian concept of *Sollen*. According to Kelsen (1945, p. 60):

If the legal norm is expressed by saying that when certain conditions are fulfilled the organ ought to order and execute the sanction, then the word "ought" only denotes the specific sense in which the sanction is "stipulated", "provided", "determined", in the norm. Nothing is thereby said on the question of whether is "obligated" to enact the sanction.

2.2. Kelsen seems to maintain that in his primary norm, the verb "*sollen*" ("ought") doesn't have a deontic sense (doesn't *prescribe* enacting the sanction). The Ought (*Sollen*) of the primary norm, according to Kelsen, is an adeontic normative Ought (*Sollen*). Adeontic is a neologism by Amedeo G. Conte (1990): the elements of which it consists are an *alpha privativum* and the adjective deontic introduced in philosophical terminology by Ernst Mally, Oskar Fechner, Charlie Dunbar Broad, Georg Henrik von Wright.

2.3. According to Kelsen, in his primary norm "*sollen*" has a *nomothetic* function: "*sollen*" seems only to denote the fact that the sanction is posited by a *legislative* (or *nomothetic*) act. Kelsen seems to argue that the use of the *prima facie* deontic linguistic form *sollen* is, in this context, only a linguistic cue, a metacommunicative cue to the legislating act (or nomothetic) act.[15]

Università di Camerino (Italy)

NOTES

[1] According to Conte 1991, the pragmatic ambivalence of deontic sentences is not a semantic *ambiguity*. The thesis of the semantic ambiguity (*Zweideutigkeit*) is maintained by Sigwart (1873). According to him, sentences in terms of "*sollen*" (*déon* sentences, ought-sentences) are ambiguous: in his own words "*zweideutig*". This semantic *Zweideutigkeit* does not exist, according to Sigwart, in the case of imperatives.

[2] The relevance of von Wright's distinction (1963) between "descriptively interpreted deontic sentences" and "prescriptively interpreted deontic sentences" for the discussion on the foundations of deontic logic is stressed by von Wright himself: "My view was then that Deontic Logic is a logic of descriptively interpreted formalized norm-formulations. This made the application of truth-connectives and of such meta-logical notions as entailment, consistency, and contradiction uncontroversial." (1983, p. 131).

[3] See Spiegelberg 1935 a; 1935 b; 1937.

[4] The adjective "thetic" derives from the Greek verb that means "to pose".

[5] English translation: Let "S" signify the subject of the proposition.

[6] Spiegelberg 1958, pp. 244–45.

[7] See Hilbert and Ackermann 1959[4], p. 11.

[8] See Eike von Repgow [1180–1233] *Sachsenspiegel*. English translation: Let this book be called the Mirror of the Saxons.

[9] See Wittgenstein 1980, II, § 535, p. 95.

[10] Spiegelberg 1958, p. 244.

[11] *Ibidem*, pp. 244–45.

[12] *Ibidem*, p. 294.

[13] Driedger 1976, p. 13.

[14] Spiegelberg 1935 a, p. 74.

[15] On metacommunication see Caffi 1984 and M.-E. Conte 1995 b.

BIBLIOGRAPHY

Caffi 1984
Caffi, Claudia: "Some Remarks on Illocution and Metacommunication", *Journal of Pragmatics*, 8, pp. 449–67.

Conte 1970
Conte, Amedeo G.: "Studio per una teoria della validità", *Rivista internazionale di filosofia del diritto*, 47, pp. 331–54. Reprinted in A. G. Conte, *Filosofia del linguaggio normativo*, I, Giappichelli, Torino, 1989, pp. 55–74.

Conte 1990
Conte, Amedeo G.: "Adeontic Negation", in: L. Gianformaggio (ed.): *Hans Kelsen's Legal Theory. A Diachronic Point of View*, Giappichelli, Torino, pp. 75–9.

Conte 1991
Conte, Amedeo G.: "Deon in Deontics", *Ratio juris*, 4, pp. 349–54.

Conte 1997 a
Conte, Amedeo G.: "Eidetic-Constitutive Rules", in: M. Jori and A. Pintore (eds.): *Law and Language*, Deborah Charles Publications, Liverpool, pp. 133–46.

Conte 1997 b
Conte, Amedeo G.: *Filosofia dell'ordinamento normativo*, Giappichelli, Torino.

Conte 1997 c
Conte, Amedeo G.: "Hans Kelsen's Deontics", in Stanley L. Paulson (ed.): *Normativity and Norms. Critical Perspectives on Kelsenian Themes*, Clarendon Press, Oxford.

Conte, M.-E. 1995 a
Conte, Maria-Elisabeth: "Epistemico, deontico, anankastico", in A. Giacalone Ramat, G. Crocco Galéas (eds.): *From Pragmatics to Syntax. Modality in Second Language Acquisition*, Günter Narr, Tübingen, pp. 3–9.

Conte M.-E. 1995 b
Conte, Maria-Elisabeth: "Pragmatica della promessa", in G. Galli (ed.): *Interpretazione e promessa*, Giardini, Pisa, pp. 94–128.

Di Lucia 1992
Di Lucia, Paolo: *Deontica in von Wright*, Giuffré, Milano.
Di Lucia 1998
Di Lucia, Paolo: "Pragmatica de los actos y ontologia del derecho", *Nóesis*, 18, 1998, pp. 55–68.
Driedger 1976[2]
Driedger, Elmer A.: *The Composition of Legislation. Legislative Forms and Precedents*, The Department of Justice, Ottawa.
Hedenius 1941
Hedenius, Ingemar: *Om rätt och moral*, Tidens Vorlag, Stockholm.
Hilbert and Ackermann 1938
Hilbert, David and Ackermann, W.: *Grundzüge der theoretischen Logik*, Springer, Berlin 1959[4].
Kelsen 1945
Kelsen, Hans: *General Theory of Law and State*, Harvard University Press, Cambridge, Mass.
Kelsen 1960
Kelsen, Hans: *Reine Rechtslehre*, F. Deuticke, Wien.
Losano 1967
Losano M. G.: "Per un'analisi del 'Sollen' in Hans Kelsen", *Rivista internazionale di filosofia del diritto*, 44, pp. 546–68.
Sigwart 1873
Sigwart, Christoph: *Logik* (1873), ed. by H. Maier, Mohr, Tübingen, 1921[4].
Spiegelberg 1935 a
Spiegelberg, Herbert: *Gesetz und Sittengesetz*, M. Niehans, Zürich.
Spiegelberg 1935 b
Spiegelberg, Herbert: *Antirelativismus*, M. Niehans, Zürich.
Spiegelberg 1937
Spiegelberg, Herbert: *Sollen und Dürfen. Philosophische Grundlagen der ethischen Rechte und Pflichten* (1937), bearbeitet und herausgegeben von K. Schuhmann, Kluwer, Dordrecht 1989.
Spiegelberg 1958
Spiegelberg, Herbert: "Zur Ontologie des idealen Sollens", *Philosophisches Jahrbuch der Görres-Gesellschaft*, 66, pp. 243–53.
Spiegelberg 1968
Spiegelberg, Herbert: "Rules and Order. Toward a Phenomenology of Order", in P. Kuntz (ed.): *The Grinnell Symposium*, Washington University Press, Washington, pp. 290–308.
von Wright 1951
von Wright, Georg Henrik: "Deontic Logic", *Mind*, 60, pp. 1–15.
von Wright 1963
von Wright, Georg Henrik: *Norm and Action. An Essay in Logical Analysis*, Routledge & Kegan Paul, London.
von Wright 1983
von Wright, Georg Henrik: *Practical Reason. Philosophical Papers*, Vol. I, Blackwell, Oxford.
Wittgenstein 1980
Wittgenstein Ludwig: *Bemerkungen über die Philosophie der Psychologie. Remarks on the Philosophy of Psychology*, vol. II, ed. by G. H. von Wright and H. Nyman, Blackwell, Oxford.

SELECTED BIBLIOGRAPHY

A. WRITINGS OF G. H. VON WRIGHT

1. "On Probability", *Mind*, 49, 1940, pp. 265–83.
2. "The Logical Problem of Induction", *Acta Philosophica Fennica*, Fasc. 3, Helsingfors 1941, 258 pp. (Blackwell, Oxford 1957[2])
3. "Georg Christoph Lichtenberg als Philosoph", *Theoria*, 8, 1942, pp. 201–17.
4. *Über Wahrscheinlichkeit. Eine logische und philosophische Untersuchung*, Acta Societatis Scientiarum Fennicae Nova Series A, Vol. 3, 11, Helsingfors 1945, 66 pp.
5. "Paideia", *Nya Argus*, 40, 1947, pp. 229–31. Reprinted with revisions in item **22**.
6. "On the Idea of Logical Truth", **I**, Societas Scientiarum Fennica. Commentationes Physico–Mathematicae, Vol. 14, 4, Helsingfors 1948, 20 pp. Reprinted in item **24**.
7. "Dostojevskij", *Nya Argus*, 42, 1949, pp. 56–70. Reprinted with revisions in item **22**.
8. *Form and Content in Logic*, Cambridge University Press, London 1949, 35 pp. Reprinted in item **24**.
9. "Some Principles of Eliminative Induction", *Ajatus*, 15, 1949, pp. 315–28.
10. "On the Idea of Logical Truth", II, Societas Scientiarum Fennica. Commentationes Physico-Mathematicae, Vol. 15, 10, Helsingfors 1950, 45 pp. See also item **6**.
11. "Descartes och den vetenskapliga idéutvecklingen" [Descartes and the Evolution of Scientific Ideas], *Ajatus*, 16, 1950, pp. 103–71.
12. "Spengler och Toynbee", *Nya Argus*, 44, 1951, pp. 47–50. Reprinted with revisions in item **22**.
13. *A Treatise on Induction and Probability*, Routledge & Kegan Paul, London 1951, 310 pp.
14. *An Essay in Modal Logic*, North-Holland Publishing Co., Amsterdam 1951, 90 pp.
15. "Deontic Logic", *Mind*, 60, 1951, pp. 1–15.
16. (With P. T. Geach) "On the Extended Logic of Relation", Societas Scientiarum Fennica. Commentationes Physico-Mathematicae, Vol. 16, 1, Helsingfors 1952, 37 pp.
17. "On Double Quantification", Societas Scientiarum Fennica. Commentationes Physico-Mathematicae, Vol. 16, 3, Helsingfors 1952, 14 pp.
18. "Interpretations of Modal Logic", *Mind*, 61, 1952, pp. 165–77.
19. "On the Logic of Some Axiological and Epistemological Concepts", *Ajatus* 17, 1952, pp. 213–34.
20. "A New System of Modal Logic", in *Proceedings of the 11th International Congress of Philosophy*, Brussels, Vol. 5, 1953, pp. 59–63. Reprinted in item **24**.
21. "Ludwig Wittgenstein. A Biographical Sketch", *The Philosophical Review*, 64, 1955, pp. 527–45. Reprinted in N. Malcolm: *Ludwig Wittgenstein. A Memoir*, Oxford University Press, London 1958, pp. 1–22 and in item **89**.
22. *Tanke och förkunnelse* [Thought and Prophecy] Söderströms, Helsingfors 1955 (Gleerups, Lund 1964[2]).
23. "A Note on Deontic Logic and Derived Obligation", *Mind*, 65, 1956, pp. 507–9.
24. *Logical Studies*, Routledge & Kegan Paul, London 1957, ix + 195 pp. Contents: items **6, 5, 14, 12, 15, 20** and the essays "On Conditionals", "The Concept of Entailment", written for this volume.
25. *Logik, filosofi och sprak. Strömningar och gestalter i modern filosofi* [Logic, Philosophy and Language. Trends and Personalities in Modern Philosophy] Söderströms, Helsingfors 1957, 250 pp.
26. "Eino Kaila", *Theoria*, 24, 1958, pp. 137–8.
27. "On the Logic of Negation", Societas Scientiarum Fennica. Commentationes Physico-Mathematicae, Vol. 22, 4, Helsingfors 1959, 30 pp.

221

R. Egidi (ed.), In Search of a New Humanism, 221–228.
© 1999 *Kluwer Academic Publishers. Printed in Great Britain.*

28. "Broad on Induction and Probability", in *The Philosophy of C. D. Broad*, ed. by P. A. Schilpp, Tudor Publishing Co., New York 1959, pp. 313–52.

29. "The Heterological Paradox", Societas Scientiarum Fennica. Commentationes Physico-Mathematicae, Vol. 24, 5, Helsingfors 1960, 28 pp. Reprinted in item **94**.

30. "Kunskapens träd" [The Tree of Knowledge] *Historiska och Litteraturhistoriska Studier*, 35, 1960, pp. 43–76. Reprinted with revisions in item **76**. See also item **132**.

31. "On Promises", *Theoria*, 28, 1962, pp. 277–97. Reprinted in item **93**.

32. *Essay om naturen, människan och den vetenskapligt-tekniska revolutionen* [Essay on Nature, Man, and the Scientific Revolution] Gleerups, Lund 1963, 25 pp. Reprinted, with revisions, in item **76**.

33. *Norm and Action. A Logical Inquiry*, Routledge & Kegan Paul, London 1963, xviii + 214 pp.

34. *The Varieties of Goodness*, Routledge & Kegan Paul-The Humanities Press, London-New York 1963, xviii + 222 pp.

35. *The Logic of Preference. An Essay*, At the University Press, Edinburgh, 1963, 68 pp.

36. "Remarks on the Paradox of the Liar", in *Philosophical Essays*, ed. by H. Bratt *et al.*, Gleerups, Lund 1963, pp. 295–306.

37. "Practical Inference", *The Philosophical Review*, 72, 1963, pp. 159–79. Reprinted in item **93**.

38. "Normit ja logiikka", *Ajatus*, 26, 1964, pp. 255–76.

39. "The Foundations of Norms and Normative Statements", in *The Foundations of Statements and Decisions*. Proceedings of the International Colloquium on Methodology of Science, ed. by K. Ajdukiewicz, Warsaw 1965, pp. 351–67.

40. "Remarks on the Epistemology of Subjective Probability", in *Logic, Methodology and Philosophy of Science: Proceedings of the 1960 International Congress*, Stanford University Press, Stanford, CA 1965, pp. 330–39.

41. " 'And Next' ", in *Studia Logico-Mathematica et Philosophica in Honorem R. Nevanlinna, Acta Philosophica Fennica*, Fasc. 18, Helsinki 1965, pp. 293–304. Reprinted in item **94**.

42. "The Paradox of Confirmation", *Theoria*, 31, 1965, pp. 255–74.

43. " 'And Then' ", Societas Scientiarum Fennica. Commentationes Physico-Mathematicae, Vol. 32, 7, Helsingfors 1966, 11 pp. Reprinted in item **94**.

44. "The Logic of Action. A Sketch", in *The Logic of Decision and Action*, ed. N. Rescher, Pittsburgh University Press, Pittsburgh 1967, pp. 121–36.

45. "Deontic Logics", *American Philosophical Quarterly*, 4, 1967, pp. 136–43.

46. "Quelques remarks sur la logique du temps et les systèmes modales", *Scientia,* 102, 1967, pp. 565–72.

47. *An Essay in Deontic Logic and the General Theory of Action*, North-Holland Publishing Co., Amsterdam 1968, 110 pp.

48. "The Logic of Practical Discourse", in R. Klibansky (ed.): *Contemporary Philosophy. A Survey*, Vol. I, La Nuova Italia, Firenze, 1968, pp. 141–67.

49. "Deontic Logic and the Theory of Conditions", *Critica*, 2, 1968, pp. 3–25. Reprinted with some revisions in *Deontic Logic: Introductory and Systematic Readings*, ed. by R. Hilpinen, Reidel, Dordrecht 1971, pp. 159–77.

50. "Always", *Theoria*, 34, 1968, pp. 208–21.

51. *Time, Change, and Contradiction*, Cambridge University Press, London 1969, 32 pp. Reprinted in item **94**.

52. "On the Logic and Ontology of Norms", in *Philosophical Logic*, ed. by J. W. Davis *et al.*, Reidel, Dordrecht 1969, pp. 89–107.

53. "Wittgenstein's View of Probability", *Revue Internationale de Philosophie*, 23, 1969, pp. 259–79. Reprinted in item **89**.

54. "The Wittgenstein Papers", *The Philosophical Review*, 78, 1969, pp. 483–501. Reprinted in item **89**.

55. "A Note on Confirmation Theory and on the Concept of Evidence", *Scientia*, 105, 1970, pp. 595–606. Reprinted in a revised version in item **94**.

56. "A New System of Deontic Logic", in *Deontic Logic: Introductory and Systematic Readings*, ed. by R. Hilpinen, Reidel, Dordrecht 1971, pp. 105–20.

57. "Historical Introduction: The Origin of Wittgenstein's Tractatus", in L. Wittgenstein: *Proto-tractatus. An early version of Tractatus Logico-philosophicus*, Routledge & Kegan Paul, London

1971, pp. 1–34. See item **08**. Reprinted with some revisions in *Wittgenstein: Sources and Perspectives*, ed. by C. G. Luckhardt, Cornell University Press, Ithaca, N.Y. 1979, pp. 99–137 and in item **89**.

58. *Explanation and Understanding*, Routledge & Kegan Paul, London 1971.

59. "On so Called Practical Inference", *Acta Sociologica*, 15, 1972, pp. 46–72. Reprinted in item **93**.

60. "Some Observations on Modal Logic and Philosophical Systems", in *Contemporary Philosophy in Scandinavia*, ed. by R. E. Olson and A. M. Paul, The Johns Hopkins Press, Baltimore and London 1972, pp. 17–26. Reprinted in item **89**.

61. "Wittgenstein on Certainty", in *Problems in the Theory of Knowledge*, ed. by G. H. von Wright, Nijhoff, The Hague 1972, pp. 47–60. Reprinted in item **89**.

62. "The Logic of Preference Reconsidered", *Theory and Decision*, 3, 1972, pp. 140–69. Reprinted in item **94**.

63. "Truth as Modality. A Contribution to the Logic of Sense and Nonsense", in *Modality, Morality and Other Problems of Sense and Nonsense*, Gleerups, Lund 1973, pp. 142–50.

64. "On the Logic and Epistemology of Causal Relation", in *Logic, Methodology and Philosophy of Science, IV*, ed. by P. Suppes *et al.*, North–Holland Publishing Co., 1973, pp. 293–312. Reprinted in *Causation and Conditionals*, ed. by E. Sosa, Oxford University Press, London 1975, pp. 95–113.

65. "Deontic Logic Revisited", *Rechtstheorie*, 4, 1973, pp. 37–46.

66. "Remarks on the Logic of Predication", *Ajatus*, 35, 1973, pp. 158–67.

67. *Causality and Determinism*, Columbia University Press, New York and London 1974, xxii + 143 pp.

68. "Handlungslogik", in *Normenlogik. Grundprobleme der deontischen Logik*, Verlag Dokumentation, Münich-Pullach 1974, pp. 9–24. Reprinted in item **74**.

69. "Normenlogik", *ibidem*, pp. 25–38. Reprinted in item **74**.

70. "Determinismus, Wahrheit und Zeitlichkeit, ein Beitrag zum Problem der zukünftigen kontigenten Wahrheiten", *Studia Leibnitiana*, 6, 1974, pp. 161–78.

71. "Replies to Commentators. Second Thoughts on Explanation and Understanding", in *Essays on Explanation and Understanding*, ed. by J. Manninen and R. Tuomela, Reidel, Dordrecht 1976, pp. 371–413.

72. "Determinism and the Study of Man", *ibidem*, pp. 415–35. Reprinted in item **93**.

73. *What is Humanism?*, The Lindlay Lecture, University of Kansas, Lawrence, Kansas 1977, 25 pp.

74. *Handlung, Norm und Intention. Untersuchungen zur deontischen Logik*, de Gruyter, Berlin and New York 1977. It contains translations into German of items **15, 37, 44, 49, 59, 68, 69**, and **72**.

75. "A Modal Logic of Place", in *The Philosophy of N. Rescher*, ed. by E. Sosa, Reidel, Dordrecht 1979, pp. 65–73. Reprinted in item **94**.

76. *Humanismen som livshållning och andra essayer* [What is Humanism? and Other Essays] Söderströms, Helsingfors 1978, 175 pp.

77. "Wittgenstein in Relation to his Times", in E. Leinfellner *et al.* (eds.): *Wittgenstein and its Impact on Contemporary Thought*, Hölder-Pichler-Tempsky, 1978, pp. 73–8. Reprinted in item **89**.

78. "The Origin and Composition of Wittgenstein's *Investigations*", in *Wittgenstein: Sources and Perspectives*, ed. by C. G. Luckhardt, Cornell University Press, Ithaca, N.Y. 1979, pp. 138–60. Reprinted in item **89**.

79. "The 'Master Argument' of Diodoros", in *Essays in Honour of J. Hintikka*, ed. by E. Saarinen *et al.*, Reidel, Dordrecht 1979, pp. 297–307.

80. "Time, Truth and Necessity", in *Intention and Intentionality. Essays in Honour of G. E. M. Anscombe*, ed. by C. Diamond and J. Teichman, The Harvester Press, Brighton 1979, pp. 237–50.

81. "Diachronic and Synchronic Modalities", *Teorema*, 9, 1979, pp. 231–45. Reprinted in a revised version in item **99** as "Diachronic and Synchronic Modality".

82. "Das menschliche Handlung im Lichte seiner Ursachen und Gründe", in *Handlungstheorien-Interdisziplinär*, Vol. 2, Zweiter Halbband, ed. by H. Lenk, W. Fink Verlag, Munich 1979, pp. 417–30.

83. "The Determinants of Action", in *Reason, Action and Experience. Essays in Honor of R. Klibansky*, ed. by H. Kohlenberger, Meiner, Hamburg 1979, pp. 107–19.

84. *Freedom and Determination*, North-Holland Publishing Co., Amsterdam 1980 (*Acta Philosophica Fennica*, Vol. 31), 88 pp.

85. "Humanism and the Humanities", in *Philosophy and Grammar*, ed. by S. Kanger and S. Öhman, Reidel, Dordrecht 1981, pp. 1–16. Reprinted in item **132**.

86. "Problems and Prospects of Deontic Logic", in *Modern Logic. A Survey*, ed. by E. Agazzi, Reidel, Dordrecht 1981, pp. 399–423.

87. "Explanation and Understanding of Action", *Revue Internationale de Philosophie*, 35, 1981, pp. 127–42. Reprinted in item **93**.

88. "On the Logic of Norms and Actions", in *New Studies in Deontic Logic*, ed. by R. Hilpinen, Reidel, Dordrecht, 1981, pp. 3–35. Reprinted, with revisions, in item **93**.

89. *Wittgenstein*, Blackwell, Oxford 1982, vi + 218 pp. Contents: Revised versions of the items **21, 54, 57, 78, 53, 61, 77,** and of item **60** with the title "Modal Logic and the *Tractatus*".

90. "Determinism and Knowledge of the Future", *Tulevaisuuden Tutkimuksen Seuran Julkaisu* A4, Turku, 1982, 25 pp. Reprinted in item **99**.

91. "Norms, Truth, and Logic", in *Deontic Logic, Computational Linguistics and Legal Information Systems*, ed. by A. A. Martino, North-Holland Publishing Co., 1982, pp. 3–20. Reprinted in item **93**.

92. "Musil and Mach", in R. Musil, *On Mach's Theories*, Philosophia Verlag, München 1982, pp. 7–14. Reprinted in item **132**.

93. *Practical Reason. Philosophical Papers*, Vol. I, Blackwell, Oxford 1983, x + 214 pp. Revised versions of items **31, 36, 39, 59, 72, 87, 88, 91.**

94. *Philosophical Logic. Philosophical Papers*, Vol. II, Blackwell, Oxford 1983, xiii + 143 pp. Revised versions of items **29, 36, 42, 55, 40, 62, 41, 43, 51, 75**.

95. "Technology and the Legitimation Crisis of Industrial Society", *Epistemologia*, 6, 1983, Special Issue, pp. 17–27.

96. "Proposizioni normative condizionali", *Epistemologia*, 6, 1983, pp. 187–200.

97. "On Causal Knowledge", in *Knowledge and Mind*, ed. by C. Ginet and S. Shoemaker, Oxford University Press, New York-Oxford 1983, pp. 50–62. Reprinted in item **99**.

98. "The Origin and Development of Westermarck's Moral Philosophy", in *Edward Westermarck's. Essay on His Life and Works*, ed. by T. Stroup, Societas Philosophica Fennica, Vammala 1983, pp. 25–61 (*Acta Philosophica Fennica*, Vol. 34).

99. *Truth, Knowledge, and Modality. Philosophical Papers*, Vol. III, Blackwell, Oxford 1984, ix + 155 pp. Contains revised versions of items **66, 81, 90, 97** and the hitherto unpublished essays "Determinism and Future Truth", "Demystifying Propositions", "Truth and Logic", "Knowledge and Necessity", "Omne quod est quando est necesse est esse", "Logical Modality", "Natural Modality", "Laws of Nature".

100. "Bedingungsnormen: ein Prüfstein für die Normenlogik", in W. Krawietz *et al.* (eds.): *Theorie der Normen. Festgabe für Ota Weinberger zum 65. Geburtstag*, Duncker und Humblot, Berlin 1984, pp. 447–56.

101. "A Pilgrim's Progress. Voyage d'un pélerin", in *Philosophes critiques d'eux-mêmes*, Vol. 12, ed. by A. Mercier and M. Svilar, Verlag P. Lang, Bern 1985, pp. 257–94. Reprinted in item **132.**

102. "Probleme des Erklärens und Verstehens von Handlungen", *Conceptus*, 18, 1985, pp. 3–19.

103. "Is and Ought", in *Man, Law, and Modern Forms of Life*, ed. by E. Bulygin *et al.*, Reidel, Dordrecht 1985, pp. 263–81. Reprinted in *Facts and Values*, ed. by M. C. Doeser and J. N. Kraay, Nijhoff, Dordrecht 1986, pp. 31–48; in *Normativity and Norms. Critical Perspectives on Kelsenian Themes*, ed. by S.L. Paulson, Clarendon Press, Oxford 1998, pp. 265–82.

104. "Of Human Freedom", in *The Tanner Lectures on Human Values*, Vol. VI, ed. by S. M. McMurrin, University of Utah Press, Salt Lake City, 1985, pp. 107–70. Reprinted in item **150.**

105. "Truth, Negation and Contradiction", *Synthese*, 66, 1986, pp. 3–14.

106. "Rationality: Means and Ends", *Epistemologia*, 9, 1986, pp. 57–71.

107. *Vetenskapen och förnuftet. Ett försök till orientering* [Science and Reason. An Attempt to Orientation] Söderströms, Helsingfors 1986, 154 pp.

108. *Logiko-filosofskie Issledovanija. Izbrannye Trudy* [Logico-Philosophical Investigations. Selected Works] Prog ress, Moscow 1986, 595 pp.

109. "Wissenschaft und Vernunft", *Rechtstheorie*, 18, 1987, pp. 15–33. Translated into English in item ms **115** and **132**.

110. "Truth-Logics", *Logique et Analyse*, 30, 1987, pp. 311–34. Reprinted in item **142**.

111. "If-then", in *Intensional Logic, History of Philosophy, and Methodology*, ed. by I. M. Bodnàr *et al.*, Akadémiai Kiadò Idegennye, Budapest 1988, pp. 91–99. See "On Conditionality", in item **142**.

112. "Reflections on Psycho-Physical Parallelism", in *Perspectives on Human Conduct*, ed. by L. Hertzberg and J. Pietarinen, E. J. Brill, Leiden-New York-Toronto 1988, pp. 22–32.

113. "An Essay on Door-Knocking", *Rechtstheorie*, 19, 1988, pp. 275–88. Reprinted in item **150**.

114. "The Myth of Progress", in *Architecture and Cultural Values*, Report of the 4th A. Aalto Symposium, held in Jyväskylä (Finland) 1988, pp. 66–89. Reprinted in item **132**.

115. "Images of Science and Forms of Rationality", in *Images of Science*, ed. by S. J. Doorman, Gower Publishing Co., Southampton 1989, pp. 11–29.

116. (With G. Meggle) "Das Verstehen von Handlungen", *Rechtstheorie*, 20, 1989, pp. 3–37. Reprinted in item **135**.

117. "Science, Reason, and Value", *Documenta 49*, The Royal Swedish Academy of Sciences, Stockholm 1989, pp. 7–28. Reprinted in item **132**.

118. "Intellectual Autobiography", in *The Philosophy of G. H. von Wright*, ed. by P. A. Schilpp and L. E. Hahn, Open Court, La Salle, Ill. 1989, pp. 1–55 and "A Reply to my Critics", *ibidem*, pp. 731–75.

119. "Dante between Ulysses and Faust", in *Knowledge and the Sciences in Medieval Philosophy*, ed. by M. Aszalos *et al.*, Helsinki 1990, pp. 1–9. Reprinted in item **132**.

120. "Wittgenstein and the Twentieth Century", in *Language, Knowledge, and Intentionality: Perspectives on the Philosophy of J. Hintikka*, ed. by L. Haaparanta *et al.*, Acta Philosophica Fennica, Vol. 49, Helsinki, 1990, pp. 47–67. Reprinted in *Wittgenstein: Mind and Language*, ed. by R. Egidi, Kluwer, Dordrecht 1995, pp. 1–19.

121. "Possibility, Plenitude and Determinism", in *Peter Geach: Philosophical Encounters*, ed. by H. A. Lewis, Kluwer, Dordrecht 1991, pp. 83–98.

122. "Is there a Logic of Norms?", *Ratio Juris*, 4, 1991, pp. 265–83. Reprinted in item **142**.

123. "Eino Kaila's Monism", in *Eino Kaila and Logical Empiricism*, ed. by I. Niiniluoto *et al.*, Kluwer, Dordrecht 1992, pp. 71–91.

124. "Wissenschaft, Wirtschaftssystem und Gerechtigkeit", in *Öffentliche oder private Moral? Vom Geltungsgrunde und der Legitimität des Rechts. Festschrift für E. Garzón Valdés*, ed. by W. Krawietz and G. H. von Wright, Duncker & Humblot, Berlin 1992, pp. 369–75.

125. "Analytische Philosophie. Eine historisch-kritische Betrachtung", *Rechtstheorie*, 23, 1992, pp. 3–25. Reprinted in a slightly abridged form in *Information Philosophie*, 2, 1993, pp. 2–21. Translated into English in item **132**.

126. "Norman Malcom", *Philosophical Investigations*, 15, 1992, pp. 215–22. Reprinted in item **029**.

127. *Minervan pöllö. Esseitä vuosilta 1987–1991* [The Owl of Minerva. Essays 1987–1991] Otava, Helsinki 1992, 208 pp. Contains Finnish translations of previously published papers and of items **125, 123, 114, 117**.

128. "The Troubled History of Part II of the Investigations", in *Criss-Crossing a Philosophical Landscape. Essays on Wittgensteinian Themes. Dedicated to Brian McGuinness*, ed. by J. Schulte and G. Sundholm, Rodopi, Amsterdam 1992, pp. 181–92.

129. "Un discorso improvvisato", in *Il Circolo di Vienna, ricordi e riflessioni*, ed. by M. C. Galavotti and R. Simili, Pratiche Editrice, Parma 1992, 1992, pp. 3–25.

130. *Myten om framsteget. Tankar 1987–1992 med en intellektu självbiografi* [The Myth of Progress. Thoughts from the years 1987–1992 with an Intellectual Autobiography] Bonniers, Stockholm 1993, 174 pp. Contains Swedish translations of previously published papers and of revised versions of (parts of) items **119, 114, 134, 117, 120**.

131. "Two Traditions", in *Social Research, Philosophy, Politics and Practice*, ed. by M. Hammersley, Sage Publications, London 1993, pp. 9–13.

132. *The Tree of Knowledge and Other Essays*, E. J. Brill, Leiden 1993, 254 pp. Contains revised versions of items **114, 125, 92, 123, 120, 101, 30, 88, 115, 119, 114, 117** and an unpublished essay "A Philosophical Logician's Itinerary". See also item **136**.

133. "Gibt es eine Logik der Normen?", in *Rechtsnorm und Rechtswirklichkeit*, ed. by A. Aarnio *et al.*, Duncker & Humblot, Berlin 1993, pp. 101–23. Reprinted in items **142** and **135**.

134. "Logic and Philosophy in the Twentieth Century", in *Logic, Methodology, and Philosophy of Science*, Vol. X, ed. by D. Prawitz *et al.*, Elsevier Science Publishing Co., Amsterdam-New York 1994, pp. 9–25.

135. *Normen, Werte und Handlungen*, Suhrkamp, Frankfurt 1994, 259 pp. Contains sometimes revised versions of items **103, 100, 133, 62, 106, 102, 116, 104** translated into German. "Einleitung" by G. H. von Wright, pp. 1–15.

136. *Erkenntnis als Lebensform. Zeitgenössische Wanderungen eines philosophischen Logikers*, Böhlau Verlag, Wien 1994, 323 pp. Contents: German translation of item **132**.

137. "On Conditional Obligations", *Juridisk Tidskrift vid Stockholms Universitet*, 1994–95, n. 1, pp. 1–17. Reprinted in item **142**.

138. *Att förstå sin samtid. Tanke och förkunnelse och andra försök. 1945–1994*, Bonniers, Stockholm 1994, 362 pp. Contains revised version of item **22**, and of two hitherto unpublished essays "Afterthoughts in the Twilight" and "Berdjajev" translated into Swedish.

139. "On Mind and Matter", *Journal of Theoretical Biology*, 171, 1994, pp. 101–10. Reprinted in item **150**.

140. "Der Fortschritt und das Fortschrittsdenken", *Rechtstheorie*, 26, 1995, pp. 9–20.

141. *Ihminen kulttuurin murroksessa*, Otava, Helsinki 1996, 350 pp. Includes the essays on Dostoyevsky, Spengler and Toynbee, Tolstoy in item **22** and other essays translated into Finnish. "Preface" by G. H. von Wright.

142. *Six Essays in Philosophical Logic*, Acta Philosophica Fennica, Vol. 60, Helsinki 1996, 92 pp. Contains item **133, 137**, a revised version of item **110** and three previously unpublished essays "On Colour"; "Conditionality"; "Ought to Be-Ought to Do".

143. "Logica senza verità", in *Logica, Informatica, Diritto*, ed. by A. A. Martino, Servizio Editoriale Universitario di Pisa, Pisa 1996, pp. 38–58.

144. "Descartes et l'être humain", in *René Descartes. Aux sources de la philosophie moderne*, Swedish Science Press, Uppsala 1997, pp. 7–19.

145. "Progress: Fact and Fiction", in *The Idea of Progress*, ed. by A. Burgen, *et al.*, W. de Gruyter, Berlin 1997, pp. 1–18.

146. "Die Stellung der Psychologie unter den Wissenschaften", *Rechtstheorie*, 27, 1997, pp. 145–56.

147. "Ought to Be-Ought to Do", in *Normative Systems in Legal and Moral Theory*, ed. by E. Garzón Valdés *et al.*, Duncker & Humblot, Berlin 1997, pp. 427–35. Reprinted in *Actions, Norms, Values. Discussions with Georg Henrik von Wright*, ed. by G. Meggle. Assisted by A. Wojcik, W. de Gruyter, Berlin-New York, 1999, pp. 3–9.

148. "Begriffsanalyse ist eine schaffende Tätigkeit", *Deutsche Zeitschrift für Philosophie*, 45, 1997, pp. 265–77.

149. "On the Location of Mental States", in *Horizons of Humanity. Essays in Honour of I. Supek*, ed. by Z. Radman, Verlag P. Lang, Bern, 1997, pp. 131–34.

150. *In the Shadow of Descartes: Essays in the Philosophy of Mind*, Kluwer, Dordrecht 1998, xii + 176 pp. Contains items **104, 113, 139** and hitherto unpublished papers.

151. *Logiikka ja humanismi* [Logic and Humanism] Otava, Helsinki 1998, 510 pp. A reprint of previous papers anf of item **76**.

152. "Deontic Logic – as I See It", in *Norms, Logics and Information Systems. New Studies in Deontic Logic*, ed. by P. McNamara and H. Prakken, IOS Press, Amsterdam, pp. 15–25.

153. "Value, Norm, Action in my Philosophical Writings. With a Cartesian Epilogue", in *Actions, Norms, Values. Discussions with Georg Henrik von Wright*, ed. by G. Meggle. Assisted by A. Wojcik, W. de Gruyter, Berlin-New York, 1999, pp. 11–33.

B. WORKS PUBLISHED BY G. H. VON WRIGHT AS EDITOR AND CO-EDITOR

01. (With R. Rhees and G. E. M. Anscombe) L. Wittgenstein: *Bemerkungen über die Grundlagen der Mathematik. Remarks on the Foundations of Mathematics*, Blackwell, Oxford 1956.

02   (With G. E. M. Anscombe) L. Wittgenstein: *Notebooks 1914–1916*, Blackwell, Oxford 1961.

03. Eino Kaila: *Die perzeptuellen und konzeptuellen Komponenten der Alltagserfahrung*, Acta Philosophica Fennica, Fasc. 13, Helsinki 1962.

04. (With G. E. M. Anscombe) L. Wittgenstein: *Zettel*, Blackwell, Oxford 1967.

05. (With G. E. M. Anscombe) L. Wittgenstein: *Über Gewißheit. On Certainty*, Blackwell, Oxford 1969.

06. (With the Assistance of W. Methlagl) L. Wittgenstein: *Briefe an Ludwig von Ficker*, O. Müller Verlag, Salzburg 1969.

07. (With B. F. McGuinness and T. Nyberg) L. Wittgenstein: *Prototractatus*, Routledge & Kegan Paul, London 1971.

08. *Problems in the Theory of Knowledge*, Nijhoff, The Hague 1972.

09. L. Wittgenstein: *Letters to C. K. Ogden with Comments on the Englih Translation of the "Tractatus Logico-Philosophicus"*, Routledge & Kegan Paul, London 1973.

010. (With the Assistance of B. F. McGuinness) L. Wittgenstein: *Letters to Russell, Keynes, and Moore*, Blackwell, Oxford 1974, 1977.[2]

011. (With the Assistance of H. Nyman) L. Wittgenstein: *Vermischte Bemerkungen*, Suhrkamp, Frankfurt 1977, 1978[2]; *Vermischte Bemerkungen. Culture and Value*, Blackwell, Oxford 1980; *Vermischte Bemerkungen*, Neubearbeitung des Textes durch A. Pichler. With a poem by Wittgenstein, Suhrkamp, Frankfurt 1994.

012. (With A. Conte and R. Hilpinen) *Deontische Logik und Semantik*, Athenaion, Wiesbaden 1977.

013. *Logic and Philosophy*, Nijhoff, The Hague 1980.

014. (With B. F. McGuinness) L. Wittgenstein: *Briefwechsel mit B. Russell, G. E. Moore, J. M. Keynes, F. P. Ramsey, W. Eccles, P. Engelmann und L. von Ficker*, Suhrkamp, Frankfurt 1980.

015. (With G. E. M. Anscombe) L. Wittgenstein: *Bemerkungen über die Philosophie der Psychologie. Remarks on the Philosophy of Psychology*, Vol. I, Blackwell, Oxford 1980.

016. (With H. Nyman) L. Wittgenstein: *Bemerkungen über die Philosophie der Psychologie. Remarks on the Philosophy of Psychology*, Vol. II, Blackwell, Oxford 1980.

017. (With G. Fløistad) *Contemporary Philosophy. A Survey*, Vol. I, Part Two (Philosophical Logic), Nijhoff, The Hague 1981.

018. (With H. Nyman) L. Wittgenstein: *Letzte Schriften über die Philosophie der Psychologie. Last Writings on the Philosophy of Psychology*, Vol. I, Blackwell, Oxford 1982.

019. "Letters from L. Wittgenstein to G. H. von Wright", *The Cambridge Review*, 104, 1983, pp. 56–64.

020. *A Portrait of Wittgenstein as a Young Man. From the Diary of David Hume Pinsent 1912–1914*, Blackwell, Oxford 1990.

021. (With B. F. McGuinness) "Unpublished Correspondence between Russell and Wittgenstein", *Russell. The Journal of B. Russell Archives*, 10, n. 2, 1990–91.

022. (With H. Nyman) L. Wittgenstein: *Letzte Schriften über die Philosophie der Psychologie. Last Writings on the Philosophy of Psychology*, Vol. II, Blackwell, Oxford 1992.

023. (With I. Niiniluoto and M. Sintonen) *Eino Kaila and Logical Empiricism*, Societas Philosophica Fennica, Helsinki 1992 (*Acta Filosofica Fennica*, Vol. 52).

024. (With W. Krawietz) *Öffentliche oder private Moral? Vom Geltungsgrunde und der Legitimität des Rechts. Festschrift für E. Garzón Valdés*, ed. by W. Krawietz and G. H. von Wright, Duncker & Humblot, Berlin 1992, 486 pp.

025. (With A. Aarnio *et al.*) *Rechtsnorm und Rechtswirklichkeit. Festschrift für W. Krawietz*, Duncker & Humblot, Berlin 1993, 834 pp.

026. (With W. Krawietz *et al.*) *Prescriptive Formality and Normative Rationality in Modern Legal Systems. Festschrift für Robert S. Summers*, Duncker & Humblot, Berlin 1994, xxx–705 pp.

027. (With K. O. Åmås) Ludwig Wittgenstein's Correspondence with Skjolden, in *Wittgenstein and Norway*, ed. by K. Johannessen *et al.*, Solum Forlag, Oslo 1994, pp. 83–162.

028. *Norman Malcolm: Wittgensteinian Themes*, Cornell University Press, Ithaca, N.Y. 1995, 210 pp.

029. (With B. F. McGuinness) *Ludwig Wittgenstein: Cambridge Letters*, Blackwell, Oxford 1995, 349 pp.

INDEX OF NAMES

229

INDEX OF SUBJECTS

1. J. M. Bochénski, *A Precis of Mathematical Logic*. Translated from French and German by O. Bird. 1959   ISBN 90-277-0073-7
2. P. Guiraud, *Problèmes et méthodes de la statistique linguistique*. 1959   ISBN 90-277-0025-7
3. H. Freudenthal (ed.), *The Concept and the Role of the Model in Mathematics and Natural and Social Sciences*. 1961   ISBN 90-277-0017-6
4. E. W. Beth, *Formal Methods*. An Introduction to Symbolic Logic and to the Study of Effective Operations in Arithmetic and Logic. 1962   ISBN 90-277-0069-9
5. B. H. Kazemier and D. Vuysje (eds.), *Logic and Language*. Studies dedicated to Professor Rudolf Carnap on the Occasion of His 70th Birthday. 1962   ISBN 90-277-0019-2
6. M. W. Wartofsky (ed.), *Proceedings of the Boston Colloquium for the Philosophy of Science, 1961–1962*. [Boston Studies in the Philosophy of Science, Vol. I] 1963 ISBN 90-277-0021-4
7. A. A. Zinov'ev, *Philosophical Problems of Many-valued Logic*. A revised edition, edited and translated (from Russian) by G. Küng and D.D. Comey. 1963   ISBN 90-277-0091-5
8. G. Gurvitch, *The Spectrum of Social Time*. Translated from French and edited by M. Korenbaum and P. Bosserman. 1964   ISBN 90-277-0006-0
9. P. Lorenzen, *Formal Logic*. Translated from German by F.J. Crosson. 1965
                                                            ISBN 90-277-0080-X
10. R. S. Cohen and M. W. Wartofsky (eds.), *Proceedings of the Boston Colloquium for the Philosophy of Science, 1962–1964*. In Honor of Philipp Frank. [Boston Studies in the Philosophy of Science, Vol. II] 1965   ISBN 90-277-9004-0
11. E. W. Beth, *Mathematical Thought*. An Introduction to the Philosophy of Mathematics. 1965
                                                            ISBN 90-277-0070-2
12. E. W. Beth and J. Piaget, *Mathematical Epistemology and Psychology*. Translated from French by W. Mays. 1966   ISBN 90-277-0071-0
13. G. Küng, *Ontology and the Logistic Analysis of Language*. An Enquiry into the Contemporary Views on Universals. Revised ed., translated from German. 1967   ISBN 90-277-0028-1
14. R. S. Cohen and M. W. Wartofsky (eds.), *Proceedings of the Boston Colloquium for the Philosophy of Sciences, 1964–1966*. In Memory of Norwood Russell Hanson. [Boston Studies in the Philosophy of Science, Vol. III] 1967   ISBN 90-277-0013-3
15. C. D. Broad, *Induction, Probability, and Causation*. Selected Papers. 1968
                                                            ISBN 90-277-0012-5
16. G. Patzig, *Aristotle's Theory of the Syllogism*. A Logical-philosophical Study of *Book A* of the *Prior Analytics*. Translated from German by J. Barnes. 1968   ISBN 90-277-0030-3
17. N. Rescher, *Topics in Philosophical Logic*. 1968   ISBN 90-277-0084-2
18. R. S. Cohen and M. W. Wartofsky (eds.), *Proceedings of the Boston Colloquium for the Philosophy of Science, 1966–1968, Part I*. [Boston Studies in the Philosophy of Science, Vol. IV] 1969   ISBN 90-277-0014-1
19. R. S. Cohen and M. W. Wartofsky (eds.), *Proceedings of the Boston Colloquium for the Philosophy of Science, 1966–1968, Part II*. [Boston Studies in the Philosophy of Science, Vol. V] 1969   ISBN 90-277-0015-X
20. J. W. Davis, D. J. Hockney and W. K. Wilson (eds.), *Philosophical Logic*. 1969
                                                            ISBN 90-277-0075-3
21. D. Davidson and J. Hintikka (eds.), *Words and Objections*. Essays on the Work of W. V. Quine. 1969, rev. ed. 1975   ISBN 90-277-0074-5; Pb 90-277-0602-6
22. P. Suppes, *Studies in the Methodology and Foundations of Science. Selected Papers from 1951 to 1969*. 1969   ISBN 90-277-0020-6

23. J. Hintikka, *Models for Modalities*. Selected Essays. 1969
ISBN 90-277-0078-8; Pb 90-277-0598-4
24. N. Rescher *et al.* (eds.), *Essays in Honor of Carl G. Hempel*. A Tribute on the Occasion of His 65th Birthday. 1969
ISBN 90-277-0085-0
25. P. V. Tavanec (ed.), *Problems of the Logic of Scientific Knowledge*. Translated from Russian. 1970
ISBN 90-277-0087-7
26. M. Swain (ed.), *Induction, Acceptance, and Rational Belief*. 1970   ISBN 90-277-0086-9
27. R. S. Cohen and R. J. Seeger (eds.), *Ernst Mach: Physicist and Philosopher*. [Boston Studies in the Philosophy of Science, Vol. VI]. 1970
ISBN 90-277-0016-8
28. J. Hintikka and P. Suppes, *Information and Inference*. 1970   ISBN 90-277-0155-5
29. K. Lambert, *Philosophical Problems in Logic*. Some Recent Developments. 1970
ISBN 90-277-0079-6
30. R. A. Eberle, *Nominalistic Systems*. 1970   ISBN 90-277-0161-X
31. P. Weingartner and G. Zecha (eds.), *Induction, Physics, and Ethics*. 1970 ISBN 90-277-0158-X
32. E. W. Beth, *Aspects of Modern Logic*. Translated from Dutch. 1970   ISBN 90-277-0173-3
33. R. Hilpinen (ed.), *Deontic Logic*. Introductory and Systematic Readings. 1971
See also No. 152.   ISBN Pb (1981 rev.) 90-277-1302-2
34. J.-L. Krivine, *Introduction to Axiomatic Set Theory*. Translated from French. 1971
ISBN 90-277-0169-5; Pb 90-277-0411-2
35. J. D. Sneed, *The Logical Structure of Mathematical Physics*. 2nd rev. ed., 1979
ISBN 90-277-1056-2; Pb 90-277-1059-7
36. C. R. Kordig, *The Justification of Scientific Change*. 1971
ISBN 90-277-0181-4; Pb 90-277-0475-9
37. M. Čapek, *Bergson and Modern Physics*. A Reinterpretation and Re-evaluation. [Boston Studies in the Philosophy of Science, Vol. VII] 1971   ISBN 90-277-0186-5
38. N. R. Hanson, *What I Do Not Believe, and Other Essays*. Ed. by S. Toulmin and H. Woolf. 1971
ISBN 90-277-0191-1
39. R. C. Buck and R. S. Cohen (eds.), *PSA 1970*. Proceedings of the Second Biennial Meeting of the Philosophy of Science Association, Boston, Fall 1970. In Memory of Rudolf Carnap. [Boston Studies in the Philosophy of Science, Vol. VIII] 1971
ISBN 90-277-0187-3; Pb 90-277-0309-4
40. D. Davidson and G. Harman (eds.), *Semantics of Natural Language*. 1972
ISBN 90-277-0304-3; Pb 90-277-0310-8
41. Y. Bar-Hillel (ed.), *Pragmatics of Natural Languages*. 1971
ISBN 90-277-0194-6; Pb 90-277-0599-2
42. S. Stenlund, *Combinators, γ Terms and Proof Theory*. 1972   ISBN 90-277-0305-1
43. M. Strauss, *Modern Physics and Its Philosophy*. Selected Paper in the Logic, History, and Philosophy of Science. 1972   ISBN 90-277-0230-6
44. M. Bunge, *Method, Model and Matter*. 1973   ISBN 90-277-0252-7
45. M. Bunge, *Philosophy of Physics*. 1973   ISBN 90-277-0253-5
46. A. A. Zinov'ev, *Foundations of the Logical Theory of Scientific Knowledge (Complex Logic)*. Revised and enlarged English edition with an appendix by G. A. Smirnov, E. A. Sidorenka, A. M. Fedina and L. A. Bobrova. [Boston Studies in the Philosophy of Science, Vol. IX] 1973
ISBN 90-277-0193-8; Pb 90-277-0324-8
47. L. Tondl, *Scientific Procedures*. A Contribution concerning the Methodological Problems of Scientific Concepts and Scientific Explanation. Translated from Czech by D. Short. Edited by R.S. Cohen and M.W. Wartofsky. [Boston Studies in the Philosophy of Science, Vol. X] 1973
ISBN 90-277-0147-4; Pb 90-277-0323-X

48. N. R. Hanson, *Constellations and Conjectures*. 1973   ISBN 90-277-0192-X
49. K. J. J. Hintikka, J. M. E. Moravcsik and P. Suppes (eds.), *Approaches to Natural Language.*
    1973   ISBN 90-277-0220-9; Pb 90-277-0233-0
50. M. Bunge (ed.), *Exact Philosophy.* Problems, Tools and Goals. 1973   ISBN 90-277-0251-9
51. R. J. Bogdan and I. Niiniluoto (eds.), *Logic, Language and Probability.* 1973
                                          ISBN 90-277-0312-4
52. G. Pearce and P. Maynard (eds.), *Conceptual Change.* 1973
                                    ISBN 90-277-0287-X; Pb 90-277-0339-6
53. I. Niiniluoto and R. Tuomela, *Theoretical Concepts and Hypothetico-inductive Inference.* 1973
                                        ISBN 90-277-0343-4
54. R. Fraissé, *Course of Mathematical Logic* – Volume 1: *Relation and Logical Formula.* Trans-
    lated from French. 1973   ISBN 90-277-0268-3; Pb 90-277-0403-1
    (For *Volume 2* see under No. 69).
55. A. Grünbaum, *Philosophical Problems of Space and Time.* Edited by R.S. Cohen and M.W.
    Wartofsky. 2nd enlarged ed. [Boston Studies in the Philosophy of Science, Vol. XII] 1973
                                    ISBN 90-277-0357-4; Pb 90-277-0358-2
56. P. Suppes (ed.), *Space, Time and Geometry.* 1973   ISBN 90-277-0386-8; Pb 90-277-0442-2
57. H. Kelsen, *Essays in Legal and Moral Philosophy.* Selected and introduced by O. Weinberger.
    Translated from German by P. Heath. 1973   ISBN 90-277-0388-4
58. R. J. Seeger and R. S. Cohen (eds.), *Philosophical Foundations of Science.* [Boston Studies in
    the Philosophy of Science, Vol. XI] 1974   ISBN 90-277-0390-6; Pb 90-277-0376-0
59. R. S. Cohen and M. W. Wartofsky (eds.), *Logical and Epistemological Studies in Contemporary
    Physics.* [Boston Studies in the Philosophy of Science, Vol. XIII] 1973
                                    ISBN 90-277-0391-4; Pb 90-277-0377-9
60. R. S. Cohen and M. W. Wartofsky (eds.), *Methodological and Historical Essays in the Natural
    and Social Sciences. Proceedings of the Boston Colloquium for the Philosophy of Science,
    1969–1972.* [Boston Studies in the Philosophy of Science, Vol. XIV] 1974
                                    ISBN 90-277-0392-2; Pb 90-277-0378-7
61. R. S. Cohen, J. J. Stachel and M. W. Wartofsky (eds.), *For Dirk Struik. Scientific, Historical
    and Political Essays.* [Boston Studies in the Philosophy of Science, Vol. XV] 1974
                                    ISBN 90-277-0393-0; Pb 90-277-0379-5
62. K. Ajdukiewicz, *Pragmatic Logic.* Translated from Polish by O. Wojtasiewicz. 1974
                                          ISBN 90-277-0326-4
63. S. Stenlund (ed.), *Logical Theory and Semantic Analysis.* Essays dedicated to Stig Kanger on
    His 50th Birthday. 1974   ISBN 90-277-0438-4
64. K. F. Schaffner and R. S. Cohen (eds.), *PSA 1972. Proceedings of the Third Biennial Meeting of
    the Philosophy of Science Association.* [Boston Studies in the Philosophy of Science, Vol. XX]
    1974   ISBN 90-277-0408-2; Pb 90-277-0409-0
65. H. E. Kyburg, Jr., *The Logical Foundations of Statistical Inference.* 1974
                                    ISBN 90-277-0330-2; Pb 90-277-0430-9
66. M. Grene, *The Understanding of Nature.* Essays in the Philosophy of Biology. [Boston Studies
    in the Philosophy of Science, Vol. XXIII] 1974   ISBN 90-277-0462-7; Pb 90-277-0463-5
67. J. M. Broekman, *Structuralism: Moscow, Prague, Paris.* Translated from German. 1974
                                          ISBN 90-277-0478-3
68. N. Geschwind, *Selected Papers on Language and the Brain.* [Boston Studies in the Philosophy
    of Science, Vol. XVI] 1974   ISBN 90-277-0262-4; Pb 90-277-0263-2

69. R. Fraissé, *Course of Mathematical Logic* – Volume 2: *Model Theory*. Translated from French. 1974   ISBN 90-277-0269-1; Pb 90-277-0510-0
(For *Volume 1* see under No. 54)

70. A. Grzegorczyk, *An Outline of Mathematical Logic*. Fundamental Results and Notions explained with all Details. Translated from Polish. 1974   ISBN 90-277-0359-0; Pb 90-277-0447-3

71. F. von Kutschera, *Philosophy of Language*. 1975   ISBN 90-277-0591-7

72. J. Manninen and R. Tuomela (eds.), *Essays on Explanation and Understanding*. Studies in the Foundations of Humanities and Social Sciences. 1976   ISBN 90-277-0592-5

73. J. Hintikka (ed.), *Rudolf Carnap, Logical Empiricist*. Materials and Perspectives. 1975   ISBN 90-277-0583-6

74. M. Čapek (ed.), *The Concepts of Space and Time*. Their Structure and Their Development. [Boston Studies in the Philosophy of Science, Vol. XXII] 1976   ISBN 90-277-0355-8; Pb 90-277-0375-2

75. J. Hintikka and U. Remes, *The Method of Analysis*. Its Geometrical Origin and Its General Significance. [Boston Studies in the Philosophy of Science, Vol. XXV] 1974   ISBN 90-277-0532-1; Pb 90-277-0543-7

76. J. E. Murdoch and E. D. Sylla (eds.), *The Cultural Context of Medieval Learning*. [Boston Studies in the Philosophy of Science, Vol. XXVI] 1975   ISBN 90-277-0560-7; Pb 90-277-0587-9

77. S. Amsterdamski, *Between Experience and Metaphysics*. Philosophical Problems of the Evolution of Science. [Boston Studies in the Philosophy of Science, Vol. XXXV] 1975   ISBN 90-277-0568-2; Pb 90-277-0580-1

78. P. Suppes (ed.), *Logic and Probability in Quantum Mechanics*. 1976   ISBN 90-277-0570-4; Pb 90-277-1200-X

79. H. von Helmholtz: *Epistemological Writings. The Paul Hertz / Moritz Schlick Centenary Edition of 1921 with Notes and Commentary by the Editors*. Newly translated from German by M. F. Lowe. Edited, with an Introduction and Bibliography, by R. S. Cohen and Y. Elkana. [Boston Studies in the Philosophy of Science, Vol. XXXVII] 1975   ISBN 90-277-0290-X; Pb 90-277-0582-8

80. J. Agassi, *Science in Flux*. [Boston Studies in the Philosophy of Science, Vol. XXVIII] 1975   ISBN 90-277-0584-4; Pb 90-277-0612-2

81. S. G. Harding (ed.), *Can Theories Be Refuted?* Essays on the Duhem-Quine Thesis. 1976   ISBN 90-277-0629-8; Pb 90-277-0630-1

82. S. Nowak, *Methodology of Sociological Research*. General Problems. 1977   ISBN 90-277-0486-4

83. J. Piaget, J.-B. Grize, A. Szemińsska and V. Bang, *Epistemology and Psychology of Functions*. Translated from French. 1977   ISBN 90-277-0804-5

84. M. Grene and E. Mendelsohn (eds.), *Topics in the Philosophy of Biology*. [Boston Studies in the Philosophy of Science, Vol. XXVII] 1976   ISBN 90-277-0595-X; Pb 90-277-0596-8

85. E. Fischbein, *The Intuitive Sources of Probabilistic Thinking in Children*. 1975   ISBN 90-277-0626-3; Pb 90-277-1190-9

86. E. W. Adams, *The Logic of Conditionals*. An Application of Probability to Deductive Logic. 1975   ISBN 90-277-0631-X

87. M. Przełęcki and R. Wójcicki (eds.), *Twenty-Five Years of Logical Methodology in Poland*. Translated from Polish. 1976   ISBN 90-277-0601-8

88. J. Topolski, *The Methodology of History*. Translated from Polish by O. Wojtasiewicz. 1976   ISBN 90-277-0550-X

114. H. A. Simon, *Models of Discovery and Other Topics in the Methods of Science.* [Boston Studies in the Philosophy of Science, Vol. LIV] 1977   ISBN 90-277-0812-6; Pb 90-277-0858-4

115. R. D. Rosenkrantz, *Inference, Method and Decision.* Towards a Bayesian Philosophy of Science. 1977   ISBN 90-277-0817-7; Pb 90-277-0818-5

116. R. Tuomela, *Human Action and Its Explanation.* A Study on the Philosophical Foundations of Psychology. 1977   ISBN 90-277-0824-X

117. M. Lazerowitz, *The Language of Philosophy.* Freud and Wittgenstein. [Boston Studies in the Philosophy of Science, Vol. LV] 1977   ISBN 90-277-0826-6; Pb 90-277-0862-2

118. Not published 119.   J. Pelc (ed.), *Semiotics in Poland, 1894–1969.* Translated from Polish. 1979   ISBN 90-277-0811-8

120. I. Pörn, *Action Theory and Social Science.* Some Formal Models. 1977 ISBN 90-277-0846-0

121. J. Margolis, *Persons and Mind.* The Prospects of Nonreductive Materialism. [Boston Studies in the Philosophy of Science, Vol. LVII] 1977   ISBN 90-277-0854-1; Pb 90-277-0863-0

122. J. Hintikka, I. Niiniluoto, and E. Saarinen (eds.), *Essays on Mathematical and Philosophical Logic.* 1979   ISBN 90-277-0879-7

123. T. A. F. Kuipers, *Studies in Inductive Probability and Rational Expectation.* 1978   ISBN 90-277-0882-7

124. E. Saarinen, R. Hilpinen, I. Niiniluoto and M. P. Hintikka (eds.), *Essays in Honour of Jaakko Hintikka on the Occasion of His 50th Birthday.* 1979   ISBN 90-277-0916-5

125. G. Radnitzky and G. Andersson (eds.), *Progress and Rationality in Science.* [Boston Studies in the Philosophy of Science, Vol. LVIII] 1978   ISBN 90-277-0921-1; Pb 90-277-0922-X

126. P. Mittelstaedt, *Quantum Logic.* 1978   ISBN 90-277-0925-4

127. K. A. Bowen, *Model Theory for Modal Logic.* Kripke Models for Modal Predicate Calculi. 1979   ISBN 90-277-0929-7

128. H. A. Bursen, *Dismantling the Memory Machine.* A Philosophical Investigation of Machine Theories of Memory. 1978   ISBN 90-277-0933-5

129. M. W. Wartofsky, *Models.* Representation and the Scientific Understanding. [Boston Studies in the Philosophy of Science, Vol. XLVIII] 1979   ISBN 90-277-0736-7; Pb 90-277-0947-5

130. D. Ihde, *Technics and Praxis.* A Philosophy of Technology. [Boston Studies in the Philosophy of Science, Vol. XXIV] 1979   ISBN 90-277-0953-X; Pb 90-277-0954-8

131. J. J. Wiatr (ed.), *Polish Essays in the Methodology of the Social Sciences.* [Boston Studies in the Philosophy of Science, Vol. XXIX] 1979   ISBN 90-277-0723-5; Pb 90-277-0956-4

132. W. C. Salmon (ed.), *Hans Reichenbach: Logical Empiricist.* 1979   ISBN 90-277-0958-0

133. P. Bieri, R.-P. Horstmann and L. Krüger (eds.), *Transcendental Arguments in Science.* Essays in Epistemology. 1979   ISBN 90-277-0963-7; Pb 90-277-0964-5

134. M. Marković and G. Petrović (eds.), *Praxis.* Yugoslav Essays in the Philosophy and Methodology of the Social Sciences. [Boston Studies in the Philosophy of Science, Vol. XXXVI] 1979   ISBN 90-277-0727-8; Pb 90-277-0968-8

135. R. Wójcicki, *Topics in the Formal Methodology of Empirical Sciences.* Translated from Polish. 1979   ISBN 90-277-1004-X

136. G. Radnitzky and G. Andersson (eds.), *The Structure and Development of Science.* [Boston Studies in the Philosophy of Science, Vol. LIX] 1979   ISBN 90-277-0994-7; Pb 90-277-0995-5

137. J. C. Webb, *Mechanism, Mentalism and Metamathematics.* An Essay on Finitism. 1980   ISBN 90-277-1046-5

138. D. F. Gustafson and B. L. Tapscott (eds.), *Body, Mind and Method.* Essays in Honor of Virgil C. Aldrich. 1979   ISBN 90-277-1013-9

139. L. Nowak, *The Structure of Idealization*. Towards a Systematic Interpretation of the Marxian Idea of Science. 1980   ISBN 90-277-1014-7

140. C. Perelman, *The New Rhetoric and the Humanities*. Essays on Rhetoric and Its Applications. Translated from French and German. With an Introduction by H. Zyskind. 1979
ISBN 90-277-1018-X; Pb 90-277-1019-8

141. W. Rabinowicz, *Universalizability*. A Study in Morals and Metaphysics. 1979
ISBN 90-277-1020-2

142. C. Perelman, *Justice, Law and Argument*. Essays on Moral and Legal Reasoning. Translated from French and German. With an Introduction by H.J. Berman. 1980
ISBN 90-277-1089-9; Pb 90-277-1090-2

143. S. Kanger and S. Öhman (eds.), *Philosophy and Grammar*. Papers on the Occasion of the Quincentennial of Uppsala University. 1981   ISBN 90-277-1091-0

144. T. Pawlowski, *Concept Formation in the Humanities and the Social Sciences*. 1980
ISBN 90-277-1096-1

145. J. Hintikka, D. Gruender and E. Agazzi (eds.), *Theory Change, Ancient Axiomatics and Galileo's Methodology*. Proceedings of the 1978 Pisa Conference on the History and Philosophy of Science, Volume I. 1981   ISBN 90-277-1126-7

146. J. Hintikka, D. Gruender and E. Agazzi (eds.), *Probabilistic Thinking, Thermodynamics, and the Interaction of the History and Philosophy of Science*. Proceedings of the 1978 Pisa Conference on the History and Philosophy of Science, Volume II. 1981 ISBN 90-277-1127-5

147. U. Mönnich (ed.), *Aspects of Philosophical Logic*. Some Logical Forays into Central Notions of Linguistics and Philosophy. 1981   ISBN 90-277-1201-8

148. D. M. Gabbay, *Semantical Investigations in Heyting's Intuitionistic Logic*. 1981
ISBN 90-277-1202-6

149. E. Agazzi (ed.), *Modern Logic – A Survey*. Historical, Philosophical, and Mathematical Aspects of Modern Logic and Its Applications. 1981   ISBN 90-277-1137-2

150. A. F. Parker-Rhodes, *The Theory of Indistinguishables*. A Search for Explanatory Principles below the Level of Physics. 1981   ISBN 90-277-1214-X

151. J. C. Pitt, *Pictures, Images, and Conceptual Change*. An Analysis of Wilfrid Sellars' Philosophy of Science. 1981   ISBN 90-277-1276-X; Pb 90-277-1277-8

152. R. Hilpinen (ed.), *New Studies in Deontic Logic*. Norms, Actions, and the Foundations of Ethics. 1981   ISBN 90-277-1278-6; Pb 90-277-1346-4

153. C. Dilworth, *Scientific Progress*. A Study Concerning the Nature of the Relation between Successive Scientific Theories. 3rd rev. ed., 1994   ISBN 0-7923-2487-0; Pb 0-7923-2488-9

154. D. Woodruff Smith and R. McIntyre, *Husserl and Intentionality*. A Study of Mind, Meaning, and Language. 1982   ISBN 90-277-1392-8; Pb 90-277-1730-3

155. R. J. Nelson, *The Logic of Mind*. 2nd. ed., 1989   ISBN 90-277-2819-4; Pb 90-277-2822-4

156. J. F. A. K. van Benthem, *The Logic of Time*. A Model-Theoretic Investigation into the Varieties of Temporal Ontology, and Temporal Discourse. 1983; 2nd ed., 1991   ISBN 0-7923-1081-0

157. R. Swinburne (ed.), *Space, Time and Causality*. 1983   ISBN 90-277-1437-1

158. E. T. Jaynes, *Papers on Probability, Statistics and Statistical Physics*. Ed. by R. D. Rozenkrantz. 1983   ISBN 90-277-1448-7; Pb (1989) 0-7923-0213-3

159. T. Chapman, *Time: A Philosophical Analysis*. 1982   ISBN 90-277-1465-7

160. E. N. Zalta, *Abstract Objects*. An Introduction to Axiomatic Metaphysics. 1983
ISBN 90-277-1474-6

161. S. Harding and M. B. Hintikka (eds.), *Discovering Reality*. Feminist Perspectives on Epistemology, Metaphysics, Methodology, and Philosophy of Science. 1983
ISBN 90-277-1496-7; Pb 90-277-1538-6

162. M. A. Stewart (ed.), *Law, Morality and Rights*. 1983   ISBN 90-277-1519-X
163. D. Mayr and G. Süssmann (eds.), *Space, Time, and Mechanics*. Basic Structures of a Physical Theory. 1983   ISBN 90-277-1525-4
164. D. Gabbay and F. Guenthner (eds.), *Handbook of Philosophical Logic*. Vol. I: Elements of Classical Logic. 1983   ISBN 90-277-1542-4
165. D. Gabbay and F. Guenthner (eds.), *Handbook of Philosophical Logic*. Vol. II: Extensions of Classical Logic. 1984   ISBN 90-277-1604-8
166. D. Gabbay and F. Guenthner (eds.), *Handbook of Philosophical Logic*. Vol. III: Alternative to Classical Logic. 1986   ISBN 90-277-1605-6
167. D. Gabbay and F. Guenthner (eds.), *Handbook of Philosophical Logic*. Vol. IV: Topics in the Philosophy of Language. 1989   ISBN 90-277-1606-4
168. A. J. I. Jones, *Communication and Meaning*. An Essay in Applied Modal Logic. 1983
           ISBN 90-277-1543-2
169. M. Fitting, *Proof Methods for Modal and Intuitionistic Logics*. 1983   ISBN 90-277-1573-4
170. J. Margolis, *Culture and Cultural Entities*. Toward a New Unity of Science. 1984
           ISBN 90-277-1574-2
171. R. Tuomela, *A Theory of Social Action*. 1984   ISBN 90-277-1703-6
172. J. J. E. Gracia, E. Rabossi, E. Villanueva and M. Dascal (eds.), *Philosophical Analysis in Latin America*. 1984   ISBN 90-277-1749-4
173. P. Ziff, *Epistemic Analysis*. A Coherence Theory of Knowledge. 1984
           ISBN 90-277-1751-7
174. P. Ziff, *Antiaesthetics*. An Appreciation of the Cow with the Subtile Nose. 1984
           ISBN 90-277-1773-7
175. W. Balzer, D. A. Pearce, and H.-J. Schmidt (eds.), *Reduction in Science*. Structure, Examples, Philosophical Problems. 1984   ISBN 90-277-1811-3
176. A. Peczenik, L. Lindahl and B. van Roermund (eds.), *Theory of Legal Science*. Proceedings of the Conference on Legal Theory and Philosophy of Science (Lund, Sweden, December 1983). 1984   ISBN 90-277-1834-2
177. I. Niiniluoto, *Is Science Progressive?* 1984   ISBN 90-277-1835-0
178. B. K. Matilal and J. L. Shaw (eds.), *Analytical Philosophy in Comparative Perspective*. Exploratory Essays in Current Theories and Classical Indian Theories of Meaning and Reference. 1985   ISBN 90-277-1870-9
179. P. Kroes, *Time: Its Structure and Role in Physical Theories*. 1985   ISBN 90-277-1894-6
180. J. H. Fetzer, *Sociobiology and Epistemology*. 1985   ISBN 90-277-2005-3; Pb 90-277-2006-1
181. L. Haaparanta and J. Hintikka (eds.), *Frege Synthesized*. Essays on the Philosophical and Foundational Work of Gottlob Frege. 1986   ISBN 90-277-2126-2
182. M. Detlefsen, *Hilbert's Program*. An Essay on Mathematical Instrumentalism. 1986
           ISBN 90-277-2151-3
183. J. L. Golden and J. J. Pilotta (eds.), *Practical Reasoning in Human Affairs*. Studies in Honor of Chaim Perelman. 1986   ISBN 90-277-2255-2
184. H. Zandvoort, *Models of Scientific Development and the Case of Nuclear Magnetic Resonance*. 1986   ISBN 90-277-2351-6
185. I. Niiniluoto, *Truthlikeness*. 1987   ISBN 90-277-2354-0
186. W. Balzer, C. U. Moulines and J. D. Sneed, *An Architectonic for Science*. The Structuralist Program. 1987   ISBN 90-277-2403-2
187. D. Pearce, *Roads to Commensurability*. 1987   ISBN 90-277-2414-8
188. L. M. Vaina (ed.), *Matters of Intelligence*. Conceptual Structures in Cognitive Neuroscience. 1987   ISBN 90-277-2460-1

189. H. Siegel, *Relativism Refuted*. A Critique of Contemporary Epistemological Relativism. 1987
ISBN 90-277-2469-5

190. W. Callebaut and R. Pinxten, *Evolutionary Epistemology*. A Multiparadigm Program, with a
Complete Evolutionary Epistemology Bibliograph. 1987 ISBN 90-277-2582-9

191. J. Kmita, *Problems in Historical Epistemology*. 1988 ISBN 90-277-2199-8

192. J. H. Fetzer (ed.), *Probability and Causality*. Essays in Honor of Wesley C. Salmon, with an
Annotated Bibliography. 1988 ISBN 90-277-2607-8; Pb 1-5560-8052-2

193. A. Donovan, L. Laudan and R. Laudan (eds.), *Scrutinizing Science*. Empirical Studies of
Scientific Change. 1988 ISBN 90-277-2608-6

194. H.R. Otto and J.A. Tuedio (eds.), *Perspectives on Mind*. 1988 ISBN 90-277-2640-X

195. D. Batens and J.P. van Bendegem (eds.), *Theory and Experiment*. Recent Insights and New
Perspectives on Their Relation. 1988 ISBN 90-277-2645-0

196. J. Österberg, *Self and Others*. A Study of Ethical Egoism. 1988 ISBN 90-277-2648-5

197. D.H. Helman (ed.), *Analogical Reasoning*. Perspectives of Artificial Intelligence, Cognitive
Science, and Philosophy. 1988 ISBN 90-277-2711-2

198. J. Woleński, *Logic and Philosophy in the Lvov-Warsaw School*. 1989 ISBN 90-277-2749-X

199. R. Wójcicki, *Theory of Logical Calculi*. Basic Theory of Consequence Operations. 1988
ISBN 90-277-2785-6

200. J. Hintikka and M.B. Hintikka, *The Logic of Epistemology and the Epistemology of Logic*.
Selected Essays. 1989 ISBN 0-7923-0040-8; Pb 0-7923-0041-6

201. E. Agazzi (ed.), *Probability in the Sciences*. 1988 ISBN 90-277-2808-9

202. M. Meyer (ed.), *From Metaphysics to Rhetoric*. 1989 ISBN 90-277-2814-3

203. R.L. Tieszen, *Mathematical Intuition*. Phenomenology and Mathematical Knowledge. 1989
ISBN 0-7923-0131-5

204. A. Melnick, *Space, Time, and Thought in Kant*. 1989 ISBN 0-7923-0135-8

205. D.W. Smith, *The Circle of Acquaintance*. Perception, Consciousness, and Empathy. 1989
ISBN 0-7923-0252-4

206. M.H. Salmon (ed.), *The Philosophy of Logical Mechanism*. Essays in Honor of Arthur W.
Burks. With his Responses, and with a Bibliography of Burk's Work. 1990
ISBN 0-7923-0325-3

207. M. Kusch, *Language as Calculus vs. Language as Universal Medium*. A Study in Husserl,
Heidegger, and Gadamer. 1989 ISBN 0-7923-0333-4

208. T.C. Meyering, *Historical Roots of Cognitive Science*. The Rise of a Cognitive Theory of
Perception from Antiquity to the Nineteenth Century. 1989 ISBN 0-7923-0349-0

209. P. Kosso, *Observability and Observation in Physical Science*. 1989 ISBN 0-7923-0389-X

210. J. Kmita, *Essays on the Theory of Scientific Cognition*. 1990 ISBN 0-7923-0441-1

211. W. Sieg (ed.), *Acting and Reflecting*. The Interdisciplinary Turn in Philosophy. 1990
ISBN 0-7923-0512-4

212. J. Karpiński, *Causality in Sociological Research*. 1990 ISBN 0-7923-0546-9

213. H.A. Lewis (ed.), *Peter Geach: Philosophical Encounters*. 1991 ISBN 0-7923-0823-9

214. M. Ter Hark, *Beyond the Inner and the Outer*. Wittgenstein's Philosophy of Psychology. 1990
ISBN 0-7923-0850-6

215. M. Gosselin, *Nominalism and Contemporary Nominalism*. Ontological and Epistemological
Implications of the Work of W.V.O. Quine and of N. Goodman. 1990 ISBN 0-7923-0904-9

216. J.H. Fetzer, D. Shatz and G. Schlesinger (eds.), *Definitions and Definability*. Philosophical
Perspectives. 1991 ISBN 0-7923-1046-2

217. E. Agazzi and A. Cordero (eds.), *Philosophy and the Origin and Evolution of the Universe*.
1991 ISBN 0-7923-1322-4

218. M. Kusch, *Foucault's Strata and Fields*. An Investigation into Archaeological and Genealogical Science Studies. 1991   ISBN 0-7923-1462-X
219. C.J. Posy, *Kant's Philosophy of Mathematics*. Modern Essays. 1992   ISBN 0-7923-1495-6
220. G. Van de Vijver, *New Perspectives on Cybernetics*. Self-Organization, Autonomy and Connectionism. 1992   ISBN 0-7923-1519-7
221. J.C. Nyíri, *Tradition and Individuality*. Essays. 1992   ISBN 0-7923-1566-9
222. R. Howell, *Kant's Transcendental Deduction*. An Analysis of Main Themes in His Critical Philosophy. 1992   ISBN 0-7923-1571-5
223. A. García de la Sierra, *The Logical Foundations of the Marxian Theory of Value*. 1992
                                                                                   ISBN 0-7923-1778-5
224. D.S. Shwayder, *Statement and Referent*. An Inquiry into the Foundations of Our Conceptual Order. 1992   ISBN 0-7923-1803-X
225. M. Rosen, *Problems of the Hegelian Dialectic*. Dialectic Reconstructed as a Logic of Human Reality. 1993   ISBN 0-7923-2047-6
226. P. Suppes, *Models and Methods in the Philosophy of Science: Selected Essays*. 1993
                                                                                   ISBN 0-7923-2211-8
227. R. M. Dancy (ed.), *Kant and Critique: New Essays in Honor of W. H. Werkmeister*. 1993
                                                                                   ISBN 0-7923-2244-4
228. J. Woleński (ed.), *Philosophical Logic in Poland*. 1993   ISBN 0-7923-2293-2
229. M. De Rijke (ed.), *Diamonds and Defaults*. Studies in Pure and Applied Intensional Logic. 1993   ISBN 0-7923-2342-4
230. B.K. Matilal and A. Chakrabarti (eds.), *Knowing from Words*. Western and Indian Philosophical Analysis of Understanding and Testimony. 1994   ISBN 0-7923-2345-9
231. S.A. Kleiner, *The Logic of Discovery*. A Theory of the Rationality of Scientific Research. 1993
                                                                                   ISBN 0-7923-2371-8
232. R. Festa, *Optimum Inductive Methods*. A Study in Inductive Probability, Bayesian Statistics, and Verisimilitude. 1993   ISBN 0-7923-2460-9
233. P. Humphreys (ed.), *Patrick Suppes: Scientific Philosopher*. Vol. 1: Probability and Probabilistic Causality. 1994   ISBN 0-7923-2552-4
234. P. Humphreys (ed.), *Patrick Suppes: Scientific Philosopher*. Vol. 2: Philosophy of Physics, Theory Structure, and Measurement Theory. 1994   ISBN 0-7923-2553-2
235. P. Humphreys (ed.), *Patrick Suppes: Scientific Philosopher*. Vol. 3: Language, Logic, and Psychology. 1994   ISBN 0-7923-2862-0
                                                        Set ISBN (Vols 233–235) 0-7923-2554-0
236. D. Prawitz and D. Westerståhl (eds.), *Logic and Philosophy of Science in Uppsala*. Papers from the 9th International Congress of Logic, Methodology, and Philosophy of Science. 1994
                                                                                   ISBN 0-7923-2702-0
237. L. Haaparanta (ed.), *Mind, Meaning and Mathematics*. Essays on the Philosophical Views of Husserl and Frege. 1994   ISBN 0-7923-2703-9
238. J. Hintikka (ed.), *Aspects of Metaphor*. 1994   ISBN 0-7923-2786-1
239. B. McGuinness and G. Oliveri (eds.), *The Philosophy of Michael Dummett*. With Replies from Michael Dummett. 1994   ISBN 0-7923-2804-3
240. D. Jamieson (ed.), *Language, Mind, and Art*. Essays in Appreciation and Analysis, In Honor of Paul Ziff. 1994   ISBN 0-7923-2810-8
241. G. Preyer, F. Siebelt and A. Ulfig (eds.), *Language, Mind and Epistemology*. On Donald Davidson's Philosophy. 1994   ISBN 0-7923-2811-6
242. P. Ehrlich (ed.), *Real Numbers, Generalizations of the Reals, and Theories of Continua*. 1994
                                                                                   ISBN 0-7923-2689-X

243. G. Debrock and M. Hulswit (eds.), *Living Doubt*. Essays concerning the epistemology of Charles Sanders Peirce. 1994   ISBN 0-7923-2898-1
244. J. Srzednicki, *To Know or Not to Know*. Beyond Realism and Anti-Realism. 1994
                                                                                ISBN 0-7923-2909-0
245. R. Egidi (ed.), *Wittgenstein: Mind and Language*. 1995   ISBN 0-7923-3171-0
246. A. Hyslop, *Other Minds*. 1995   ISBN 0-7923-3245-8
247. L. Pólos and M. Masuch (eds.), *Applied Logic: How, What and Why*. Logical Approaches to Natural Language. 1995   ISBN 0-7923-3432-9
248. M. Krynicki, M. Mostowski and L.M. Szczerba (eds.), *Quantifiers: Logics, Models and Computation*. Volume One: Surveys. 1995   ISBN 0-7923-3448-5
249. M. Krynicki, M. Mostowski and L.M. Szczerba (eds.), *Quantifiers: Logics, Models and Computation*. Volume Two: Contributions. 1995   ISBN 0-7923-3449-3
                                                        Set ISBN (Vols 248 + 249) 0-7923-3450-7
250. R.A. Watson, *Representational Ideas from Plato to Patricia Churchland*. 1995
                                                                                ISBN 0-7923-3453-1
251. J. Hintikka (ed.), *From Dedekind to Gödel*. Essays on the Development of the Foundations of Mathematics. 1995   ISBN 0-7923-3484-1
252. A. Wiśniewski, *The Posing of Questions*. Logical Foundations of Erotetic Inferences. 1995
                                                                                ISBN 0-7923-3637-2
253. J. Peregrin, *Doing Worlds with Words*. Formal Semantics without Formal Metaphysics. 1995
                                                                                ISBN 0-7923-3742-5
254. I.A. Kieseppä, *Truthlikeness for Multidimensional, Quantitative Cognitive Problems*. 1996
                                                                                ISBN 0-7923-4005-1
255. P. Hugly and C. Sayward: *Intensionality and Truth*. An Essay on the Philosophy of A.N. Prior. 1996   ISBN 0-7923-4119-8
256. L. Hankinson Nelson and J. Nelson (eds.): *Feminism, Science, and the Philosophy of Science*. 1997   ISBN 0-7923-4162-7
257. P.I. Bystrov and V.N. Sadovsky (eds.): *Philosophical Logic and Logical Philosophy*. Essays in Honour of Vladimir A. Smirnov. 1996   ISBN 0-7923-4270-4
258. Å.E. Andersson and N-E. Sahlin (eds.): *The Complexity of Creativity*. 1996
                                                                                ISBN 0-7923-4346-8
259. M.L. Dalla Chiara, K. Doets, D. Mundici and J. van Benthem (eds.): *Logic and Scientific Methods*. Volume One of the Tenth International Congress of Logic, Methodology and Philosophy of Science, Florence, August 1995. 1997   ISBN 0-7923-4383-2
260. M.L. Dalla Chiara, K. Doets, D. Mundici and J. van Benthem (eds.): *Structures and Norms in Science*. Volume Two of the Tenth International Congress of Logic, Methodology and Philosophy of Science, Florence, August 1995. 1997   ISBN 0-7923-4384-0
                                                        Set ISBN (Vols 259 + 260) 0-7923-4385-9
261. A. Chakrabarti: *Denying Existence*. The Logic, Epistemology and Pragmatics of Negative Existentials and Fictional Discourse. 1997   ISBN 0-7923-4388-3
262. A. Biletzki: *Talking Wolves*. Thomas Hobbes on the Language of Politics and the Politics of Language. 1997   ISBN 0-7923-4425-1
263. D. Nute (ed.): *Defeasible Deontic Logic*. 1997   ISBN 0-7923-4630-0
264. U. Meixner: *Axiomatic Formal Ontology*. 1997   ISBN 0-7923-4747-X
265. I. Brinck: *The Indexical 'I'*. The First Person in Thought and Language. 1997
                                                                                ISBN 0-7923-4741-2
266. G. Hölmström-Hintikka and R. Tuomela (eds.): *Contemporary Action Theory*. Volume 1: Individual Action. 1997   ISBN 0-7923-4753-6; Set: 0-7923-4754-4

267. G. Hölmström-Hintikka and R. Tuomela (eds.): *Contemporary Action Theory*. Volume 2: Social Action. 1997   ISBN 0-7923-4752-8; Set: 0-7923-4754-4
268. B.-C. Park: *Phenomenological Aspects of Wittgenstein's Philosophy*. 1998
          ISBN 0-7923-4813-3
269. J. Paśniczek: *The Logic of Intentional Objects*. A Meinongian Version of Classical Logic. 1998   ISBN 0-7923-4880-X
270. P.W. Humphreys and J.H. Fetzer (eds.): *The New Theory of Reference*. Kripke, Marcus, and Its Origins. 1998   ISBN 0-7923-4898-2
271. K. Szaniawski, A. Chmielewski and J. Woleński (eds.): *On Science, Inference, Information and Decision Making*. Selected Essays in the Philosophy of Science. 1998
          ISBN 0-7923-4922-9
272. G.H. von Wright: *In the Shadow of Descartes*. Essays in the Philosophy of Mind. 1998
          ISBN 0-7923-4992-X
273. K. Kijania-Placek and J. Woleński (eds.): *The Lvov–Warsaw School and Contemporary Philosophy*. 1998   ISBN 0-7923-5105-3
274. D. Dedrick: *Naming the Rainbow*. Colour Language, Colour Science, and Culture. 1998
          ISBN 0-7923-5239-4
275. L. Albertazzi (ed.): *Shapes of Forms*. From Gestalt Psychology and Phenomenology to Ontology and Mathematics. 1999   ISBN 0-7923-5246-7
276. P. Fletcher: *Truth, Proof and Infinity*. A Theory of Constructions and Constructive Reasoning. 1998   ISBN 0-7923-5262-9
277. M. Fitting and R.L. Mendelsohn (eds.): *First-Order Modal Logic*. 1998
          ISBN 0-7923-5334-X
278. D. Dedrick: *Naming the Rainbow*. Colour Language, Colour Science, and Culture. 1998
          ISBN 0-7923-5239-4
279. F. Vollmer: *Agent Causality*. 1999   ISBN 0-7923-5848-1
280. A. Cantini, E. Casari and P. Minari (eds.): *Logic and Foundations of Mathematics*. 1999
          ISBN 0-7923-5659-4
281. M.L. Dalla Chiara, R. Giuntini and F. Laudisa (eds.): *Language, Quantum, Music*. 1999
          ISBN 0-7923-5727-2
282. R. Egidi (ed.): *In Search of a New Humanism*. The Philosophy of Georg Hendrik von Wright. 1999   ISBN 0-7923-5810-4
283. F. Vollmer: *Agent Causality*. 1999   ISBN 0-7923-5848-1
284. J. Peregrin (ed.): *Truth and Its Nature (if Any)*. 1999   ISBN 0-7923-5865-1
285. M. De Caro (ed.): *Interpretations and Causes*. New Perspectives on Donald Davidson's Philosophy. 1999   ISBN 0-7923-5869-4

Previous volumes are still available.

KLUWER ACADEMIC PUBLISHERS – DORDRECHT / BOSTON / LONDON